TEN PLAYS

TEN PLAYS

ANTON CHEKHOV

DOVER PUBLICATIONS, INC.
Mineola, New York

Copyright

Theatrical Rights

This Dover edition may be used in its entirety, in adaptation, or in any other way for theatrical productions, professional and amateur, in the United States, without permission, fee, or acknowledgment. (This may not apply outside of the United States, as copyright conditions may vary.)

Bibliographical Note

This Dover edition, first published in 2008, is an unabridged republication of English translations of ten plays by Anton Chekhov from standard editions: *Ivanov, The Bear, The Proposal, An Unwilling Martyr, The Wedding, The Anniversary* (Constance Garnett, translator); *The Sea Gull, Uncle Vanya* (Marian Fell, translator); *The Three Sisters, The Cherry Orchard* (Black's Readers Service Company). The introductory Note was specially prepared for this edition.

Library of Congress Cataloging-in-Publication Data

Chekhov, Anton Pavlovich, 1860–1904.
    [Plays. English. Selections]
    Ten plays / Anton Chekhov.
        p. cm.
    "This Dover edition, first published in 2008, is an unabridged republication of English translations of ten plays by Anton Chekhov from standard editions: Ivanov, The Bear, The Proposal, An Unwilling Martyr, The Wedding, The Anniversary (Constance Garnett, translator); The Sea Gull, Uncle Vanya (Marian Fell, translator); The Three Sisters, The Cherry Orchard (Black's Readers Service Company). The introductory Note was specially prepared for this edition."
    ISBN-13: 978-0-486-46560-9
    ISBN-10: 0-486-46560-8
    1. Chekhov, Anton Pavlovich, 1860–1904—Translations into English. I. Garnett, Constance Black, 1862–1946. II. Fell, Marian. III. Black's Readers Service Company. IV. Title.

PG3456.A13G375 2008
891.72'3—dc22

2007046747

Manufactured in the United States of America
Dover Publications, Inc., 31 East 2nd Street, Mineola, N.Y. 11501

Note

ANTON PAVLOVICH CHEKHOV (1860–1904), one of Russia's greatest dramatists and short story writers, was a key figure in the development of modern drama. This collection of plays showcases ten of Chekhov's greatest works *Ivanov, The Sea Gull, Uncle Vanya, The Three Sisters, The Cherry Orchard,* and five of his one-act masterpieces—all arranged in chronological order for easy reference.

Chekhov was born in the town of Taganrog in south Russia, and as a young boy, worked in his father's grocery store. Unfortunately, his father had to declare bankruptcy in 1876. Chekhov attended a Greek school for boys and then a local grammar school.

In 1876 his father moved the rest of the family to Moscow in hopes of making a fresh start. Anton continued at school in Taganrog, living alone and supporting himself by tutoring younger boys. He graduated in 1879, joined his family in Moscow, and began studying at the Moscow University Medical School, earning his M.D. in 1884. While a medical student, he was the main support of his mother and two younger siblings, as his father could obtain only low-paying employment. Chekhov became quite popular as a prolific writer of comic short stories, which were published in several St. Petersburg journals and newspapers.

After earning his medical degree, Chekhov began writing short stories on tragic themes, but humor remained an underlying element in much of his work. He always insisted that his major dramas were comedies, not tragedies.

Contents

IVANOV

Characters

NIKOLAY ALEXEYEVITCH IVANOV, *permanent member of the Rural Board*

ANNA PETROVNA, *his wife, before her baptism and marriage called* SARRA ABRAMSON

COUNT MATVEY SEMYONITCH SHABELSKY, *his maternal uncle*

PAVEL KIRILLITCH LEBEDYEV, *Chairman of the District Zemstvo*

ZINAIDA SAVISHNA, *his wife*

SASHA, *their daughter, aged twenty*

YEVGENY KONSTANTINOVITCH LVOV, *a young Zemstvo Doctor*

MARFA YEGOROVNA BABAKIN, *the young widow of a landowner, daughter of a rich merchant*

DMITRI NIKITITCH KOSSIH, *Excise officer*

MIHAIL MIHAILOVITCH BORKIN, *a distant relative of* IVANOV *and Steward of his estate*

AVDOTYA NAZAROVNA, *an old woman of no definite occupation*

YEGORUSHKA, *a dependant of the* LEBEDYEVS

FIRST GUEST   SECOND GUEST   THIRD GUEST   FOURTH GUEST

PYOTR, IVANOV's *manservant*

GAVRIL, LEBEDYEV's *manservant*

VISITORS, *of both sexes*   MENSERVANTS

The action takes place in one of the provinces of Central Russia.

ACT I

The garden on IVANOV's *estate. On the left, the front of the house with the verandah. One window is open. In front of the verandah is a wide semicircular space, from which an avenue at right angles to the house, and another to the right, run into the garden. On the right side of the verandah are garden seats and tables. On one of the latter a lamp is burning. Evening is coming on. As the curtain rises there is the sound of a duet of piano and 'cello being practiced indoors.*

IVANOV *is sitting at a table reading.* BORKIN, *wearing high boots and carrying a gun, comes into sight at the further end of the garden—he is a little drunk; seeing* IVANOV, *he advances on tiptoe towards him, and when he reaches him aims his gun at his face.*

IVANOV [*seeing* BORKIN, *starts and jumps up*].   Misha, what are you about? . . . You gave me a fright. . . . I am worried as it is, and then you come with your stupid jokes . . . [*sits down*]. He has frightened me, and is delighted . . .

BORKIN [*laughs*].   There, there. . . . I am sorry, I am sorry [*sits down beside him*]. I won't do it again, I really won't . . . [*takes off his cap*]. I'm hot. Would you believe it, my dear soul, I've done nearly twelve miles in three hours! . . . Just feel how my heart is beating! . . .

IVANOV [*reading*].   All right, presently. . . .

BORKIN.   No, feel now [*takes* IVANOV's *hand and lays it on his chest*]. Do you hear? Too-too-too-too-too-too. . . . It shows I've got heart-disease, you know. I might die suddenly, any minute. I say, will you be sorry if I die?

IVANOV.   I am reading . . . presently. . . .

BORKIN.   No, seriously, will you be sorry if I die? Nikolay Alexeyevitch, will you be sorry if I die?

IVANOV.   Don't pester me!

BORKIN.   My dear fellow, do tell me whether you will be sorry.

IVANOV.   I am sorry you smell of vodka. Misha, it's disgusting!

3

BORKIN [*laughs*]. Do I smell of it? How surprising! . . . Though there is nothing surprising in it, really. At Plesniki I met the examining magistrate, and I must own we put away eight glasses or so each. Drinking is very bad for one, really. I say, it is bad for one, isn't it? It is, isn't it?

IVANOV. This is really intolerable. . . . You must see that it's simply maddening. . . .

BORKIN. There, there. . . . I am sorry, I am sorry. . . . God bless you; sit still . . . [*gets up and walks away*]. Queer people; there's no talking to them! [*Comes back*] Oh yes, I was almost forgetting. . . . Give me the eighty-two rubles.

IVANOV. What eighty-two rubles?

BORKIN. To pay the laborers to-morrow.

IVANOV. I haven't got it.

BORKIN. Very much obliged! [*Mimicking*] I haven't got it. . . . But the laborers must be paid, mustn't they?

IVANOV. I don't know. I haven't the money to-day. Wait till the first of next month, when I get my salary.

BORKIN. Much good it is talking to such a specimen! . . . The laborers won't come for the money on the first; they will come to-morrow morning! . . .

IVANOV. Well, what am I to do? You may cut my throat, hack me to pieces. . . . And what a revolting habit it is of yours to pester me just when I am reading or writing, or . . .

BORKIN. I ask you, must the laborers be paid or not? But what's the use of talking to you! [*waves his hand*]. And he is a country gentleman—hang it all, a landowner! . . . Up-to-date agricultural methods. . . . Three thousand acres, and not a penny in his pocket! . . . There is a winecellar, and no corkscrew. . . . I'll go and sell the three horses to-morrow! Yes! I have sold the standing oats, and now I'll sell the rye! [*strides about the stage*]. Do you suppose I'd hesitate? Eh? No; you've hit on the wrong man for that. . . .

[SHABELSKY's *voice inside:* "*It is impossible to play with you. . . . You have no more ear than a stuffed pike, and your touch is appalling!*"]

ANNA PETROVNA [*appears at the open window*]. Who was talking here just now? Was it you, Misha? Why are you striding about like that?

BORKIN. Your *Nicolas-voilà* is enough to drive one to anything!

ANNA PETROVNA. I say, Misha, tell them to bring some hay on to the croquet lawn.

BORKIN [*waving her off*]. Please let me alone. . . .

ANNA PETROVNA. Goodness! what a way to speak! . . . That tone doesn't suit you at all. If you want women to like you, you must never let them see you cross or standing on your dignity. [*To her husband*] Nikolay, let us roll about on the hay!

IVANOV.   It's bad for you to stand at an open window, Anyuta. Please go in . . . [*Calls*] Uncle, shut the window. [*The window is shut.*]

BORKIN.   Don't forget that in two days' time you have to pay Lebedyev his interest.

IVANOV.   I remember. I shall be at Lebedyev's to-day, and I will ask him to wait [*looks at his watch*].

BORKIN.   When are you going?

IVANOV.   Directly.

BORKIN [*eagerly*].   Wait a minute! I do believe it is Sasha's birthday to day . . . tut—tut—tut . . . and I forgot it. . . . What a memory! [*skips about*]. I am going—I am going [*sings*]. I am going. . . . I'll go and have a bathe, chew some paper, take three drops of spirits of ammonia—and I shall be ready to begin all over again. . . . Nikolay Alexeyevitch darling, my precious, angel of my heart, you are always in a state of nerves, complaining, and in the dismal doldrums, and yet the devil only knows what we two might bring off together! I am ready to do anything for you. . . . Would you like me to marry Marfusha Babakin for you? Half her dowry shall be yours . . . no, not half, all, all shall be yours!

IVANOV.   Do shut up with your silly rot.

BORKIN.   No, seriously! Would you like me to marry Marfusha? We'll go halves over the dowry. . . . But there, why do I talk about it to you? As though you would understand! [*Mimicking*] "Shut up with your silly rot." You are a fine man, an intelligent man, but you've none of that streak in you, you know—none of that go . . . To have a fling to make the devils sick with envy. . . . You are a neurotic, a drooper, but if you were a normal man you would have a million in a year. For instance, if I had at this moment two thousand three hundred rubles, I would have twenty thousand in a fortnight. You don't believe it? You call that silly rot too? No, it's not silly rot. . . . There, give me two thousand three hundred rubles and in a week I'll bring you twenty thousand. On the other side of the river Ovsyanov is selling a strip of land just opposite us for two thousand three hundred rubles. If we were to buy that strip, both sides of the river would be ours, and if both banks were ours, you know, we should have the right to dam up the river, shouldn't we? We'd set about building a mill, and, as soon as we let people know we were going to make a dam, all the people living down the river would make a hullaballoo, and we'd say—*kommen sie hier,* if you don't want to have a dam, buy us off. Do you understand? Zarevsky's factory would give us five thousand, Korolkov three thousand, the monastery five thousand. . . .

IVANOV.   That's all stuff and nonsense, Misha. . . . If you don't want to quarrel with me, keep such schemes to yourself.

BORKIN [*sits down to the table*].   Of course! . . . I knew it would be so! . . . You won't do anything yourself, and you won't let me.

[*Enter* SHABELSKY *and* LVOV.]

SHABELSKY [*coming out of the house with* LVOV].   Doctors are just the same as lawyers; the only difference is that the lawyers rob you, and the doctors rob you and murder you. . . . I am not speaking of present company [*sits down on the garden-seat*]. Charlatans, exploiters. . . . Perhaps in Arcadia there may be some exceptions to the general rule, but . . . In the course of my life I've spent twenty thousand or so on doctors, and I never met a single one who did not seem to me a licensed swindler.

BORKIN [*to* IVANOV].   Yes, you do nothing yourself, and you won't let me do anything. That's why we have no money. . . .

SHABELSKY.   I repeat that I am not speaking of present company. . . . Perhaps there are exceptions, though indeed . . . [*yawns*].

IVANOV [*shutting his book*].   What do you say, doctor?

LVOV [*looking round towards the window*].   What I said to you this morning: she must go to the Crimea at once [*paces about the stage*].

SHABELSKY [*giggles*].   Crimea! . . . Why don't you and I go in for being doctors, Misha? It's so simple. . . . As soon as some Madame Angot or Ophelia begins wheezing and coughing because she has nothing better to do, you've to take a sheet of paper and prescribe according to the rules of your science: first, a young doctor, then a trip to the Crimea, a Tatar guide in the Crimea. . . .

IVANOV [*to* SHABELSKY].   Oh, do stop it! How you do keep on! [*to* LVOV] To go to the Crimea one must have money. Even if I do manage to get it, she absolutely refuses to go.

LVOV.   Yes, she does [*pause*].

BORKIN.   I say, doctor, is Anna Petrovna really so ill that it is necessary for her to go to the Crimea?

LVOV [*looking round towards the window*].   Yes, it's consumption.

BORKIN.   Ss—ss! . . . That's bad. . . . For some time past I've thought she looked as though she wouldn't last long.

LVOV.   But . . . don't talk so loud . . . you will be heard in the house [*pause*].

BORKIN [*sighing*].   Such is life. . . . The life of man is like a flower growing luxuriantly in a field: a goat comes and eats it, and the flower is no more.

SHABELSKY.   It's all nonsense, nonsense, nonsense . . . [*yawns*]. Nonsense and fraud [*pause*].

BORKIN.   And here, gentlemen, I keep showing Nikolay Alexeyevitch how to make money. I've just given him a glorious idea, but as usual he throws cold water on it. There's no moving him. . . . Just look at him: melancholy, spleen, depression, hypochondria, dejection. . . .

SHABELSKY [*stands up and stretches*].   You've got some scheme for everyone, you genius; you teach everyone how to live, you might try it on me for once. . . . Give me a lesson, you brainy person, show me a way of escape. . . .

BORKIN [*getting up*].   I'm going to bathe. . . . Good-bye, gentlemen. [*To the* COUNT] There are twenty things you could do. . . . If I were in your place I would have twenty thousand within a week [*is going*].

SHABELSKY [*follows him*].   How's that? Come, show me how to do it.

BORKIN.   It doesn't need showing. It's very simple [*coming back*]. Nikolay Alexeyevitch, give me a ruble!

[IVANOV *gives him the money in silence.*]

BORKIN.   *Merci!* [*To the* COUNT] You've still lots of trump cards in your hand.

SHABELSKY [*following him*].   Well, what are they?

BORKIN.   If I were in your place, within a week I would have thirty thousand, if not more [*goes out with the* COUNT].

IVANOV [*after a pause*].   Superfluous people, superfluous words, the necessity of answering foolish questions—all this has so exhausted me that I am quite ill, doctor. I have grown irritable, hasty, harsh, and so petty that I don't know myself. For days together my head aches; I cannot sleep, there's a noise in my ears. . . . And there's no getting away from it all . . . simply nothing I can do. . . .

LVOV.   I want to talk to you seriously, Nikolay Alexeyevitch.

IVANOV.   What is it?

LVOV.   It's about Anna Petrovna [*sits down*]. She won't consent to go to the Crimea, but with you she would go.

IVANOV [*pondering*].   To go together we must have the means to do it. Besides, they won't give me a long leave. I've taken my holiday this year already . . .

LVOV.   Well, supposing that is so. Now for the next point.

The most important condition for the treatment of consumption is absolute peace of mind, and your wife never has a moment's peace of mind. She is in continual agitation over your attitude to her. Forgive me, I am excited and am going to speak frankly to you. Your conduct is killing her [*pause*]. Nikolay Alexeyevitch, allow me to think better of you!

IVANOV. It's all true, quite true. . . . I expect I am terribly to blame, but my thoughts are in a tangle, my soul is paralyzed by inertia, and I am incapable of understanding myself. I don't understand others or myself . . . [*looks at the window*]. We may be overheard, let us go for a stroll. [*They get up.*] I'd tell you the whole story from the beginning, my dear fellow, but it's a long story and so complicated that I shouldn't be finished by to-morrow morning. [*They are walking away.*] Anyuta is a remarkable, exceptional woman. . . . For my sake she has changed her religion, given up her father and mother, abandoned wealth, and if I wanted a hundred more sacrifices she would make them without the quiver of an eyelash. Well, and I am in no way remarkable, and I have made no sacrifices. But it's a long story. . . . The point of it all is, dear doctor [*hesitates*], is that . . . The long and the short of it is that I was passionately in love when I married and vowed I would love her for ever; but . . . five years have passed, she still loves me, and I . . . [*makes a gesture of despair*]. Here you tell me that she is soon going to die, and I feel neither love nor pity, but a sort of emptiness and weariness. . . . If one looks at me from outside it must be horrible. I don't myself understand what is happening in my soul. [*They go out along the avenue.*]

[*Enter* SHABELSKY.]

SHABELSKY [*laughing*]. Upon my honor, he is no common rascal, he is a genius, an expert! We ought to put up a statue to him. He combines in himself every form of modern rottenness: the lawyer's and the doctor's, and the huckster's and the cashier's [*sits down on the lowest step of the verandah*]. And yet I believe he has never finished his studies! That's what is so surprising. . . . What a rascal of genius he would have been if he had absorbed culture and learning! "You can have twenty thousand in a week," says he. "You've still the ace of trumps in your hands," says he, "your title" [*laughs*]. "Any girl with a dowry would marry you. . . ."

[ANNA PETROVNA *opens the window and looks down.*]

SHABELSKY. "Would you like me to make a match for you with Marfusha?" says he. *Qui est-ce que c'est Marfusha?* Ah, it's that Balabalkin . . . Babakalkin . . . who looks like a washer-woman. . . .

ANNA PETROVNA.   Is that you, Count?

SHABELSKY.   What is it?

[ANNA PETROVNA *laughs*.]

SHABELSKY [*with a Jewish accent*].   Vot for you laugh?

ANNA PETROVNA.   I thought of something you said. Do you remember you said at dinner: "A thief that is forgiven, a horse . . ." What is it?

SHABELSKY.   A Jew that is christened, a thief that is forgiven, a horse that is doctored—are worth the same price.

ANNA PETROVNA [*laughs*].   You can't make even a simple joke without spite in it. You are a spiteful man. [*Earnestly*] Joking apart, Count, you are very spiteful. It's dull and dreadful living with you. You are always snarling and grumbling. You think all men are scoundrels and rascals. Tell me honestly, have you ever said anything good about anyone?

SHABELSKY.   Why this cross-examination?

ANNA PETROVNA.   We've been living under the same roof for five years and I've never once heard you speak of people calmly, without malice and derision. What harm have people done you? And do you really imagine that you are better than anyone else?

SHABELSKY.   I don't imagine it at all. I am just as great a blackguard and pig in a skull-cap as everyone else, *mauvais ton* and an old rag. I always abuse myself. Who am I? What am I? I was rich, free and rather happy, but now . . . I am a dependant, a hanger-on, a degraded buffoon. I am indignant, I am contemptuous, and people laugh at me: I laugh and they shake their heads at me mournfully and say the old chap is cracked . . . and most often they don't hear me, don't heed me. . . .

ANNA PETROVNA [*calmly*].   It is screeching again.

SHABELSKY.   Who is screeching?

ANNA PETROVNA.   The owl. It screeches every evening.

SHABELSKY.   Let it screech. Nothing can be worse than what is now [*stretching*]. Ah, my dear Sarra, if I were to win a hundred or two hundred thousand I'd show you a thing or two! You'd see no more of me here. I'd get away from this hole, away from the bread·of charity . . . and wouldn't set foot here again till the day of judgment. . . .

ANNA PETROVNA.   And what would you do if you did win a lot of money?

SHABELSKY [*after a moment's thought*].   First of all I would go to Moscow to hear the gypsies. Then . . . then I should be off to Paris. I should take a flat there, I should go to the Russian church. . . .

ANNA PETROVNA.   And what else?

SHABELSKY.   I should sit for days together on my wife's grave and think. I should sit there till I died. My wife is buried in Paris. . . . [*pause*].

ANNA PETROVNA.   How awfully dull it is! Shall we play another duet?

SHABELSKY.   Very well, get the music ready.

[ANNA PETROVNA *goes out. Enter* IVANOV *and* LVOV.]

IVANOV [*comes into sight with* LVOV *in the avenue*].   You took your degree only last year, my dear friend, you are still young and vigorous while I am five and thirty. I have the right to advise you. Don't marry a Jewess nor a neurotic nor a blue stocking, but choose what is commonplace, gray, with no vivid colors or super- fluous flourishes. In fact, build your whole life on the conventional pattern. The grayer and the more monotonous the background the better, my dear boy. Don't fight with thousands single-handed, don't wage war on windmills, don't batter your head against the wall. . . . God preserve you from all sorts of scientific farming, wonderful schools, enthusiastic speeches. . . . Shut yourself up in your shell, do the humble duty God has laid upon you. . . . That's snugger, happier and more honest. But the life that I have led, how tiring it is! Ah, how tiring! . . . How many mistakes, how much that was unjust and absurd. . . . [*Seeing the* COUNT, *irritably*] You are always in the way, Uncle, you never let one have a talk in peace!

SHABELSKY [*in a tearful voice*].   Oh, the devil take me, there's no refuge for me anywhere! [*jumps up and goes into the house*].

IVANOV [*calls after him*].   Oh, I am sorry! [*To* LVOV] What made me hurt his feelings? Yes, I must be out of gear. I must do something with myself, I really must. . . .

LVOV [*in agitation*].   Nikolay Alexeyevitch, I have listened to you and . . . and forgive me, I will speak plainly, without beating about the bush. Your voice, your intonation, to say nothing of your words, are full of such soulless egoism, such cold heartlessness. . . . Someone very near to you is dying through her love for you, her days are num- bered, and you . . . you can be cold to her, can walk about and give advice, and pose. . . . I cannot tell you, I have no gift for words, but . . . but you are intensely repulsive to me!

IVANOV.   Very likely, very likely. . . . You can see it all more clearly from outside. . . . It's very possible that you understand. . . . I daresay I am horribly to blame, horribly . . . [*listens*]. I fancy I hear the carriage. I am going to get ready . . . [*goes to the house and stops*].

You dislike me, doctor, and don't conceal your dislike. It does credit to your heart . . . [*goes into the house*].

LVOV [*alone*]. My cursed weakness! Again I've missed the chance and haven't said what I ought to have said. . . . I cannot speak to him calmly! As soon as I open my mouth and say a word I feel such a suffocation, such a heaving here [*points to his chest*], and my tongue sticks to the roof of my mouth. I hate this Tartuffe, this highflown scoundrel, I hate him. . . . Here he is going away. . . . His poor wife's only happiness is to have him near her, she lives in him, she implores him to spend one evening with her, and he . . . he cannot! He feels stifled and cramped at home, if you please. If he were to spend a single evening at home, he'd be so depressed that he'd blow his brains out. Poor fellow . . . he must have freedom to contrive some new villainy. . . . Oh, I know why you go to these Lebedyevs every evening! I know!

[*Enter* IVANOV *in his hat and overcoat,* ANNA PETROVNA *and* SHABELSKY.]

SHABELSKY [*as he comes out of the house with* ANNA PETROVNA *and* IVANOV]. Really, *Nicolas,* this is positively inhuman! You go out every evening and we are left alone. We are so bored we go to bed at eight o'clock. It's hideous, it's not life at all! And why is it that you can go and we mayn't? Why?

ANNA PETROVNA. Leave him alone! Let him go, let him. . . .

IVANOV [*to his wife*]. How can you go when you are ill? You are ill and you mustn't be out after sunset. . . . Ask the doctor. You are not a child, Anyuta, you must be sensible. . . . [*To the* COUNT] And what do you want to go there for?

SHABELSKY. I'd go to hell, into the jaws of a crocodile, so long as I need not stay here! I am bored! I am bored to stupefaction! Everybody is sick of me. You leave me at home so that she should not be bored alone, but I do nothing but snap and nag at her!

ANNA PETROVNA. Leave him alone, Count, leave him alone! Let him go if he enjoys it.

IVANOV. Anyuta, why do you speak like that? You know I am not going for pleasure! I have to speak about the loan.

ANNA PETROVNA. I don't know why you justify yourself! Go! No one is keeping you!

IVANOV. Come, don't let us nag at each other! Surely it isn't necessary?

SHABELSKY [*in a tearful voice*]. Nicolas, dear boy, I implore you, take me with you! I shall have a look at the knaves and fools there and perhaps it will amuse me! I haven't been anywhere since Easter!

IVANOV [*irritably*].   Oh, very well, come along! How sick I am of
you all!

SHABELSKY.   Yes? Oh, *merci, merci* . . . [*cheerfully takes him by the
arm and leads him aside*]. May I wear your straw hat?

IVANOV.   Yes, only make haste!

[*The* COUNT *runs indoors.*]

IVANOV.   How sick I am of you all! But, good God, what am I
saying? Anyuta, I talk to you in an unpardonable way. I never used
to be like this before. Well, good-bye, Anyuta, I shall be back by
one.

ANNA PETROVNA.   Kolya, darling, stay at home!

IVANOV [*agitated*].   My precious, my poor unhappy darling, I entreat you, don't prevent my going out in the evening. It's cruel and
unfair of me, but let me be unfair! I feel miserably depressed at home!
As soon as the sun sets, I am overcome by acute misery. Such misery!
Don't ask why it is. I don't know myself. I swear I don't! Here it is
misery; I go to the Lebedyevs and there it is worse still; I come back
and here misery again, and it goes on like that all night. . . . It's simply desperate!

ANNA PETROVNA.   Kolya . . . but if you stay? We will talk as we
used to. . . . We'll have supper together; we will read. . . . The old
grumbler and I have learned a lot of duets for you . . . [*puts her arms
round him*]. Do stay! [*pause*]. I don't understand you. This has been
going on for a whole year. Why have you changed?

IVANOV.   I don't know, I don't know. . . .

ANNA PETROVNA.   And why don't you want me to go with you
in the evening?

IVANOV.   If you will have it, I'll tell you. It's rather cruel to say it,
but it is better to speak out. . . . When I am depressed I . . . I begin
not to love you. I run away even from you at such times. In short, I
must get away from home.

ANNA PETROVNA.   Depression! I understand—I understand. . . .
Do you know what, Kolya? Try to sing, to laugh, to get cross, as you
used to. . . . Stay, we will laugh, drink home-made wine, and we'll
drive away your depression in an instant. Shall I sing to you? Or we'll
go and sit in your study in the dark as we used to, and you shall
tell me about your depression. . . . Your eyes are so full of suffering!
I will look into them and weep, and we shall both feel better . . . [*she
laughs and cries*]. Oh, Kolya, what is it? The flowers come again every
spring, but joys do not? Yes? Well, go, go. . . .

IVANOV.   Pray for me, Anyuta! [*he moves forward, stops, and ponders*]. No, I cannot [*goes out*].

ANNA PETROVNA.   Go . . . [sits down at the table].
LVOV [pacing up and down the stage]. Anna Petrovna, you must make it a rule as soon as the clock strikes six to come indoors and stay there till morning. The damp of the evening is bad for you.
ANNA PETROVNA.   Yes, sir!
LVOV.   What do you mean by that? I am speaking seriously.
ANNA PETROVNA.   And I don't want to be serious [coughs].
LVOV.   There, you see, you are coughing already.

[Enter SHABELSKY].

SHABELSKY [comes out in a hat and overcoat].   Where is Nikolay? Is the carriage there? [goes up quickly and kisses ANNA PETROVNA's hand]. Good-night, my charmer! [grimacing]. Gewalt! Vill you pardon me? [goes out quickly].
LVOV.   The buffoon!

[Pause; the sound of a concertina far away.]

ANNA PETROVNA.   How dull it is! The coachmen and the cooks have got up a ball, while I . . . I seem to be forsaken. . . . Yevgeny Konstantinitch, why are you striding up and down? Come here, sit down!
LVOV.   I can't sit still [pause].
ANNA PETROVNA.   They are playing the Greenfinch in the kitchen.
    [Sings] Greenfinch, greenfinch, where have you been?
        Drinking vodka under the hill?
[pause] Doctor, have you got a father and mother?
LVOV.   My father is dead, but I have a mother.
ANNA PETROVNA.   Do you miss your mother?
LVOV.   I have no time to miss her.
ANNA PETROVNA [laughs].   The flowers come again every spring, but joys do not. Who was it said that to me? Let me see. . . . I believe it was Nikolay himself [listens]. There's the owl screeching again!
LVOV.   Well, let it screech.
ANNA PETROVNA.   I begin to think, doctor, that fate has been unfair to me. Numbers of people who are perhaps no better than I are happy and pay nothing for their happiness. I have paid for everything, absolutely everything! And what a price! Why take from me such terribly high interest? . . . My good friend, you are all on your guard with me—you are so considerate, you are afraid to tell me the truth; but do you suppose I don't know what's the matter with me? I know very well. But it's boring to talk about it. [In a Jewish accent] Vill you pardon me, please? Can you tell funny stories?

LVOV. No.

ANNA PETROVNA. Nikolay can. And I begin to be surprised at people's injustice. Why don't they return love for love, and why do they repay truth with falsehood? Tell me, how long will my father and mother hate me? They live forty miles from here, but day and night, even in my sleep, I feel their hatred. And what would you have me make of Nikolay's depression? He says that he doesn't love me only in the evenings, when he is overwhelmed with depression. That I understand and can allow for. But only imagine if he should tire of me altogether! Of course it's impossible, but—if he did? No, no, I must not even think about it. [*Sings*] Greenfinch, greenfinch, where have you been? . . . [*starts*]. What dreadful ideas come into my mind! You are not married, doctor, and there are many things you can't understand. . . .

LVOV. You are surprised . . . [*sits down beside her*]. No, I . . . I am surprised—I am surprised at you! Come, explain, make me understand, how is it that you, intelligent, honest, almost a saint, have allowed yourself to be so shamelessly deceived and dragged into this owl's nest? Why are you here? What have you in common with this cold, soulless . . . but let us leave your husband out! What have you in common with these vulgar, empty surroundings? Oh, good heavens! . . . that everlastingly grumbling, rusty, mad Count, that knave Misha—a scoundrel if ever there was one—with his revolting countenance. . . . Explain to me what you are here for. How did you come here?

ANNA PETROVNA [*laughs*]. That's just how he used once to talk. Word for word. . . . But his eyes are larger, and when he began talking of anything with excitement they glowed like coals. . . . Go on, go on!

LVOV [*gets up with a wave of his hand*]. What am I to say? Go indoors!

ANNA PETROVNA. You say that Nikolay is this and that, one thing and another. How do you know him? Do you suppose that you can get to know a man in six months? He is a remarkable man, doctor, and I am sorry that you did not meet him two or three years ago. Now he is depressed and melancholy, he doesn't talk or do anything; but in the old days . . . how charming he was! I loved him at first sight [*laughs*]. I looked and the mousetrap went bang! He said "Come" . . . I cut off everything as, you know, one cuts off dead leaves with scissors, and followed him [*pause*]. But now it is different. Now he goes to the Lebedyevs to distract his mind with other women, while I . . . sit in the garden and listen to the owl screeching . . . [*A watchman's tap*.] And have you any brothers, doctor?

Lvov.   No.

[Anna Petrovna *breaks into sobs.*]

Lvov.   Well, what now? What's the matter?

Anna Petrovna [*gets up*].   I can't bear it, doctor . . . I am going. . . .

Lvov.   Where?

Anna Petrovna.   Where he is . . . I am going. Tell them to put the horses in [*runs into the house*].

Lvov.   No, I must absolutely decline to treat a patient under such conditions! It's not enough that they don't pay me a farthing, but they turn my soul inside out as well! . . . No, I decline! It's too much . . . [*goes into the house*].

CURTAIN.

ACT II

*A drawing-room in LEBEDYEV's house; facing the stage a door into the gar-
den; doors on right and left. Old-fashioned expensive furniture. A
chandelier, candelabras, and pictures—all under covers.*

ZINAIDA SAVISHNA, KOSSIH, AVDOTYA NAZAROVNA, YEGORUSHKA,
GAVRIL, *a* MAIDSERVANT, OLD LADY VISITORS, YOUNG PEOPLE,
and MADAME BABAKIN.

ZINAIDA SAVISHNA *is sitting on the sofa.* OLD LADIES *are sitting in arm-
chairs on either side of her, and* YOUNG PEOPLE *on ordinary chairs. In
the background, near the way out into the garden, they are playing cards;
among the players are* KOSSIH, AVDOTYA NAZAROVNA *and*
YEGORUSHKA. GAVRIL *is standing by the door on right; a* MAID-
SERVANT *carries round a tray full of sweets. Throughout the act*
GUESTS *pass across the stage from the garden to door on right and back
again.* MADAME BABAKIN *comes in from door on right and goes up to*
ZINAIDA SAVISHNA.

ZINAIDA [*joyfully*].   My darling Marfa Yegorovna!

MADAME BABAKIN.   How are you, Zinaida Savishna? I have the
honor to congratulate you on your daughter's birthday. [*They kiss.*]
God grant that . . .

ZINAIDA.   Thank you, darling, I am so glad. . . . Well, how are
you?

MADAME BABAKIN.   Thank you very much indeed [*sits down beside her on the sofa*]. How do you do, young people?

[*The* GUESTS *get up and bow.*]

FIRST GUEST [*laughs*].   Young people! . . . Why, are you old,
then?

MADAME BABAKIN [*with a sigh*].   Well, I am sure I don't claim to
be young. . . .

FIRST GUEST [*laughing respectfully*].   Upon my word, what next!
You don't look like a widow; you can give points to any young
girl.

[GAVRIL *hands* MADAME BABAKIN *tea.*]

16

ZINAIDA [*to* GAVRIL].   Why do you bring it like that? Fetch some jam. Gooseberry or something.

MADAME BABAKIN.   Please don't trouble.   Thanks ever so much. . . .

[*Pause*]

FIRST GUEST.   Did you drive through Mushkino, Marfa Yegorovna?

MADAME BABAKIN.   No, through Zaimishtche. The road is better that way.

FIRST GUEST.   To be sure.

KOSSIH.   Two spades.

YEGORUSHKA.   Pass.

AVDOTYA.   Pass.

SECOND GUEST.   Pass.

MADAME BABAKIN.   Lottery tickets have gone up shockingly, Zinaida Savishna, darling. It's unheard of: the first drawings are worth two hundred and seventy and the second nearly two hundred and fifty. It has never been so much before. . . .

ZINAIDA [*sighs*].   It's a good thing for those who have plenty of them.

MADAME BABAKIN.   Don't say that, darling. Though the price is so high, it does not pay to put one's money into them. The insurance alone is enough to drive you crazy.

ZINAIDA.   That may be so; but still, my dear, one has hopes . . . [*she sighs*]. God is merciful.

THIRD GUEST.   From my point of view, *mesdames,* I maintain that it does not pay to have capital at all nowadays. Investments yield a very small dividend and to put money into business is extremely risky. The way I look at it, *mesdames,* is that the man who has capital in the present day is in a much more critical position than a man who . . .

MADAME BABAKIN [*sighing*].   That's true!

[FIRST GUEST *yawns.*]

MADAME BABAKIN.   Is that the way to behave before ladies?

FIRST GUEST.   Pardon, *mesdames,* it was an accident.

[ZINAIDA SAVISHNA *gets up and goes out at the door on right. Prolonged silence.*]

YEGORUSHKA.   Two of diamonds.

AVDOTYA.   Pass.

SECOND GUEST.   Pass.

KOSSIH.   Pass.

MADAME BABAKIN [*aside*].   O Lord, how deadly dull it is!

[*Enter* ZINAIDA SAVISHNA *and* LEBEDYEV.]

ZINAIDA [*coming out of door on right with* LEBEDYEV, *quietly*].   What do you want to stick there for all alone! As though you were a prima-donna! Sit with your visitors [*sits down in the same place as before*].

LEBEDYEV [*yawns*].   Oh dear, oh dear! [*Seeing* MADAME BABAKIN] Saints alive, here is strawberry cream! Turkish delight! [*shakes hands*]. How is your precious self?

MADAME BABAKIN.   All right, thanks ever so much.

LEBEDYEV.   Well, thank God for that! [*sits down*]. Yes, yes . . . Gavril!

[GAVRIL *brings him a wineglass of vodka and a tumbler of water; he drinks up the vodka and sips the water.*]

FIRST GUEST.   To your very good health!

LEBEDYEV.   Very good health indeed! . . . I must be thankful I've not snuffed it altogether. [*To his wife*] Zyuzushka, where is the queen of the day?

KOSSIH [*plaintively*].   I should like to know why it is we have taken no tricks [*jumps up*]. Why have we lost every game? May the devil flay me entirely!

AVDOTYA [*jumps up and says angrily*].   Why, because if you can't play, my good man, you had better not take a hand. Whatever busi-ness had you to lead your opponent's suit? That's why you were left with your ace in pickle! [*They both run forward from the table.*]

KOSSIH [*in a tearful voice*].   Listen. . . . I had the ace, king, queen and eight more diamonds, the ace of spades and one little heart, you know. . . . And she could not declare a little slam—the devil knows why! I said no trumps . . .

AVDOTYA.   It was I who said no trumps! You said two and no trumps. . . .

KOSSIH.   It's revolting! . . . Excuse me . . . you had . . . I had . . . you had . . . [*To* LEBEDYEV] Just think, Pavel Kirillitch . . . I had the ace, king, queen and eight more diamonds. . . .

LEBEDYEV [*putting his fingers in his ears*].   Let me alone, if you don't mind . . .

AVDOTYA [*shouts*].   It was I said no trumps!

KOSSIH [*ferociously*].   May I be damned and disgraced if I ever sit down again to play with that cross old crab! [*goes quickly into the gar-den.* SECOND GUEST *goes after him.* YEGORUSHKA *is left at the table*].

AVDOTYA.   Ugh! I am hot all over. . . . A crab! . . . You are a crab yourself!

MADAME BABAKIN.   You are a hasty one, too, Granny. . . .

AVDOTYA [*seeing* MADAME BABAKIN, *flings up her hands*].   My joy, my beauty! She is here, and me so blind as not to see her! . . . My darling . . . [*kisses her on the shoulder and sits down beside her*]. How delightful! Let me have a look at you, my white swan! . . . I'll knock on the wood!

LEBEDYEV.   Now you are off. . . . You'd much better be finding her a husband. . . .

AVDOTYA.   I will find her one! I won't lay my sinful old bones in my coffin till I have married her off, and Sasha too! . . . I won't! . . . [*a sigh*]. Only where are they to be found nowadays, these husbands? Here they sit ruffling up their feathers like cocks in the rain, our young men!

THIRD GUEST.   A very unhappy comparison. In my opinion, *mesdames,* if young men nowadays prefer a bachelor existence, the reason is to be found in social conditions, so to say. . . .

LEBEDYEV.   Come, come, no moralizing! . . . I don't care for it . . .

[*Enter* SASHA.]

SASHA [*goes up to her father*].   Such glorious weather, and you all sit here in this stuffy room.

ZINAIDA.   Sashenka, don't you see that Marfa Yegorovna is here?

SASHA.   I am sorry [*goes up to* MADAME BABAKIN *and shakes hands*].

MADAME BABAKIN.   You are growing proud, Sasha. You have not been to see me once [*kisses her*]. I congratulate you, darling. . . .

SASHA.   Thank you [*sits down beside her father*].

LEBEDYEV.   Yes, Avdotya Nazarovna, it is a difficult job with the young men nowadays. One can't get a decent best man for a wedding, let alone a husband. Nowadays young people (no offense to present company) are so limp and flabby, God help them! . . . They can't talk, they can't dance, they can't drink. . . .

AVDOTYA.   Oh, they are all equal to drinking if they have the chance.

LEBEDYEV.   There's no great art in drinking—even a horse can drink. . . . The thing is to drink like a gentleman. In our time we used to be struggling all day with lectures, and as soon as evening came on we would go off anywhere and be twirling like a top till morning . . . and we danced and amused the young ladies and had a good drink too. We talked nonsense or talked philosophy till our tongues were tired. . . . But the young men nowadays . . . [*waves his hand*]. I can't make them out. . . . Neither a candle to God nor a poker to the devil. There's only one sensible fellow in the district, and he is married [*sighs*], and I fancy he is beginning to go off his head too. . . .

MADAME BABAKIN.   Who is that?

LEBEDYEV.   Nikolasha Ivanov.

MADAME BABAKIN.   Yes, he is a nice gentleman [*makes a grimace*]. Only unfortunate! . . .

ZINAIDA.   How could he be fortunate, my dear? [*sighs*]. What a mistake he made, poor fellow! He married his Jewess and reckoned, poor fellow! that her father and mother would give mountains of gold with her; but it has turned out quite the other way. . . . Ever since she changed her religion her father and mother have cast her off— they cursed her. . . . So he hasn't got a farthing. Now he is sorry, but it is too late. . . .

SASHA.   Mother, that's not true.

MADAME BABAKIN [*hotly*].   Sasha! not true? Why, everybody knows it. If it weren't for money why ever should he have married a Jewess? There are plenty of Russian girls, aren't there? He made a mistake, darling, he made a mistake . . . [*Eagerly*] And, I say, how she catches it from him now! It is simply too funny. As soon as he comes home he is at her at once: "Your father and mother have cheated me! Get out of my house!" And where is she to go? Her father and mother won't take her; she would go for a housemaid, but she has never been trained to do anything . . . And he goes on from one thing to another till the Count takes her part. If it were not for the Count he would have been the death of her long ago. . . .

AVDOTYA.   And sometimes he will shut her in the cellar and make her eat garlic. . . . She will eat it and eat it till she is sick [*laughter*].

SASHA.   Father, that's a lie, you know!

LEBEDYEV.   Well, what of it? Let them babble as they like . . . [*Shouts*] Gavril!

[GAVRIL *hands him vodka and water.*]

ZINAIDA.   That's how it is he has come to ruin, poor fellow! His affairs are in a bad way, my dear. . . . If Borkin did not look after the estate he and his Jewess would have nothing to eat [*sighs*]. And what we have had to put up with on his account, my dear. . . . God only knows what we have had to put up with! Would you believe it, dear, he has been owing us nine thousand for these three years!

MADAME BABAKIN [*with horror*].   Nine thousand!

ZINAIDA.   Yes. . . . It was my precious Pashenka's idea to give it to him. He never knows whom one can lend to and whom one can't.

I say nothing of the capital—it's no good worrying about that—but he might at least pay the interest regularly.

SASHA [*hotly*].   Mother, you have talked of that thousands of times already!

ZINAIDA.   What is it to you? Why do you defend him?

SASHA [*getting up*].   But how can you have the face to talk like that about a man who has done you no sort of harm? Why, what has he done to you?

THIRD GUEST.   Alexandra Pavlovna, allow me to say a couple of words. I respect Nikolay Alexeyevitch, and always considered it an honor . . . but, speaking *entre nous,* my opinion is that he is an adventurer.

SASHA.   Well, I congratulate you on your opinion.

THIRD GUEST.   In support of it I beg to mention the following fact which was reported to me by his *attaché* or, so to speak, *cicerone,* Borkin. Two years ago at the time of the cattle plague he bought cattle, insured them . . .

ZINAIDA.   Yes, yes, yes! I remember the incident. I was told of it too.

THIRD GUEST.   Insured them—mark that—then infected them with the cattle plague and got the insurance money.

SASHA.   Ugh, that's all such rubbish! No one bought cattle or infected them! That was all Borkin's invention, and he boasted of the plan everywhere. When Ivanov heard of it, Borkin was begging his pardon for a fortnight before he would forgive him. Ivanov is only to blame for being weak and not having the heart to kick that Borkin out, and he is to blame for putting too much trust in people too! He has been robbed and plundered on all sides: everyone who could made money out of his generous schemes.

LEBEDYEV.   Sasha, you little spitfire, shut up!

SASHA.   Why do they talk such nonsense? It's so dull—so boring! Ivanov, Ivanov, Ivanov—you talk of nothing else [*goes to the door and turns back*]. I wonder! [*to the young men*]. I positively wonder at your patience, gentlemen! Aren't you tired of sitting still like this? The very air is heavy with boredom! Do say something; entertain the young ladies; move about a little! Come, if you have no other subject but Ivanov, laugh, sing, dance or something. . . .

LEBEDYEV [*laughing*].   Give it to them, give it to them well!

SASHA.   Come, I say, do something for me! If you don't care to dance, to laugh, to sing, if all that bores you, I beg you, I entreat you, just for once in your life—as a curiosity—to surprise or amuse us: make a great effort and all together think of something witty and brilliant; say something, even if it is rude or vulgar, so long as it is amusing and new! Or all together do some little thing, however inconspicuous, so long as it is just conceivably worth doing, so that for once in their lives the young ladies may cry "Oh!" as they look at you. You do want to please, don't you? So why don't you try to be pleasing? Ah! my friends, you are not up to much—not up to much, any of you. . . . The very flies die of boredom and the lamps begin smoking when they look at you. . . . You are not up to much, any of you. . . . I have told you so a thousand times already, and I shall always say so.

[*Enter* IVANOV *and* SHABELSKY.]

SHABELSKY [*entering with* IVANOV *by door on right*]. Who is preaching here? You, Sasha? [*laughs and shakes hands with her*]. Happy returns, my angel. God grant that you die as late as possible and are not born again. . . .

ZINAIDA [*delightedly*]. Nikolay Alexeyevitch! Count!

LEBEDYEV. Bah! Whom do I see? . . . The Count! [*goes to meet him*].

SHABELSKY [*seeing* ZINAIDA SAVISHNA *and* MADAME BABAKIN, *stretches out his hands to them*]. Two gold mines on one sofa! . . . Delightful spectacle! [*shakes hands. To* ZINAIDA SAVISHNA] How do you do, Zyuzushka! [*To* MADAME BABAKIN] How do you do, dumpling!

ZINAIDA. I am glad. You are such a rare visitor, Count! [*Shouts*] Gavril, tea! Please sit down [*gets up, goes out of door on right and at once returns; she looks extremely preoccupied.* SASHA *sits down in the same place as before.* IVANOV *greets everyone in silence*].

LEBEDYEV [*to* SHABELSKY]. Where have you dropped from? What brought you here? It is a surprise! [*kisses him*]. Count, you are a rascal! Is that the way for decent people to behave? [*leads him by the hand to the footlights*]. Why do you never come and see us? Are you cross, or what?

SHABELSKY. How can I come and see you? Astride a stick? I have no horses, and Nikolay won't bring me with him: he tells me to stay with Sarra, to keep her company. Send your horses for me, and then I will come. . . .

LEBEDYEV [*with a wave of his hand*]. Oh, well! Zyuzushka would burst before she'd let me have the horses. You dear creature, you darling, you know you are nearer and dearer to me than anyone! Of all the old set there is no one left but you and me! In you I love my sorrows of past years, and my fair youth so idly flung away. . . . Joking apart, I feel ready to cry! [*kisses the* COUNT].

SHABELSKY.   Let go—let go! You smell like a winecellar. . . .

LEBEDYEV.   My dear soul, you can't think how I miss my old friends! I could hang myself, I am so miserable [*softly*]. Zyuzushka, with her money-grubbing, has driven all decent people away, and as you see we have none but Zulus left . . . these Dudkins and Budkins. . . . Come, drink your tea!

[GAVRIL *brings* SHABELSKY *tea.*]

ZINAIDA [*anxiously to* GAVRIL].   What are you doing? Bring some jam . . . gooseberry, or something . . .

SHABELSKY [*laughs; to* IVANOV].   There; did I not tell you? [*To* LEBEDYEV] I bet him on the way that as soon as we got here Zyuzushka would regale us with gooseberry jam. . . .

ZINAIDA.   You are just as fond of your joke as ever, Count [*sits down*].

LEBEDYEV.   She has made two barrels of gooseberry jam, so what is she to do with it?

SHABELSKY [*sitting down near the table*].   You are saving money, Zyuzushka, aren't you? I suppose you are a millionaire by now, eh?

ZINAIDA [*with a sigh*].   Yes, to outsiders it seems as though we are richer than anyone, but where could we get money from? That's all gossip. . . .

SHABELSKY.   Come, come! We know all about that! . . . We know what a poor hand you are at the game . . . [*To* LEBEDYEV] Pasha, tell the truth, have you saved a million?

LEBEDYEV.   I don't know. Ask Zyuzushka. . . .

SHABELSKY [*to* MADAME BABAKIN].   And our fat little dumpling will soon have a million too! She gets plumper and prettier, not every day, but every hour! That's what it is to have plenty of money. . . .

MADAME BABAKIN.   I am very much obliged to your Excellency, but I am not fond of being jeered at.

SHABELSKY.   My dear gold-mine, do you suppose it was a jeer? It was simply a cry from the heart. Out of the fullness of the heart the mouth speaketh. . . . There is no limit to my affection for you and Zyuzushka [*gaily*]. It's rapture, ecstasy! I can't look at either of you unmoved!

ZINAIDA.   You are just the same as ever. [*To* YEGORUSHKA] Yegorushka, put out the candles! Why let them burn for nothing when you are not playing? [YEGORUSHKA *starts; puts out the candles and sits down. To* IVANOV] Nikolay Alexeyevitch, how is your wife?

IVANOV.   She is very ill. The doctor told us today that it is certainly consumption.

ZINAIDA.   Really? What a pity! [*a sigh*]. We are all so fond of her.

SHABELSKY.   Nonsense, nonsense, nonsense! . . . There is no consumption at all: it's all quackery—doctors' tricks. The learned gentleman likes to hang about the house, so he makes out it's consumption. Luckily for him the husband is not jealous. [IVANOV *makes a gesture of impatience.*] As for Sarra herself, I don't trust a word she says or a thing she does. All my life I've never trusted doctors, lawyers, or women. It's all nonsense and nonsense, quackery and tricks!

LEBEDYEV [*to* SHABELSKY].   You are a strange individual, Matvey! . . . You've taken up this affectation of misanthropy and play about with it like a fool with a new hat. You are a man like anyone else, but you are as peevish in your talk as though you had a blister on your tongue, or indigestion. . . .

SHABELSKY.   Why, would you have me kiss rogues and scoundrels, or what?

LEBEDYEV.   Where do you see rogues and scoundrels?

SHABELSKY.   I don't refer to present company, of course, but . . .

LEBEDYEV.   There you are with your buts. . . . It's all affectation.

SHABELSKY.   Affectation? . . . It's a good thing you've no philosophy of life.

LEBEDYEV.   What philosophy could I have? I sit every minute expecting to kick the bucket. That's my philosophy of life. It's too late for you and me, old man, to talk of philosophies of life. Yes, indeed! [*Shouts*] Gavril!

SHABELSKY.   You have had too much of Gavril as it is. . . . Your nose is like beetroot already.

LEBEDYEV [*drinks*].   Never mind, my dear soul . . . it's not my wedding day.

ZINAIDA.   It is a long while since Dr. Lvov has been to see us. He has quite deserted us.

SASHA.   My pet aversion. The walking image of honesty. He can't ask for a glass of water or smoke a cigarette without displaying his extraordinary honesty. If he walks about or talks, his face is always labelled "I am an honest man." He bores me.

SHABELSKY.   He is a stiff-necked, narrow-minded individual! [*Mimicking*] "Make way for honest labor!" He shouts like a cockatoo at every step, and he fancies he is really a second Dobrolyubov. If a man does not shout as he does, he is a scoundrel. His views are wonderfully profound. If a peasant is well off and lives like a human being, he is a scoundrel and a blood-sucker. I put on a velvet jacket and am dressed by a valet, so I am a scoundrel and a slave-owner. He is simply bursting with honesty. Nothing is good enough for him. I am positively afraid of him. . . . Yes, indeed! any minute he may slap you in the face or call you a scoundrel from a sense of duty.

IVANOV.   He wearies me dreadfully, but at the same time I like him; he is so sincere.

SHABELSKY.   Nice sort of sincerity! He came up to me yesterday evening, and *apropos* of nothing at all: "You are deeply repulsive to me, Count!" I am very much obliged! And all that not simply, but from principle: his voice shakes, his eyes flash, and he is all of a tremor. . . . Damnation take his wooden sincerity! He may find me hateful and disgusting; it's natural enough. . . . I can see that, but why tell me so to my face? I am a wretched creature, but anyway my hair is gray. . . . A stupid, pitiless honesty!

LEBEDYEV.   Come, come, come! . . . You've been young yourself, and can make allowances.

SHABELSKY.   Yes, I've been young and foolish: I've played the Tchatsky in my day. I've denounced rascals and blackguards, but never in my life have I called a man a thief to his face, or talked of the gallows in the house of a man who has been hanged. I was decently brought up. But your dull-witted doctor would be in the seventh heaven and feel that he was fulfilling his mission, if fate would grant him the opportunity of publicly slapping me in the face and punching me in the pit of the stomach for the sake of principle and the great ideals of humanity.

LEBEDYEV.   Young people are always self-assertive. I had an uncle, a Hegelian . . . he would invite a houseful of visitors, drink with them, stand up on a chair like this and begin: "You are ignorant! You are the powers of darkness! The dawn of a new life," etc., etc., etc. . . . He would go on and on at them.

SASHA.   And what did the visitors do?

LEBEDYEV.   Oh, nothing . . . they just listened and went on drinking. Once, though, I challenged him to a duel . . . my own uncle. It was about Bacon. I remember, if I am right, I was sitting where Matvey is now, and my uncle and Gerassim Nilitch were standing as it might be here, where Nikolay is. . . . And Gerassim Nilitch, if you please, puts the question . . .

[BORKIN, *foppishly dressed, with a parcel in his hand, comes in at door on right, humming and skipping about. A murmur of approval.*]

YOUNG LADIES.   Mihail Mihailitch!

LEBEDYEV.   Mihail Mihailitch! My ears tell me . . .

SHABELSKY.   The soul of the party!

BORKIN.   Here I am! [*runs up to* SASHA] Noble lady! I venture to make so bold as to congratulate the universe on the birth of so marvellous a flower as you. . . . As the tribute of my enthusiasm may I dare to offer you [*gives her the parcel*] some fireworks and Bengal fires of my own manufacture? May they illuminate the night as you lighten the gloom of the kingdom of darkness [*makes a theatrical bow*].

SASHA. Thank you. . . .

LEBEDYEV [*laughing, to* IVANOV]. Why don't you get rid of that Judas?

BORKIN [*to* LEBEDYEV]. My respects to Pavel Kirillitch! [*To* IVANOV] To my patron! [*Sings.*] *Nicolas, voilà, ho-hi-ho.* [*Makes the round of the whole party*] To the most honored Zinaida Savishna! Divine Marfa Yegorovna . . . most ancient Avdotya Nazarovna . . . most illustrious Count. . . .

SHABELSKY [*laughs*]. The soul of the party. . . . As soon as he comes in the atmosphere grows lighter. Have you noticed it?

BORKIN. Ough, I am tired. . . . I believe I have greeted everybody now. Well, what's the news, ladies and gentlemen? Is there nothing special to wake us up? [*Briskly to* ZINAIDA SAVISHNA] I say, mamma . . . as I was on the way here . . . [*To* GAVRIL] Give me some tea, Gavril, but no gooseberry jam! [*To* ZINAIDA SAVISHNA] As I was on the way here I saw the peasants stripping the bark of your osiers on the river. Why don't you let a dealer have them?

LEBEDYEV [*to* IVANOV]. Why don't you get rid of that Judas?

ZINAIDA [*aghast*]. I might, that's true, the idea never struck me!

BORKIN [*does drill exercises with his arms*]. I can't get on without exercise. . . . What can I do that's extra special, mamma? Marfa Yegorovna, I *am* in form to-night . . . wild with excitement! [*Sings.*] "Once more I stand before thee. . . ."

ZINAIDA. Get up something, for we are all bored.

BORKIN. Really! Why are you all so down in the mouth? You sit like jurymen! . . . Let us do something. What would you like? Forfeits? Hide the ring? Touch third? Dancing? Fireworks?

YOUNG LADIES [*clap their hands*]. Fireworks! Fireworks! [*they run into the garden*].

SASHA [*to* IVANOV]. Why are you so depressed this evening?

IVANOV. My head aches, Sasha, and I am bored. . . .

SASHA. Come into the drawing-room. [*They go towards door on right; everyone goes into the garden except* ZINAIDA SAVISHNA *and* LEBEDYEV.]

ZINAIDA. Well, that's something like a young man—before he has been here a minute he has cheered them up [*turns down the big lamp*]. While they are all out in the garden it is no use wasting the candles [*puts out the candles*].

LEBEDYEV [*following her*].   Zyuzushka, we ought to give our visitors something to eat. . . .

ZINAIDA.   There, what a lot of candles . . . no wonder people think we are rich [*puts out the candles*].

LEBEDYEV [*following her*].   Zyuzushka, you ought to give the people something to eat. . . . They are young people, I bet they are hungry, poor things. . . . Zyuzushka. . . .

ZINAIDA.   The Count has not finished his glass. Simply wasting sugar! [*goes towards door on left*].

LEBEDYEV.   Tfoo! [*goes out into the garden*].

[*Enter* IVANOV *and* SASHA.]

SASHA [*comes in with* IVANOV *from door on right*].   They have all gone into the garden.

IVANOV.   That's how it is, Sasha. In old days I did a lot of work and a lot of thinking and never got tired; now I do nothing and think of nothing, and I am weary body and soul. My conscience aches night and day, I feel that I am terribly to blame, but exactly in what way I am to blame I don't know. And then my wife's illness, no money, the everlasting nagging and gossip, unnecessary talk, that fool Borkin. . . . My home has grown hateful to me, and living in it is worse than torture. I tell you openly, Sasha, even to be with my wife who loves me has become unbearable. You are my old friend, and won't be angry with me for speaking the truth. I have come to you to distract my mind, but I am bored here too, and I am longing to get home again. Forgive me, I will just slip away.

SASHA.   Nikolay Alexeyevitch, I understand you. Your misfortune is that you are all alone. You ought to have someone by you whom you love and who understands you. Nothing can renew you but love.

IVANOV.   What next, Sasha! That would be the last straw for a wretched bedraggled old creature like me to start a new love affair! God preserve me from such a calamity! No, my wise little friend, it is not a case for love affairs. I tell you in all solemnity, I can put up with everything—misery and neurasthenia and bankruptcy and the loss of my wife and my premature old age and my loneliness—but I cannot endure my contempt for myself. I could die with shame at the thought that I, a strong healthy man, have turned into a sort of Hamlet or a Manfred or a superfluous man . . . the devil knows what. There are pitiful creatures who are flattered at being called Hamlets or superfluous men, but to me it is a disgrace! It wounds my pride, I am crushed by shame, and I am miserable. . . .

SASHA [*jestingly through tears*]. Nikolay Alexeyevitch, let us run off to America.

IVANOV. I am too lazy to move to this door, and you talk of America. . . . [*They go to the door into the garden.*] Of course, Sasha, you don't have an easy time of it here. When I look at the people that surround you, I feel horrified at the thought of whom you can marry. The only hope is that some lieutenant or student will pass this way and carry you off. . . .

[ZINAIDA SAVISHNA *comes in from door on left with a jar of jam.*]

IVANOV. Excuse me, Sasha, I will come after you. . . .

[SASHA *goes out into the garden*]

IVANOV. Zinaida Savishna, I've come to ask you a favor.

ZINAIDA. What is it, Nikolay Alexeyevitch?

IVANOV [*hesitates*]. Well, you see, the fact is that the day after to-morrow the interest on your loan is due. You would very greatly oblige me if you would give me a little longer, or would let me add the interest on to the principal. I have no money at all at the moment. . . .

ZINAIDA [*alarmed*]. Nikolay Alexeyevitch, how is that possible? That's not the way to do things! No, don't think of such a thing. For God's sake don't worry me, I have troubles enough. . . .

IVANOV. I am sorry, I am sorry . . . [*goes out into the garden*].

ZINAIDA. Ough, he has upset me! I am all of a shake . . . all of a shake . . . [*goes out at door on right*].

[*Enter* KOSSIH.]

KOSSIH [*enters from left door and crosses the stage*]. I had the ace, king, queen, and eight more diamonds, the ace of spades and just one . . . one little heart, and she could not declare a little slam, the devil take her entirely . . . [*goes out at door on right*].

[*Enter* AVDOTYA NAZAROVNA *and* FIRST GUEST.]

AVDOTYA [*coming from the garden with* FIRST GUEST]. I could tear her to pieces, I could tear her to pieces, the old skinflint! It's no joke. I've been sitting here since five o'clock and she has not offered us as much as a stale herring! . . . It is a house! . . . It is a way to manage!

FIRST GUEST. I am so bored that I could run and bash my head against the wall! They are people, Lord have mercy upon us! One is so hungry and so bored; it's enough to make one howl like a wolf and begin snapping at people.

AVDOTYA.   Couldn't I tear her to pieces, sinful woman that I am!

FIRST GUEST.   I'll have a drink, old lady, and get home! I don't want your eligible young ladies. How the devil is one to think of love when one has not had one glass of wine since dinner?

AVDOTYA.   Let's go and look for something. . . .

FIRST GUEST.   Sh-sh! Quietly! I believe there is vodka in the sideboard in the dining-room. We'll get hold of Yegorushka. . . . Sh-sh! [*They go out by door on left.*]

[ANNA PETROVNA *and* LVOV *come out of door on right.*]

ANNA PETROVNA.   It's all right, they will be pleased to see us. Nobody here. They must be in the garden.

LVOV.   I wonder why you have brought me here into this nest of vultures? This is no place for you or me. Honest people ought to keep out of this atmosphere!

ANNA PETROVNA.   Listen, Mr. honest man! It is not polite to take a lady out and to talk to her of nothing but your honesty all the way! It may be honest, but to say the least of it, it is wearisome. You should never talk to women about your virtues. Let them see those for themselves. When my Nikolay was your age he did nothing but sing songs and tell stories in the company of ladies, but they could all see what sort of man he was.

LVOV.   Oh, don't talk to me about your Nikolay. I understand him perfectly!

ANNA PETROVNA.   You are a good man, but you don't understand anything. Let us go into the garden. He never used such expressions as "I am honest! I am stifled in this atmosphere! Vultures! Owl's nest! Crocodiles!" He used to leave the menagerie alone, and when he had been indignant all I heard from him was, "Ah, how unjust I was to-day!" or "Anyuta, I am sorry for that man!" That's what he was like, while you . . . [*They go out.*]

[*Enter* AVDOTYA NAZAROVNA *and* FIRST GUEST.]

FIRST GUEST [*coming in from door on left*].   It's not in the dining-room, so it must be somewhere in the larder. We must try Yegorushka. Let us go through the drawing-room.

AVDOTYA.   Couldn't I tear her to pieces! [*They go out at door on right.*]

[MADAME BABAKIN *and* BORKIN *run out of the garden, laughing;* SHABELSKY *comes tripping after them, laughing, and rubbing his hands*]

MADAME BABAKIN.   How dull it is! [*laughs*]. It is dull! They all sit
and walk about as though they had swallowed a poker. I am stiff with
boredom [*skips about*]. I must stretch my legs! [BORKIN *puts his arm
round her waist and kisses her on the cheek.*]

SHABELSKY [*laughs and snaps his fingers*].   Dash it all! [*clears his
throat*]. After all . . .

MADAME BABAKIN.   Let go, take away your arm, you shameless
fellow, or goodness knows what the Count will think! Leave
off! . . .

BORKIN.   Angel of my soul, jewel of my heart! . . . [*kisses her*]. Do
lend me two thousand three hundred rubles! . . .

MADAME BABAKIN.   N-no, n-no, n-no. . . . You may say what
you like, but as regards money, no thank you. . . . No, no, no! Oh,
take your arms away!

SHABELSKY [*prances round them*].   The little dumpling. . . . She has
her charm. . . .

BORKIN [*gravely*].   Come, that's enough. Let us come to the
point. Let us discuss things straightforwardly, in a businesslike way.
Give me a direct answer, without any tricks or subtleties: yes or no?
Listen [*points to the* COUNT]. He wants money, at least three thousand
rubles a year. You want a husband. Would you like to be a
Countess?

SHABELSKY [*laughs*].   A wonderful cynic!

BORKIN.   Would you like to be a Countess? Yes or no?

MADAME BABAKIN [*agitated*].   Do think what you are saying,
Misha, really! And such things aren't done in this slap-dash way. . . .
If the Count wishes it he can himself . . . and I don't know really
how, all of a minute. . . .

BORKIN.   Come, come, that's enough airs and graces! It's a business matter. . . . Yes or no?

SHABELSKY [*laughing and rubbing his hands*].   Yes, really, eh? Dash
it all, why not play this dirty trick? What? The dumpling! [*kisses
MADAME BABAKIN on the cheek*]. Charmer! Peach!

MADAME BABAKIN.   Wait a minute, wait a minute. . . . You've
quite upset me. . . . Go away, go away! No, don't go! . . .

BORKIN.   Make haste! Yes or no? We've no time to waste. . . .

MADAME BABAKIN.   I tell you what, Count. You come and stay
with me for two or three days. . . . You'll find it jolly, it's not like
this house. Come to-morrow. . . . [*To* BORKIN] No, you are joking,
aren't you?

BORKIN [*angrily*].   As though one would joke about serious
things!

MADAME BABAKIN.   Wait a minute, wait a minute. . . . Oh, I feel

faint! I feel faint! Countess . . . I am fainting . . . I shall drop. . . .
[BORKIN *and the* COUNT, *laughing, take her arm-in-arm and, kissing her on the cheek, lead her out by door on right.*]

[IVANOV *and* SASHA *run in from the garden.*]

IVANOV [*clutching his head in despair*].   It cannot be! Don't, don't, Sasha! . . . Oh, don't!

SASHA [*carried away*].   I love you madly. . . . There is no meaning in life, no joy, no happiness without you! You are everything to me! . . .

IVANOV.   What's the use, what's the use? My God! I don't understant it! Sasha, don't! . . .

SASHA.   In my childhood you were my only joy; I loved you and your soul like myself, but now . . . I love you, Nikolay Alexeyevitch! . . . I'll go with you to the ends of the earth, where you like, to the grave, if you will, but for God's sake let it be soon or I shall be stifled. . . .

IVANOV [*breaks into a happy laugh*].   What is it? Beginning life again then, Sasha, yes? . . . My happiness! [*draws her to him*]. My youth, my freshness! . . .

[ANNA PETROVNA *comes in from the garden and, seeing her husband and* SASHA, *stands rooted to the spot.*]

IVANOV.   I am to live then? Yes? To get to work again? [*A kiss. After the kiss* IVANOV *and* SASHA *look round and see* ANNA PETROVNA.]

IVANOV [*in horror*].   Sarra!

CURTAIN.

ACT III

IVANOV's *study. A writing-table on which papers, books, official envelopes, knick-knacks and revolvers are lying in disorder; near the papers a lamp, a decanter of vodka, a plate of herring, pieces of bread and cucumber. On the walls maps, pictures, guns, pistols, sickles, whips, etc. It is midday.*

SHABELSKY, LEBEDYEV, BORKIN *and* PYOTR. SHABELSKY *and* LEBEDYEV *are sitting by the writing-table,* BORKIN *in the middle of the stage astride a chair.* PYOTR *is standing at the door.*

LEBEDYEV.   The policy of France is clear and definite. . . . The French know what they want. All they want is to flay the sausage-eaters, while it is quite a different story with Germany. Germany has plenty of specks in her eye besides France. . . .

SHABELSKY.   Nonsense! . . . What I think is that the Germans are cowards and the French are cowards too. They are simply putting out their tongues at each other on the sly. Believe me, things won't go further than that. They won't come to fighting.

BORKIN.   And to my mind, there is no need to fight. What is the use of all these armaments, congresses, expenditure? I tell you what I should do. I should collect dogs from all over the country, innoculate them with a good dose of Pasteur's virus and let them loose in the enemy's country. All the enemy would run mad with hydrophobia in a month.

LEBEDYEV [*laughs*].   His head is small to look at, but there are as many great ideas in it as fish in the sea.

SHABELSKY.   He is a specialist in them!

LEBEDYEV.   God bless you, you do amuse me, Mihail Mihailovitch. [*Stops laughing*] We keep chattering away, but what about vodka? *Repetatur!* [*fills three wine-glasses*]. To our good health! [*They drink and eat a little.*] Good old red herring is the best sort of snack one can have.

SHABELSKY.   No, cucumber is better. . . . The learned men have been busy thinking since the creation of the world, but they have

32

thought of nothing better than salted cucumber. [*To* PYOTR] Pyotr, go and get some more cucumbers and tell the cook to fry us four onion turnovers, and send them hot.

[PYOTR *goes out.*]

LEBEDYEV.   Caviare is not bad with vodka either. But you want to use it properly. . . . You want to take a quarter of a pound of pressed caviare, two spring onions, olive oil, mix it all together . . . and just a little wee drop of lemon on the top of it, you know. Gorgeous! The very smell of it is stunning.

BORKIN.   A dish of fried gudgeon is good after vodka too. Only one must know how to fry them. They must be cleaned, then dipped in sifted breadcrumbs and fried till they are dry, so that they crunch in the teeth. . . . Kroo-kroo-kroo. . . .

SHABELSKY.   We had a good dish at Madame Babakin's yesterday—mushrooms.

LEBEDYEV.   I daresay. . . .

SHABELSKY.   Only it was prepared in some special way. You know, with onion and bay leaves and all sorts of condiments. As soon as the cover was taken off there was a steam, a smell . . . delicious!

LEBEDYEV.   Well, what do you say? *Repetatur,* gentlemen. [*They drink.*] To our good health! [*Looks at his watch*] I am afraid I can't wait for Nikolay. It's time I was off. You say you had mushrooms at Madame Babakin's, and we have not seen a mushroom yet. And just tell me, if you please, why the devil are you so often at Marfa's?

SHABELSKY [*nods towards* BORKIN].   Why, he wants to marry me to her.

LEBEDYEV.   Marry? Why, how old are you?

SHABELSKY.   Sixty-two.

LEBEDYEV.   The very time to get married. And Marfa is just the match for you.

BORKIN.   It is not a question of Marfa, but of Marfa's rubles.

LEBEDYEV.   Anything else! Marfa's rubles! You will be crying for the moon next!

BORKIN.   When the man is married and has stuffed his pockets, you will see whether it's crying for the moon! You will envy his luck.

SHABELSKY.   And you know he is in earnest. This genius is convinced that I'll do what he tells me and marry her.

BORKIN.   Why, of course! Aren't you convinced of it too?

SHABELSKY.   You are crazy. . . . When was I convinced? Phew!

BORKIN.   Thank you. . . . Thank you very much! So you want to make a fool of me? First, it's I'll marry and then I won't marry. . . .

Who the devil is to make you out? And I have given my word of
honor! So you won't marry her?

SHABELSKY [*shrugging his shoulders*].   He is in earnest! Amazing
person!

BORKIN [*indignant*].   In that case what do you want to upset a
respectable woman for? She is mad on being a countess, can't sleep or
eat. . . . Is it a subject to joke about? Is it honest?

SHABELSKY [*snapping his fingers*].   Well, and how if I do play this
dirty trick after all? What? Just for mischief? I'll go and do it! On my
word. . . . It will be fun!

[*Enter* LVOV.]

LEBEDYEV.   Doctor, our humble respects! [*gives* LVOV *his hand and
sings*]. Doctor, save me kindly, sir, I am in deadly fear of death!

LVOV.   Nikolay Alexeyevitch has not come in yet?

LEBEDYEV.   Why no, I have been waiting for him for more than
an hour. [LVOV *strides impatiently up and down the stage.*] Well, my dear
fellow, how is Anna Petrovna?

LVOV.   Very ill.

LEBEDYEV [*sighs*].   Can I go and pay her my respects?

LVOV.   No, please don't go. I believe she is asleep . . . [*Pause*].

LEBEDYEV.   She is a nice, sweet woman [*sighs*]. On Sasha's birthday, when she fainted at our house, I looked at her face and I saw
she had not long to live, poor dear. I don't know why she was taken
ill then. I ran up, I looked at her and she was lying pale as death,
with Nikolay on his knees beside her as pale as she, and Sasha in
tears. Sasha and I went about as though we were dazed for a week
after.

SHABELSKY [*to* LVOV].   Tell me, honored votary of science, what
learned sage was it discovered that ladies with delicate chests are
benefited by the frequent visits of a young doctor? It's a great dis-
covery, great! To which is it to be ascribed: to the allopaths or the
homeopaths?

[LVOV *is on the point of answering, but with a contemptuous gesture walks
away.*]

SHABELSKY.   What a withering glance. . . .

LEBEDYEV.   And what devil sets your tongue wagging? Why did
you insult him?

SHABELSKY [*irritably*].   And what does he tell lies for? Consumption,
no hope, she is dying. . . . It's all lies! I can't endure it!

LEBEDYEV.   What makes you think he is lying?

SHABELSKY [*gets up and walks about*].   I can't admit the idea that a living creature should suddenly, *à propos* of nothing, go and die. Let us drop the subject!

[*Enter* KOSSIH.]

KOSSIH [*runs in, breathless*].   Is Nikolay Alexeyevitch at home? Good morning! [*rapidly shakes hands with everyone*]. Is he at home?

BORKIN.   No; he is out.

KOSSIH [*sits down and leaps up*].   If that's so, good-bye! [*drinks a glass of vodka and hurriedly eats something*]. I'll go on . . . I am busy . . . I am worn out . . . I can hardly stand up. . . .

LEBEDYEV.   Where have you dropped from?

KOSSIH.   From Barabanov's. . . . We were playing vint all night, and have only just finished. . . . I am cleaned out. . . . That Barabanov plays like a cobbler! [*In a weeping voice*] Just listen: all the time I was playing hearts. . . . [*Addresses* BORKIN, *who skips away from him*] He leads diamonds, but I play hearts again; he diamonds. . . . Well, I made no tricks. [*To* LEBEDYEV] We play four clubs. I had the ace, the queen, and five more clubs in my hand, the ace, the ten, and two more spades. . . .

LEBEDYEV [*putting his fingers in his ears*].   Spare me, for mercy's sake, spare me!

KOSSIH [*to the* COUNT].   Do you see: the ace, the queen, and five more clubs, the ace, the ten, and two more spades. . . .

SHABELSKY [*waving him off*].   Go away; I don't want to hear you!

KOSSIH.   And all at once such ill-luck: my ace of spades was trumped in the first round.

SHABELSKY [*picking up a revolver from the table*].   Go away, I'll shoot! . . .

KOSSIH [*waves his hand*].   Damnation take it. . . . Is there nobody one can say a word to? One might be in Australia: no common interests, no sympathy. . . . They are all absorbed in themselves. . . . I must go, though . . . it's time [*snatches up his cap*]. Time is precious [*shakes hands with* LEBEDYEV]. Pass! [*laughter*].

[KOSSIH *goes out, and in the doorway stumbles against* AVDOTYA NAZAROVNA.]

AVDOTYA [*screams*].   Plague take you! Knocking me off my feet!

ALL.   A-ah! she is everywhere at once!

AVDOTYA.   So this is where they are, and I have been looking all over the house. Good morning! my bright falcons, enjoying your meal? [*greets them*].

LEBEDYEV.   What have you come about?

AVDOTYA.   Business, my good sir. [*To the* COUNT] Business that concerns you, your Excellency [*bows*]. I was told to greet you and inquire after your health. . . . And my pretty poppet bid me say that if you don't come and see her this evening, she will cry her eyes out. Take him aside, my dear, she said, and whisper it into his ear in secret. But what's the need of secrets? We are old friends here. Besides, it's not as if we were robbing a hen-roost, but aiming at lawful wedlock with the love and mutual consent of both parties. Sinful woman that I am, I never touch a drop, but on such an occasion, I will have a glass!

LEBEDYEV.   And I'll have one too [*fills the glasses*]. And you, old crow, seem none the worse for wear. You were an old woman when I met you first, thirty years ago.

AVDOTYA.   I've lost count of the years. . . . I've buried two husbands, and would marry a third, but no one cares to take me without a dowry. I had eight children . . . [*takes the glass*]. Well, please God, we've begun a good work and God grant we finish it! They will live and prosper and we shall look at them and rejoice. God give them love and good counsel! [*drinks*]. It's stiff vodka!

SHABELSKY [*laughing, to* LEBEDYEV].   But what's the oddest thing of all, you know, is that they seriously think that I . . . It's amazing! [*gets up*]. What do you think, Pasha—shall I really play this dirty trick? For mischief. . . . Why should not the old dog snap up his bone, Pasha, eh?

LEBEDYEV.   You are talking nonsense, Count. It's time for you and me to think of kicking the bucket; the time for Marfas and rubles has passed long ago. . . . Our day is over.

SHABELSKY.   No, I will do it—on my honor, I will!

[*Enter* IVANOV *and* LVOV.]

LVOV.   I beg you to spare me only five minutes.

LEBEDYEV.   Nikolasha! [*goes up to* IVANOV *and kisses him*]. Good morning, my dear boy. I have been waiting for you for a good hour.

AVDOTYA [*bows*].   Good morning, sir.

IVANOV [*bitterly*].   Gentlemen, again you've turned my study into a drinking bar! . . . A thousand times I have asked each and all of you not to do it . . . [*goes up to the table*]. There, now . . . you've spilt vodka over my papers . . . here are crumbs and bits of cucumber. . . . It's disgusting!

LEBEDYEV.   I am sorry, Nikolasha, I am sorry. . . . Forgive us. I want to talk to you, dear boy, about something very important. . . .

BORKIN.   And I, too.

LVOV.   Nikolay Alexeyevitch, can I have a word with you?

IVANOV [*pointing to* LEBEDYEV].   You see he wants me too. Wait a little; you can come afterwards. . . . [*To* LEBEDYEV] What is it?

LEBEDYEV.   Gentlemen, I want to have a confidential talk. Please. . . .

[*The* COUNT *goes out with* AVDOTYA NAZAROVNA, BORKIN *follows them, then* LVOV.]

IVANOV.   Pasha, you may drink as much as you like—it's an illness with you; but I beg you not to lead Uncle into it. He never used to drink before. It's bad for him.

LEBEDYEV [*alarmed*].   My dear, I did not know. . . . I did not even notice. . . .

IVANOV.   If, which God forbid, the old baby should die, it wouldn't matter to you, but it would to me. . . . What is it you want? [*Pause*].

LEBEDYEV.   You see, my dear friend. . . . I don't know how to begin to make it sound less shameless. . . . Nikolasha, I am ashamed, I blush, I can't bring myself to say it, but, my dear boy, put yourself in my position—realize that I am a man in bondage, a nigger, a rag. . . . Forgive me. . . .

IVANOV.   What is it?

LEBEDYEV.   My wife has sent me . . . Do me a favor—be a friend, pay her your interest! You wouldn't believe how she nags at me, drives me, wears me out! Do get rid of her, for goodness' sake! . . .

IVANOV.   Pasha, you know I have no money just now.

LEBEDYEV.   I know, I know; but what am I to do? She won't wait. If she summons you, how can Sasha and I ever look you in the face again?

IVANOV.   I am ashamed myself, Pasha—I should like to sink into the earth; but . . . but where am I to get it? Tell me, where? The only thing is to wait till the autumn, when I sell the corn.

LEBEDYEV [*shouts*].   She won't wait! [*Pause*].

IVANOV.   Your position is unpleasant and difficult, and mine is worse still [*walks up and down thinking*]. And there is no plan one can think of. . . . There's nothing to sell. . . .

LEBEDYEV.   You might go to Milbach and ask him; he owes you sixteen thousand, you know.

[IVANOV *waves his hand hopelessly*.]

LEBEDYEV.   I tell you what, Nikolasha. . . . I know you will begin scolding, but . . . do a favor to an old drunkard. Between friends. . . . Look upon me as a friend. . . . We have both been students, liberals. . . . We have common ideas and interests. . . . We both studied in

Moscow. . . . *Alma mater* . . . [*takes out his pocket-book*]. Here I've got
a secret hoard; no one at home knows of it. Let me lend it to you . . .
[*takes out money and lays it on the table*]. Drop your pride and look at
it as a friend. . . . I would take it from you—on my honor, I would
[*Pause*]. Here it is, on the table, eleven hundred. You go to her to-day
and give it with your own hands. . . . Take it, Zinaida Savishna, and
may it choke you! Only mind you don't make a sign that it comes
from me, God preserve you! or I shall get it hot from old Gooseberry
Jam [*looks into* IVANOV's *face*]. Oh, all right, never mind! [*hastily takes
the money from the table and puts it into his pocket*]. Never mind! I was
joking. . . . Forgive me, for Christ's sake! [*Pause*]. You are sick at
heart?

[IVANOV *makes a gesture of despair.*]

LEBEDYEV.   Yes, it is a business . . . [*sighs*]. A time of woe and
tribulation has come for you. A man is like a samovar, old boy. It is
not always in the cool on the shelf—there are times when they put
hot coals into it. . . . The comparison is not worth much, but I can't
think of anything better . . . [*sighs*]. Troubles strengthen the spirit. I
am not sorry for you, Nikolasha—you'll get out of your difficulties,
things will come right; but I feel vexed and offended with people. . . .
I should like to know where these scandals come from! There are
such stories going about you all over the district that you might get a
call from the public prosecutor any day. . . . You are a murderer and
a blood-sucker and a robber. . . .

IVANOV.   That doesn't matter; what does matter is that my head
aches.

LEBEDYEV.   That's all from thinking too much.

IVANOV.   I don't think at all.

LEBEDYEV.   You just snap your fingers at everything, Nikolasha,
and come over to us. Sasha is fond of you; she understands you and
appreciates you. She is a good, fine creature, Nikolasha. She takes
neither after father nor mother, but after some passing stranger. . . .
Sometimes I look at her and can't believe that a bottle-nosed old
drunkard like me can have such a treasure. Come over; you can talk
about intellectual subjects with her, and it will be a change for you.
She has a faithful, sincere nature . . . [*Pause*].

IVANOV.   Pasha, my dear soul, leave me alone.

LEBEDYEV.   I understand, I understand . . . [*looks hurriedly at his
watch*]. I understand [*kisses* IVANOV]. Good-bye. I've got to go to the
dedication of a school [*goes to the door and stops*]. She is a clever girl.
. . . Yesterday she and I were talking about gossip [*laughs*]. And she
made an epigram: "Father," she said, "glow-worms shine at night

simply so that the night birds may see and devour them more easily; and good people exist to provide food for gossip and slander." What do you say to that? A genius! A George Sand!

IVANOV.   Pasha! [*stops him*]. What is the matter with me?

LEBEDYEV.   I wanted to ask you that myself, but, to tell you the truth, I did not like to. I don't know, dear boy! On the one hand, it seemed to me that you were crushed by misfortunes of all sorts, and on the other hand, I know you are not the sort to . . . You are not the one to be mastered by trouble. There is something else in it, Nikolasha, but what it is I don't know.

IVANOV.   I don't know myself. I fancy it is either . . . but no! [*Pause*]. You see, what I meant to say was this. I had a workman called Semyon—you remember him. One day at threshing time he wanted to show the girls how strong he was, put two sacks of rye on his back, and ruptured himself. He died soon after. It seems to me that I have ruptured myself, too. The high-school, university, then managing my estate, plans, schools. . . . My beliefs were not like other people's, my marriage was not like other people's. I was enthusiastic, I took risks, threw away my money right and left, as you know. I have had more happiness and more misery than anyone in the whole district. All this was like those sacks for me, Pasha. . . . I took a burden on my back, and my back was broken. At twenty we are heroes—we tackle anything, we can do anything; and at thirty we are already exhausted and good for nothing. How do you explain that liability to exhaustion, tell me? But perhaps it's not that, though. . . . That's not it, that's not it! . . . Go along, Pasha, God bless you; I have been boring you.

LEBEDYEV [*eagerly*].   You know what it is, old boy? It's your environment has destroyed you.

IVANOV.   Oh, that's stupid, Pasha, and stale. Run along!

LEBEDYEV.   Yes, it is certainly stupid. I can see for myself now it is stupid. I am going! I am going! [*goes out*].

IVANOV [*alone*].   I am a bad, abject, worthless man. One has to be as abject, broken and shattered as Pasha to like and respect me. How I despise myself, my God! How I hate my voice, my step, my hands, these clothes, my thoughts! Isn't it absurd, isn't it mortifying? It's not a year since I was strong and well, I was inexhaustible, full of warmth and confidence, I worked with these same hands, I could speak so as to move even the ignorant to tears, I could weep at the sight of sorrow, was moved to wrath at the sight of wrong-doing. I knew the meaning of inspiration, I felt the charm and poetry of still nights when from sunset to sunrise one sits at one's writing-table or gladdens one's soul with dreams. I had faith, I could look into the future as into my mother's eyes. . . . But now, oh, my God! I am worn out, I have no faith, I spend days and nights doing nothing. My brains do not obey me, nor my hands nor my feet. My property is going to ruin, the forest is falling under the axe [*weeps*]. My land looks at me like a deserted child. I expect nothing, I regret nothing; my soul shudders with fear of the morrow. . . . And the way I have treated Sarra! I swore to love her for ever, I promised her happiness, I displayed before her a future she had not imagined in her dreams. She believed me. For five years I've seen her pining away under the weight of her sacrifice, and worn out by the struggle with her conscience, but, as God is above, there has not been one doubtful glance, not one word of reproach! And here I've ceased to love her. . . . How? Why? What for? I don't understand it. Here she is suffering; her days are numbered, and I, like the meanest sneak, run away from her pale face, her sunken chest, her supplicating eyes. It's shameful, shameful! [*Pause*]. Sasha, a child, is touched by my misery. She tells me, at my age, that she loves me, and I am intoxicated, forget everything in the world, enchanted as though by music, and shout "A new life! happiness!" And next day I believe as little in that new life and happiness as in goblins. . . . What's the matter with me? To what depths am I making myself sink? What has brought this weakness on me? What has happened to my nerves? If my sick wife wounds my vanity or a servant does not please me, or my gun misses fire, I become brutal, angry and unlike myself [*Pause*]. I don't understand, I don't understand! I might as well shoot myself and have done with it!

LVOV [*enters*]. I must have things out with you, Nikolay Alexeyevitch.

IVANOV. If we are to have things out every day, Doctor, it's more than anyone could stand.

LVOV. Will you hear me out?

IVANOV. I hear you out every day, and I still can't make out what it is you want of me.

LVOV. I speak clearly and definitely, and no one but a heartless man could fail to understand me.

IVANOV. That my wife is dying—I know; that I am hopelessly to blame in regard to her, I know also. That you are an honest, upright man, I know too! What more do you want?

LVOV. I am revolted by human cruelty. . . . A woman is dying. She has a father and mother whom she loves and would like to see before her death; they know quite well that she will soon die and that she still loves them, but, damnable cruelty! they seem to want to impress people by their religious hardness—they still persist in cursing her! You are the man to whom she has sacrificed everything—her home and her peace of conscience; yet in the most undisguised way, with the most undisguised objects, you go off every day to those Lebedyevs! . . .

IVANOV.   Oh, I have not been there for a fortnight. . . .

LVOV [not heeding him].   With people like you one must speak plainly without beating about the bush, and if you don't care to listen to me, then don't listen! I am accustomed to call a spade a spade. . . . Her death will suit you and pave the way for your new adventures; so be it, but surely you might wait? If you would let her die naturally without persistently worrying her by your open cynicism, surely you would not lose the Lebedyev girl and her dowry? If not now, then in a year or two you would succeed, you marvellous hypocrite, in turning the girl's head and getting her money just as easily. . . . Why are you in such a hurry? Why do you want your wife to die now, and not in a month or in a year? . . .

IVANOV.   This is simply agony. . . . You can't be a very good doctor if you imagine that a man can restrain himself indefinitely. It's a fearful effort to me not to answer your insults.

LVOV.   Come, whom do you think you are taking in? Throw off your mask!

IVANOV.   You clever person, think a little! You suppose there is nothing easier than understanding me, yes? I married Anna for the sake of her fortune . . . they did not let me have it. I made a blunder, and now I am getting rid of her so as to marry another girl and get her money, yes? How simple and straightforward! Man is such a simple, uncomplicated machine. . . . No, doctor, there are too many wheels and screws and levers in any one of us for us to be able to judge each other from the first impression or from two or three external signs. I don't understand you, you don't understand me, and we don't understand ourselves. One may be a good doctor and at the same time utterly ignorant of human nature. Don't be too self-confident, and do see that.

LVOV.   Can you really imagine that you are so difficult to see through, and that I am so brainless that I can't see the difference between a rogue and an honest man?

IVANOV.   It is evident that we shall never come to an understanding. For the last time I ask you the question, and please answer it without any preliminary words: what exactly do you want of me? What are you trying to get at? [Irritably] And to whom have I the honor of speaking—my judge or my wife's doctor?

LVOV.   I am a doctor, and as a doctor I insist on your behaving differently. Your behavior is killing Anna Petrovna.

IVANOV.   But what am I to do? What? Since you understand me better than I understand myself, tell me definitely, what am I to do?

Lvov. At least you might keep up appearances.

IVANOV. Oh, my God! Do you suppose you understand what you are saying? [*drinks water*]. Leave me alone. I am infinitely to blame: I must answer for it to God; but no one has authorized you to torment me every day. . . .

Lvov. And who has authorized you to outrage my sense of justice? You torture and poison my soul. Before I came into this district I admitted that silly, mad, impulsive people did exist, but I never believed that there were people so criminal as intentionally, consciously, wilfully to choose the path of evil. . . . I loved and respected mankind, but since I have known you . . .

IVANOV. I have heard about that already.

[*Enter* SASHA.]

Lvov. Oh, have you? [*seeing* SASHA; *she is in a riding habit*]. Now I trust we quite understand each other! [*shrugs his shoulders and goes out*].

IVANOV [*with alarm*]. Sasha, is it you?

SASHA. Yes, it is me. How are you? You did not expect me? Why haven't you been to see us for so long?

IVANOV. Sasha, for goodness' sake, this is unwise! Your coming may have a terrible effect on my wife.

SASHA. She won't see me. I came by the back way. I am just going. I am uneasy: are you well? Why is it you haven't come all this time?

IVANOV. My wife is distressed as it is; she is almost dying, and you come here. Sasha, Sasha, it's thoughtless and inhuman!

SASHA. I couldn't help it. You haven't been to see us for a fortnight, you haven't answered my letters. I was worried to death. I fancied that you were unbearably miserable here, ill, dying. I haven't had one good night's sleep. I am just going. . . . Tell me, anyway, are you well?

IVANOV. No. I torment myself, and people torment me endlessly. . . . It's simply more than I can bear! And now you on the top of it all! How morbid, how abnormal it all is! How guilty I feel, Sasha—how guilty! . . .

SASHA. How fond you are of saying dreadful and tragic things! So you are guilty. . . . Yes? Guilty? Tell me then, what of?

IVANOV. I don't know, I don't know. . . .

SASHA. That's not an answer. Every sinner ought to know what his sins are. Have you forged notes, or what?

IVANOV. That's stupid.

SASHA.   Are you guilty because you have changed to your wife? Perhaps, but man is not master of his feelings, you didn't want your feelings to change. Are you guilty because she saw me telling you that I love you? No, you did not want her to see. . . .

IVANOV [*interrupting*].   And so on, so on. . . . In love, out of love, not master of his feelings—these are commonplaces, stock phrases, which don't help. . . .

SASHA.   It's wearisome talking to you [*looks at a picture*]. How well that dog is drawn. Is that from life?

IVANOV.   Yes. And all our love story is commonplace and hackneyed: he has lost heart and is plunged in despair, she appears on the scene, full of strength and courage—holds out a helping hand. That's fine and sounds all right in novels, but in real life . . .

SASHA.   In real life it's the same.

IVANOV.   I see, you've such a subtle understanding of life! My whining excites your reverent awe, you fancy you have discovered a second Hamlet in me, but to my mind my morbid state with all accessories provides good material for ridicule and nothing else! You ought to laugh at my antics while you cry "Help!" To save me, to do something heroic! Oh, how cross I am with myself to-day! I feel this nervous strain will make me do something. . . . Either I shall smash something, or . . .

SASHA.   That's it, that's it, just what you ought to do. Break something, smash things, or scream. You are angry with me; it was silly of me to think of coming here. Well, be angry, shout at me, stamp! Well? Begin to rage! [*Pause*]. Well?

IVANOV.   Ridiculous girl!

SASHA.   Excellent! I believe you are smiling! Be kind and graciously smile again!

IVANOV [*laughs*].   I've noticed when you begin saving me and giving me good advice your face becomes very, very naïve and your eyes as big as though you were looking at a comet. Wait a minute, your shoulder is dusty [*brushes some dust off her shoulder*]. A naïve man is a fool, but you women have the art of being naïve so that it is sweet and natural and warm and not so silly as it seems. But isn't it a queer trick in all of you—so long as a man is strong and well and cheerful, you take no notice of him, but as soon as he begins running rapidly downhill and sets up a whine, you throw yourselves upon his neck! Is it worse to be the wife of a strong, brave man than to be the nurse of some lachrymose failure?

SASHA.   Yes, it is.

IVANOV.   Why is it? [*laughs*]. Darwin knows nothing about it, or he would give it to you! You are ruining the race. Thanks to you there will soon be none but snivellers and neurotics born into the world!

SASHA.   There is a great deal men don't understand. Any girl will prefer a man who is a failure to one who is a success, because every woman longs to love actively. . . . Do you understand, actively? A man is absorbed in his work and so love with him is in the background. To talk to his wife, to walk in the garden and spend the time pleasantly with her and weep on her grave—that's all he wants. While with us love is life. I love you, that means that I am dreaming how I shall heal you of your misery, how I shall go to the ends of the earth with you. If you go uphill, I go uphill too; if you go down into a pit, I go down into the pit too. To me, for instance, it would be a great happiness to spend a whole night copying your papers, or the whole night watching that no one should wake you, or walking a hundred miles with you! I remember once three years ago at threshing time you came to see us, all covered with dust, sunburnt and exhausted and asked for water. By the time I brought you a glass, you were lying on the sofa, sleeping like the dead. You slept for twelve hours, and all the time I stood on guard at the door that no one should come in. And how happy I was! The harder the work, the better the love, that is, the more strongly it's felt, you understand.

IVANOV.   Active love. . . . Hm. Decadence, a young girl's philosophy or perhaps that's how it should be . . . [*shrugs his shoulders*]. Devil only knows! [*gaily*]. Sasha, on my honor I am a decent man! . . . Think of this: I have always been fond of generalizing, but I have never in my life said that "our women were demoralised" or that "woman was on the wrong track." I have only been grateful to them and nothing else! Nothing else! My good little girl, how amusing you are! And what an absurd duffer I am! I shock good people and do nothing but whine for days together [*laughs*]. Oo-oo! Oo-oo! [*walks quickly away*]. But do go, Sasha! we are forgetting . . .

SASHA.   Yes, I must go. Good-bye! I am afraid your honest doctor's sense of duty may make him tell Anna Petrovna that I am here. Listen to me: go to your wife at once and sit by her, sit by her. . . . If you have to sit by her for a year, sit by her for a year. . . . If it is ten years—sit ten years. Do your duty. Grieve and beg her forgiveness and weep—all that is only right. And, above all, don't neglect your work.

IVANOV.   Again I have that feeling as though I were poisoned. Again!

SASHA.   Well, God bless you! You need not think about me at all.

If you send me a line once a fortnight, that will do for me. I will write
to you. . . .

[BORKIN *peeps in at the door.*]

BORKIN.   Nikolay Alexeyevitch, may I come in? [*Seeing* SASHA] I
beg your pardon, I did not see you . . . [*comes in*]. Bong jour! [*bows*].
SASHA [*in confusion*].   How do you do?
BORKIN.   You have grown plumper and prettier.
SASHA [*to* IVANOV].   I am just going, Nikolay Alexeyevitch. . . . I
am going [*goes out*].
BORKIN.   Lovely vision! I came for prose and stumbled on poetry.
. . . [*Sings*] "Thou dids't appear like a bird at dawn.". . .

[IVANOV *walks up and down the stage in agitation.*]

BORKIN [*sits down*].   There is a certain something about her, you
know, *Nicolas,* unlike other girls. Isn't there? Something special . . .
phantasmagoric . . . [*sighs*]. As a matter of fact she is the wealthiest
match in the countryside, but the mother is such a bitter radish that
no one cares to be mixed up with her. When she is dead everything
will be left to Sasha, but till then she will give nothing but a miserable
ten thousand, with flat irons and gophering tongs, and one will have
to go down on one's knees to her for that too [*fumbles in his pockets*].
I'll smoke *De-los-mahoros*. Wouldn't you like one? [*offers his cigar-case*].
They are good. . . . They are worth smoking.
IVANOV [*goes up to* BORKIN, *breathless with anger*].   Clear out of my
house this minute and do not set foot in it again! This minute!

[BORKIN *gets up and drops his cigar.*]

IVANOV.   Get out! This minute!
BORKIN.   *Nicolas,* what's the matter? Why are you angry?
IVANOV.   What for? Where did you get those cigars? And do you
suppose I don't know where you are taking the old man every day
and what your object is?
BORKIN [*shrugging his shoulders*].   But what has that to do with
you?
IVANOV.   You blackguard! The vile projects which you scatter all
over the district have disgraced my name in the eyes of everyone! We
have nothing in common, and I beg you to leave my house this minute! [*strides rapidly up and down*].
BORKIN.   I know you are saying all this because you are irritated
and so I am not angry with you. You can insult me as much as you
like [*picks up his cigar*]. But it's time to shake off your melancholy. You
are not a schoolboy. . . .

IVANOV.   What did I say to you? [*trembling*]. Are you playing with me?

[*Enter* ANNA PETROVNA.]

BORKIN.   Well, here is Anna Petrovna. . . . I will go [*goes out*].

[IVANOV *stops at the table and stands with bowed head.*]

ANNA PETROVNA [*after a pause*].   What did she come for just now? [*Pause*]. I ask you, what did she come for?

IVANOV.   Don't ask me, Anyuta. . . . [*Pause*]. I am terribly to blame. You can think of anything you like to punish me, I'll bear anything, but . . . don't question me. . . . I am not equal to talking.

ANNA PETROVNA [*angrily*].   What has she been here for? [*Pause*]. Ah, so that's what you are like! Now I understand you. At last I see what sort of man you are. Dishonorable, mean. . . . Do you remember you came and told a lie, saying that you loved me. . . . I believed you; I gave up my father and mother and my religion and followed you. . . . You told me lies about truth and goodness and your noble plans. I believed every word. . . .

IVANOV.   Anyuta, I've never told you a lie.

ANNA PETROVNA.   I have lived with you five years. I have been depressed and ill, but I have loved you, and have never left you for a moment. . . . You have been my idol. . . . And all the while you have been deceiving me in the most shameless way. . . .

IVANOV.   Anyuta, don't say what is untrue. I have made mistakes, yes, but I have never told a lie in my life. . . . You dare not reproach me with that. . . .

ANNA PETROVNA.   I see it all now. . . . You married me thinking my father and mother would forgive me and give me money . . . that was what you expected. . . .

IVANOV.   Oh, my God! Anyuta, to try my patience like this . . . [*weeps*].

ANNA PETROVNA.   Hold your tongue! When you saw the money was not coming, you started a fresh game. . . . Now I remember it all and understand [*weeps*]. You never loved me, and were never faithful to me. . . . Never!

IVANOV.   Sarra, that's a lie! Say what you like, but don't insult me with lies. . . .

ANNA PETROVNA.   Mean, dishonorable man! . . . You are in debt to Lebedyev, and now to wriggle out of your debt you are trying to turn his daughter's head, to deceive her as you did me. Isn't that true?

IVANOV [*gasping*].   For God's sake, hold your tongue! I can't answer for myself. . . . I am choking with rage, and I . . . I may say something to hurt you. . . .

ANNA PETROVNA. You have always shamelessly deceived people, not only me. You put down everything discreditable to Borkin, but now I know who is responsible.

IVANOV. Sarra, be quiet! Go away, or I may say something! I feel tempted to say to you something horrible, insulting. . . . [*Shouts*] Hold your tongue, Jewess!

ANNA PETROVNA. I won't be silent. . . . You've deceived me too long, and I must speak. . . .

IVANOV. So you won't hold your tongue [*struggling with himself*]. For God's sake . . .

ANNA PETROVNA. Now you can go and deceive the Lebedyev girl. . . .

IVANOV. Well, let me tell you that you . . . are going to die. . . . The doctor told me that you can't last long. . . .

ANNA PETROVNA [*sits down; in a sinking voice*]. When did he say that? [*Pause*].

IVANOV [*clutches his head*] What a brute I am! My God, what a brute! [*sobs*].

CURTAIN.

[*Between the Third and the Fourth Acts about a year elapses.*]

ACT IV

A drawing-room in LEBEDYEV'*s house. In foreground an arch dividing the
front drawing-room from the back drawing-room; doors to right and to
left. Old bronzes, family portraits. Everything has a festive look. A
piano; lying on it a violin; near it stands a 'cello. Throughout the act*
GUESTS *cross the stage dressed as for a ball.*

LVOV [*comes in, looking at his watch*].   It's past four. I suppose it is
just time for the blessing. . . . They will bless her, and take her to
church to be married. Here is the triumph of virtue and justice! He
did not succeed in robbing Sarra; he worried her into her grave, and
now he has found another. He will play a part to her too until he has
plundered her, and then he will lay her in her grave like poor Sarra.
It's the old money-grubbing story . . . [*Pause*]. He is in the seventh
heaven of bliss: will live happily to old age, and will die with an easy
conscience. No, I'll expose you! When I tear off your damnable mask
and all learn what sort of a creature you are, you will fall headlong
from the seventh heaven into depths such as the very devil cannot
pull you out of! I am an honest man: it's my duty to interfere and
open their blind eyes. I will do my duty, and to-morrow leave this
cursed district for ever! [*Muses*] But how am I to do it? Talking to the
Lebedyevs is waste of time. Challenge him to a duel? Make a row?
My God, I am as nervous as a schoolboy and have quite lost all power
of reflection! What am I to do? A duel?

KOSSIH [*coming in, joyfully to* LVOV].   Yesterday I declared a little
slam in clubs and took a grand slam. Only that Barabanov spoiled it
all again! We were playing. I said "No trumps." He said "Pass." I
played the two of clubs. He said "Pass." I played the two of diamonds
. . . the three of clubs . . . and would you believe it—can you imagine it!—I declared a slam, and he did not show his ace! If he had
shown his ace—the blackguard!—I could have declared a grand slam
on no trumps. . . .

LVOV.   Excuse me, I don't play cards, and so I cannot share your
enthusiasm. Will the blessing be soon?

48

KOSSIH.   It must be soon. They are bringing Zyuzushka to her senses. . . . She is howling like a calf: she is sorry to lose the dowry.

LVOV.   And not her daughter?

KOSSIH.   It's the dowry. Besides, it's galling for her. If he marries into the family, he won't pay what he owes her. You cannot summon your own son-in-law.

MADAME BABAKIN [*grandly dressed, with a dignified air, walks across the stage past* LVOV *and* KOSSIH; *the latter guffaws into his fist; she looks round*].   How stupid!

[KOSSIH *touches her waist with his finger and laughs.*]

MADAME BABAKIN.   You lout! [*goes out*].

KOSSIH [*laughs*].   The silly woman has gone right off her head! Before she set her cap at a title she was a woman like any other, and now there is no approaching her. [*Mimicking her*] "You lout!"

LVOV [*agitated*].   I say, tell me honestly, what is your opinion of Ivanov?

KOSSIH.   He is no good. He plays like a cobbler. I'll tell you what happened last year in Lent. We were all sitting down to cards—the Count, Borkin, he and I—and I was dealing . . .

LVOV [*interrupting*].   Is he a good man?

KOSSIH.   He? He is a shark! He is a tricky fellow; he has seen some ups and downs. . . . The Count and he—they are a pair of them. They have a keen scent for what they can lay their hands on. He put his foot in it with the Jewess, came a cropper, and now he has got his eye on Zyuzushka's money-bags. I'll bet anything, damn my soul, if he does not bring Zyuzushka to beggary within a year. He'll do for Zyuzushka and the Count for the widow. They'll grab the money and live happy ever afterwards. Doctor, why are you so pale to-day? You don't look like yourself.

LVOV.   Oh, it's nothing! I drank a little too much yesterday.

[*Enter* LEBEDYEV *and* SASHA.]

LEBEDYEV [*coming in with* SASHA].   We can talk here [*to* LVOV *and* KOSSIH]. You can go and join the ladies, you Zulus. We want to talk secrets.

KOSSIH [*snaps his fingers enthusiastically as he passes* SASHA].   A picture! A queen of trumps.

LEBEDYEV.   Run along, you cave-man—run along!

[LVOV *and* KOSSIH *go out.*]

LEBEDYEV.   Sit down, Sasha; that's right . . . [*sits down and looks round*]. Listen attentively and with befitting reverence. It's like this:

your mother has told me to make this communication. . . . You understand, I am not going to say this from myself: it's your mother's orders.

SASHA.   Father, do be brief!

LEBEDYEV.   You are to have fifteen thousand rubles at your marriage. There. . . . Mind that there is no talk about it afterwards! Wait a minute; be quiet! There are more treats to come. Your portion is fifteen thousand, but, since Nikolay Alexeyevitch owes your mother nine thousand, that is to be deducted from your dowry. . . . Well, besides that . . .

SASHA.   What are you telling me this for?

LEBEDYEV.   Your mother told me to.

SASHA.   Do leave me alone! If you had the slightest respect for me or for yourself, you could not bring yourself to speak to me in this way. I don't want your dowry! I did not ask for it, and do not ask for it!

LEBEDYEV.   Why do you fly out at me? In Gogol the two rats first sniffed, then went away, but you are so advanced you fly at me without sniffing.

SASHA.   Leave me alone! Don't insult my ears with your reckonings of halfpence!

LEBEDYEV [*firing up*].   Tfoo! The way you all go on will drive me to murder someone or stick a knife into myself! One is howling from morning to night, nagging and jawing away, counting her farthings, while the other's so clever, and humane and emancipated—dash it all!—she can't understand her own father! I insult her ears! Why, before coming here to insult your ears, out there [*points to the door*] I was torn to pieces, hacked into bits. She cannot understand! Her head is turned, and she has lost all sense. . . . Confound you all! [*goes to the door and stops*]. I dislike it—I dislike everything in you!

SASHA.   What do you dislike?

LEBEDYEV.   I dislike everything—everything!

SASHA.   What everything?

LEBEDYEV.   Do you suppose I am going to sit down and begin telling you? There is nothing I like about it, and I can't bear to see your wedding! [*Goes up to* SASHA *and says caressingly*] Forgive me, Sasha, perhaps your marriage is all very clever, honorable, elevated, full of high principles, but there is something all wrong in it—all wrong! It's not like other marriages. You are young and fresh and clear as a bit of glass, and beautiful, while he is a widower, rather frayed and shabby, and I don't understand him, God bless the man! [*kisses his daughter*]. Sasha, forgive me, but there is something not quite straight. People are saying all sorts of things. The way his Sarra died,

and then the way he was set on marrying you all at once . . . [*briskly*].
But there, I am an old woman—an old woman! I am as womanish as
an old crinoline. Don't listen to me. Listen to no one but yourself.

SASHA.   Father, I feel myself that there is something wrong. . . .
There is—there is! If only you knew how heavy my heart is! It's
unbearable! I am ashamed and frightened to admit it. Father darling,
do help me to be brave, for God's sake . . . tell me what to do.

LEBEDYEV.   What is it? What is it?

SASHA.   I am frightened as I have never been before [*looks round*].
It seems as though I don't understand him and never shall. All the
while I have been engaged to him he has never once smiled, has
never looked me straight in the face. He is full of complaints, remorse
for something, shudderings, hints at some wrong he has done. . . . I
am exhausted. There are minutes when I even fancy that I . . . that I
don't love him as I ought. And when he comes to us or talks to me
I am bored. What does it all mean, father? I am frightened.

LEBEDYEV.   My darling, my only one, listen to your old father.
Break it off.

SASHA [*in alarm*].   What are you saying?

LEBEDYEV.   Yes, really, Sasha. There will be a scandal, all the
countryside will be wagging their tongues, but it is better to face a
scandal than to ruin your whole life.

SASHA.   Don't speak of it, father. I won't listen. I must struggle
against gloomy thoughts. He is a fine man, unhappy and misunder-
stood. I will love him; I will understand him; I will set him on his
feet; I will carry out my task. That's settled!

LEBEDYEV.   It's not a task—it's neurosis.

SASHA.   That's enough. I have confessed to you what I would not
admit to myself. Don't tell anyone. Let us forget it.

LEBEDYEV.   I can't make head or tail of it. Either I've gone dotty
with old age, or you have all grown too clever. Anyway, I can make
nothing of it; I'll be hanged if I can.

SHABELSKY [*entering*].   The devil take them all and me into the
bargain. It's revolting.

LEBEDYEV.   What's wrong with you?

SHABELSKY.   No, seriously, come what may, I must play some
dirty, shabby trick so that other people may be as sick as I am. And I
will too. Honor bright! I've told Borkin to announce my engagement
to-day [*laughs*]. Everyone is a scoundrel, and I'll be a scoundrel too.

LEBEDYEV.   Oh, you bore me! Do you know what, Matvey?—
you will talk yourself into such a state that, excuse my saying so, they
will clap you into a madhouse.

SHABELSKY.   And is a madhouse worse than any other house? You can take me there to-day if you like; I don't care. Everyone is mean, petty, trivial and dull. I am disgusting to myself; I don't believe a word I say. . . .

LEBEDYEV. I tell you what, Matvey—you should take some tow in your mouth, put a match to it, and breathe out fire and flame. Or, better still, take your cap and go home. This is a wedding; everyone is making merry, while you croak like a crow. Yes, really. . . .

[SHABELSKY *bends over the piano and sobs.*]

LEBEDYEV. Holy saints! Matvey! Count! What is the matter with you? Matyusha, my dear . . . my angel . . . I have offended you? Come, you must forgive an old dog like me. . . . Forgive a drunkard . . . have some water.

SHABELSKY. I don't want it [*raises his head*].

LEBEDYEV. Why are you crying?

SHABELSKY. Oh, it's nothing! . . .

LEBEDYEV. Come, Matyusha, don't tell stories. What's the reason?

SHABELSKY. I happened to look at that 'cello . . . and thought of the poor little Jewess. . . .

LEBEDYEV. Phew! you've pitched on the right minute to think of her! The kingdom of heaven and eternal peace be hers! But this is not the time to remember her.

SHABELSKY. We used to play duets together. . . . She was a wonderful, splendid woman!

[SASHA *sobs.*]

LEBEDYEV. What's the matter with you now? Give over! Lord, they are both howling! And I—I . . . You might at least go somewhere else; people may see you.

SHABELSKY. Pasha, when the sun shines it's merry in the churchyard. If one has hope one may be happy in old age. But I have no hopes left, not one!

LEBEDYEV. Yes, things really aren't very bright for you. . . . You've no children, no money, no work. . . . Well, it can't be helped. [*To* SASHA] And what's the matter with you?

SHABELSKY. Pasha, give me some money. We'll settle accounts in the next world. I'll go to Paris and look at my wife's grave. I've given away a lot in my day: I gave away half my property, and so I have a right to ask. Besides, I am asking a friend. . . .

LEBEDYEV [*in a fluster*]. My dear boy, I haven't a penny! But all right, all right! That is, I don't promise anything, but you understand . . . very good, very good! . . . [*Aside*] They worry the life out of me.

MADAME BABAKIN [*coming in*].   Where is my partner? Count, how dare you leave me alone? Ah, horrid man! [*taps the* COUNT *on the hand with her fan*].

SHABELSKY [*shrinking away*].   Leave me alone! I hate you!

MADAME BABAKIN [*aghast*].   What? . . . Eh? . . .

SHABELSKY.   Go away!

MADAME BABAKIN [*sinks into a chair*].   Oh! [*weeps*].

ZINAIDA SAVISHNA [*enters, weeping*].   Somebody has arrived. . . . I believe it's the best man. It's time for the blessing [*sobs*].

SASHA [*in a voice of entreaty*].   Mother!

LEBEDYEV.   Well, they are all howling! It's a quartet! Oh, leave off, you are making the place so damp! Matvey . . . Marfa Yegorovna! . . . Why, I shall cry myself in a minute . . . [*weeps*]. My goodness!

ZINAIDA.   Well, since you don't care for your mother, since you are disobedient . . . I'll comply with your wishes and give you my blessing.

[IVANOV *comes in; he is in a dress-suit and gloves*.]

LEBEDYEV.   This is the last straw! What is it?

SASHA.   Why have you come?

IVANOV.   I am sorry. May I speak to Sasha alone?

LEBEDYEV.   That's not at all the thing for you to come to the bride before the wedding! You ought to be on your way to the church!

IVANOV.   Pasha, I beg you . . .

[LEBEDYEV *shrugs his shoulders; he,* ZINAIDA SAVISHNA, SHABELSKY *and* MADAME BABAKIN *go out*.]

SASHA [*severely*].   What do you want?

IVANOV.   I am choking with fury, but I can speak coolly. Listen! Just now I was dressing for the wedding. I looked in the glass and saw that I had gray hairs on my temples. . . . Sasha, it's not right! While there is still time we ought to break off this senseless farce. . . . You are young and pure, your life is before you, while I . . .

SASHA.   That's all stale. I have heard it a thousand times and I am sick of it! Go to the church! Don't keep people waiting.

IVANOV.   I am going home at once, and you tell your people that there will be no wedding. Give them some explanation. We have been foolish long enough. I've played the Hamlet and you the noble maiden, and that will do.

SASHA [*flaring up*].   What do you mean by speaking like that? I won't listen.

IVANOV.   But I am speaking, and I will speak.

SASHA.   What have you come for? Your whining is turning into jeering.

IVANOV.   No, I am not whining now. Jeering? Yes, I am jeering. And if I could jeer at myself a thousand times more bitterly and set the whole world laughing, I would do it. I looked at myself in the looking-glass and it was as though a shell exploded in my conscience! I laughed at myself and almost went out of my mind with shame [*laughs*]. Melancholy! Noble sorrow! Mysterious sadness! To crown it all I ought to write verses. . . . To whine, to lament, to make people miserable, to recognize that vital energy is lost for ever, that I have gone to seed, outlived my day, that I have given in to weakness and sunk over my ears in this loathsome apathy—to feel all this when the sun is shining brightly, when even the ant is dragging his little load and is satisfied with himself—no, thanks! To see some people thinking you a fraud, others sorry for you, others holding out a helping hand, while some—worst of all—listen with reverence to your sighs, look upon you as a prophet, and are all agog for you to reveal some new religion. . . . No, thank God I have still some pride and conscience! As I came here, I laughed at myself and felt as though the very birds, the trees, were laughing at me. . . .

SASHA.   This is not anger, it's madness.

IVANOV.   Do you think so? No, I am not mad. Now I see things in their true light and my mind is as clear as your conscience. We love each other, but we shall never be married! I can rave and be melancholy as much as I like, but I have no right to ruin other people. I poisoned the last year of my wife's life with my whining. While you have been engaged to me, you have forgotten how to laugh and have grown five years older. Your father, to whom everything in life was clear, is at a loss to understand people, thanks to me. Whether I go to a meeting, or on a visit, or shooting, wherever I am, I bring boredom, depression, and dissatisfaction with me. Wait, don't interrupt me! I am harsh and savage, but forgive me, I am choked with fury and cannot speak in any other way. I used never to tell lies about life or abuse it, but now that I have become an old grumbler I unconsciously abuse life falsely, repine against destiny and complain, and everyone who hears me is affected by the distaste for life and begins abusing it too. And what an attitude! As though I were doing a favor to nature by living! Damnation take me!

SASHA.   Wait a minute. . . . From what you said just now it follows that you are weary of repining and that it's time to begin a new life! . . . And a good thing too. . . .

IVANOV.   I see nothing good, and what's the use of talking about a new life? I am lost beyond all hope! It is time for us both to realize it. A new life!

SASHA.   Nikolay, pull yourself together! What makes you think that you are lost? Why this cynicism? No, I won't speak or listen. . . . Go to the church!

IVANOV.   I am lost!

SASHA.   Don't shout like that, the visitors will hear you!

IVANOV.   If an educated, healthy man who is not a fool begins, for no apparent reason, lamenting and rolling downhill, he will roll down without stopping, and nothing can save him! Come, where can I look for help? In what? I can't drink—wine makes my head ache; I can't write bad verse; I can't worship my spiritual sloth and see something lofty in it. Sloth is sloth, weakness is weakness—I have no other names for them. I am done for, done for—and it's no good talking about it! [looks round]. We may be interrupted. Listen! If you love me, help me. This very minute, at once, break it off with me. Make haste! . . .

SASHA.   Oh, Nikolay, if you knew how you exhaust me! How you weary my soul! You are a good, clever man: judge for yourself, how can you set me such tasks? Every day there is some fresh problem, each harder than the one before. . . . I wanted active love, but this is martyrdom!

IVANOV.   And when you are my wife the problems will be more complicated still. Break it off! You must understand; it is not love but the obstinacy of an honest nature that is working in you. You've made it your aim at all costs to make a man of me again, to save me. It flattered you to think you were doing something heroic. . . . Now you are ready to draw back but are hindered by a false sentiment. Do understand that!

SASHA.   What queer, mad logic! Why, can I break it off with you? How can I break it off? You have neither mother, nor sister, nor friends. . . . You are ruined, you have been robbed right and left, everyone is telling lies about you. . . .

IVANOV.   It was stupid of me to have come here . . . I ought to have done as I meant. . . .

[Enter LEBEDYEV.]

SASHA [runs to her father].   Father, for mercy's sake! He has rushed here as though he were frantic and is torturing me! He insists on my breaking it off; he doesn't want to spoil my life. Tell him that I won't accept his generosity. I know what I am doing.

LEBEDYEV.   I can't make head or tail of it. . . . What generosity?

IVANOV.   There will be no marriage!

SASHA.   There shall be! Father, tell him that there shall be!

LEBEDYEV.   Wait a minute, wait a minute! . . . Why don't you want to marry her?

IVANOV.   I told her why, but she refuses to understand.

LEBEDYEV.   No, don't explain to her, but to me, and explain it so that I can understand! Ah, Nikolay Alexeyevitch, God be your judge! You've brought such a lot of muddle into our life that I feel as though I were living in a museum of curiosities: I look about and I can make nothing of it. . . . It is an infliction. . . . What is an old man to do with you? Challenge you to a duel or what?

IVANOV.   There's no need of a duel. All that is needed is to have a head on your shoulders and to understand Russian.

SASHA [*walks up and down the stage in agitation*].   This is awful, awful! Simply like a child. . . .

LEBEDYEV.   One can only throw up one's hands in amazement, that's all. Listen, Nikolay! To you all this seems clever, subtle, and according to all the rules of psychology, but to me it seems a scandal and a misfortune. Listen to an old man for the last time! This is what I advise you: give your mind a rest! Look at things simply, like everyone else! Everything is simple in this world. The ceiling is white, the boots are black, sugar is sweet. You love Sasha, she loves you. If you love her—stay; if you don't love her—go; we won't make a fuss. Why, it's so simple! You are both healthy, clever, moral, and you have food to eat and clothes to wear, thank God. . . . What more do you want? You've no money? As though that mattered. . . . Money does not give happiness. . . . Of course I understand . . . your estate is mortgaged, you have no money to pay the interest, but I am a father, I understand. . . . Her mother can do as she likes, bless the woman; if she won't give the money, she need not. Sasha says she does not want a dowry. Principles, Schopenhauer. . . . That's all tosh . . . I have a private ten thousand in the bank [*looks round*]. Not a dog in the house knows of it. . . . Granny's money . . . that is for you too. . . . Take it, only on one condition: give Matvey two thousand. . . .

[GUESTS *assemble in the back drawing-room.*]

IVANOV.   Pasha, it's no use talking. I shall act as my conscience tells me.

SASHA.   And I shall act as my conscience tells me. You can say what you like, I won't give you up. I'll go and call mother [*goes out*].

LEBEDYEV.   I can't make head or tail of it.

IVANOV.   Listen, poor fellow. . . . I am not going to tell you what I am—honest or a fraud, healthy or a neurotic. There is no making

you understand. I used to be young, ardent, earnest, and not a fool: I
loved, I hated, and I believed not as others do; I hoped and did the
work of ten; I fought with windmills, I knocked my head against the
wall; not measuring my strength, not considering, knowing nothing
of life, I took up a burden which broke my back and strained my
muscles; I made haste to spend all of myself in my youth; I was intoxicated, I worked myself up, I toiled, I knew no moderation. And
tell me, could I have done otherwise? We are few, you know, and
there is so much to do, so much! My God! how much! And see how
cruelly the life with which I struggled has paid me out! I have over-
strained myself. At thirty came the awakening, I was already old and
slothful. Exhausted, overstrained, broken, with my head heavy and
my soul indolent, without faith, without love, without an object in
life, I linger like a shadow among men and don't know what I am,
what I am living for, what I want. . . . And I fancy that love is nonsense and tenderness, mawkish, that there is no sense in work, that
songs and words of enthusiasm are vulgar and stale, and everywhere
I bring with me misery, chilly boredom, dissatisfaction, distaste for
life. . . . I am lost beyond all hope! Before you stands a man worn out
at thirty-five; disillusioned, crushed by his own paltry efforts; he is
burning with shame, mocking at his own feebleness. . . . Oh, how
my pride revolts, how I choke with rage! [*staggering*]. There, what I
have brought myself to! I am simply reeling. . . . I feel ill. Where is
Matvey? Let him take me home.

[*Voices in the back room: "The best man has come!"*]

SHABELSKY [*entering*].   In a shabby, borrowed coat . . . with no
gloves . . . and how many jeering looks, silly jokes, vulgar grins on
account of it! . . . Disgusting cads!

BORKIN [*enters hurriedly, with a bouquet; he is in evening dress and
wearing a flower as the badge of the best man*].   Ough! Where is he? [*To
*IVANOV] They have been waiting for you at the church for ever so
long and here you are airing your views. He is a funny chap! He really
is a funny chap! You mustn't go to church with your bride, but
separately, with me, and I will come back from the church and fetch
the bride. Do you mean to say you don't even know that? He really
is a funny chap!

LVOV [*entering, to *IVANOV].   Ah, you are here? [*Loudly*] Nikolay
Alexeyevitch Ivanov, I proclaim in the hearing of all that you are a
scoundrel!

IVANOV [*coldly*].   I am very much obliged to you.

[*General perturbation.*]

BORKIN [*to* LVOV].   Sir, this is contemptible! I challenge you to a duel!

LVOV.   Mr. Borkin, I regard it as degrading not only to fight, but even to speak with you! But Mr. Ivanov may receive satisfaction whenever he chooses.

SHABELSKY.   Sir, I shall fight you!

SASHA [*to* LVOV].   What have you insulted him for? What is it for? Gentlemen, please, let him tell me what made him do it.

LVOV.   Alexandra Pavlovna, I did not insult him without grounds. I came here as an honest man to open your eyes, and I beg you to hear me.

SASHA.   What can you say? That you are an honest man? The whole world knows that! You had better tell me on your conscience whether you understand yourself or not! You have come in here just now as an honest man and flung at him a terrible insult which has almost killed me; in old days, when you used to follow him about like a shadow and poisoned his life, you were convinced that you were doing your duty, that you were an honest man. You have meddled in his private life, you have blackened his name and condemned him; whenever you could you pelted me and all his friends with anonymous letters—and all the time you thought you were a conscientious man. You, a doctor, thought it honorable and did not spare even his sick wife; you gave her no peace with your suspicions. And whatever outrage, whatever cruel meanness you may commit, you will always believe that you are a conscientious and advanced man!

IVANOV [*laughing*].   This is not a wedding, but a debate! Bravo, bravo!

SASHA [*to* LVOV].   So now think a little: do you understand yourself or not? Dull-witted, heartless people! [*Takes* IVANOV *by the hand*] Come away, Nikolay! Father, come!

IVANOV.   Come where? Wait a minute, I will make an end of it all! My youth is awakened in me, my old self is roused! [*takes out his revolver*].

SASHA [*screams*].   I know what he means to do! Nikolay, for God's sake!

IVANOV.   I've been rolling down hill long enough, now a halt! It's time to know when to take leave! Stand back! Thanks, Sasha!

SASHA [*screams*].   Nikolay, for God's sake! Hold him!

IVANOV.   Let me alone! [*runs aside and shoots himself*].

CURTAIN.

THE BEAR

A JEST IN ONE ACT

Characters

YELENA IVANOVNA POPOV, *a widow with dimples in her cheeks, owner of an estate in the country*

GRIGORY STEPANITCH SMIRNOV, *a middle-aged landowner*

LUKA, MADAME POPOV's *old manservant*

The action takes place in a drawing-room in MADAME POPOV's *house.*

MADAME POPOV (*in deep mourning, keeps her eyes fixed on a photograph*) *and* LUKA.

LUKA. It's not right, madam. . . . You are simply killing yourself. . . . The cook and the housemaid have gone to the wood to pick strawberries, every breathing thing rejoices, the very cat, even she knows how to enjoy herself and walks about the yard catching birds, while you sit all day indoors as though you were in a nunnery and have no pleasure in anything. Yes, indeed! If you come to think of it, it's nearly a year since you've been out of the house!

MADAME POPOV. And I shall never go out. . . . Why should I? My life is over. He lies in his grave; I have buried myself within four walls. . . . We are both dead.

LUKA. Well, there it is! I don't like to hear it. Nikolay Mihailitch is dead, so it had to be, it is God's will. The kingdom of heaven be his! . . . You have grieved, and that's enough; you must know when to stop. You can't weep and wear mourning all your life. I buried my old woman, too, in my time. . . . Well, I was grieved and cried for a month or so, and that was enough for her; but if I had been doleful all my life, it is more than the old woman herself was worth. [*Sighs*] You have forgotten all your neighbors. . . . You don't go out yourself or receive visitors. We live like spiders, if I may say so—we don't see the light of day. The mice have eaten my livery. . . . It's not as though you had no nice people about you: the district is full of gentry. . . . There's a regiment at Ryblovo—the officers are perfect sugar-plums, a sight for sore eyes! And in the camp there is a ball every Friday, and the band plays almost every day. . . . Ah! madam, my dear, you are young and lovely, blooming like a rose—you have only to live and enjoy yourself. . . . Beauty won't last all your life, you know. In another ten years you may want to be as gay as a peacock and dazzle the officers, but then it will be too late. . . .

MADAME POPOV [*resolutely*]. I beg you never to speak like that to me! You know that ever since Nikolay Mihailitch died life has lost all value for me. It appears to you that I am alive, but it is only an appearance! I have taken a vow not to put off this mourning, nor to look upon the world outside as long as I live. . . . Do you hear? May his shade see how I love him! . . . Yes, I know it was no secret to you: he was often unjust to me, cruel and . . . and even unfaithful; but I will be true to the grave, and will show him how I can love. Yonder, on the other side of the grave, he will see me just the same as I was before his death. . . .

LUKA. Instead of talking like that you had better go for a walk in the garden, or order Toby or Giant to be put into the carriage and go to visit your neighbors. . . .

MADAME POPOV. Ach! [*weeps*].

LUKA. Madam! My dear! What is it? Christ be with you!

MADAME POPOV. He was so fond of Toby! He always used to drive him when he went to the Kortchagins or the Vlassovs. How wonderfully he drove! What grace there was in his figure when he tugged at the reins with all his might! Do you remember? Toby, Toby! Tell them to give him an extra gallon of oats to-day!

LUKA. Yes, madam.

[*An abrupt ring at the bell.*]

MADAME POPOV [*starts*]. Who is that? Say that I see no one.

LUKA. Yes, madam [*goes out*].

MADAME POPOV [*looking at the photograph*]. You will see, Nicolas, how I can love and forgive. . . . My love will die only with me when my poor heart leaves off beating [*laughing through her tears*]. And aren't you ashamed? I am a good girl—a true wife. I have locked myself up, and will be true to you to the grave, while you . . . aren't you ashamed, you chubby? You deceived me, you made scenes, left me alone for weeks together. . . .

[LUKA *enters in a fluster.*]

LUKA. Madam, there is someone asking for you. He wants to see you.

MADAME POPOV. But didn't you tell him that since my husband's death I see no one?

LUKA. I did, but he won't listen; he says it is on very urgent business.

MADAME POPOV. I see no-bo-dy!

LUKA. I told him so, but . . . he is a regular devil. He swears and just shoves himself into the room . . . he is in the dining-room now.

MADAME POPOV [*irritably*]. Oh, very well! Show him in. How rude!

[LUKA *goes out.*]

MADAME POPOV. How wearisome these people are! What do they want of me? Why should they disturb my peace? [*sighs*]. It seems I shall really have to go into a nunnery . . . [*Ponders*] Yes, a nunnery. . . .

[*Enter* LUKA *with* SMIRNOV.]

SMIRNOV [*as he enters, to* LUKA]. Blockhead, you are too fond of talking! Ass! [*Seeing* MADAM POPOV, *with dignity*] Madam, I have the honor to introduce myself: Grigory Stepanitch Smirnov, landowner and retired lieutenant of artillery. I am compelled to trouble you about a very important matter.

MADAME POPOV [*not offering her hand*]. What can I do for you?

SMIRNOV. Your late husband, whom I had the honor of knowing, owed me twelve hundred rubles on two bills. As I have to-morrow to pay my interest to the land bank, I am obliged to ask you to repay me that sum to-day.

MADAME POPOV. Twelve hundred! . . . And what did my husband owe you that money for?

SMIRNOV. He bought oats from me.

MADAME POPOV [*sighing, to* LUKA]. Don't forget, Luka, to tell them to give Toby an extra gallon of oats [LUKA *goes out. To* SMIRNOV] If Nikolay Mihailitch owed you money, of course I will pay it, but you must please excuse me—I haven't the cash in hand to-day. My steward will be coming back from the town the day after to-morrow, and I will tell him to pay you what is owing; but till then I cannot do what you want. . . . Besides, it is exactly seven months to-day since my husband died, and I am in such a state of mind that I don't feel equal to attending to money matters.

SMIRNOV. And I am in such a state of mind that if I don't pay my interest to-morrow I shall have to put a bullet through my brains. They'll sell up my estate.

MADAME POPOV. The day after to-morrow you shall have the money.

SMIRNOV. I want the money, not the day after to-morrow, but to-day.

MADAME POPOV. Excuse me, I cannot pay you to-day.

SMIRNOV. And I can't wait till the day after to-morrow.

MADAME POPOV. What am I to do if I haven't the money?

SMIRNOV. Then you can't pay it?

MADAME POPOV. I cannot.

SMIRNOV. H'm! Is that your final answer?

MADAME POPOV.   Yes.

SMIRNOV.   The final? Positively?

MADAME POPOV.   Positively.

SMIRNOV.   Very much obliged to you. I'll make a note of it [*shrugs his shoulders*]. And I am expected to keep cool! I met the excise officer on the road just now, and he asked me, "Why are you always so angry, Grigory Stepanitch?" Upon my soul, how can I help being angry? I am in deadly need of money. I set off almost before daylight yesterday morning, I went round to all who owed me money, and not one has paid me! I am as tired as a dog. Goodness knows where I spent the night—in a wretched Jewish pot-house, beside a barrel of vodka. . . . At last I get here, over fifty miles from home, hoping to be paid my money, and all I am offered is a state of mind! How am I to keep my temper?

MADAME POPOV.   I believe I have told you distinctly that when my steward comes back from the town you will be paid.

SMIRNOV.   I have come to see you, and not your steward! What the devil—excuse the expression—do I want with your steward?

MADAME POPOV.   Excuse me, sir, I am not accustomed to such strange expressions and such a tone. I will not listen to you [*goes out quickly*].

SMIRNOV.   Upon my soul! A state of mind! . . . It's seven months since her husband died. . . . But am I to pay the interest, or not? I ask you, am I to pay the interest, or not? To be sure, your husband is dead, and you are in a state of mind, and all sorts of nonsense. Your steward has gone off somewhere—the devil take him!—but what am I to do? Fly away from my creditors on a balloon, or what? Or run and smash my skull against the wall? I went to Gruzdyov—not at home. Yaroshevitch was in hiding. With Kuritsin I had an awful row, and nearly flung him out of a window. Mazutov had a bilious attack, and this one has got a state of mind! Not one of the wretches has paid me! And all because I have been too soft with them—because I am a noodle, a rag, an old woman! I've been too gentle with them. But wait a bit! I'll show you what I can do. I won't let them make a fool of me, damnation take it! I'll stay and stick on here till she does pay. Brr! How cross I feel to-day! I am in such a rage that I'm twitching all over, and I can hardly breathe. . . . Phew! Hang it, I feel positively sick! [*Shouts*] Hi, there!

[*Enter* LUKA.]

LUKA.   What is it?

SMIRNOV.   Give me some kvass or some water.

[LUKA *goes out.*]

SMIRNOV.   Yes, what logic! A man is in deadly need of money—nothing left but to hang himself—and she won't pay because, if you please, she is not equal to attending to money matters! . . . Typical petticoat logic! That is why I never like, and never have liked, talking to women. I'd rather sit on a barrel of gunpowder than talk to a woman! Brr! I am chicken-flesh all over—that feminine creature has put me in such a rage! I have only to see a poetic being like that in the distance for my legs to begin twitching with fury. I feel like shouting "Help!"

[LUKA *enters and gives him water.*]

LUKA.   My lady is unwell and sees no one.
SMIRNOV.   Be off!

[LUKA *goes out.*]

SMIRNOV.   Unwell and sees no one! Very good, you needn't. . . . I'll stay on and sit here till you do pay me. If you are ill a week, I'll stay here for a week. If you are ill for a year, I'll stay for a year. . . . I'll get my own back, my good woman! You won't touch me with your mourning and the dimples in your cheeks. We all know about those dimples! [*Shouts out of window*] Semyon! Take the horses out. We shan't be leaving just directly. I am staying here. Tell them at the stable to give the horses a feed of oats. You've let the left trace horse get its legs into the reins again, you brute! [*Mimicking*] It's a—a—all right. I'll show you if it's all right! [*moves away from the window*]. It's a bad look-out! The heat is insufferable, no one will pay, I had a bad night, and now this mourning female with her state of mind! . . . My head aches. . . . Shall I have some vodka? Perhaps I will. [*Shouts*] Hi, there!

[*Enter* LUKA.]

LUKA.   What is it?
SMIRNOV.   Bring me a glass of vodka. [LUKA *goes out*]. Ough! [*sits down and examines himself*]. I must say, I am a nice sight! Covered with dust, muddy boots, unwashed, uncombed, straws on my waistcoat! The lady thought I was a highwayman, I expect [*yawns*]. . . . It's not quite polite to come into a drawing-room looking like this—but there, it doesn't matter. I am not a visitor—I am a creditor and there is no regulation dress for a creditor.

[*Enter* LUKA.]

LUKA [*giving him vodka*].   You take liberties, sir.

SMIRNOV [*angrily*].   What?

LUKA.   Nothing. I only . . .

SMIRNOV.   To whom are you speaking? Shut up!

LUKA [*aside*].   Well, here's an infliction! It's an ill wind brought him [*goes out*].

SMIRNOV.   Ach, how furious I am! I feel as though I should like to pound the whole world into powder. . . . I feel positively sick. . . . [*Shouts*] Hi, there!

[MADAME POPOV *enters, looking down.*]

MADAME POPOV.   Sir, in my solitude I have long been unused to the human voice, and cannot endure shouting. I beg you most earnestly not to disturb my peace.

SMIRNOV.   Pay me my money, and I will go.

MADAME POPOV.   I've told you in plain Russian I have no money in hand at the moment. Wait till the day after to-morrow.

SMIRNOV.   I too had the honor of telling you in plain Russian that I need the money, not the day after to-morrow, but to-day. If you don't pay me to-day, I shall have to hang myself to-morrow.

MADAME POPOV.   But what am I to do if I have no money? How strange it is!

SMIRNOV.   So you won't pay me at once . . . you won't?

MADAME POPOV.   I can't. . . .

SMIRNOV.   In that case I shall stop here, and shall go on staying here till I get it [*sits down*]. You will pay me the day after to-morrow! Very good! I shall sit here till the day after to-morrow. I shall sit here like this . . . [*leaps up*]. I ask you, am I obliged to pay my interest to-morrow, or not? Or do you think I am joking?

MADAME POPOV.   Sir, I beg you not to shout! This is not a stable.

SMIRNOV.   I am not asking you about a stable. I am asking—have I got to pay my interest to-morrow, or not?

MADAME POPOV.   You don't know how to behave in the society of ladies.

SMIRNOV.   Yes, I do know how to behave in the society of ladies.

MADAME POPOV.   No, you don't! You are a coarse, ill-bred man. Decent people don't speak like that to ladies.

SMIRNOV.   Oh, that's curious! How would you like me to speak to you? In French, or what? [*Growing angry and speaking with a lisp*] *Madame, je vous prie,* how happy I am that you are not paying me my money. Ach, *pardon* for having troubled you! What a lovely day it is! And how that mourning suits you! [*bows and scrapes*].

MADAME POPOV.   That's rude and not clever.

SMIRNOV [*mimicking her*].   Rude and not clever! I don't know how to behave in the society of ladies! Madam, I have seen more women in my day than you have sparrows. I have fought three duels over women. I have thrown over twelve women, and nine have thrown me over. Yes! There was a time when I played the fool—when I was all sentiment and honey, did the polite, was all bowing and scraping. . . . I loved and suffered, sighed at the moon, was all thrills and raptures. . . . I loved passionately, frantically in all sorts of ways, confound me!—chattered like a magpie about the rights of women, spent half my fortune on the tender passion; but now—no, thank you! You won't get round me now. I've had enough. Black eyes, eyes full of passion, crimson lips, dimples, moonlight, whisperings, timid breathing—I would not give a brass farthing for all that, madam! Present company excepted, of course, all women, young and old, are affected, mincing, gossiping, spiteful, liars to the marrow of their bones, trivial, petty, pitiless; their logic is most revolting, and as for this department [*slaps himself on the forehead*]—excuse me for my candor—a sparrow can give points to any philosopher in petticoats! One looks at some poetical creature, all in muslin, an ethereal being, a goddess, a million raptures, but if one peeps into her soul she is the most commonplace crocodile! [*takes hold of the back of a chair; the chair cracks and breaks*]. But what's most revolting is that this crocodile, for some reason, imagines that her *chef-d'œuvre,* her monopoly and privilege, is the tender passion! But, damnation take me, you may hang me on this nail, head downwards, if a woman has ever been capable of loving anyone but a lap-dog! In love all she can do is to whine and whimper. While a man suffers and makes sacrifices, all her love expresses itself in trailing her skirts and trying to keep a tight hold on him. You have the misfortune to be a woman, and so you know a woman's nature from yourself. Tell me honestly, have you ever in your life seen a woman who was sincere, true, and constant? You haven't! None but old women and frights are true and constant. It is easier to find a cat with horns or a white snipe than a constant woman!

MADAME POPOV.   Allow me to ask, then, who is true and constant in love according to you? Not man, surely!

SMIRNOV.   Yes, man.

MADAME POPOV.   Man! [*laughs maliciously*]. Man true and constant in love! That's something new, I must say. [*Hotly*] What right have you to say such a thing? Men true and constant! If it comes to that, I'll tell you that of all the men that I know, or have ever known, the best was my late husband. . . . I loved him passionately, with all my being, as none but a young, spiritual-minded woman can love; I gave him my youth, my life, my happiness, my fortune. He was the breath of my being, the idol I worshipped like a heathen, and—and that best of men deceived me in the most shameless fashion at every step! After his death I found in his table a drawer full of love-letters, and when he was alive—it is dreadful to remember!—he left me alone for weeks at a time. Before my very eyes he made love to other women and deceived me, squandered my money, mocked at my feelings. . . . And in spite of all that I loved him and was faithful to him. . . . What is more, I am still true and faithful to him. I have buried myself within four walls for ever, and I will not cast aside this mourning as long as I live.

SMIRNOV [*laughing contemptuously*].   Mourning! I don't know what you take me for. As though I don't know why you masquerade in black and shut yourself up within four walls! I should think so! It's so mysterious—so romantic! If some young ensign or unfledged poet passes your estate, he will look up at the windows and think, "Here lives the mysterious Tamara who from love for her husband has shut herself within four walls." I know all such tricks.

MADAME POPOV [*flushing crimson*].   What? How dare you say such things to me!

SMIRNOV.   You have buried yourself alive, but you have not forgotten to put powder on your face!

MADAME POPOV.   How dare you speak to me like that!

SMIRNOV.   Don't shout at me, please—I am not your steward! Allow me to call things by their real names. I am not a woman, and am accustomed to say what I think plainly. So don't shout, please.

MADAME POPOV.   I am not shouting—it's you who shout. Kindly let me alone!

SMIRNOV.   Pay me my money, and I will go away.

MADAME POPOV.   I won't give you the money.

SMIRNOV.   Yes, you will give it to me!

MADAME POPOV.   Just to spite you, I won't give you a farthing! You may as well leave me in peace.

SMIRNOV.   I haven't the pleasure of being married or engaged to you, and so please do not make a scene [*sits down*]. I don't like it.

MADAME POPOV [*gasping with indignation*].   You are sitting down?

SMIRNOV.   I am.

MADAME POPOV.   I beg you to go away.

SMIRNOV.   Give me my money! [*Aside*] Oh, how furious I feel!

MADAME POPOV.   I don't care to talk to insolent people. Be so good as to take yourself off [*Pause*]. You won't go—you won't?

SMIRNOV.   No.

MADAME POPOV.   No?

SMIRNOV.   No.

MADAME POPOV.   Very good, then [*rings the bell*].

[*Enter* LUKA.]

MADAME POPOV.   Luka, remove this gentleman.

LUKA [*approaches* SMIRNOV].   Sir, kindly go when you are told. It's no use staying here—

SMIRNOV [*leaping up*].   Hold your tongue! To whom are you speaking? I'll make mincemeat of you!

LUKA [*puts his hands on his heart*].   Holy Saints! [*sinks into an armchair*]. Oh, I feel ill! I feel ill! I can't breathe!

MADAME POPOV.   Where's Dasha? Dasha! [*Shouts*] Dasha! Pelageya! Dasha! [*rings the bell*].

LUKA.   Ach! they've all gone to pick strawberries. There's no one in the house. I feel ill! Water!

MADAME POPOV.   Kindly take yourself off.

SMIRNOV.   Please be more polite.

MADAME POPOV [*clenching her fists and stamping*].   You are a boor! A coarse bear! A bully! A monster!

SMIRNOV.   What? What did you say?

MADAME POPOV.   I said that you were a bear—a monster!

SMIRNOV [*stepping up to her*].   Excuse me, what right have you to insult me?

MADAME POPOV.   Yes, I am insulting you—what of it? Do you suppose I am afraid of you?

SMIRNOV.   And do you think that because you are a poetical creature you have a right to insult people with impunity? Yes? I challenge you!

LUKA.   Saints and holy martyrs! Water!

SMIRNOV.   Pistols!

MADAME POPOV.   If you have got strong fists and can bellow like a bull, do you think I am afraid of you, eh? You bully!

SMIRNOV.   I challenge you! I allow no one to insult me, and it's nothing to me that you are a woman, a weak creature!

MADAME POPOV [*trying to shout him down*].   Bear! bear! bear!

SMIRNOV.   It's time to abandon the prejudice that only men must pay for an insult. If there is to be equality, then let it be equality. Damn it all! I challenge you!

MADAME POPOV.   You want a duel? By all means!

SMIRNOV.   This minute!

MADAME POPOV.   This minute! My husband had pistols. . . . I'll fetch them at once [*goes out and hurriedly returns*]. . . . What pleasure I shall have in putting a bullet through your brazen head! Damnation take you! [*goes out*].

SMIRNOV.   I'll shoot her like a chicken! I am not a boy, I am not a sentimental puppy—feminine frailty means nothing to me.

LUKA.   My good gentleman [*drops on his knees*], for mercy's sake, have pity on an old man! Go away! You've frightened me to death, and now you are going to fight!

SMIRNOV [*not heeding him*].   Fight a duel! That really is equality, emancipation! That does make the sexes equal! I shall shoot her on principle. But what a woman! [*Mimics her*] "Damnation take you! Put a bullet through your brazen head!" . . . What a woman! Her cheeks were flushed, her eyes sparkled. . . . She accepted the challenge! Honor bright, I've never seen anyone like her in my life! . . .

LUKA.   Kind sir, go away! I'll remember you in my prayers!

SMIRNOV.   She is something like a woman! I like that! A real woman! Not a mush of sentiment, but flame, gunpowder, fireworks! I shall be sorry to kill her.

LUKA [*weeps*].   My good sir, go away!

SMIRNOV.   I really like her. I really do! Though she has dimples in her cheeks, I like her! I would forgive her the debt even, and all my anger is gone. . . . A wonderful woman!

[*Enter* MADAME POPOV *with pistols.*]

MADAME POPOV.   Here they are, the pistols. . . . But before we begin the duel, kindly show me how to fire. . . . I've never handled a pistol in my life.

LUKA.   The Lord save us and have mercy upon us! I'll go and look for the gardener and the coachman. What's brought this trouble on us? [*goes out*].

SMIRNOV [*examining the pistols*].   You see, there are several sorts of pistols. . . . There are special duelling pistols, the Mortimer pattern, with capsules. . . . But yours are the Smith-Wesson make, triple action with extractor. . . . They are fine pistols. They are worth at least ninety rubles the brace. . . . You have to hold the revolver like this. [*Aside*] What eyes! what eyes! A ravishing woman!

MADAME POPOV.   Is that right?

SMIRNOV.   Yes, that's it. . . . Then you raise the cock . . . take aim like this. . . . Throw your head a little back! . . . Stretch out your arm full length—that's it. . . . Then with this finger press on that little thing—and that's all. But the chief rule is not to get excited and to take aim slowly. Try not to let your hand shake.

MADAME POPOV.   Very well. It's not convenient to fight indoors; let us go into the garden.

SMIRNOV. Let us. Only I warn you beforehand I shall fire into the air.

MADAME POPOV. That's the last straw! Why?

SMIRNOV. Because . . . because . . . that's my affair.

MADAME POPOV. You funk it, do you? A-a-ah! No, sir, no wriggling! Kindly follow me. I shall not be satisfied till I have put a bullet through your head—that head that's so hateful to me! Are you funking it?

SMIRNOV. Yes, I am.

MADAME POPOV. That's a lie. Why won't you fight?

SMIRNOV. Because . . . because . . . I like you.

MADAME POPOV [with a malicious laugh]. He likes me! He dares to say that he likes me! [Pointing to the door] You can go!

SMIRNOV [in silence puts down the revolver, takes up his cap and is going; near the door he stops. For half a minute they look at each other in silence; then, going irresolutely towards MADAME POPOV]. I say—are you still angry? I, too, am devilish angry, but you know—how shall I put it? The fact is, you see—it's something like this, to put it plainly. [Shouts] Well, it's not my fault that I like you! [Clutches at the back of the chair; the chair cracks and breaks] Damnation, what fragile furniture you have! I like you. Do you understand? I—I am almost in love.

MADAME POPOV. Go away! I hate you!

SMIRNOV. Good God, what a woman! I have never seen anyone like her. I am lost! I am done for! I am caught like a mouse in a trap!

MADAME POPOV. Go away, or I'll fire.

SMIRNOV. Fire away! You can't imagine what joy it would be to die in the sight of those wonderful eyes—to be shot by a revolver held by that little velvety hand! . . . I have gone crazy! Think and decide at once, for if I go away from here, we shall never meet again. Decide! . . . I come of a good family, I am a gentleman, I have ten thousand rubles a year. . . . I can put a bullet through a halfpenny tossed in the air. . . . I've got first-rate horses. . . . Will you be my wife?

MADAME POPOV [indignant, brandishes the revolver]. A duel! Let us fight!

SMIRNOV. I've gone crazy. I can't understand. [Shouts] Hi, there! Water!

MADAME POPOV [shouts]. I challenge you!

SMIRNOV. I've gone crazy. I am in love like a boy—like a fool! [Snatches her hand; she shrieks with pain] I love you! [Falls on his knees] I love you as I have never loved before! I have thrown over twelve women, nine have thrown me over, but I never loved one of them as I love you. . . . I am getting maudlin, I am limp all over, I am a mush! Here I am on my knees like a fool and offering you my hand! . . . It's a shame, a disgrace! I've not been in love for five years. I vowed I wouldn't, and here I am completely bowled over! I offer you my hand. Yes or no? Won't you have it? Very well, you needn't! [*gets up and goes quickly to the door*].

MADAME POPOV. Stay!

SMIRNOV [*stopping*]. Well?

MADAME POPOV. Nothing—go! But stay, though—no, go, go! I hate you! Oh, no!—don't go away! Oh, if you knew how angry I am! [*Throws the revolver on the table*] My fingers are numb from the horrid thing. [*Tears her handkerchief in a fury*] Why are you standing there? Go away!

SMIRNOV. Good-bye!

MADAME POPOV. Yes, yes, go away! [*Shouts*] Where are you going? Stay—you can go, though. Oh, how angry I feel! Don't come near me! Don't come near me!

SMIRNOV [*going up to her*]. How angry I am with myself! I am in love like a schoolboy. I've been on my knees—it makes me feel cold all over. . . . [*Rudely*] I love you! As though I wanted to fall in love with you! To-morrow I have to pay my interest, the haymaking has begun, and now you on the top of it all. . . . [*Puts his arm round her waist*] I shall never forgive myself for this!

MADAME POPOV. Go away! Take your arms away! I—hate you! I chal-challenge you! [*A prolonged kiss.*]

[*Enter* LUKA *with an axe, the gardener with a rake, the coachman with a fork, and laborers with poles.*]

LUKA [*seeing the embracing couple*]. Holy Saints!

[*Pause*]

MADAME POPOV [*dropping her eyes*]. Luka, tell them in the stable not to give Toby any oats to-day.

CURTAIN.

THE PROPOSAL

A JEST IN ONE ACT

Characters

STEPAN STEPANOVITCH TCHUBUKOV, *a landowner*

NATALYA STEPANOVNA, *his daughter, age 25*

IVAN VASSILYEVITCH LOMOV, *a neighbor of* TCHUBUKOV'*s, a healthy, well-nourished, but hypochondriacal landowner*

Drawing-room in TCHUBUKOV's *house.* TCHUBUKOV *and* LOMOV; *the latter enters wearing evening dress and white gloves.*

TCHUBUKOV [*going to meet him*]. My darling, whom do I see? Ivan Vassilyevitch! Delighted! [*shakes hands*]. Well, this is a surprise, dearie. . . . How are you?

LOMOV. I thank you. And pray, how are you?

TCHUBUKOV. We are getting on all right, thanks to your prayers, my angel, and all the rest of it. Please sit down. . . . It's too bad, you know, to forget your neighbors, darling. But, my dear, why this ceremoniousness? A swallow-tail, gloves, and all the rest of it! Are you going visiting, my precious?

LOMOV. No, I have only come to see you, honored Stepan Stepanovitch.

TCHUBUKOV. Then why the swallow-tail, my charmer? As though you were paying calls on New Year's Day!

LOMOV. You see, this is how it is [*takes his arm*]. I have come, honored Stepan Stepanovitch, to trouble you with a request. I have more than once had the honor of asking for your assistance, and you have always, so to speak—but pardon me, I am agitated. I will have a drink of water, honored Stepan Stepanovitch [*drinks water*].

TCHUBUKOV [*aside*]. Come to ask for money! I am not going to give it to him. [*To him*] What is it, my beauty?

LOMOV. You see, Honor Stepanovitch—I beg your pardon, Stepan Honoritch. . . . I am dreadfully agitated, as you see. In short, no one but you can assist me, though, of course, I have done nothing to deserve it, and . . . and . . . have no right to reckon upon your assistance. . . .

TCHUBUKOV. Oh, don't spin it out, dearie. Come to the point. Well?

LOMOV. Immediately—in a moment. The fact is that I have come to ask for the hand of your daughter, Natalya Stepanovna.

TCHUBUKOV [*joyfully*]. You precious darling! Ivan Vassilyevitch, say it again! I can't believe my ears.

LOMOV. I have the honor to ask . . .

TCHUBUKOV [*interrupting*]. My darling! I am delighted, and all the rest of it. Yes, indeed, and all that sort of thing [*embraces and kisses him*]. I have been hoping for it for ages. It has always been my wish [*sheds a tear*]. And I have always loved you, my angel, as though you were my own son. God give you both love and good counsel, and all the rest of it. I have always wished for it. . . . Why am I standing here like a post? I am stupefied with joy, absolutely stupefied! Oh, from the bottom of my heart. . . . I'll go and call Natasha and that sort of thing.

LOMOV [*touched*]. Honored Stepan Stepanovitch, what do you think? May I hope that she will accept me?

TCHUBUKOV. A beauty like you, and she not accept you! I'll be bound she is as love-sick as a cat, and all the rest of it. . . . In a minute [*goes out*].

LOMOV. I am cold—I am trembling all over, as though I were in for an examination. The great thing is to make up one's mind. If one thinks about it too long, hesitates, discusses it, waits for one's ideal or for real love, one will never get married. . . . Brr! I am cold. Natalya Stepanovna is an excellent manager, not bad looking, educated— what more do I want? But I am beginning to have noises in my head. I am so upset [*sips water*]. And get married I must. To begin with, I am thirty-five—a critical age, so to speak. And, secondly, I need a regular, well-ordered life. . . . I have valvular disease of the heart, continual palpitations. I am hasty, and am very easily upset. . . . Now, for instance, my lips are quivering and my right eyelid is twitching. . . . But my worst trouble is with sleep. No sooner have I got into bed and just begun to drop asleep, than I have a shooting pain in my left side and a stabbing at my shoulder and my head. . . . I leap up like a madman. I walk about a little and lie down again, but no sooner do I drop off than there's the shooting pain in my side again. And the same thing twenty times over! . . .

[*Enter* NATALYA STEPANOVNA.]

NATALYA. Well, so it's you! Why, and papa said a purchaser had come for the goods! How do you do, Ivan Vassilyevitch?

LOMOV. How do you do, honored Natalya Stepanovna!

NATALYA. Excuse my apron and *négligé*. We are shelling peas for drying. How is it you have not been to see us for so long? Sit down. [*They sit down*.]. Will you have some lunch?

LOMOV. No, thank you, I have already lunched.

NATALYA. Won't you smoke? Here are the matches. . . . It's a magnificent day, but yesterday it rained so hard that the men did no work at all. How many hay-cocks have you got out? Only fancy, I have been too eager and had the whole meadow mown, and now I am sorry—I am afraid the hay will rot. It would have been better to wait. But what's this? I do believe you have got on your dress-coat! That's something new. Are you going to a ball, or what? And, by the way, you are looking nice. . . . Why are you such a swell, really?

LOMOV [in agitation]. You see, honored Natalya Stepanovna. . . . The fact is that I have made up my mind to ask you to listen to me. . . . Of course, you will be surprised, and even angry, but I . . . It's horribly cold!

NATALYA. What is it? [Pause] Well?

LOMOV. I will try to be brief. You are aware, honored Natalya Stepanovna, that from my earliest childhood I had the honor of knowing your family. My late aunt and her husband, from whom, as you know, I inherited the estate, always entertained a profound respect for your papa and your late mamma. The family of the Lomovs and the family of the Tchubukovs have always been on the most friendly and, one may say, intimate terms. Moreover, as you are aware, my land is in close proximity to yours. If you remember, my Volovyi meadows are bounded by your birch copse.

NATALYA. Excuse my interrupting you. You say "my Volovyi meadows." . . . But are they yours?

LOMOV. Yes, mine.

NATALYA. Well, what next! The Volovyi meadows are ours, not yours!

LOMOV. No, they are mine, honored Natalya Stepanovna.

NATALYA. That's news to me. How do they come to be yours?

LOMOV. How do they come to be mine? I am speaking of the Volovyi meadows that run like a wedge between your birch copse and the Charred Swamp.

NATALYA. Quite so. Those are ours.

LOMOV. No, you are mistaken, honored Natalya Stepanovna, they are mine.

NATALYA. Think what you are saying, Ivan Vassilyevitch! Have they been yours long?

LOMOV. What do you mean by "long"? As long as I can remember they have always been ours.

NATALYA. Well, there you must excuse me.

LOMOV. There is documentary evidence for it, honored Natalya Stepanovna. The Volovyi meadows were once a matter of dispute, that is true, but now everyone knows that they are mine. And there can be no dispute about it. Kindly consider . . . my aunt's grandmother gave over those meadows to the peasants of your father's grandfather for their use, rent free, for an indefinite period, in return for their firing her bricks. The peasants of your father's grandfather enjoyed the use of the meadows, rent free, for some forty years, and grew used to looking upon them as their own; afterwards, when the settlement came about after the emancipation . . .

NATALYA. It is not at all as you say! Both my grandfather and my great-grandfather considered their land reached to the Charred Swamp—so the Volovyi meadows were ours. I can't understand what there is to argue about. It's really annoying!

LOMOV. I will show you documents, Natalya Stepanovna.

NATALYA. No, you are simply joking, or trying to tease me. . . . A nice sort of surprise! We have owned the land nearly three hundred years, and all of a sudden we are told that the land is not ours! Forgive me, Ivan Vassilyevitch, but I positively cannot believe my ears. . . . I don't care about the meadows. They are not more than fifteen acres, and they are only worth some three hundred rubles, but I am revolted by injustice. You may say what you like, but I cannot endure injustice!

LOMOV. Listen to me, I implore you. The peasants of your father's grandfather, as I had already the honor to inform you, made bricks for my aunt's grandmother. My aunt's grandmother, wishing to do something for them . . .

NATALYA. Grandfather, grandmother, aunt. . . . I don't understand a word of it. The meadows are ours, and that's all about it.

LOMOV. They are mine.

NATALYA. They are ours. If you go on arguing for two days, if you put on fifteen dress-coats, they are still ours, ours, ours! . . . I don't want what's yours, but I don't want to lose what's mine. . . . You can take that as you please!

LOMOV. I do not care about the meadows, Natalya Stepanovna, but it is a matter of principle. If you like, I will make you a present of them.

NATALYA. I might make you a present of them, they are mine. All this is very queer, Ivan Vassilyevitch, to say the least of it. Hitherto we have looked upon you as a good neighbor—a friend. Last year we lent you our threshing-machine, and through that we couldn't finish our threshing till November; and you treat us as if we were gypsies! Make me a present of my own land! Excuse me, but that is not neighborly. To my thinking it is positively impertinent, if you care to know. . . .

LOMOV. According to you I am a usurper, then? I've never snatched other people's land, madam, and I will allow no one to accuse me of such a thing . . . [*goes rapidly to the decanter and drinks water*]. The Volovyi meadows are mine!

Natalya.   It's not true: they are ours!

Lomov.   They are mine!

Natalya.   That's not true. I'll prove it. I'll send our mowers to cut the hay there to-day!

Lomov.   What?

Natalya.   My laborers will be there to-day.

Lomov.   I'll kick them out.

Natalya.   Don't you dare!

Lomov [*clutches at his heart*].   The Volovyi meadows are mine! Do you understand? Mine!

Natalya.   Don't shout, please. You can shout and choke with rage when you are at home, if you like; but here I beg you to keep within bounds.

Lomov.   If it were not for these terrible, agonizing palpitations, madam—if it were not for the throbbing in my temples, I should speak to you very differently. [*Shouts*] The Volovyi meadows are mine!

Natalya.   Ours!

Lomov.   Mine!

Natalya.   Ours!

Lomov.   Mine!

[*Enter* Tchubukov.]

Tchubukov.   What is it? What are you shouting about?

Natalya.   Papa, explain to this gentleman, please: to whom do the Volovyi meadows belong—to him or to us?

Tchubukov [*to* Lomov].   My chicken, the meadows are ours.

Lomov.   But upon my word, Stepan Stepanovitch, how did they come to be yours? Do you, at least, be reasonable. My aunt's grandmother gave over the meadows for temporary gratuitous use to your grandfather's peasants. The peasants made use of the land for forty years and got used to regarding it as their own; but when the Settlement came . . .

Tchubukov.   Allow me, my precious. . . . You forget that the peasants did not pay your grandmother rent and all the rest of it, just because the ownership of the land was in dispute, and so on. . . . And now every dog knows that they are ours. You can't have seen the map.

Lomov.   I will prove to you that they are mine.

Tchubukov.   You never will, my pet.

Lomov.   Yes, I will.

Tchubukov.   Why are you shouting, my love? You will prove nothing at all by shouting. I don't desire what is yours, and don't intend to give up what is mine. Why ever should I? If it comes to that, my dear, if you intend to wrangle over the meadows, I would rather give them to the peasants than to you, that I would!

LOMOV.   I don't understand it. What right have you to give away another man's property?

TCHUBUKOV.   Allow me to decide for myself whether I have the right or no. I may say, young man, I am not accustomed to being spoken to in that tone, and all the rest of it. I am twice as old as you are, young man, and I beg you to speak to me without getting excited and all the rest of it.

LOMOV.   Why, you simply take me for a fool and are laughing at me! You call my land yours, and then you expect me to be cool about it and to speak to you properly! That's not the way good neighbors behave, Stepan Stepanovitch. You are not a neighbor, but a usurper!

TCHUBUKOV.   What? What did you say?

NATALYA.   Papa, send the men at once to mow the meadows.

TCHUBUKOV [*to* LOMOV].   What did you say, sir?

NATALYA.   The Volovyi meadows are ours, and I won't give them up. I won't! I won't!

LOMOV.   We will see about that. I'll prove to you in court that they are mine.

TCHUBUKOV.   In court? You can take it into court, sir, and all the rest of it! You can! I know you—you are only waiting for a chance to go to law, and so on. . . . A pettifogging character! All your family were fond of litigation—all of them!

LOMOV.   I beg you not to insult my family. The Lomovs have all been honest men, and not one of them has ever been on his trial for embezzling money like your uncle!

TCHUBUKOV.   Well, you Lomovs have all been mad!

NATALYA.   Every one of them—every one of them!

TCHUBUKOV.   Your grandfather was a dipsomaniac, and your youngest aunt, Nastasya Mihailovna, ran away with an architect, and so on.

LOMOV.   And your mother was a hunchback [*clutches at his heart*]. The shooting pain in my side! . . . The blood has rushed to my head. . . . Holy Saints! . . . Water!

TCHUBUKOV.   And your father was a gambler and a glutton!

NATALYA.   And there was no one like your aunt for talking scandal!

LOMOV.   My left leg has all gone numb. . . . And you are an intriguer! . . . Oh, my heart! . . . And it is no secret that before the elections you . . . There are flashes before my eyes! . . . Where is my hat?

NATALYA.   It's mean! It's dishonest! It's disgusting!

TCHUBUKOV.   And you yourself are a viperish, double-faced, mischief-making man. Yes, indeed!

LOMOV.   Here is my hat. . . . My heart! . . . Which way am I to go? Where's the door? Oh! I believe I am dying! I've lost the use of my leg [*goes towards the door*].

TCHUBUKOV [*calling after him*].   Never set foot within my door again!

NATALYA.   Take it into court! We shall see!

[LOMOV *goes out, staggering.*]

TCHUBUKOV.   Damnation take him! [*walks about in excitement*].

NATALYA.   What a wretch! How is one to believe in good neighbors after that!

TCHUBUKOV.   Blackguard! Scarecrow!

NATALYA.   The object! Collars other people's land—then abuses them!

TCHUBUKOV.   And that noodle—that eyesore—had the face to make a proposal, and all the rest of it. Just fancy, a proposal!

NATALYA.   What proposal?

TCHUBUKOV.   Why, he came here on purpose to propose to you!

NATALYA.   To propose? To me? Why didn't you tell me so before?

TCHUBUKOV.   And he had got himself up in his dress-coat on purpose! The sausage! The shrimp!

NATALYA.   To me? A proposal! Ah! [*She falls into an armchair and moans*] Bring him back! Bring him back! Oh, bring him back!

TCHUBUKOV.   Bring whom back?

NATALYA.   Make haste, make haste! I feel faint! Bring him back! [*Hysterics.*]

TCHUBUKOV.   What is it! What's the matter? [*clutches at his head*] I do have a life of it! I shall shoot myself! I shall hang myself! They'll be the death of me!

NATALYA.   I am dying! Bring him back!

TCHUBUKOV.   Tfoo! Directly. Don't howl [*runs off*].

NATALYA [*alone, moans*].   What have we done! Bring him back! Bring him back!

TCHUBUKOV [*runs in*].   He is just coming in, and all the rest of it. Damnation take him! Ough! Talk to him yourself, I don't want to. . . .

NATALYA [*moans*].   Bring him back!

TCHUBUKOV [*shouts*].   He is coming, I tell you! What a task it is,

O Lord, to be the father of a grown-up daughter! I shall cut my throat! I shall certainly cut my throat! We've abused the man, put him to shame, kicked him out, and it is all your doing—your doing!

NATALYA.   No, it was yours!

TCHUBUKOV.   Oh, it's my fault, so that's it! [LOMOV *appears at the door*]. Well, talk to him yourself [*goes out*].

[*Enter* LOMOV *in a state of collapse.*]

LOMOV.   Fearful palpitations! My leg is numb . . . there's a stitch in my side. . . .

NATALYA.   Forgive us; we were too hasty, Ivan Vassilyevitch. I remember now: the Volovyi meadows really are yours.

LOMOV.   My heart is throbbing frightfully. . . . The meadows are mine. . . . There's a twitching in both my eyelids.

NATALYA.   Yes, they are yours, they are. Sit down. [*They sit down.*] We were wrong.

LOMOV.   I acted from principle. . . . I do not value the land, but I value the principle. . . .

NATALYA.   Just so, the principle. . . . Let us talk of something else.

LOMOV.   Especially as I have proofs. My aunt's grandmother gave the peasants of your father's grandfather . . .

NATALYA.   Enough, enough about that. . . . [*Aside*] I don't know how to begin. [*To him*] Shall you soon be going shooting?

LOMOV.   I expect to go grouse shooting after the harvest, honored Natalya Stepanovna. Oh! did you hear? Only fancy, I had such a misfortune! My Tracker, whom I think you know, has fallen lame.

NATALYA.   What a pity! How did it happen?

LOMOV.   I don't know. . . . He must have put his paw out of joint, or perhaps some other dog bit it. . . . [*Sighs*] My very best dog, to say nothing of the money I have spent on him! You know I paid Mironov a hundred and twenty-five rubles for him.

NATALYA.   You gave too much, Ivan Vassilyevitch!

LOMOV.   Well, to my mind it was very cheap. He is a delightful dog.

NATALYA.   Father gave eighty-five rubles for his Backer, and Backer is a much better dog than your Tracker.

LOMOV.   Backer a better dog than Tracker? What nonsense! [*laughs*]. Backer a better dog than Tracker!

NATALYA.   Of course he is better. It's true that Backer is young yet—he is hardly a full-grown dog—but for points and cleverness even Voltchanetsky hasn't one to beat him.

LOMOV.   Excuse me, Natalya Stepanovna, but you forget that your Backer has a pug-jaw, and a dog with a pug-jaw is never any good for gripping.

NATALYA.   A pug-jaw! That's the first time I've heard so.

LOMOV.   I assure you the lower jaw is shorter than the upper.

NATALYA.   Why, have you measured?

LOMOV.   Yes. He is all right for coursing, no doubt, but for gripping he'd hardly do.

NATALYA.   In the first place, our Backer is a pedigree dog, son of Harness and Chisel, but you can't even tell what breed your spotty piebald is. . . . Then he is as old and ugly as a broken-down horse.

LOMOV.   He is old, but I wouldn't exchange him for half a dozen of your Backers. . . . How could I? Tracker is a dog, but Backer—there can be no question about it. Every huntsman has packs and packs of dogs like your Backer. Twenty-five rubles would be a good price for him.

NATALYA.   There is a demon of contradictoriness in you to-day, Ivan Vassilyevitch. First you make out that the meadows are yours, then that your Tracker is a better dog than Backer. I don't like a man to say what he does not think. You know perfectly well that Backer is worth a hundred of your . . . stupid Trackers. Why, then, say the opposite?

LOMOV.   I see, Natalya Stepanovna, that you think I am blind or a fool. Do you understand that your Backer has a pug-jaw?

NATALYA.   It's not true!

LOMOV.   It is!

NATALYA [shouts].   It's not true!

LOMOV.   Why are you shouting, madam?

NATALYA.   Why do you talk nonsense? This is revolting! It's time your Tracker was shot—and you compare him to Backer!

LOMOV.   Excuse me, I cannot continue this argument. I have palpitations.

NATALYA.   I have noticed that men argue most about hunting who know least about it.

LOMOV.   Madam, I beg you to be silent. My heart is bursting. [Shouts] Be silent!

NATALYA.   I will not be silent till you own that Backer is a hundred times better than your Tracker.

LOMOV.   A hundred times worse! Plague take your Backer! My temples . . . my eyes . . . my shoulder. . . .

NATALYA.   There's no need for plague to take your fool of a Tracker—he is as good as dead already.

LOMOV [weeping].   Be silent! My heart is bursting!

NATALYA.   I won't be silent.

[*Enter* TCHUBUKOV.]

TCHUBUKOV [*coming in*].   What now?

NATALYA.   Papa, tell me truly, on your conscience, which is the better dog—our Backer or his Tracker?

LOMOV.   Stepan Stepanovitch, I implore you tell me one thing only: has your Backer a pug-jaw or not? Yes or no?

TCHUBUKOV.   And what if he has? It's of no consequence. Anyway, there's no better dog in the whole district, and all the rest of it.

LOMOV.   But my Tracker is better, isn't he? Honestly?

TCHUBUKOV.   Don't excite yourself, my precious. Your Tracker certainly has his good qualities. . . . He is a well-bred dog, has good legs, and is well set-up, and all the rest of it. But the dog, if you care to know, my beauty, has two serious defects: he is old and is snub-nosed.

LOMOV.   Excuse me, I have palpitations. . . . Let us take the facts. . . . If you will kindly remember, at Maruskin's my Tracker kept shoulder to shoulder with the Count's Swinger, while your Backer was a good half-mile behind.

TCHUBUKOV.   Yes, he was, because the Count's huntsman gave him a crack with his whip.

LOMOV.   He deserved it. All the other dogs were after the fox, but Backer got hold of a sheep.

TCHUBUKOV.   That's not true! . . . Darling, I am hot-tempered, and I beg you to drop this conversation. He lashed him because everyone is jealous of another man's dog. . . . Yes, they are all envious! And you are not free from blame on that score either, sir. As soon as you notice, for instance, that someone's dog is better than your Tracker, at once you begin with this and that, and all the rest of it. I remember it all!

LOMOV.   I remember it too!

TCHUBUKOV [*mimics him*].   "I remember it too!" And what do you remember?

LOMOV.   Palpitations! . . . My leg has no feeling in it. I can't . . .

NATALYA [*mimicking him*].   "Palpitations!" . . . A fine sportsman! You ought to be lying on the stove in the kitchen squashing black-beetles instead of hunting foxes. Palpitations!

TCHUBUKOV.   Yes, you are a fine sportsman, really! With your palpitations you ought to stay at home, instead of jolting in the saddle. It wouldn't matter if you hunted, but you only ride out to wrangle and interfere with other men's dogs and all the rest of it. I am hot-tempered; let us drop this subject. You are not a sportsman at all.

LOMOV.   And you—are you a sportsman? You only go to the hunt to intrigue and make up to the Count. . . . My heart! . . . You are an intriguer!

TCHUBUKOV.   What? Me an intriguer? [*Shouts*] Hold your tongue!

LOMOV.   Intriguer!

TCHUBUKOV.   Milksop! Puppy!

LOMOV.   Old rat! Jesuit!

TCHUBUKOV.   Hold your tongue, or I'll shoot you with a filthy gun like a partridge! Noodle!

LOMOV.   Everyone knows—oh, my heart!—that your wife used to beat you. . . . My leg . . . my forehead . . . my eyes! I shall drop! I shall drop!

TCHUBUKOV.   And you go in terror of your housekeeper!

LOMOV.   Oh, oh, oh! My heart has burst! I can't feel my shoulder—what has become of my shoulder? I am dying! [*falls into an armchair*]. A doctor! [*swoons*].

TCHUBUKOV.   Puppy! Milksop! Noodle! I feel faint! [*drinks water*]. Faint!

NATALYA.   You are a fine sportsman! You don't know how to sit on your horse. [*To her father*] Papa, what's the matter with him? Papa! Look, papa! [*shrieks*]. Ivan Vassilyevitch! He is dead!

TCHUBUKOV.   I feel faint! I can't breathe! Give me air!

NATALYA.   He is dead! [*shakes* LOMOV *by the sleeve*]. Ivan Vassilyevitch! Ivan Vassilyevitch! What have we done! He is dead! [*falls into an armchair*]. A doctor! a doctor! [*hysterics*].

TCHUBUKOV.   Och! What is it? What do you want?

NATALYA [*moans*].   He is dead! He is dead!

TCHUBUKOV.   Who is dead? [*looking at* LOMOV] He really is dead! Holy Saints! Water! A doctor! [*Holds a glass of water to* LOMOV's *lips*] Drink! . . . No, he won't drink. So he is dead, and all the rest of it. I do have a life of it! Why don't I put a bullet through my brains? Why is it I haven't cut my throat? What am I waiting for? Give me a knife! Give me a pistol! [LOMOV *makes a slight movement.*] I believe he is reviving. . . . Have a drink of water. That's right.

LOMOV.   Flashes—dizziness—where am I?

TCHUBUKOV.   You'd better make haste and get married—and go to the devil! She consents [*joins the hands of* LOMOV *and his daughter*]. She accepts you, and all the rest of it. I give you my blessing, and so on. Only leave me in peace.

LOMOV.   Eh? What? [*getting up*] Who?

TCHUBUKOV.   She accepts you. Well? Kiss each other and . , , be damned to you!

NATALYA [*moans*].   He is alive! Yes, yes, I accept.

TCHUBUKOV.   Kiss!

LOMOV.   Eh? Whom? [*kisses* NATALYA STEPANOVNA]. Delighted!
Excuse me, what's the point? Oh, yes, I understand! Palpitations . . .
dizziness . . . I am happy, Natalya Stepanovna [*kisses her hand*]. My leg
is numb!

NATALYA.   I . . . I too am happy.

TCHUBUKOV.   It's a load off my heart! Ough!

NATALYA.   But . . . still you must admit now that Tracker is not
as good a dog as Backer.

LOMOV.   He is better!

NATALYA.   He is worse!

TCHUBUKOV.   Well, here's the beginning of family happiness!
Champagne!

LOMOV.   He is better!

NATALYA.   He is not! He is not! He is not!

TCHUBUKOV [*trying to shout them down*].   Champagne!
Champagne!

CURTAIN.

AN UNWILLING MARTYR
(A HOLIDAY EPISODE)
A JEST IN ONE ACT

Characters

IVAN IVANITCH TOLKATCHOV, *father of a family*
ALEXEY ALEXEYITCH MURASHKIN, *his friend*

The action takes place in Petersburg, in MURASHKIN'S *flat.*

MURASHKIN's *study. Upholstered furniture.* MURASHKIN *is sitting at the writing-table. Enter* TOLKATCHOV, *holding in his arms a glass globe for a lamp, a toy bicycle, three hat-boxes, a large parcel of clothes, a fish-basket containing bottles of beer, and many small parcels. He looks about him in a dazed way and sinks exhausted on the sofa.*

MURASHKIN.   Hullo, Ivan Ivanitch! Delighted to see you! Where do you hail from?

TOLKATCHOV [*breathing hard*].   My dear fellow . . . I have a favor to ask you. . . . I entreat you . . . lend me a revolver till to-morrow. Be a friend!

MURASHKIN.   What do you want with a revolver?

TOLKATCHOV.   I need one. . . . Oh, holy saints! . . . Give me some water. . . . Make haste, water! I need it. . . . I have to pass through a dark wood to-night and so . . . to be ready for anything. Lend it me, there's a good fellow!

MURASHKIN.   Oh, nonsense, Ivan Ivanitch! What the devil's this about a dark wood? You've got something in your mind, I suppose? I can see from your face you are up to no good! But what's the matter with you? Are you ill?

TOLKATCHOV.   Stop, let me get my breath. . . . Oh, holy saints! I am as tired as a dog. I have a sensation all over my head and body as though I'd been beaten like a beefsteak. I can bear no more. Be a friend, ask no questions, don't go into details . . . give me a revolver! I implore you!

MURASHKIN.   Come, come, Ivan Ivanitch! What weakness! You, the father of a family, a civil councillor! For shame!

TOLKATCHOV.   Me the father of a family? I'm a martyr! I'm a beast of burden, a nigger, a slave, a coward who keeps waiting for something instead of despatching himself to the other world! I am a rag, a blockhead, an idiot! What am I living for? What's the object of it? [*leaps up*]. Tell me, please, what is it I am living for? Why this endless succession of moral and physical miseries? I can understand being a martyr for an idea, yes! but to be a martyr for goodness knows what, for lamp-shades and ladies' petticoats. No! I'd rather not, thanks! No, no, no! I've had enough of it! Enough!

MURASHKIN.   Don't talk so loud, the neighbors will hear!

TOLKATCHOV.   The neighbors may hear for all I care! If you won't give me a revolver, someone else will—anyway, I shan't be long among the living! That's settled!

MURASHKIN.   Stop, you have pulled off my button. Speak coolly. I still don't understand what's wrong with your life.

TOLKATCHOV.   What's wrong? You ask what's wrong? Certainly, I'll tell you! By all means. Perhaps if I have it out, it will make me feel better. . . . Let us sit down. Come, listen. . . . Oh, dear, I can't get my breath! . . . Take to-day, for example. Take it. As you know from ten o'clock in the morning till four o'clock in the afternoon, I have to stick in the office. Baking hot, stuffy, flies, hopeless muddle and confusion. The secretary has taken a holiday, Hrapov has gone off to get married, the small fry of the office have gone dotty over week-ends, love affairs and amateur theatricals. . . . They are all worn out, sleepy and exhausted so that you can get no sense out of them. . . . The secretary's duties are being carried on by an individual deaf in the left ear and in love; the people who come to the office seem to have lost their wits, they are always in a hurry and a fluster—ill-tempered, threatening—such a regular Bedlam that you want to scream for help. Confusion and muddle! And the work is hellish: the same thing over and over again, enquiries and references—all the same like the waves of the sea. Your eyes are ready to drop out of your head, you know. Give me some water. . . . You come out of the office shattered, torn to rags. . . . You ought to have your dinner and a good snooze—but no, you've to remember that it's the summer holidays; that is, that you are a slave, a wretched rag, a miserable lost creature, and must run like a chicken, carrying out commissions. There is a charming custom in our country retreat: if the summer visitor is going to town, not only his wife, but every wretched holiday-maker is privileged and entitled to burden him with masses of commissions. My spouse insists on my going to the dressmaker and giving her a good scolding, because she has made the bodice too full and the shoulders too narrow; Sonitchka's shoes must be changed; my sister-in-law wants twenty kopecks' worth of crimson silk to match a pattern and two and a half yards of tape. . . . But wait a minute, here I'll read it to you. [*Takes a note out of his pocket and reads it*] A globe for the lamp; one pound of ham sausage; five kopecks' worth of cloves and nutmeg; castor-oil for Misha; ten pounds of granulated sugar; fetch from home the copper stewpan and the mortar for pounding sugar; carbolic acid, insect powder, ten kopecks' worth of face powder; twenty bottles of beer; vinegar and a pair of corsets, size 82, for Mlle. Chanceau. . . . Ough! and fetch from home Misha's greatcoat and goloshes. Those are the orders from my wife and family. Now for the commissions from my dear friends and neighbors, damnation take them. The Vlassins are keeping Volodya's name-day to-morrow; he is to have a bicycle bought him; Madame Vihrin, the wife of the lieutenant-colonel, is in an interesting condition, and so I have to go every day to the midwife and beg her to come. And so on, and so on. I have five lists in my pocket, and my handkerchief is nothing but knots. And so, my dear fellow, in the time between the office and the train, one's tearing about the town like a dog with its tongue out—tearing about and cursing one's life. From the draper's to the chemist's, from the chemist's to the dressmaker's, from the dressmaker's to the pork butcher's, and then back to the chemist's again. In one place you trip up, in another you lose your money, in the third you forget to pay and they run after you and make a row, in the fourth you tread on a lady's skirt . . . pfoo! Such a form of exercise sends one dotty and makes one such a wreck that every bone aches all night afterwards, and one dreams of crocodiles. Well, your tasks have been performed and everything has been bought—now kindly tell me how is one to pack all this truck? How, for instance, are you going to pack a heavy copper pan and a mortar with a globe for the lamp, or carbolic with tea? How are you going to combine bottles of beer and a bicycle? It's a labor of Hercules, a problem, a riddle! You may rack your brains and do your utmost, but in the end you are sure to break or spill something, and at the station and in the railway carriage you will have to stand with your legs straddling and your arms out, propping up some package with your chin, all hung with fish baskets, cardboard boxes, and such trumpery. And when the train starts the passengers begin hustling your parcels out of the way, for your luggage is all over other people's seats. They make a fuss, call the guard, threaten to have you turned out, but what am I to do? I simply stand and blink at them like a donkey when it is beaten. Now let me tell you what comes next. I get home to my summer villa. Then one does deserve a good drink after one's day of toil, a meal—a good snooze—doesn't one?—but not a bit of it! My wife keeps a sharp eye on me. You've scarcely swallowed your soup before she pounces on you and you must go, if you please, to private theatricals or a dancing club. Don't dare to protest. You are a husband, and the word "husband," translated into holiday language, means a dumb animal who can be driven and laden as you please, with no risk of interference from the Society for the Prevention of Cruelty to Animals. You go and stare at "A Scandal in a Respectable Family" or at "Motya"; you clap your hands at your wife's prompting while you grow weaker, and weaker, and weaker, and feel every minute as though you will expire. And at the club you have to look on at the dancing and find partners for your better-half, and if there are not gentlemen enough, you have to dance the quadrille yourself. You get home from the theatricals or the dancing after midnight, feeling more like a dead sheep than a human being. But now, at last, you reach the longed-for end; you have undressed and get into bed. Excellent, you can shut your eyes and go to sleep. . . . It's all so nice, so poetical, so snug, you know; the children are not screaming in the next room, and your wife is not there, and your conscience is at ease—you could wish for nothing better. You drop asleep—and all at once . . . all at once you hear, dz-z-z-z! The gnats! [*leaps up*]. The gnats, double damnation to them! [*shakes his fists*]. Gnats! They beat the plagues of Egypt, the tortures of the Inquisition! Dz-z-z! It buzzes so plaintively, so mournfully, as though it were asking your forgiveness; but it bites you, the rascal, so that you are scratching for an hour after. You smoke, you slaughter them, you cover up your head—there is no escape! In the end you curse and give yourself up to be devoured: let the damned brutes bite away! No sooner are you resigned to the gnats than another plague is upon you: your spouse begins practicing songs with her tenors in the drawing-room. They sleep all day and spend the night getting up amateur concerts. Oh, my God! Those tenors are a torture, the gnats aren't in it! [*Sings*] "Tell me not thy youth is ru-ined!" . . . "Spellbound again I stand before thee." . . . Oh, the be-easts! They wring the very soul out of my body! To deaden the sound of them a little I have to practice this trick: I tap myself with my finger just by my ear. I go on tapping like that till they go away at four o'clock. Och! Another drink of water, my boy. . . . I can't bear it. . . . Well, so after a night without sleep you get up at six o'clock and—off to the station for your train! You run, you are afraid of being late, and the mud! the fog! the cold—brr! When you get to town, it is the same old hurdy-gurdy over again! There it is! It's a beastly life, I tell you. I wouldn't wish my worst enemy such a life. It has made me ill, do you understand? Asthma, heartburn, I am always in a panic about something; my stomach won't work, my eyes are dizzy. . . . Would you believe it, I have become a regular neurotic . . . [*looks about him*]. Only this is strictly between ourselves. I should like to consult Tchetchott or Merzheyovsky. A sort of frenzy comes over me, my boy. When I am annoyed or driven silly, when the gnats bite or the tenors sing, I have a sudden dizziness before my eyes. I leap up and run all over the house as though I were crazy, shouting, "I thirst for blood! Blood!" And at such moments I really long to stick a knife into somebody or bash his head in with a chair. You see what this holiday life may bring one to! And no one is sorry for me, no one feels for me—they all take it for granted. They actually laugh. But can't you understand, I am a living creature, I want to live! This isn't a farce, it is a tragedy! If you won't give me a revolver, you might at least feel for me!

MURASHKIN.   I do feel for you.

TOLKATCHOV.   I see how you feel for me. . . . Good-bye, I must go and get anchovies, sausage . . . there's still the tooth-powder to get, too, and then to the station.

MURASHKIN.   Where are you staying for the holidays?

TOLKATCHOV.   At the Putrid River.

MURASHKIN [gleefully].   Really? I say, do you happen to know Olga Pavlovna Finberg who is staying there?

TOLKATCHOV.   I know her. She is a friend of ours, in fact.

MURASHKIN.   You don't say so! What luck! How fortunate! It would be nice of you . . .

TOLKATCHOV.   What is it?

MURASHKIN.   My dear friend, would it be possible for you to do me a small favor? Be a friend! Promise me you will do it?

TOLKATCHOV.   What is it?

MURASHKIN.   As a friend, I ask you! I entreat you, my dear boy. In the first place give my greetings to Olga Pavlovna, tell her that I am alive and well and that I kiss her hand. And in the second, take her something for me. She commissioned me to buy her a hand sewing-machine, and there is nobody to take it her. . . . Take it, my dear fellow! And while you are about it, you might as well take this cage with the canary . . . only do be careful, or the little door will get broken. . . . Why do you look at me like that?

TOLKATCHOV.   A sewing-machine . . . a bird-cage and canary . . . greenfinches . . . linnets . . .

MURASHKIN.   Ivan Ivanitch, what is the matter with you? Why are you so red in the face?

TOLKATCHOV [stamping].   Give me the sewing-machine! Where is the bird-cage? Get on my back yourself! Tear a man to pieces! Eat him up! Make an end of him! [clenches his fists]. I thirst for blood! for blood! for blood!

MURASHKIN.   You are mad!

TOLKATCHOV [bearing down upon him].   I thirst for blood! for blood!

MURASHKIN [in terror].   He's gone out of his mind! [Shouts] Petrusha! Marya! Where are you? Save me!

TOLKATCHOV [chasing him about the room].   I thirst for blood! For blood!

CURTAIN.

THE WEDDING

A FARCE IN ONE ACT

Characters

YEVDOKIM ZAHAROVITCH ZHIGALOV, *retired collegiate registry-clerk*

NASTASYA TIMOFEYEVNA, *his wife*

DASHENKA, *their daughter*

EPAMINOND MAXIMOVITCH APLOMBOV, *her bridegroom*

FYODOR YAKOVLEVITCH REVUNOV-KARAULOV, *retired naval captain of the second rank*

ANDREY ANDREYEVITCH NYUNIN, *insurance agent*

ANNA MARTYNOVNA ZMEYUKIN, *a midwife, about thirty, in a bright magenta dress*

IVAN MIHAILOVITCH YAT, *a telegraph clerk*

HARLAMPY SPIRIDONOVITCH DYMBA, *a Greek keeper of a confectioner's shop*

DMITRY STEPANOVITCH MOZGOVOY, *a sailor in the volunteer fleet*

BEST MAN, Dancing Gentlemen, Waiters, *etc.*

The action takes place in one of the rooms of a second-class restaurant.

A brilliantly lighted room. A big table laid for supper. Waiters in swallow-tails are busy at the tables. Behind the scenes a band is playing the last figure of the quadrille.

MADAME ZMEYUKIN, YAT, *and the bridegroom's* BEST MAN *walk across the stage.*

MADAME ZMEYUKIN.   No, no, no!

YAT [*following her*].   Have pity on me!

MADAME ZMEYUKIN.   No, no, no!

THE BEST MAN [*hastening after them*].   I say, you can't go on like that! Where are you off to? And the *Grand-rond? Grand-rond*, silvoo-play! [*They go out*].

[*Enter* NASTASYA TIMOFEYEVNA *and* APLOMBOV.]

NASTASYA.   Instead of worrying me, saying all sorts of things, you had much better go and dance.

APLOMBOV.   I am not a Spinoza, to go twirling my legs like a top. I am a practical man and a man of character, and I find no entertainment in idle diversions. But dancing is not what I am talking about. Forgive me, *maman,* but there's a great deal I can't make out in your conduct. For instance, apart from objects of household utility, you promised to give me two lottery tickets with your daughter. Where are they?

NASTASYA.   I've got a shocking headache. . . . It must be the weather. . . . There's going to be a thaw!

APLOMBOV.   Don't try to put me off. I found out to-day that your tickets are pawned. Excuse me, *maman,* no one but an exploiter would do a thing like that. I don't say this from egoisticism—I don't want your lottery tickets—but it's matter of principle, and I won't allow anyone to do me. I've made your daughter's happiness, and if you don't give me the tickets to-day, I'll make it hot for her! I am a man of honor!

NASTASYA [*looking round the table and counting the places laid*].   One, two, three, four, five . . .

A WAITER.   The cook told me to ask you how you will have the ices served: with rum, with Madeira, or with nothing.

APLOMBOV.   With rum. And tell the manager there is not enough wine. Tell him to send some Haut-Sauterne as well. [*To* NASTASYA TIMOFEYEVNA] You promised, too, and it was an agreed thing, that at supper to-night there should be a general. And where is he, I should like to know?

NASTASYA.   That's not my fault, my dear.

APLOMBOV.   Whose then?

NASTASYA.   Andrey Andreyevitch's. He was here yesterday and promised to bring a real general [*sighs*]. I suppose he could not find one anywhere, or he would have brought him. As though we were mean about it! There's nothing we'd grudge for our child's happiness. A general by all means, if you want one. . . .

APLOMBOV.   And another thing. . . . Everybody knows, and so do you, *maman,* that that telegraph clerk Yat was courting Dashenka before I made her an offer. Why have you invited him? Surely you must have known I should dislike it?

NASTASYA.   Oh, what's your name? Epaminond Maximitch, here you have not been married one day, and already you've worn me out, and Dashenka too, with your talk. And what will it be in a year? You are a trying man, you really are!

APLOMBOV.   You don't like to hear the truth? A-ha! So that's how it is. But you should behave honorably! All I want of you is to be honorable!

[*Couples dancing the* Grand-rond *come in at one door, cross the stage, and go out at another. The first couple are* DASHENKA *and the* BEST MAN, *the last* YAT *and* MADAME ZMEYUKIN. *The last couple drop behind and remain in the room.* ZHIGALOV *and* DYMBA *enter and go up to the table.*]

THE BEST MAN [*shouts*].   Promenade! Messieurs, promenade! [*Behind the scenes*] Promenade!

[*The couples dance out.*]

YAT [*to* MADAME ZMEYUKIN].   Have pity, have pity, enchanting Anna Martynovna!

MADAME ZMEYUKIN.   Oh, what a man! . . . I have told you already that I am not in voice to-day.

YAT.   I entreat you, do sing! If it's only one note! Have pity! If only one note!

MADAME ZMEYUKIN.   You worry me . . . [*sits down and waves her fan*].

YAT. Yes, you really are pitiless! To think of such a cruel creature, if I may use the expression, having such a lovely voice! With such a voice you oughtn't to be a midwife, if you'll allow me to say so, but to sing at public concerts! How divine is your rendering of this phrase, for instance . . . this one . . . [*hums*] . . . "I loved you, love that was in vain" . . . Exquisite!

MADAME ZMEYUKIN [*hums*]. "I loved you, and still it may be love" . . . Is that it?

YAT. Yes, that's it. Exquisite!

MADAME ZMEYUKIN. No, I am not in voice to-day. . . . There, fan me . . . it's hot! [*To* APLOMBOV] Epaminond Maximitch, why are you so melancholy? That's not the thing on your wedding day! You ought to be ashamed, you horrid man! Why, what are you thinking about?

APLOMBOV. Marriage is a serious step. It needs serious consideration from every point of view.

MADAME ZMEYUKIN. What hateful sceptics you all are! I cannot breathe in your society. . . . Give me atmosphere! Do you hear? Give me atmosphere! [*Hums*]

YAT. Exquisite! exquisite!

MADAME ZMEYUKIN. Fan me, fan me! I feel as though my heart were going to burst. . . . Tell me, please, why is it I feel suffocated?

YAT. It's because you are in a sweat. . . .

MADAME ZMEYUKIN. Ough, what vulgarity! Don't dare to use such expressions!

YAT. I beg your pardon! Of course you are used to aristocratic society, if you'll excuse the expression. . . .

MADAME ZMEYUKIN. Oh, let me alone! Give me poetry, raptures! Fan me, fan me! . . .

ZHIGALOV [*to* DYMBA]. Shall we repeat? [*Fills glasses.*] One can drink at any minute. The great thing is not to neglect one's business, Harlampy Spiridonitch. Drink, but keep your wits about you! . . . But as for drinking, why not drink? There's no harm in a drink. . . . To your good health! [*They drink.*] And are there tigers in Greece?

DYMBA. Dere are.

ZHIGALOV. And lions?

DYMBA. Yes, lions too. In Russia dere's noding, but in Greece dere's everyding. Dere I have fader, and uncle, and broders, and here I have noding.

ZHIGALOV. Hm. . . . And are there whales in Greece?

DYMBA. Dere's everyding.

NASTASYA [*to her husband*]. Why are you eating and drinking all anyhow? It's time for everyone to sit down. Don't stick your fork into the tinned lobster. . . . That's for the general. Perhaps he may come yet. . . .

ZHIGALOV. And are there lobsters in Greece, too?

DYMBA. Yes . . . dere's everyding dere.

ZHIGALOV. Hm. . . . And collegiate registry clerks too?

MADAME ZMEYUKIN. I can imagine what the atmosphere is in Greece!

ZHIGALOV. And I expect there's a lot of roguery. . . . Greeks are much the same as Armenians or gypsies. They sell you a sponge or a goldfish, and are all agog to fleece you over it. Shall we repeat?

NASTASYA. What's the good of repeating? It's time we were all sitting down. It's past eleven. . . .

ZHIGALOV. Well, let us sit down, then. Ladies and gentlemen, pray come to supper! [*Shouts*] Supper! Young people!

NASTASYA. Dear friends, please come! Sit down!

MADAME ZMEYUKIN [*sitting down at the table*]. Give me poetry! "His restless spirit seeks the storm as though in tempest there were peace!" Give me tempest!

YAT [*aside*]. A remarkable woman! I am in love! head over ears in love!

[*Enter* DASHENKA, MOZGOVOY, *the* BEST MAN, *gentlemen and ladies. They all sit down noisily; a moment's pause; the band plays a march.*]

MOZGOVOY [*getting up*]. Ladies and gentlemen, I have something to say. . . . We have a great many toasts to drink and speeches to make. Don't let us put them off, but begin at once. Ladies and gentlemen, I propose the toast of the bride and bridegroom!

[*The band plays a flourish. Shouts of "Hurrah!" and clinking of glasses.*]

MOZGOVOY. It needs sweetening!

ALL. It needs sweetening!

[APLOMBOV *and* DASHENKA *kiss*.]

YAT. Exquisite! exquisite! I must declare, ladies and gentlemen—and it's only paying credit where credit is due—that this room and the establishment generally is magnificent! Superb, enchanting! But, you know, there's one thing wanting to complete it: electric lighting, if you will excuse the expression! In all countries they have electric light now, and only Russia lags behind.

ZHIGALOV [*with an air of profundity*]. Electric light. . . . Hm. . . . But to my mind electric light is nothing but roguery. . . . They stick a bit of coal in, and think they will hoax you with that! No, my good man, if you are going to give us light, don't give us a little bit of coal, but give us something substantial, something solid that you can get hold of! Give us light—you understand—light that's natural and not intellectual!

YAT.   If you had seen an electric battery, and what it's made of, you'd think differently.

ZHIGALOV.   I don't want to see it. It's roguery. They take simple folks in. . . . Squeeze the last drop out of them. . . . We know all about them. . . . Instead of sticking up for roguery, young man, you had better have a drink and fill other people's glasses. Yes, indeed!

APLOMBOV.   I quite agree with you, Pa. What's the use of trotting out these learned subjects? I am quite ready to talk of all sorts of discoveries in the scientific sense, but there's a time for everything! [*To* DASHENKA] What do you think about it, *ma chère?*

DASHENKA.   He wants to show off his learning, and always talks of things no one can understand.

NASTASYA.   Thank God, we have lived all our lives without learning, and this is the third daughter we are marrying to a good husband. And if you think we are so uneducated, why do you come to see us? You should go to your learned friends!

YAT.   I've always had a respect for your family, Nastasya Timofeyevna, and if I did say a word about electric lighting, it doesn't mean I spoke out of conceit. I am ready enough to have a drink! I have always wished Darya Yevdokimovna a good husband with all the feelings of my heart. It's difficult to find a good husband nowadays, Nastasya Timofeyevna. Nowadays everybody is keen on marrying for money. . . .

APLOMBOV.   That's a hint at me!

YAT [*scared*].   Not the slightest hint intended. . . . I was not speaking of present company. . . . I meant it as a general remark. . . . Upon my word! Everyone knows you are marrying for love. . . . The dowry is not worth talking about!

NASTASYA.   Not worth talking about, isn't it? You mind what you are saying, sir. Besides a thousand rubles in cash, we are giving three pelisses, the bedding and all the furniture. You try and find a dowry to match that!

YAT.   I didn't mean anything. . . . The furniture is certainly nice . . . and . . . and the pelisses, of course; I only spoke in the sense that they're offended as though I'd dropped a hint.

NASTASYA.   Well, you shouldn't drop hints. It's out of regard for your parents we asked you to the wedding, and you keep saying all sorts of things. And if you knew that Epaminond Maximovitch was after her money, why didn't you speak before? [*Tearfully*] I have reared and nurtured her. . . . I've watched over her like a diamond or an emerald, my sweet child. . . .

APLOMBOV.   And you believe him? Much obliged, I am sure! Very much obliged. [*To* YAT] And as for you, Mr. Yat, though you are a friend, I won't allow you to behave so disgracefully in other people's houses! Kindly take yourself off!

YAT.   What do you mean?

APLOMBOV.   I could wish you were as much of a gentleman as I am! In fact, kindly take yourself off.

[*The band plays a flourish.*]

GENTLEMEN [*to* APLOMBOV].   Oh, stop it! Leave off! It doesn't matter! Sit down! Let him alone!

YAT.   I wasn't saying anything . . . why, I . . . In fact, I don't understand it. . . . Certainly, I'll go. . . . But first pay me the five rubles you borrowed from me a year ago to buy yourself a piqué waistcoat; excuse the expression. I'll have another drink and I'll . . . I'll go, only first pay me what you owe me.

GENTLEMEN.   Come, stop it, stop it! That's enough! Making such a fuss about nothing!

THE BEST MAN [*shouts*].   To the health of the bride's parents, Yevdokim Zaharitch and Nastasya Timofeyevna!

[*The band plays a flourish. Shouts of "*Hurrah!*"*]

ZHIGALOV [*touched, bows in all directions*].   Thank you, good friends! I am very grateful to you for not forgetting us and not being too proud to come! . . . Don't think that I am a knave or that it's roguery. I speak merely as I feel! In the simplicity of my heart! For my friends I grudge nothing! I thank you sincerely! [*Kisses those near him.*]

DASHENKA [*to her mother*].   Ma, why are you crying? I am so happy.

APLOMBOV.   Maman is upset at the approaching separation. But I would advise her to think over our conversation.

YAT.   Don't cry, Nastasya Timofeyevna! Think what human tears are! Neurotic weakness, that's all!

ZHIGALOV.   And are there mushrooms in Greece?

DYMBA.   Yes, dere is everyding dere.

ZHIGALOV.   But, I bet, there are no brown ones, like ours.

DYMBA.   Yes, dere are.

MOZGOVOY.   Harlampy Spiridonitch, it's your turn to make a speech! Ladies and gentlemen, let him make a speech!

ALL.   A speech! a speech! It's your turn.

DYMBA.   Why? What for? I not understand what it is. . . .

MADAME ZMEYUKIN.   No, no! Don't dare to refuse! It's your turn! Get up!

DYMBA [*stands up, in confusion*].   I can say dis. . . . Dere's Russia and dere's Greece. Dere's people in Russia and dere's people in Greece. . . . And *caravies* floating on de sea, dat is in Russia, ships, and on de earth de different railways. I know very well. . . . We Greeks, you Russians, and not want noding. I can tell you . . . dere's Russia and dere's Greece.

[*Enter* NYUNIN.]

NYUNIN.   Stay, ladies and gentlemen, don't eat yet! Wait a bit! Nastasya Timofeyevna, one minute; Come this way! [*Draws* NASTASYA TIMOFEYEVNA *aside, breathlessly.*] I say, the general is just coming. . . . At last I've got hold of him. . . . I am simply worn out. . . . A real general, so dignified, elderly, eighty I should think, or perhaps ninety. . . .

NASTASYA.   When is he coming?

NYUNIN.   This minute! You will be grateful to me to the end of your days. Not a general but a peach, a Boulanger! Not a common general, not an infantry man, but a naval one! In grade he is a captain of the second rank, but in their reckoning, in the fleet, it's equal to a major-general, or, in the civil service, to an actual civil councillor. It's exactly the same; higher, in fact.

NASTASYA.   You are not deceiving me, Andryushenka?

NYUNIN.   What next! Am I a swindler? Set your mind at rest.

NASTASYA [*with a sigh*].   I don't want to spend my money for nothing, Andryushenka. . . .

NYUNIN.   Set your mind at rest! He is a perfect picture of a general! [*Raising his voice*] I said to him: "You have quite forgotten us, your Excellency! It's too bad, your Excellency, to forget your old friends! Nastasya Timofeyevna," I said, "is quite huffy!" [*Goes to the table and sits down.*] And he said to me: "Upon my soul, my boy, how can I go when I don't know the bridegroom?" "What next, your Excellency! why stand on ceremony? The bridegroom is a splendid fellow, an open-hearted chap. He is a valuer in a pawnbroker's shop," I told him, "but don't imagine, your Excellency, that he is a paltry beggar or a cad. Even well-born ladies serve in pawnshops nowadays." He slapped me on the shoulder, we each had a Havana cigar, and here he is coming now. . . . Wait a minute, ladies and gentlemen, don't eat. . . .

APLOMBOV.   And when will he be here?

NYUNIN.   This minute. He was putting on his goloshes when I came away.

APLOMBOV. Then we must tell them to play a march.

NYUNIN [*shouts*]. Hey, bandmaster! A march! [*The band plays a march for a minute.*]

A WAITER [*announces*]. Mr. Revunov-Karaulov!

[ZHIGALOV, NASTASYA TIMOFEYEVNA, *and* NYUNIN *hasten to meet him. Enter* REVUNOV-KARAULOV.]

NASTASYA [*bowing*]. You are very welcome, your Excellency! Delighted to see you!

REVUNOV. Delighted!

ZHIGALOV. We are not distinguished or wealthy people, your Excellency, we are plain folks; but don't think there's any roguery on our part. We grudge nothing for nice people, nothing is too good for them. You are very welcome!

REVUNOV. Delighted!

NYUNIN. Allow me to introduce, your Excellency! The bridegroom Epaminond Maximitch Aplombov, with his newborn. . . . I mean newly married bride! Ivan Mihailitch Yat, of the telegraph department. Harlampy Spiridonitch Dymba, a foreigner of Greek extraction, in the confectionery line! Osip Lukitch Babelmandebsky! and so on . . . and so on. . . . The rest are not much account. Sit down, your Excellency.

REVUNOV. Delighted! Excuse me, ladies and gentlemen, I want to say a couple of words to Andryusha [*leads* NYUNIN *aside*]. I feel rather awkward, my boy. . . . Why do you call me "your Excellency"? Why, I am not a general! A captain of the second rank; it isn't even as good as a colonel.

NYUNIN [*speaks into his ear as to a deaf man*]. I know, but, Fyodor Yakovlevitch, be so good as to let us say "your Excellency"! They are a patriarchal family here, you know; they honor their betters, and like to show respect where respect is due. . . .

REVUNOV. Well, if that's how it is, of course . . . [*going to the table*]. Delighted!

NASTASYA. Sit down, your Excellency! Do us the honor! What will you take, your Excellency? Only you must excuse us, you are accustomed to dainty fare at home, while we are plain people!

REVUNOV [*not hearing*]. What? Hm. . . . Yes. . . . [*Pause*] Yes. . . . In old days people all lived plainly and were satisfied. I am a man of rank in the service, but I live plainly. . . . Andryusha came to me to-day and invited me here to the wedding. "How can I go," said I, "when I don't know them? That would be awkward!" But, he said, "They are plain people, a patriarchal family, always glad to see a visitor." "Oh well, of course if that is how it is . . . Why not? I am delighted. It's dull for me at home all alone, and if my being at the wedding can give pleasure to anyone, well, by all means," I said.

ZHIGALOV.   So it was in the kindness of your heart, your Excellency? I honor you! I am a plain man, with no sort of roguery about me, and I respect those that are the same. Pray take something, your Excellency.

APLOMBOV.   Have you long left the service, your Excellency?

REVUNOV.   Eh? Yes, yes . . . to be sure. That's true. Yes. . . . But how is this? The herring is bitter and the bread is bitter, I can't eat it.

ALL.   It needs sweetening!

[APLOMBOV *and* DASHENKA *kiss*.]

REVUNOV.   He-he-he! . . . Your health! [*Pause*] Yes. . . . In old days everything was plain, and everyone was satisfied. . . . I like plain ways. . . . I am an old man. Of course, I retired from the service in 1865. I am seventy-two . . . Yes. In old days to be sure, they liked, too, on occasion to make a show, but . . . [*seeing* MOZGOVOY]. You . . . er . . . are a sailor, aren't you?

MOZGOVOY.   Yes, sir.

REVUNOV.   Aha! . . . To be sure. . . . Yes. . . . The naval service was always a hard one. You've something to think about and rack your brains over. Every trivial word has, so to say, a special meaning. For instance: Mast-hands, to the top-sail lifts and the mainsail braces! What does that mean? A sailor understands, no fear about that! Ha-ha! It's as hard as any mathematics.

NYUNIN.   To the health of his Excellency, Fyodor Yakovlevitch Revunov-Karaulov!

[*Band plays a flourish*.]

ALL.   Hurrah!

YAT.   Well, your Excellency, you've just been pleased to tell us something about the difficulties of the naval service. But is the telegraph service any easier? Nowadays, your Excellency, no one can go in for the telegraph service unless he can read and write French and German. But the hardest job for us is transmitting the telegrams! It's awfully difficult! Just listen [*taps with his fork on the table, imitating the telegraph code*].

REVUNOV.   And what does that mean?

YAT.   That means: I respect you, your Excellency, for your noble qualities. Do you suppose that's easy? And now listen [*taps*].

REVUNOV.   A little louder. . . . I don't hear.

YAT. That means: Madam, how happy I am to hold you in my arms.

REVUNOV. What madam are you talking about? Yes . . . [*to* MOZGOVOY]. And now if you are sailing with a strong wind and want to hoist the top-gallant sail and the royal, then you must shout: Sail hands, on the cross-trees to the top-gallant sail and the royal sail! . . . and while they pay out the sails on the yards below, they are at the top-gallant and royal halyards, stays and braces. . . .

THE BEST MAN [*getting up*]. Ladies and gentle . . .

REVUNOV [*interrupting*]. Yes . . . there are all sorts of orders to be given. . . . Yes. . . . Top-gallant sheets and royal sheets taut, let go the lifts! Sounds fine, doesn't it? But what does it mean? Oh, it's very simple. They pull the top-gallant and royal sheets and raise the lifts. . . . All at once! And at the same time as they raise them, level the royal sheets and the royal lifts, and, where necessary, slacken the braces of those sails, and when the sheets are taut and all the lifts have been raised to their places, the top-gallant braces and the royal braces are taut and the yards are turned the way of the wind. . . .

NYUNIN [*to* REVUNOV]. Fyodor Yakovlevitch! our hostess begs you to talk of something else. Our guests can't understand this, they are bored. . . .

REVUNOV. What? Who is bored? [*To* MOZGOVOY] Young man! Now, if the ship is lying with the wind on the starboard tack, under full sail, and you want to bring her round before the wind, what order must you give? Why, pipe all hands on deck, bring her round before the wind.

NYUNIN. Fyodor Yakovlevitch, that's enough, eat your supper!

REVUNOV. As soon as they have all run up, you give the command at once: Stand to your places, bring her round before the wind! Ah, what a life! You give the command and see the sailors run like lightning to their places and pull the stays and the braces, then you can't help shouting, Bravo, lads! [*Chokes and coughs.*]

THE BEST MAN [*hastening to take advantage of the ensuing pause*]. On this, so to speak, festive occasion, on which we, all gathered together here, to do honor to our beloved . . .

REVUNOV [*interrupting*]. Yes! And you have to remember all that! For instance: let out the fore-top-sail-sheet, top-gallant-sail sheet! . . .

THE BEST MAN [*offended*]. Why does he interrupt? At this rate we shan't get through a single speech!

NASTASYA. We are ignorant people, your Excellency, we don't understand a word of all this. If you would tell us something that would amuse . . .

REVUNOV [*not hearing*].   Thank you, I have had some. Did you say goose? Thank you. . . . Yes. I was recalling old days. It's a jolly life, young man! You float over the sea without a care in your heart and . . . [*In a shaking voice*] Do you remember the excitement of tacking? What sailor isn't fired by the thought of that manœuvre! Why, as soon as the command is given: Pipe all hands on deck, it's like an electric shock running through them all. From the commanding officer to the lowest sailor they are all in a flutter. . . .

MADAME ZMEYUKIN.   I am bored, I am bored! [*A general murmur*].

REVUNOV [*not hearing*].   Thank you, I have had some. [*With enthusiasm*] Everyone is ready and all eyes are fixed on the senior officer. . . . "Fore-topsail and mainsail braces to starboard, mizzen-braces to larboard, counter-braces to port," shouts the senior officer. Every order is carried out instantly. "Slacken fore-sheet and jib-stay . . . right to starboard!" [*Gets up.*] Then the ship rolls to the wind and the sails begin to flap. The senior officer shouts "To the braces! to the braces! look alive!" While he fixes his eyes on the topsail and when at last it begins to flap, that is, when the ship begins to turn, a terrific yell is heard: "Loose the mainsail-stays, let go the braces!" Then everything is flying and creaking—a regular tower of Babel! it's all done without a break. The ship is turned!

NASTASYA [*flaring up*].   For all you are a general, you've no manners! You should be ashamed at your age!

REVUNOV.   Greengage? No, I have not had any. . . . Thank you.

NASTASYA [*aloud*].   I say, you ought to be ashamed at your age! You are a general, but you have no manners!

NYUNIN [*in confusion*].   Come, friends! . . . why make a fuss? . . . really.

REVUNOV.   To begin with, I am not a general, but a captain of the second rank, which corresponds to a lieutenant-colonel of military rank.

NASTASYA.   If you are not a general, what did you take the money for? We did not pay you money to be rude to us!

REVUNOV [*in perplexity*].   What money?

NASTASYA.   You know very well what money. You got the twenty-five rubles from Andrey Andreyevitch right enough . . . [*to* NYUNIN]. It's too bad of you, Andryusha! I didn't ask you to engage a fellow like this.

NYUNIN.   Oh, come. . . . Drop it! Why make a fuss?

REVUNOV.   Engaged . . . Paid . . . What does it mean?

APLOMBOV.   Allow me. . . . You've received twenty-five rubles from Andrey Andreyevitch, haven't you?

REVUNOV.   Twenty-five rubles? [*Grasping the situation*] So that's how it is! Now I understand it! What a dirty trick! What a dirty trick!

APLOMBOV.   Well, you had the money, hadn't you?

REVUNOV.   I've had no money! Get away with you! [*Gets up from the table.*] What a dirty trick! What a mean trick! To insult an old man like this—a sailor—an officer who has seen honorable service! . . . If these were decent people I might challenge someone to a duel, but as it is, what can I do? [*Distractedly*] Where is the door? Which way do I go? Waiter! show me out! Waiter! [*Going*] What a mean trick! What a dirty trick! [*Goes out.*]

NASTASYA.   Andryusha, where is that twenty-five rubles, then?

NYUNIN.   Oh, don't make a fuss about such a trifle! As though it matters! Here everyone is rejoicing, while you keep on about this silly business. [*Shouts*] To the health of the happy pair! Band, a march! [*The band plays a march.*] To the health of the happy pair!

MADAME ZMEYUKIN.   I am stifling! Give me atmosphere! At your side I am suffocated!

YAT [*delighted*].   Exquisite creature!

[*Hubbub.*]

THE BEST MAN [*trying to shout above the rest*].   Ladies and gentlemen! On this, so to say, festive occasion . . .

CURTAIN.

THE ANNIVERSARY

Characters

ANDREY ANDREYEVITCH SHIPUTCHIN, *Chairman of the Board of Management of the N— Mutual Credit Bank, a youngish man with an eyeglass*

TATYANA ALEXEYEVNA, *his wife, age 25*

KUZMA NIKOLAYEVITCH HIRIN, *the Bank Cashier, an old man*

NASTASYA FYODOROVNA MERTCHUTKIN, *an old woman in a pelisse*

Members of the Board of Management

Bank Clerks

The action takes place in the N— Mutual Credit Bank.

The chairman's office. On the left a door leading to the counting-house. Two writing-tables. The office is furnished with pretensions to refined taste: velvet upholstery, flowers, statues, rugs. Telephone. Midday.
HIRIN *alone; he is wearing felt overboots.*

HIRIN [*shouts at the door*]. Send someone to the chemist's for three pennyworth of valerian drops and tell them to bring some clean water to the chairman's office! Am I to tell you a hundred times? [*Goes to the table.*] I am utterly worn out. I have been writing for the last three days and nights without closing my eyes; from morning till night I am at work here, and from night till morning at home [*coughs*]. And I feel ill all over! Shivering, feverish, coughing, my legs ache and there are all sorts of . . . stops and dashes before my eyes [*sits down*]. That affected ass, our scamp of a chairman, will read a report to-day at the general meeting: "Our bank at present and in the future." A regular Gambetta . . . [*writes*]. Two . . . one . . . one . . . six . . . nought . . . six. . . . He wants to cut a dash and so I have to sit here and work for him like a galley-slave! . . . He has put in nothing but the lyrical touches in the report and has left me to work for days together adding up figures, the devil flay his soul . . . [*counts on reckoning frame*]. I can't endure the man [*writes*]. One . . . three . . . seven . . . two . . . one . . . nought. . . . He promised to reward me for my work. If every thing goes off well to-day and he succeeds in hoodwinking the public, he promised me a gold medal and a bonus of three hundred. . . . We shall see [*writes*]. But if I get nothing for my trouble you must look out for yourself. . . . I am a hasty man. . . . I may do anything if I am worked up. . . . Yes!

[*Behind the scenes there is a noise of applause. Voice of* SHIPUTCHIN: "Thank you, thank you! I am touched!" *Enter* SHIPUTCHIN. *He is wearing a dress-coat and white tie; in his hands an album which has just been presented to him.*]

SHIPUTCHIN [*standing in the doorway and looking towards the counting-house*]. I shall keep this present of yours, dear colleagues, to the day

111

of my death in memory of the happiest days of my life! Yes, gentlemen! I thank you once more [*waves a kiss and walks up to* HIRIN]. My dear, good Kuzma Nikolayevitch!

[*While he is on the stage* Clerks *come in occasionally with papers for him to sign, and go out again.*]

HIRIN [*getting up*].   I have the honor to congratulate you, Andrey Andreyevitch, on the fifteenth anniversary of our bank, and hope that . . .

SHIPUTCHIN [*presses his hand warmly*].   Thank you, dear old man, thank you! In honor of this glorious occasion, in honor of the anniversary, I think we might even kiss each other. [*They kiss.*] I am very glad, very. Thanks for your good work, for everything! If I've done anything useful during my period of office as chairman of the Board of Management, I am indebted for it above all to my colleagues [*sighs*]. Yes, old man, fifteen years, fifteen years as sure as my name's Shiputchin! [*Eagerly*] Well, what about my report? Is it getting on?

HIRIN.   Yes. There are only five pages left.

SHIPUTCHIN.   Good. Then by three o'clock it will be ready?

HIRIN.   If nobody hinders me, I shall get it done. There's very little left to do.

SHIPUTCHIN.   Splendid. Splendid, as sure as my name's Shiputchin! The general meeting will be at four o'clock. I say, my dear fellow, let me have the first half, I'll go over it. . . . Make haste, give it me [*takes the report*]. . . . I expect great things from this report. . . . It's my *profession de foi,* or rather my fireworks . . . fireworks, as sure as my name's Shiputchin! [*sits down and reads the report*]. I am devilish tired, though. . . . I had an attack of gout in the night, I spent all the morning racing about doing things, and then this excitement, this ovation . . . so upsetting! I am tired!

HIRIN [*writes*].   Two . . . nought . . . nought . . . three . . . nine . . . two . . . nought. . . . The figures make my eyes dizzy. . . . Three . . . one . . . six . . . four . . . one . . . five . . . [*rattles the reckoning beads*].

SHIPUTCHIN.   Another unpleasantness. . . . Your wife came to me this morning and complained of you again. She said that you ran after her and your sister-in-law with a knife yesterday. Kuzma Nikolayevitch, what next! Aie, aie!

HIRIN [*sourly*].   I will venture, Andrey Andreyevitch, in honor of the anniversary, to ask a favor of you, and beg you, if only out of consideration for my working like a slave, not to meddle in my family affairs! I beg you!

SHIPUTCHIN [*sighs*].   You have an impossible temper, Kuzma Nikolayevitch! You are an excellent, estimable person, but with women you behave like some Jack the Ripper! You really do. I can't understand why you hate them so.

HIRIN.   And I can't understand why you like them so! [*Pause*]

SHIPUTCHIN.   The clerks have just presented me with an album and the members of the Board, so I hear, are going to present me with an address and a silver tankard . . . [*playing with his eyeglass*]. It's fine, as sure as my name's Shiputchin! . . . It's all to the good. . . . We must have a bit of splash for the sake of the bank, deuce take it! You are one of ourselves, you know all about it, of course. . . . I composed the address myself, I bought the silver tankard myself too. . . . And there, the binding of the address cost 45 rubles. But we have to have that. They would never have thought of it themselves [*looks round him*]. Just look at the get-up of the place! Isn't it fine? Here they tell me that it is petty of me to want the locks on the doors to be polished and the clerks to wear fashionable ties, and to have a stout porter at the entrance. Not a bit of it, my good sir! The locks on the doors and the stout porter are not a petty matter. At home I may be a vulgarian, I may eat and sleep like a pig and drink till I am crazy. . . .

HIRIN.   No insinuations, please!

SHIPUTCHIN.   Nobody is making insinuations! What an impossible temper you have. . . . Well, as I was saying, at home I may be a vulgarian, a parvenu, and give way to my habits, but here everything must be *en grand*. This is the bank! Here every detail must be impressive, so to speak, and have an imposing air! [*Picks up a scrap of paper from the floor and throws it into the fire.*] What I do take credit for is having raised the reputation of the bank. . . . Tone is a great thing! It's a great thing as sure as my name's Shiputchin. [*Scrutinizing* HIRIN] My dear fellow, the deputation from the shareholders may be here any minute and you are in your felt overboots and that scarf . . . and a reefer jacket of some nondescript color. . . . You might have put on a dress-coat or a black frock-coat, anyway. . . .

HIRIN.   My health is more precious to me than your shareholders. I am suffering from inflammation all over.

SHIPUTCHIN [*growing excited*].   But you must own it's unsuitable? You spoil the *ensemble!*

HIRIN.   If the deputation comes in I can keep out of sight. It's no great matter . . . [*writes*]. Seven . . . one . . . seven . . . two . . . one . . . five . . . nought. I don't like anything unsuitable myself. Seven . . . two . . . nine . . . [*rattles the reckoning beads*]. I can't stand anything unsuitable. For instance, you would have done better not to have invited ladies to the anniversary dinner to-day!

SHIPUTCHIN.   What nonsense!

HIRIN.   I know you will let in a whole drawing-room full of them to make a fine show, only mind they'll spoil it all for you. They are the source of every trouble and mischief.

SHIPUTCHIN.   Quite the opposite. Feminine society has an elevating influence!

HIRIN.   Yes. . . . Your wife is highly cultured, I believe, but last Monday she said something so appalling that I couldn't get over it for two days after. All of a sudden, before outsiders, she blurted out: "Is it true that my husband has bought the Dryazhko-Pryazhky shares which have fallen on the exchange? Oh, my husband is so worried about them!" To say that before outsiders! And what you want to be so open with them for, I can't understand! Do you want them to get you into trouble?

SHIPUTCHIN.   Come, that's enough, that's enough! This is all too gloomy for an anniversary. By the way, you remind me [*looks at his watch*]. My better-half ought to be here directly. By rights I ought to have gone to the station to meet her, poor thing, but I haven't time and I'm . . . tired. To tell the truth I am not glad she is coming. That is, I am glad, but it would have been pleasanter for me if she had stayed another two days at her mother's. She will expect me to spend the whole evening with her, and meanwhile we have planned a little excursion when the dinner is over . . . [*shivers*]. There, I am in a nervous shiver already. My nerves are so over-strained that I could burst into tears at the slightest provocation! No, I must be firm, as sure as my name's Shiputchin!

[*Enter* TATYANA ALEXEYEVNA *wearing a waterproof and with a travelling satchel slung across one shoulder.*]

SHIPUTCHIN.   Bah! Talk about angels!

TATYANA ALEXEYEVNA.   Darling! [*Runs to her husband; prolonged kiss.*]

SHIPUTCHIN.   And we were just talking about you!

TATYANA ALEXEYEVNA [*breathlessly*].   Have you missed me? Are you quite well? I haven't been home yet, I've come straight here from the station. I've got ever so much to tell you, ever so much. I can't wait . . . I won't take off my things, I've only looked in for a minute. [*To* HIRIN] How are you, Kuzma Nikolayevitch? [*To her husband*] Is everything all right at home?

SHIPUTCHIN.   Quite. Why, you've grown plumper and prettier in the week. Well, what sort of journey did you have?

TATYANA ALEXEYEVNA.   Splendid! Mamma and Katya send you their love. Vassily Andreyevitch asked me to give you a kiss from him [*kisses him*]. Aunt sends you a jar of jam and they are all angry with you for not writing. Zina told me to give you a kiss from her [*kisses him*]. Ah, if only you knew what happened! What happened! I am positively afraid to tell you! Oh, such a dreadful thing happened! But I see from your face you're not glad to see me.

SHIPUTCHIN.   Quite the contrary . . . darling . . . [*kisses her*].

[HIRIN *coughs angrily*.]

TATYANA ALEXEYEVNA [*sighs*].   Ah, poor Katya, poor Katya! I am so sorry for her, so frightfully sorry!

SHIPUTCHIN.   It's our anniversary to-day, darling. The deputation from the shareholders may turn up here any minute and you are not dressed.

TATYANA ALEXEYEVNA.   Really? The anniversary? I congratulate you, gentlemen. . . . I wish you . . . So there will be a party here to-day, a dinner? I like that. . . . And do you remember that splendid address you were so long making up for the shareholders? Will they read it to you to-day?

[HIRIN *coughs angrily*.]

SHIPUTCHIN [*in confusion*].   We don't talk about that, darling. . . . Really, you had better go home.

TATYANA ALEXEYEVNA.   In a minute, in a minute . . . I'll tell you all about it in one instant and then go. I'll tell you all about it from the very beginning. Well . . . when you saw me off I sat down, do you remember, beside that stout lady and began reading? I don't like talking in the train. I went on reading for three stations and did not say a word to anyone. . . . Well, evening came on and I began to have such depressing thoughts, you know! There was a young man sitting opposite who was quite all right, not bad-looking, rather dark. . . . Well, we got into conversation. . . . A naval officer came up, then a student . . . [*laughs*]. I told them I wasn't married. . . . How they flirted with me! We talked till midnight. The dark young man told some awfully funny stories and the naval officer kept singing. . . . My chest simply ached with laughing. And when the officer—ah, those naval men!—when the officer found out accidentally that my name was Tatyana, do you know what he sang? [*Sings in a bass voice*] "Onyegin, I will not disguise it, I love Tatyana madly!" . . . [*laughs*].

[HIRIN *coughs angrily*.]

SHIPUTCHIN.   But, Tanyusha, we are hindering Kuzma Nikolayevitch. Go home, darling. Tell me later. . . .

TATYANA ALEXEYEVNA.   Never mind, never mind, let him listen, it's interesting. I shall have finished directly. Seryozha came to the station to fetch me. A young man turned up too, a tax inspector I believe he

was . . . quite all right, very nice, particularly his eyes. . . . Seryozha in-
troduced him and he drove back with us. It was glorious weather. . . .

[*Voices behind the scenes:* "You can't, you can't! What do you
want?" *Enter* MADAME MERTCHUTKIN.]

MADAME MERTCHUTKIN [*in the doorway, waving the clerks off*]. What
are you holding me for? What next! I want to see the manager! . . .
[*Comes in to* SHIPUTCHIN] . . . I have the honor, your Excellency . . .
my name is Nastasya Fyodorovna Mertchutkin, wife of a provincial
secretary.

SHIPUTCHIN.   What can I do for you?

MADAME MERTCHUTKIN.   You see, your Excellency, my husband, the provincial secretary Mertchutkin, has been ill for five
months, and while he was laid up at home in the doctor's hands he
was discharged from the service for no sort of reason, your Excellency.
And when I went for his salary, they deducted, if you please, your
Excellency, 24 rubles 36 kopecks from it. "What's that for?" I asked.
"Well," they told me, "he borrowed that from the Mutual Benefit
club and the other clerks stood security for him." How is that? How
could he borrow it without my consent? That's not the way to do
things, your Excellency! I am a poor woman, I earn my bread by
taking in lodgers. . . . I am a weak, defenseless woman. . . . I have to
put up with ill-usage from everyone and never hear a kind word.

SHIPUTCHIN.   Excuse me [*takes her petition from her and reads it
standing*].

TATYANA ALEXEYEVNA [*to* HIRIN].   But I must tell you from the
beginning. . . . Last week I suddenly got a letter from mamma. She
wrote to me that a certain Mr. Grendilevsky had made my sister
Katya an offer. An excellent, modest young man, but with no means
and no definite position. And unluckily, only fancy, Katya was very
much taken with him. What was to be done? Mamma wrote that I
was to come at once and use my influence with Katya.

HIRIN [*surlily*].   Excuse me, you put me out! You go on about
mamma and Katya and I've lost count and don't know what I am doing.

TATYANA ALEXEYEVNA.   As though that mattered! You ought to
listen when a lady talks to you! Why are you so cross to-day? Are you
in love? [*laughs.*]

SHIPUTCHIN [*to* MADAME MERTCHUTKIN].   Excuse me, what's
this? I can make nothing of it.

TATYANA ALEXEYEVNA.   You're in love! A-ha! he is blushing!

SHIPUTCHIN [*to his wife*].   Tanyusha, go into the counting-house
for a minute, darling. I shan't be long.

TATYANA ALEXEYEVNA.   Very well [*goes out*].

SHIPUTCHIN. I can make nothing of it. Evidently you have come to the wrong place, madam. Your petition has nothing to do with us at all. You will have to apply to the department in which your husband was employed.

MADAME MERTCHUTKIN. Why, my dear sir, I have been to five places already and they would not even take the petition anywhere. I'd quite lost my head, but my son-in-law, Boris Matveyitch—God bless him for it—advised me to come to you. "You go to Mr. Shiputchin, mamma," he said, "he is an influential man, he can do anything for you." . . . Help me, your Excellency!

SHIPUTCHIN. We can do nothing for you, Madame Mertchutkin. You must understand: your husband, so far as I can see, served in the Army Medical Department, and our establishment is a purely private commercial undertaking, a bank. Surely you must understand that!

MADAME MERTCHUTKIN. Your Excellency, I have the doctor's certificate that my husband was ill! Here it is, if you will kindly look at it!

SHIPUTCHIN [irritably]. Very good, I believe you, but I repeat it has nothing to do with us.

[Behind the scenes TATYANA ALEXFYEVNA's laugh; then a masculine laugh.]

SHIPUTCHIN [glancing towards the door]. She is hindering the clerks there. [To MADAME MERTCHUTKIN] It's queer and absurd, indeed. Surely your husband must know where you ought to apply.

MADAME MERTCHUTKIN. He knows nothing, your Excellency. He keeps on "It's not your business, go away"—that's all I can get out of him.

SHIPUTCHIN. I repeat, madam: your husband was in the Army Medical Department, and this is a bank, a purely private commercial undertaking.

MADAME MERTCHUTKIN. Yes, yes, yes. . . . I understand, sir. In that case, your Excellency, tell them to pay me fifteen rubles at least! I agree to take part on account.

SHIPUTCHIN [sighs]. Ough!

HIRIN. Andrey Andreyitch, at this rate I shall never have the report done!

SHIPUTCHIN. One minute. [To MADAME MERTCHUTKIN] There's no making you see reason. Do understand that to apply to us with such a petition is as strange as to send a petition for divorce to a chemist's, for instance, or to the Assaying Board.

[A knock at the door, TATYANA ALEXEYEVNA's voice: "Andrey, may I come in?"]

SHIPUTCHIN [*shouts*]. Wait a little, darling; in a minute! [*To* MADAME MERTCHUTKIN] You have not been paid your due, but what have we to do with it? Besides, madam, it's our anniversary today; we are busy . . . and someone may come in here at any minute. . . . Excuse me.

MADAME MERTCHUTKIN. Your Excellency, have pity on a lone lorn woman! I am a weak, defenseless woman. . . . I am worried to death. . . . I have a lawsuit with my lodgers, and I have to see to my husband's affairs and fly round looking after the house, and my son-in-law is out of a job.

SHIPUTCHIN. Madame Mertchutkin, I . . . No, excuse me, I cannot talk to you! My head is going round. . . . You are hindering us and wasting time . . . [*sighs, aside*]. She's an idiot, as sure as my name is Shiputchin! [*To* HIRIN] Kuzma Nikolayevitch, please will you explain to Madame Mertchutkin . . . [*with a wave of his hand goes out of the office*].

HIRIN [*going up to* MADAME MERTCHUTKIN, *surlily*]. What can I do for you?

MADAME MERTCHUTKIN. I am a weak, defenseless woman. . . . I look strong perhaps, but if you were to overhaul me there isn't one healthy fiber in me! I can scarcely keep on my feet, and my appetite is gone. I drank my cup of coffee this morning without the slightest relish.

HIRIN. I am asking you what I can do for you.

MADAME MERTCHUTKIN. Bid them pay me fifteen rubles, sir, and I'll take the rest in a month's time.

HIRIN. But you've been told already in plain words: this is a bank.

MADAME MERTCHUTKIN. Yes, yes. . . . And if necessary I can produce a medical certificate.

HIRIN. Have you got a head on your shoulders, or what?

MADAME MERTCHUTKIN. My dear man, I am asking for what is my due. I don't want other people's money.

HIRIN. I ask you, madam, have you got a head on your shoulders, or what? I'll be damned if I waste my time talking to you. I am busy. [*Points to the door*] Kindly walk out!

MADAME MERTCHUTKIN [*surprised*]. And what about the money?

HIRIN. The fact is, what you've got on your shoulders is not a head, but this . . . [*taps with his finger on the table and then on his own forehead*].

MADAME MERTCHUTKIN [*offended*]. What? Come, come! . . . Talk to your own wife like that. . . . My husband is a provincial secretary! You'd better look out!

HIRIN [*firing up, in a low voice*].   Clear out!

MADAME MERTCHUTKIN.   Come, come, come! . . . Look out!

HIRIN [*in a low voice*].   If you don't leave the room this very minute, I'll send for the porter. Clear out! [*Stamps.*]

MADAME MERTCHUTKIN.   Not a bit of it! I am not afraid of you. I've seen the likes of you . . . You screw!

HIRIN.   I don't believe I've ever in my life seen a nastier woman. . . . Ough! It makes me feel dizzy . . . [*breathing hard*]. I tell you once more . . . do you hear? If you don't leave the room, you old scarecrow! I'll pound you to a jelly. I've such a temper, I might cripple you for life! I might commit a crime!

MADAME MERTCHUTKIN.   More bark than bite. I'm not afraid of you. I've seen the likes of you.

HIRIN [*in despair*].   I can't bear the sight of her! I feel ill! I can't stand it [*goes to the table and sits down*]. They let loose a swarm of women on the bank: I can't write the report! I can't do it!

MADAME MERTCHUTKIN.   I am not asking for other people's money: I am asking for my own—for what is my lawful due. Ah, the shameless fellow! He is sitting in a public office with his overboots on. . . . The lout!

[*Enter* SHIPUTCHIN *and* TATYANA ALEXEYEVNA.]

TATYANA ALEXEYEVNA [*following her husband in*].   We went to an evening party at the Berezhnitskys'. Katya was wearing a pale blue foulard with light lace and a low neck. . . . It does suit her doing her hair up high, and I did it for her myself. . . . When she was dressed and had her hair done she looked simply fascinating!

SHIPUTCHIN [*by now suffering from migraine*].   Yes, yes . . . fascinating! . . . They may come in here in a minute.

MADAME MERTCHUTKIN.   Your Excellency!

SHIPUTCHIN [*despondently*].   What now? What can I do for you?

MADAME MERTCHUTKIN.   Your Excellency! [*Pointing to* HIRIN] Here, this man . . . he here, this man, tapped himself on the forehead and then tapped the table. . . . You told him to go into my case, and he is jeering at me and saying all sorts of things. I am a weak, defenseless woman.

SHIPUTCHIN.   Very well, madam; I will go into it. . . . I will take steps. . . . Go away! Later. [*Aside*] My gout is coming on!

HIRIN [*goes quietly up to* SHIPUTCHIN].   Andrey Andreyitch, send for the porter; let him kick her out! It's too much of a good thing!

SHIPUTCHIN [*in alarm*].   No, no! She'll set up a squeal, and there are lots of flats in the building.

MADAME MERTCHUTKIN.   Your Excellency!

HIRIN [*in a tearful voice*]. But I've got to finish the report! I shan't finish it in time! . . . [*goes back to the table*]. I can't do it!

MADAME MERTCHUTKIN. Your Excellency, when shall I receive the money? I need it to-day.

SHIPUTCHIN [*aside, with indignation*]. A re—mar—kab—ly nasty woman. [*To her, softly*] Madam, I have told you already, this is a bank—a private commercial establishment.

MADAME MERTCHUTKIN. Do me a kindness, your Excellency! Be a father to me! . . . If the medical certificate is not enough, I can produce an affidavit from the police. Tell them to give me the money!

SHIPUTCHIN [*sighs heavily*]. Ough!

TATYANA ALEXEYEVNA [*to* MADAME MERTCHUTKIN]. Granny, you've been told that you are hindering them. It's too bad of you, really.

MADAME MERTCHUTKIN. My pretty lady, I've no one to take my part. I might just as well not eat or drink. I drank my cup of coffee this morning without the slightest relish.

SHIPUTCHIN [*exhausted, to* MADAME MERTCHUTKIN]. How much do you want?

MADAME MERTCHUTKIN. Twenty-four rubles thirty-six ko-pecks.

SHIPUTCHIN. Very good [*takes a twenty-five ruble note out of his pocket-book and gives it to her*]. Here is twenty-five rubles. Take it . . . and go!

[HIRIN *coughs angrily.*]

MADAME MERTCHUTKIN. Thank you kindly, your Excellency [*puts the money away*].

TATYANA ALEXEYEVNA [*sitting down by her husband*]. It's time for me to go home [*looking at her watch*]. . . . But I haven't finished my story. It won't take me a minute to tell you the rest, and then I am going. . . . Something so dreadful happened! And so we went to an evening party at the Berezhnitskys'. . . . It was all right—very jolly—but nothing special. . . . Of course, Katya's admirer Grendilevsky was there too. . . . Well, I had talked to Katya, I had cried; I'd used my influence; she had it out with Grendilevsky on that very evening and refused him. Well, I thought, everything is settled for the best: I had set mamma's mind at rest, I had saved Katya, and now I could be comfortable myself. . . . And what do you think? Just before supper Katya and I were walking along an avenue in the garden. . . . All of a sudden . . . [*excited*] all of a sudden we hear a shot. . . . No, I can't talk of it! [*Fans herself with her handkerchief.*] No, I can't!

SHIPUTCHIN [*sighs*]. Ough!

TATYANA ALEXEYEVNA [*weeping*]. We ran into the arbor, and there . . . there lay poor Grendilevsky . . . with a pistol in his hand. . . .

SHIPUTCHIN. No, I can't stand it! I can't stand it! [*To* MADAME MERTCHUTKIN] What more do you want?

MADAME MERTCHUTKIN. Your Excellency, couldn't you find another job for my husband?

TATYANA ALEXEYEVNA [*weeping*]. He had aimed straight at his head . . . here. . . . Katya fell down fainting, poor darling! . . . And he lay there terribly frightened, and . . . and asked us to send for a doctor. Soon a doctor arrived and . . . and saved the poor fellow. . . .

MADAME MERTCHUTKIN. Your Excellency, couldn't you find another job for my husband?

SHIPUTCHIN. No, I can't stand it! [*Weeps*] I can't stand it! [*Holds out both hands to* HIRIN *in despair*.] Turn her out! Turn her out, I implore you!

HIRIN [*going up to* TATYANA ALEXEYEVNA]. Clear out!

SHIPUTCHIN. Not her, but this . . . this awful woman . . . [*points to* MADAME MERTCHUTKIN] this one!

HIRIN [*not understanding, to* TATYANA ALEXEYEVNA]. Clear out! [*Stamps*] Clear out!

TATYANA ALEXEYEVNA. What? What are you about? Have you gone off your head?

SHIPUTCHIN. This is awful! I'm done for! Turn her out! Turn her out!

HIRIN [*to* TATYANA ALEXEYEVNA]. Get out! I'll smash you! I'll make mincemeat of you! I'll do something criminal!

TATYANA ALEXEYEVNA [*runs away from him; he runs after her*]. How dare you! You insolent creature! [*screams*]. Andrey! Save me, Andrey! [*shrieks*].

SHIPUTCHIN [*runs after them*]. Leave off! I implore you! Hush! Spare me!

HIRIN [*chasing* MADAME MERTCHUTKIN]. Clear out! Catch her! Beat her! Cut her throat!

SHIPUTCHIN [*shouts*]. Leave off! I beg you! I implore!

MADAME MERTCHUTKIN. Holy saints! . . . Holy saints! [*Squeals*] Holy saints!

TATYANA ALEXEYEVNA [*screams*]. Save me! . . . Ah! Oh! . . . I feel faint! I feel faint! [*Jumps on to a chair, then falls on the sofa and moans as though in a swoon.*]

HIRIN [*chasing* MADAME MERTCHUTKIN]. Beat her! Give it her hot! Kill her!

MADAME MERTCHUTKIN.   Oh! Oh! . . . Holy saints! I feel dizzy! Oh! [*Falls fainting in* SHIPUTCHIN'*s arms.*]

[*A knock at the door and a voice behind the scenes:* "The deputation."]

SHIPUTCHIN.   Deputation . . . reputation . . . occupation! . . .

HIRIN [*stamps*].   Get out, damn my soul! [*Tucks up his sleeves.*] Let me get at her! I could do for her!

[*Enter the* Deputation, *consisting of five persons; all are in dress-coats. One holds in his hands the address in a velvet binding, another the silver tankard,* Clerks *look in at the door.* TATYANA ALEXEYEVNA *on the sofa,* MADAME MERTCHUTKIN *in* SHIPUTCHIN'*s arms, both uttering low moans.*]

ONE OF THE DELEGATES [*reads aloud*].   Dear and highly respected Andrey Andreyevitch! Casting a retrospective glance over the past of our financial institution, and taking a mental view of its gradual development, we obtain a highly gratifying impression. It is true that in the early years of its existence the limited amount of our original capital, the absence of any important transactions, and also the indefiniteness of our policy, forced into prominence Hamlet's question: To be or not to be? And at one time voices were even raised in favor of closing the bank. But then you took the management. Your knowledge, your energy, and your characteristic tact have been the cause of our extraordinary success and exceptional prosperity. The reputation of the bank [*coughs*] . . . the reputation of the bank . . .

MADAME MERTCHUTKIN [*moans*].   Oh! Oh!

TATYANA ALEXEYEVNA [*moans*].   Water! Water!

THE DELEGATE [*continues*].   The reputation . . . [*coughs*] the reputation of the bank has been raised by you to such a pinnacle that our bank may now rival the foremost institutions of the kind in foreign countries.

SHIPUTCHIN.   Deputation . . . reputation . . . occupation! Two friends one summer evening walked, and sagely of deep matters talked. . . . Tell me not thy youth is ruined, poisoned by my jealous love. . . .

THE DELEGATE [*continues in confusion*].   Then, turning an objective eye upon the present we, dear, highly respected Andrey Andreyevitch . . . [*dropping his voice*] Perhaps later . . . we'd better come again later . . . [*They walk out in confusion.*]

CURTAIN.

THE SEA GULL

Characters

IRINA ARKADINA, *an actress*

CONSTANTINE TREPLIEFF, *her son*

PETER SORIN, *her brother*

NINA ZARIETCHNAYA, *a young girl, the daughter of a rich landowner*

ILIA SHAMRAEFF, *the manager of* SORIN'*s estate*

PAULINA, *his wife*

MASHA, *their daughter*

BORIS TRIGORIN, *an author*

EUGENE DORN, *a doctor*

SIMON MEDVIEDENKO, *a schoolmaster*

JACOB, *a workman*

A COOK

A MAIDSERVANT

The scene is laid on SORIN'*s estate.*
Two years elapse between the third and fourth acts.

ACT I

The scene is laid in the park on SORIN's *estate. A broad avenue of trees leads away from the audience toward a lake which lies lost in the depths of the park. The avenue is obstructed by a rough stage, temporarily erected for the performance of amateur theatricals, and which screens the lake from view. There is a dense growth of bushes to the left and right of the stage. A few chairs and a little table are placed in front of the stage. The sun has just set.* JACOB *and some other workmen are heard hammering and coughing on the stage behind the lowered curtain.*

MASHA *and* MEDVIEDENKO *come in from the left, returning from a walk.*

MEDVIEDENKO.   Why do you always wear mourning?

MASHA.   I dress in black to match my life. I am unhappy.

MEDVIEDENKO.   Why should you be unhappy? [*Thinking it over*] I don't understand it. You are healthy, and though your father is not rich, he has a good competency. My life is far harder than yours. I only have twenty-three rubles a month to live on, but I don't wear mourning. [*They sit down.*]

MASHA.   Happiness does not depend on riches; poor men are often happy.

MEDVIEDENKO.   In theory, yes, but not in reality. Take my case, for instance; my mother, my two sisters, my little brother and I must all live somehow on my salary of twenty-three rubles a month. We have to eat and drink, I take it. You wouldn't have us go without tea and sugar, would you? Or tobacco? Answer me that, if you can.

MASHA [*looking in the direction of the stage*].   The play will soon begin.

MEDVIEDENKO.   Yes, Nina Zarietchnaya is going to act in Treplieff's play. They love one another, and their two souls will unite to-night in the effort to interpret the same idea by different means. There is no ground on which your soul and mine can meet. I love you. Too restless and sad to stay at home, I tramp here every day, six miles and back, to be met only by your indifference. I am poor, my

125

family is large, you can have no inducement to marry a man who cannot even find sufficient food for his own mouth.

MASHA.   It is not that. [*She takes snuff*] I am touched by your affection, but I cannot return it, that is all. [*She offers him the snuff-box*] Will you take some?

MEDVIEDENKO.   No, thank you. [*Pause*]

MASHA.   The air is sultry; a storm is brewing for to-night. You do nothing but moralise or else talk about money. To you, poverty is the greatest misfortune that can befall a man, but I think it is a thousand times easier to go begging in rags than to—You wouldn't understand that, though.

[SORIN *leaning on a cane, and* TREPLIEFF *come in.*]

SORIN.   For some reason, my boy, country life doesn't suit me, and I am sure I shall never get used to it. Last night I went to bed at ten and woke at nine this morning, feeling as if, from oversleep, my brain had stuck to my skull. [*Laughing*] And yet I accidentally dropped off to sleep again after dinner, and feel utterly done up at this moment. It is like a nightmare.

TREPLIEFF. There is no doubt that you should live in town. [*He catches sight of* MASHA *and* MEDVIEDENKO] You shall be called when the play begins, my friends, but you must not stay here now. Go away, please.

SORIN.   Miss Masha, will you kindly ask your father to leave the dog unchained? It howled so last night that my sister was unable to sleep.

MASHA.   You must speak to my father yourself. Please excuse me; I can't do so. [*To* MEDVIEDENKO] Come, let us go.

MEDVIEDENKO.   You will let us know when the play begins?

[MASHA *and* MEDVIEDENKO *go out.*]

SORIN.   I foresee that that dog is going to howl all night again. It is always this way in the country; I have never been able to live as I like here. I come down for a month's holiday, to rest and all, and am plagued so by their nonsense that I long to escape after the first day. [*Laughing*] I have always been glad to get away from this place, but I have been retired now, and this was the only place I had to come to. Willy-nilly, one must live somewhere.

JACOB [*to* TREPLIEFF].   We are going to take a swim, Mr. Constantine.

TREPLIEFF.   Very well, but you must be back in ten minutes.

JACOB.   We will, sir.

TREPLIEFF [*looking at the stage*].   Just like a real theater! See, there

we have the curtain, the foreground, the background, and all. No
artificial scenery is needed. The eye travels direct to the lake, and rests
on the horizon. The curtain will be raised as the moon rises at half-
past eight.

SORIN.   Splendid!

TREPLIEFF.   Of course the whole effect will be ruined if Nina is
late. She should be here by now, but her father and stepmother watch
her so closely that it is like stealing her from a prison to get her away
from home. [*He straightens* SORIN'*s collar*] Your hair and beard are all
on end. Oughtn't you to have them trimmed?

SORIN [*smoothing his beard*].   They are the tragedy of my existence.
Even when I was young I always looked as if I were drunk, and all.
Women have never liked me. [*Sitting down*] Why is my sister out of
temper?

TREPLIEFF.   Why? Because she is jealous and bored. [*Sitting down
beside* SORIN] She is not acting this evening, but Nina is, and so she
has set herself against me, and against the performance of the play, and
against the play itself, which she hates without ever having read it.

SORIN [*laughing*].   Does she, really?

TREPLIEFF.   Yes, she is furious because Nina is going to have a
success on this little stage. [*Looking at his watch*] My mother is a psy-
chological curiosity. Without doubt brilliant and talented, capable of
sobbing over a novel, of reciting all Nekrasoff's poetry by heart, and
of nursing the sick like an angel of heaven, you should see what happens if any one begins praising Duse to her! She alone must be praised
and written about, raved over, her marvellous acting in "La Dame
aux Camélias" extolled to the skies. As she cannot get all that rubbish
in the country, she grows peevish and cross, and thinks we are all
against her, and to blame for it all. She is superstitious, too. She dreads
burning three candles, and fears the thirteenth day of the month.
Then she is stingy. I know for a fact that she has seventy thousand
rubles in a bank at Odessa, but she is ready to burst into tears if you
ask her to lend you a penny.

SORIN.   You have taken it into your head that your mother dis-
likes your play, and the thought of it has excited you, and all. Keep
calm; your mother adores you.

TREPLIEFF [*pulling a flower to pieces*].   She loves me, loves me not;
loves—loves me not; loves—loves me not! [*Laughing*] You see, she
doesn't love me, and why should she? She likes life and love and gay
clothes, and I am already twenty-five years old; a sufficient reminder
to her that she is no longer young. When I am away she is only
thirty-two, in my presence she is forty-three, and she hates me for it.
She knows, too, that I despise the modern stage. She adores it, and

imagines that she is working on it for the benefit of humanity and her sacred art, but to me the theater is merely the vehicle of convention and prejudice. When the curtain rises on that little three-walled room, when those mighty geniuses, those high-priests of art, show us people in the act of eating, drinking, loving, walking, and wearing their coats, and attempt to extract a moral from their insipid talk; when playwrights give us under a thousand different guises the same, same, same old stuff, then I must needs run from it, as Maupassant ran from the Eiffel Tower that was about to crush him by its vulgarity.

SORIN.   But we can't do without a theater.

TREPLIEFF.   No, but we must have it under a new form. If we can't do that, let us rather not have it at all. [*Looking at his watch*] I love my mother, I love her devotedly, but I think she leads a stupid life. She always has this man of letters of hers on her mind, and the newspapers are always frightening her to death, and I am tired of it. Plain, human egoism sometimes speaks in my heart, and I regret that my mother is a famous actress. If she were an ordinary woman I think I should be a happier man. What could be more intolerable and foolish than my position, Uncle, when I find myself the only nonentity among a crowd of her guests, all celebrated authors and artists? I feel that they only endure me because I am her son. Personally I am nothing, nobody. I pulled through my third year at college by the skin of my teeth, as they say. I have neither money nor brains, and on my passport you may read that I am simply a citizen of Kiev. So was my father, but he was a well-known actor. When the celebrities that frequent my mother's drawing-room deign to notice me at all, I know they only look at me to measure my insignificance; I read their thoughts, and suffer from humiliation.

SORIN.   Tell me, by the way, what is Trigorin like? I can't understand him, he is always so silent.

TREPLIEFF.   Trigorin is clever, simple, well-mannered, and a little, I might say, melancholic in disposition. Though still under forty, he is surfeited with praise. As for his stories, they are—how shall I put it?—pleasing, full of talent, but if you have read Tolstoi or Zola you somehow don't enjoy Trigorin.

SORIN.   Do you know, my boy, I like literary men. I once passionately desired two things: to marry, and to become an author. I have succeeded in neither. It must be pleasant to be even an insignificant author.

TREPLIEFF [*listening*].   I hear footsteps! [*He embraces his uncle*] I cannot live without her; even the sound of her footsteps is music to me. I am madly happy. [*He goes quickly to meet* NINA, *who comes in at that moment*] My enchantress! My girl of dreams!

NINA [*excitedly*].   It can't be that I am late? No, I am not late.

TREPLIEFF [*kissing her hands*].   No, no, no!

NINA.   I have been in a fever all day, I was so afraid my father would prevent my coming, but he and my stepmother have just gone driving. The sky is clear, the moon is rising. How I hurried to get here! How I urged my horse to go faster and faster! [*Laughing*] I am so glad to see you! [*She shakes hands with* SORIN.]

SORIN.   Oho! Your eyes look as if you had been crying. You mustn't do that.

NINA.   It is nothing, nothing. Do let us hurry. I must go in half an hour. No, no, for heaven's sake do not urge me to stay. My father doesn't know I am here.

TREPLIEFF.   As a matter of fact, it is time to begin now. I must call the audience.

SORIN.   Let me call them—and all—I am going this minute. [*He goes toward the right, begins to sing "The Two Grenadiers," then stops.*] I was singing that once when a fellow-lawyer said to me: "You have a powerful voice, sir." Then he thought a moment and added, "But it is a disagreeable one!" [*He goes out laughing.*]

NINA.   My father and his wife never will let me come here; they call this place Bohemia and are afraid I shall become an actress. But this lake attracts me as it does the gulls. My heart is full of you. [*She glances about her.*]

TREPLIEFF.   We are alone.

NINA.   Isn't that some one over there?

TREPLIEFF.   No. [*They kiss one another.*]

NINA.   What is that tree?

TREPLIEFF.   An elm.

NINA.   Why does it look so dark?

TREPLIEFF.   It is evening; everything looks dark now. Don't go away early, I implore you.

NINA.   I must.

TREPLIEFF.   What if I were to follow you, Nina? I shall stand in your garden all night with my eyes on your window.

NINA.   That would be impossible; the watchman would see you, and Treasure is not used to you yet, and would bark.

TREPLIEFF.   I love you.

NINA.   Hush!

TREPLIEFF [*listening to approaching footsteps*].   Who is that? Is it you, Jacob?

JACOB [*on the stage*].   Yes, sir.

TREPLIEFF.   To your places then. The moon is rising; the play must commence.

NINA.   Yes, sir.

TREPLIEFF.   Is the alcohol ready? Is the sulphur ready? There must be fumes of sulphur in the air when the red eyes shine out. [*To* NINA] Go, now, everything is ready. Are you nervous?

NINA.   Yes, very. I am not so much afraid of your mother as I am of Trigorin. I am terrified and ashamed to act before him; he is so famous. Is he young?

TREPLIEFF.   Yes.

NINA.   What beautiful stories he writes!

TREPLIEFF [*coldly*].   I have never read any of them, so I can't say.

NINA.   Your play is very hard to act; there are no living characters in it.

TREPLIEFF.   Living characters! Life must be represented not as it is, but as it ought to be; as it appears in dreams.

NINA.   There is so little action; it seems more like a recitation. I think love should always come into every play.

[NINA *and* TREPLIEFF *go up onto the little stage;* PAULINA *and* DORN *come in.*]

PAULINA.   It is getting damp. Go back and put on your goloshes.

DORN.   I am quite warm.

PAULINA.   You never will take care of yourself; you are quite obstinate about it, and yet you are a doctor, and know quite well that damp air is bad for you. You like to see me suffer, that's what it is. You sat out on the terrace all yesterday evening on purpose.

DORN [*sings*].   "Oh, tell me not that youth is wasted."

PAULINA.   You were so enchanted by the conversation of Madame Arkadina that you did not even notice the cold. Confess that you admire her.

DORN.   I am fifty-five years old.

PAULINA.   A trifle. That is not old for a man. You have kept your looks magnificently, and women still like you.

DORN.   What are you trying to tell me?

PAULINA.   You men are all ready to go down on your knees to an actress, all of you.

DORN [*sings*].   "Once more I stand before thee." It is only right that artists should be made much of by society and treated differently from, let us say, merchants. It is a kind of idealism.

PAULINA.   When women have loved you and thrown themselves at your head, has that been idealism?

DORN [*shrugging his shoulders*].   I can't say. There has been a great deal that was admirable in my relations with women. In me they liked, above all, the superior doctor. Ten years ago, you remember, I was the only decent doctor they had in this part of the country—and then, I have always acted like a man of honor.

PAULINA [*seizes his hand*]. Dearest!

DORN. Be quiet! Here they come.

[ARKADINA *comes in on* SORIN's *arm; also* TRIGORIN, SHAMRAEFF, MEDVIEDENKO, *and* MASHA.]

SHAMRAEFF. She acted most beautifully at the Poltava Fair in 1873; she was really magnificent. But tell me, too, where Tchadin the comedian is now? He was inimitable as Rasplueff, better than Sadofski. Where is he now?

ARKADINA. Don't ask me where all those antediluvians are! I know nothing about them. [*She sits down.*]

SHAMRAEFF [*sighing*]. Pashka Tchadin! There are none left like him. The stage is not what it was in his time. There were sturdy oaks growing on it then, where now but stumps remain.

DORN. It is true that we have few dazzling geniuses these days, but, on the other hand, the average of acting is much higher.

SHAMRAEFF. I cannot agree with you; however, that is a matter of taste, *de gustibus.*

[*Enter* TREPLIEFF *from behind the stage.*]

ARKADINA. When will the play begin, my dear boy?

TREPLIEFF. In a moment. I must ask you to have patience.

ARKADINA [*quoting from* Hamlet]. My son,
      "Thou turn'st mine eyes into my very soul;
      And there I see such black grained spots
      As will not leave their tinct."

[*A horn is blown behind the stage.*]

TREPLIEFF. Attention, ladies and gentlemen! The play is about to begin. [*Pause*] I shall commence. [*He taps the door with a stick, and speaks in a loud voice*] O, ye time-honored, ancient mists that drive at night across the surface of this lake, blind you our eyes with sleep, and show us in our dreams that which will be in twice ten thousand years!

SORIN. There won't be anything in twice ten thousand years.

TREPLIEFF. Then let them now show us that nothingness.

ARKADINA. Yes, let them—we are asleep.

[*The curtain rises. A vista opens across the lake. The moon hangs low above the horizon and is reflected in the water.* NINA, *dressed in white, is seen seated on a great rock.*]

NINA.   All men and beasts, lions, eagles, and quails, horned stags, geese, spiders, silent fish that inhabit the waves, starfish from the sea, and creatures invisible to the eye—in one word, life—all, all life, completing the dreary round imposed upon it, has died out at last. A thousand years have passed since the earth last bore a living creature on her breast, and the unhappy moon now lights her lamp in vain. No longer are the cries of storks heard in the meadows, or the drone of beetles in the groves of limes. All is cold, cold. All is void, void, void. All is terrible, terrible—[*Pause*] The bodies of all living creatures have dropped to dust, and eternal matter has transformed them into stones and water and clouds; but their spirits have flowed together into one, and that great world-soul am I! In me is the spirit of the great Alexander, the spirit of Napoleon, of Cæsar, of Shakespeare, and of the tiniest leech that swims. In me the consciousness of man has joined hands with the instinct of the animal; I understand all, all, all, and each life lives again in me.

[*The will-o-the-wisps flicker out along the lake shore.*]

ARKADINA [*whispers*].   What decadent rubbish is this?
TREPLIEFF [*imploringly*].   Mother!
NINA.   I am alone. Once in a hundred years my lips are opened, my voice echoes mournfully across the desert earth, and no one hears. And you, poor lights of the marsh, you do not hear me. You are engendered at sunset in the putrid mud, and flit wavering about the lake till dawn, unconscious, unreasoning, unwarmed by the breath of life. Satan, father of eternal matter, trembling lest the spark of life should glow in you, has ordered an unceasing movement of the atoms that compose you, and so you shift and change for ever. I, the spirit of the universe, I alone am immutable and eternal. [*Pause*] Like a captive in a dungeon deep and void, I know not where I am, nor what awaits me. One thing only is not hidden from me: in my fierce and obstinate battle with Satan, the source of the forces of matter, I am destined to be victorious in the end. Matter and spirit will then be one at last in glorious harmony, and the reign of freedom will begin on earth. But this can only come to pass by slow degrees, when after countless eons the moon and earth and shining Sirius himself shall fall to dust. Until that hour, oh, horror! horror! horror! [*Pause. Two glowing red points are seen shining across the lake*] Satan, my mighty foe, advances; I see his dread and lurid eyes.

ARKADINA.   I smell sulphur. Is that done on purpose?
TREPLIEFF.   Yes.
ARKADINA.   Oh, I see; that is part of the effect.
TREPLIEFF.   Mother!

NINA. He longs for man—

PAULINA [*to* DORN]. You have taken off your hat again! Put it on, you will catch cold.

ARKADINA. The doctor has taken off his hat to Satan, father of eternal matter—

TREPLIEFF [*loudly and angrily*]. Enough of this! There's an end to the performance. Down with the curtain!

ARKADINA. Why, what are you so angry about?

TREPLIEFF [*stamping his foot*]. The curtain; down with it! [*The curtain falls*] Excuse me, I forgot that only a chosen few might write plays or act them. I have infringed the monopoly. I—I—

[*He would like to say more, but waves his hand instead, and goes out to the left.*]

ARKADINA. What is the matter with him?

SORIN. You should not handle youthful egoism so roughly, sister.

ARKADINA. What did I say to him?

SORIN. You hurt his feelings.

ARKADINA. But he told me himself that this was all in fun, so I treated his play as if it were a comedy.

SORIN. Nevertheless—

ARKADINA. Now it appears that he has produced a masterpiece, if you please! I suppose it was not meant to amuse us at all, but that he arranged the performance and fumigated us with sulphur to demonstrate to us how plays should be written, and what is worth acting. I am tired of him. No one could stand his constant thrusts and sallies. He is a wilful, egotistic boy.

SORIN. He had hoped to give you pleasure.

ARKADINA. Is that so? I notice, though, that he did not choose an ordinary play, but forced his decadent trash on us. I am willing to listen to any raving, so long as it is not meant seriously, but in showing us this, he pretended to be introducing us to a new form of art, and inaugurating a new era. In my opinion, there was nothing new about it, it was simply an exhibition of bad temper.

TRIGORIN. Everybody must write as he feels, and as best he may.

ARKADINA. Let him write as he feels and can, but let him spare me his nonsense.

DORN. Thou art angry, O Jove!

ARKADINA. I am a woman, not Jove. [*She lights a cigarette*] And I am not angry, I am only sorry to see a young man foolishly wasting his time. I did not mean to hurt him.

MEDVIEDENKO.   No one has any ground for separating life from matter, as the spirit may well consist of the union of material atoms. [*Excitedly, to* TRIGORIN] Some day you should write a play, and put on the stage the life of a schoolmaster. It is a hard, hard life.

ARKADINA.   I agree with you, but do not let us talk about plays or atoms now. This is such a lovely evening. Listen to the singing, friends, how sweet it sounds.

PAULINA.   Yes, they are singing across the water. [*Pause*]

ARKADINA [*to* TRIGORIN] Sit down beside me here. Ten or fifteen years ago we had music and singing on this lake almost all night. There are six houses on its shores. All was noise and laughter and romance then, such romance! The young star and idol of them all in those days was this man here, [*nods toward* DORN] Doctor Eugene Dorn. He is fascinating now, but he was irresistible then. But my conscience is beginning to prick me. Why did I hurt my poor boy? I am uneasy about him. [*Loudly*] Constantine! Constantine!

MASHA.   Shall I go and find him?

ARKADINA.   If you please, my dear.

MASHA [*goes off to the left, calling*].   Mr. Constantine! Oh, Mr. Constantine!

NINA [*comes in from behind the stage*].   I see that the play will never be finished, so now I can go home. Good evening. [*She kisses* ARKADINA *and* PAULINA.]

SORIN.   Bravo! Bravo!

ARKADINA.   Bravo! Bravo! We were quite charmed by your acting. With your looks and such a lovely voice it is a crime for you to hide yourself in the country. You must be very talented. It is your duty to go on the stage, do you hear me?

NINA.   It is the dream of my life, which will never come true.

ARKADINA.   Who knows? Perhaps it will. But let me present Monsieur Boris Trigorin.

NINA.   I am delighted to meet you. [*Embarrassed*] I have read all your books.

ARKADINA [*drawing* NINA *down beside her*].   Don't be afraid of him, dear. He is a simple, good-natured soul, even if he is a celebrity. See, he is embarrassed himself.

DORN.   Couldn't the curtain be raised now? It is depressing to have it down.

SHAMRAEFF [*loudly*].   Jacob, my man! Raise the curtain!

NINA [*to* TRIGORIN].   It was a curious play, wasn't it?

TRIGORIN.   Very. I couldn't understand it at all, but I watched it with the greatest pleasure because you acted with such sincerity, and the setting was beautiful. [*Pause*] There must be a lot of fish in this lake.

NINA.   Yes, there are.

TRIGORIN.   I love fishing. I know of nothing pleasanter than to sit on a lake shore in the evening with one's eyes on a floating cork.

NINA.   Why, I should think that for one who has tasted the joys of creation, no other pleasure could exist.

ARKADINA.   Don't talk like that. He always begins to flounder when people say nice things to him.

SHAMRAEFF.   I remember when the famous Silva was singing once in the Opera House at Moscow, how delighted we all were when he took the low C. Well, you can imagine our astonishment when one of the church cantors, who happened to be sitting in the gallery, suddenly boomed out: "Bravo, Silva!" a whole octave lower. Like this: [*In a deep bass voice*] "Bravo, Silva!" The audience was left breathless. [*Pause*]

DORN.   An angel of silence is flying over our heads.

NINA.   I must go. Good-bye.

ARKADINA.   Where to? Where must you go so early? We shan't allow it.

NINA.   My father is waiting for me.

ARKADINA.   How cruel he is, really. [*They kiss each other*] Then I suppose we can't keep you, but it is very hard indeed to let you go.

NINA.   If you only knew how hard it is for me to leave you all.

ARKADINA.   Somebody must see you home, my pet.

NINA [*startled*].   No, no!

SORIN [*imploringly*].   Don't go!

NINA.   I must.

SORIN.   Stay just one hour more, and all. Come now, really, you know.

NINA [*struggling against her desire to stay; through her tears*].   No, no, I can't. [*She shakes hands with him and quickly goes out.*]

ARKADINA.   An unlucky girl! They say that her mother left the whole of an immense fortune to her husband, and now the child is penniless because the father has already willed everything away to his second wife. It is pitiful.

DORN.   Yes, her papa is a perfect beast, and I don't mind saying so—it is what he deserves.

SORIN [*rubbing his chilled hands*].   Come, let us go in; the night is damp, and my legs are aching.

ARKADINA.   Yes, you act as if they were turned to stone; you can hardly move them. Come, you unfortunate old man. [*She takes his arm.*]

SHAMRAEFF [*offering his arm to his wife*].   Permit me, madame.

SORIN.   I hear that dog howling again. Won't you please have it unchained, Shamraeff?

SHAMRAEFF.   No, I really can't, sir. The granary is full of millet, and I am afraid thieves might break in if the dog were not there. [*Walking beside* MEDVIEDENKO] Yes, a whole octave lower: "Bravo, Silva!" and he wasn't a singer either, just a simple church cantor.

MEDVIEDENKO.   What salary does the church pay its singers?

[*All go out except* DORN.]

DORN.   I may have lost my judgment and my wits, but I must confess I liked that play. There was something in it. When the girl spoke of her solitude and the Devil's eyes gleamed across the lake, I felt my hands shaking with excitement. It was so fresh and naïve. But here he comes; let me say something pleasant to him.

[TREPLIEFF *comes in.*]

TREPLIEFF.   All gone already?

DORN.   I am here.

TREPLIEFF.   Masha has been yelling for me all over the park. An insufferable creature.

DORN.   Constantine, your play delighted me. It was strange, of course, and I did not hear the end, but it made a deep impression on me. You have a great deal of talent, and must persevere in your work.

[TREPLIEFF *seizes his hand and squeezes it hard, then kisses him impetuously.*]

DORN.   Tut, tut! how excited you are. Your eyes are full of tears. Listen to me. You chose your subject in the realm of abstract thought, and you did quite right. A work of art should invariably embody some lofty idea. Only that which is seriously meant can ever be beautiful. How pale you are!

TREPLIEFF.   So you advise me to persevere?

DORN.   Yes, but use your talent to express only deep and eternal truths. I have led a quiet life, as you know, and am a contented man, but if I should ever experience the exaltation that an artist feels during his moments of creation, I think I should spurn this material envelope of my soul and everything connected with it, and should soar away into heights above this earth.

TREPLIEFF.   I beg your pardon, but where is Nina?

DORN.   And yet another thing: every work of art should have a definite object in view. You should know why you are writing, for if you follow the road of art without a goal before your eyes, you will lose yourself, and your genius will be your ruin.

TREPLIEFF [*impetuously*].   Where is Nina?

DORN.   She has gone home.

TREPLIEFF [*in despair*].   Gone home? What *shall* I do? I want to see her; I must see her! I shall follow her.

DORN.   My dear boy, keep quiet.

TREPLIEFF.   I am going. I must go.

[MASHA *comes in.*]

MASHA.   Your mother wants you to come in, Mr. Constantine. She is waiting for you, and is very uneasy.

TREPLIEFF.   Tell her I have gone away. And for heaven's sake, all of you, leave me alone! Go away! Don't follow me about!

DORN.   Come, come, old chap, don't act like this; it isn't kind at all.

TREPLIEFF [*through his tears*].   Good-bye, doctor, and thank you. [TREPLIEFF *goes out.*]

DORN [*sighing*].   Ah, youth, youth!

MASHA.   It is always "Youth, youth," when there is nothing else to be said. [*She takes snuff.* DORN *takes the snuff-box out of her hands and flings it into the bushes.*]

DORN.   Don't do that, it is horrid. [*Pause*] I hear music in the house. I must go in.

MASHA.   Wait a moment.

DORN.   What do you want?

MASHA.   Let me tell you again. I feel like talking. [*She grows more and more excited*] I do not love my father, but my heart turns to you. For some reason, I feel with all my soul that you are near to me. Help me! Help me, or I shall do something foolish and mock at my life, and ruin it. I am at the end of my strength.

DORN.   What is the matter? How can I help you?

MASHA.   I am in agony. No one, no one can imagine how I suffer. [*She lays her head on his shoulder and speaks softly*] I love Constantine.

DORN.   Oh, how excitable you all are! And how much love there is about this lake of spells! [*Tenderly*] But what can I do for you, my child? What? What?

CURTAIN.

ACT II

The lawn in front of SORIN's *house. The house stands in the background, on a broad terrace. The lake, brightly reflecting the rays of the sun, lies to the left. There are flower-beds here and there. It is noon; the day is hot.* ARKADINA, DORN, *and* MASHA *are sitting on a bench on the lawn, in the shade of an old linden. An open book is lying on* DORN's *knees.*

ARKADINA [*to* MASHA]   Come, get up. [*They both get up*] Stand beside me. You are twenty-two and I am almost twice your age. Tell me, Doctor, which of us is the younger looking?

DORN.   You are, of course.

ARKADINA.   You see! Now why is it? Because I work; my heart and mind are always busy, whereas you never move off the same spot. You don't live. It is a maxim of mine never to look into the future. I never admit the thought of old age or death, and just accept what comes to me.

MASHA.   I feel as if I had been in the world a thousand years, and I trail my life behind me like an endless scarf. Often I have no desire to live at all. Of course that is foolish. One ought to pull oneself together and shake off such nonsense.

DORN [*sings softly*].   "Tell her, oh flowers—"

ARKADINA.   And then I keep myself as correct-looking as an Englishman. I am always well-groomed, as the saying is, and carefully dressed, with my hair neatly arranged. Do you think I should ever permit myself to leave the house half-dressed, with untidy hair? Certainly not! I have kept my looks by never letting myself slump as some women do. [*She puts her arms akimbo, and walks up and down on the lawn*] See me, tripping on tiptoe like a fifteen-year-old girl.

DORN.   I see. Nevertheless, I shall continue my reading. [*He takes up his book*] Let me see, we had come to the grain-dealer and the rats.

ARKADINA.   And the rats. Go on. [*She sits down*] No, give me the book, it is my turn to read. [*She takes the book and looks for the place*]

And the rats. Ah, here it is. [*She reads*] "It is as dangerous for society to attract and indulge authors as it is for grain-dealers to raise rats in their granaries. Yet society loves authors. And so, when a woman has found one whom she wishes to make her own, she lays siege to him by indulging and flattering him." That may be so in France, but it certainly is not so in Russia. We do not carry out a program like that. With us, a woman is usually head over ears in love with an author before she attempts to lay siege to him. You have an example before your eyes, in me and Trigorin.

[SORIN *comes in leaning on a cane, with* NINA *beside him.* MEDVIEDENKO *follows, pushing an arm-chair.*]

SORIN [*in a caressing voice, as if speaking to a child*].   So we are happy now, eh? We are enjoying ourselves to-day, are we? Father and step-mother have gone away to Tver, and we are free for three whole days!

NINA [*sits down beside* ARKADINA, *and embraces her*].   I am so happy. I belong to you now.

SORIN [*sits down in his arm-chair*].   She looks lovely to day.

ARKADINA.   Yes, she has put on her prettiest dress, and looks sweet. That was nice of you. [*She kisses* NINA] But we mustn't praise her too much; we shall spoil her. Where is Trigorin?

NINA.   He is fishing off the wharf.

ARKADINA.   I wonder he isn't bored. [*She begins to read again.*]

NINA.   What are you reading?

ARKADINA.   "On the Water," by Maupassant. [*She reads a few lines to herself*] But the rest is neither true nor interesting. [*She lays down the book*] I am uneasy about my son. Tell me, what is the matter with him? Why is he so dull and depressed lately? He spends all his days on the lake, and I scarcely ever see him any more.

MASHA.   His heart is heavy. [*Timidly, to* NINA] Please recite something from his play.

NINA [*shrugging her shoulders*].   Shall I? Is it so interesting?

MASHA [*with suppressed rapture*].   When he recites, his eyes shine and his face grows pale. His voice is beautiful and sad, and he has the ways of a poet.

[SORIN *begins to snore.*]

DORN.   Pleasant dreams!

ARKADINA.   Peter!

SORIN.   Eh?

ARKADINA.   Are you asleep?

SORIN.   Not a bit of it [*Pause*]

ARKADINA. You don't do a thing for your health, brother, but you really ought to.

DORN. The idea of doing anything for one's health at sixty-five!

SORIN. One still wants to live at sixty-five.

DORN [*crossly*] Ho! Take some camomile tea.

ARKADINA. I think a journey to some watering-place would be good for him.

DORN. Why, yes; he might go as well as not.

ARKADINA. You don't understand.

DORN. There is nothing to understand in this case; it is quite clear. [*Pause*]

MEDVIEDENKO. He ought to give up smoking.

SORIN. What nonsense!

DORN. No, that is not nonsense. Wine and tobacco destroy the individuality. After a cigar or a glass of vodka you are no longer Peter Sorin, but Peter Sorin plus somebody else. Your ego breaks in two: you begin to think of yourself in the third person.

SORIN. It is easy for you to condemn smoking and drinking; you have known what life is, but what about me? I have served in the Department of Justice for twenty-eight years, but I have never lived, I have never had any experiences. You are satiated with life, and that is why you have an inclination for philosophy, but I want to live, and that is why I drink my wine for dinner and smoke cigars, and all.

DORN. One must take life seriously, and to take a cure at sixty-five and regret that one did not have more pleasure in youth is, forgive my saying so, trifling.

MASHA. It must be lunch-time. [*She walks away languidly, with a dragging step*] My foot has gone to sleep.

DORN. She is going to have a couple of drinks before lunch.

SORIN. The poor soul is unhappy.

DORN. That is a trifle, your honor.

SORIN. You judge her like a man who has obtained all he wants in life.

ARKADINA. Oh, what could be duller than this dear tedium of the country? The air is hot and still, nobody does anything but sit and philosophize about life. It is pleasant, my friends, to sit and listen to you here, but I had rather a thousand times sit alone in the room of a hotel learning a role by heart.

NINA [*with enthusiasm*]. You are quite right. I understand how you feel.

SORIN. Of course it is pleasanter to live in town. One can sit in one's library with a telephone at one's elbow, no one comes in without being first announced by the footman, the streets are full of cabs, and all—

DORN [sings]. "Tell her, oh flowers—"

[SHAMRAEFF comes in, followed by PAULINA.]

SHAMRAEFF. Here they are. How do you do? [He kisses ARKADINA's hand and then NINA's] I am delighted to see you looking so well. [To ARKADINA] My wife tells me that you mean to go to town with her to-day. Is that so?

ARKADINA. Yes, that is what I had planned to do.

SHAMRAEFF. Hm—that is splendid, but how do you intend to get there, madam? We are hauling rye to-day, and all the men are busy. What horses would you take?

ARKADINA. What horses? How do I know what horses we shall have?

SORIN. Why, we have the carriage horses.

SHAMRAEFF. The carriage horses! And where am I to find the harness for them? This is astonishing! My dear madam, I have the greatest respect for your talents, and would gladly sacrifice ten years of my life for you, but I cannot let you have any horses to-day.

ARKADINA. But if I must go to town? What an extraordinary state of affairs!

SHAMRAEFF. You do not know, madam, what it is to run a farm.

ARKADINA [in a burst of anger]. That is an old story! Under these circumstances I shall go back to Moscow this very day. Order a carriage for me from the village, or I shall go to the station on foot.

SHAMRAEFF [losing his temper]. Under these circumstances I resign my position. You must find yourself another manager. [He goes out.]

ARKADINA It is like this every summer: every summer I am insulted here. I shall never set foot here again.

[She goes out to the left, in the direction of the wharf. In a few minutes she is seen entering the house, followed by TRIGORIN, who carries a bucket and fishing-rod.]

SORIN [losing his temper]. What the deuce did he mean by his impudence? I want all the horses brought here at once!

NINA [to PAULINA]. How could he refuse anything to Madame Arkadina, the famous actress? Is not every wish, every caprice even, of hers, more important than any farm work? This is incredible.

PAULINA [in despair]. What can I do about it? Put yourself in my place and tell me what I can do.

SORIN [to NINA]. Let us go and find my sister, and all beg her not to go. [*He looks in the direction in which* SHAMRAEFF *went out*] That man is insufferable; a regular tyrant.

NINA [*preventing him from getting up*]. Sit still, sit still, and let us wheel you. [*She and* MEDVIEDENKO *push the chair before them*] This is terrible!

SORIN. Yes, yes, it is terrible; but he won't leave. I shall have a talk with him in a moment. [*They go out. Only* DORN *and* PAULINA *are left.*]

DORN. How tiresome people are! Your husband deserves to be thrown out of here neck and crop, but it will all end by this old granny Sorin and his sister asking the man's pardon. See if it doesn't.

PAULINA. He has sent the carriage horses into the fields too. These misunderstandings occur every day. If you only knew how they excite me! I am ill; see! I am trembling all over! I cannot endure his rough ways. [*Imploringly*] Eugene, my darling, my beloved, take me to you. Our time is short; we are no longer young; let us end deception and concealment, even though it is only at the end of our lives [*pause*].

DORN. I am fifty-five years old. It is too late now for me to change my ways of living.

PAULINA. I know that you refuse me because there are other women who are near to you, and you cannot take everybody. I understand. Excuse me—I see I am only bothering you.

[NINA *is seen near the house picking a bunch of flowers.*]

DORN. No, it is all right.

PAULINA. I am tortured by jealousy. Of course you are a doctor and cannot escape from women. I understand.

DORN [*to* NINA, *who comes toward him*]. How are things in there?

NINA. Madame Arkadina is crying, and Sorin is having an attack of asthma.

DORN. Let us go and give them both some camomile tea.

NINA [*hands him the bunch of flowers*]. Here are some flowers for you.

DORN. Thank you. [*He goes into the house.*]

PAULINA [*following him*]. What pretty flowers! [*As they reach the house she says in a low voice*] Give me those flowers! Give them to me!

[DORN *hands her the flowers; she tears them to pieces and flings them away. They both go into the house.*]

NINA [*alone*].   How strange to see a famous actress weeping, and for such a trifle! Is it not strange, too, that a famous author should sit fishing all day? He is the idol of the public, the papers are full of him, his photograph is for sale everywhere, his works have been translated into many foreign languages, and yet he is overjoyed if he catches a couple of minnows. I always thought famous people were distant and proud; I thought they despised the common crowd which exalts riches and birth, and avenged themselves on it by dazzling it with the inextinguishable honor and glory of their fame. But here I see them weeping and playing cards and flying into passions like everybody else.

[TREPLIEFF *comes in without a hat on, carrying a gun and a dead sea gull.*]

TREPLIEFF.   Are you alone here?
NINA.   Yes.

[TREPLIEFF *lays the sea gull at her feet.*]

NINA.   What do you mean by this?
TREPLIEFF.   I was base enough to-day to kill this gull. I lay it at your feet.
NINA.   What is happening to you? [*She picks up the gull and stands looking at it.*]
TREPLIEFF [*after a pause*].   So shall I soon end my own life.
NINA.   You have changed so that I fail to recognize you.
TREPLIEFF.   Yes, I have changed since the time when I ceased to recognize you. You have failed me; your look is cold; you do not like to have me near you.
NINA.   You have grown so irritable lately, and you talk so darkly and symbolically that you must forgive me if I fail to follow you. I am too simple to understand you.
TREPLIEFF.   All this began when my play failed so dismally. A woman never can forgive failure. I have burnt the manuscript to the last page. Oh, if you could only fathom my unhappiness! Your estrangement is to me terrible, incredible; it is as if I had suddenly waked to find this lake dried up and sunk into the earth. You say you are too simple to understand me; but, oh, what is there to understand? You disliked my play, you have no faith in my powers, you already think of me as commonplace and worthless, as many are. [*Stamping his foot*] How well I can understand your feelings! And that understanding is to me like a dagger in the brain. May it be accursed, together with my stupidity, which sucks my life-blood like a snake! [*He sees* TRIGORIN, *who approaches reading a book*] There comes real genius,

striding along like another Hamlet, and with a book, too. [*Mockingly*] "Words, words, words." You feel the warmth of that sun already, you smile, your eyes melt and glow liquid in its rays. I shall not disturb you. [*He goes out.*]

TRIGORIN [*making notes in his book*].   Takes snuff and drinks vodka; always wears black dresses; is loved by a schoolteacher—

NINA.   How do you do?

TRIGORIN.   How are you, Miss Nina? Owing to an unforeseen development of circumstances, it seems that we are leaving here today. You and I shall probably never see each other again, and I am sorry for it. I seldom meet a young and pretty girl now; I can hardly remember how it feels to be nineteen, and the young girls in my books are seldom living characters. I should like to change places with you, if but for an hour, to look out at the world through your eyes, and so find out what sort of a little person you are.

NINA.   And I should like to change places with you.

TRIGORIN.   Why?

NINA.   To find out how a famous genius feels. What is it like to be famous? What sensations does it give you?

TRIGORIN.   What sensations? I don't believe it gives any. [*Thoughtfully*] Either you exaggerate my fame, or else, if it exists, all I can say is that one simply doesn't feel fame in any way.

NINA.   But when you read about yourself in the papers?

TRIGORIN.   If the critics praise me, I am happy; if they condemn me, I am out of sorts for the next two days.

NINA.   This is a wonderful world. If you only knew how I envy you! Men are born to different destinies. Some dully drag a weary, useless life behind them, lost in the crowd, unhappy, while to one out of a million, as to you, for instance, comes a bright destiny full of interest and meaning. You are lucky.

TRIGORIN. I, lucky? [*He shrugs his shoulders*] H-m—I hear you talking about fame, and happiness, and bright destinies, and those fine words of yours mean as much to me—forgive my saying so—as sweetmeats do, which I never eat. You are very young, and very kind.

NINA.   Your life is beautiful.

TRIGORIN.   I see nothing especially lovely about it. [*He looks at his watch*] Excuse me, I must go at once, and begin writing again. I am in a hurry. [*He laughs*] You have stepped on my pet corn, as they say, and I am getting excited, and a little cross. Let us discuss this bright and beautiful life of mine, though. [*After a few moments' thought*] Violent obsessions sometimes lay hold of a man: he may, for instance, think day and night of nothing but the moon. I have such a moon. Day and night I am held in the grip of one besetting thought, to write, write, write! Hardly have I finished one book than something urges me to write another, and then a third, and then a fourth—I write ceaselessly. I am, as it were, on a treadmill. I hurry for ever from one story to another, and can't help myself. Do you see anything bright and beautiful in that? Oh, it is a wild life! Even now, thrilled as I am by talking to you, I do not forget for an instant that an unfinished story is awaiting me. My eye falls on that cloud there, which has the shape of a grand piano; I instantly make a mental note that I must remember to mention in my story a cloud floating by that looked like a grand piano. I smell heliotrope; I mutter to myself: a sickly smell, the color worn by widows; I must remember that in writing my next description of a summer evening. I catch an idea in every sentence of yours or of my own, and hasten to lock all these treasures in my literary store-room, thinking that some day they may be useful to me. As soon as I stop working I rush off to the theater or go fishing, in the hope that I may find oblivion there, but no! Some new subject for a story is sure to come rolling through my brain like an iron cannonball. I hear my desk calling, and have to go back to it and begin to write, write, write, once more. And so it goes for everlasting. I cannot escape myself, though I feel that I am consuming my life. To prepare the honey I feed to unknown crowds, I am doomed to brush the bloom from my dearest flowers, to tear them from their stems, and trample the roots that bore them under foot. Am I not a madman? Should I not be treated by those who know me as one mentally diseased? Yet it is always the same, same old story, till I begin to think that all this praise and admiration must be a deception, that I am being hoodwinked because they know I am crazy, and I sometimes tremble lest I should be grabbed from behind and whisked off to a lunatic asylum. The best years of my youth were made one continual agony for me by my writing. A young author, especially if at first he does not make a success, feels clumsy, ill-at-ease, and superfluous in the world. His nerves are all on edge and stretched to the point of breaking; he is irresistibly attracted to literary and artistic people, and hovers about them unknown and unnoticed, fearing to look them bravely in the eye, like a man with a passion for gambling, whose money is all gone. I did not know my readers, but for some reason I imagined they were distrustful and unfriendly; I was mortally afraid of the public, and when my first play appeared, it seemed to me as if all the dark eyes in the audience were looking at it with enmity, and all the blue ones with cold indifference. Oh, how terrible it was! What agony!

NINA.   But don't your inspiration and the act of creation give you moments of lofty happiness?

TRIGORIN.   Yes. Writing is a pleasure to me, and so is reading the proofs, but no sooner does a book leave the press than it becomes odious to me; it is not what I meant it to be; I made a mistake to write it at all; I am provoked and discouraged. Then the public reads it and says: "Yes, it is clever and pretty, but not nearly as good as Tolstoi," or "It is a lovely thing, but not as good as Turgenieff's 'Fathers and Sons,'" and so it will always be. To my dying day I shall hear people say: "Clever and pretty; clever and pretty," and nothing more; and when I am gone, those that knew me will say as they pass my grave: "Here lies Trigorin, a clever writer, but he was not as good as Turgenieff."

NINA.   You must excuse me, but I decline to understand what you are talking about. The fact is, you have been spoilt by your success.

TRIGORIN.   What success have I had? I have never pleased myself; as a writer, I do not like myself at all. The trouble is that I am made giddy, as it were, by the fumes of my brain, and often hardly know what I am writing. I love this lake, these trees, the blue heaven; nature's voice speaks to me and wakes a feeling of passion in my heart, and I am overcome by an uncontrollable desire to write. But I am not only a painter of landscapes, I am a man of the city besides. I love my country, too, and her people; I feel that, as a writer, it is my duty to speak of their sorrows, of their future, also of science, of the rights of man, and so forth. So I write on every subject, and the public hounds me on all sides, sometimes in anger, and I race and dodge like a fox with a pack of hounds on his trail. I see life and knowledge flitting away before me. I am left behind them like a peasant who has missed his train at a station, and finally I come back to the conclusion that all I am fit for is to describe landscapes, and that whatever else I attempt rings abominably false.

NINA.   You work too hard to realize the importance of your writings. What if you are discontented with yourself? To others you appear a great and splendid man. If I were a writer like you I should devote my whole life to the service of the Russian people, knowing at the same time that their welfare depended on their power to rise to the heights I had attained, and the people should send me before them in a chariot of triumph.

TRIGORIN.   In a chariot? Do you think I am Agamemnon? [*They both smile.*]

NINA.   For the bliss of being a writer or an actress I could endure want, and disillusionment, and the hatred of my friends, and the pangs of my own dissatisfaction with myself; but I should demand in return fame, real, resounding fame! [*She covers her face with her hands*] Whew! My head reels!

THE VOICE OF ARKADINA [*from inside the house*].   Boris! Boris!

TRIGORIN.   She is calling me, probably to come and pack, but I don't want to leave this place. [*His eyes rest on the lake*] What a blessing such beauty is!

NINA.   Do you see that house there, on the far shore?

TRIGORIN.   Yes.

NINA.   That was my dead mother's home. I was born there, and have lived all my life beside this lake. I know every little island in it.

TRIGORIN.   This is a beautiful place to live. [*He catches sight of the dead sea gull*] What is that?

NINA.   A gull. Constantine shot it.

TRIGORIN.   What a lovely bird! Really, I can't bear to go away. Can't you persuade Irina to stay? [*He writes something in his notebook.*]

NINA.   What are you writing?

TRIGORIN.   Nothing much, only an idea that occurred to me. [*He puts the book back in his pocket.*] An idea for a short story. A young girl grows up on the shores of a lake, as you have. She loves the lake as the gulls do, and is as happy and free as they. But a man sees her who chances to come that way, and he destroys her out of idleness, as this gull here has been destroyed. [*Pause.* ARKADINA *appears at one of the windows.*]

ARKADINA.   Boris! Where are you?

TRIGORIN.   I am coming this minute.

[*He goes toward the house, looking back at* NINA. ARKADINA *remains at the window.*]

TRIGORIN.   What do you want?

ARKADINA.   We are not going away, after all.

[TRIGORIN *goes into the house.* NINA *comes forward and stands lost in thought.*]

NINA. It is a dream!

CURTAIN.

ACT III

The dining-room of SORIN's *house. Doors open out of it to the right and left. A table stands in the center of the room. Trunks and boxes encumber the floor, and preparations for departure are evident.* TRIGORIN *is sitting at a table eating his breakfast, and* MASHA *is standing beside him.*

MASHA.   I am telling you all these things because you write books and they may be useful to you. I tell you honestly, I should not have lived another day if he had wounded himself fatally. Yet I am courageous; I have decided to tear this love of mine out of my heart by the roots.

TRIGORIN.   How will you do it?

MASHA.   By marrying Medviedenko.

TRIGORIN.   The school-teacher?

MASHA.   Yes.

TRIGORIN.   I don't see the necessity for that.

MASHA.   Oh, if you knew what it is to love without hope for years and years, to wait for ever for something that will never come! I shall not marry for love, but marriage will at least be a change, and will bring new cares to deaden the memories of the past. Shall we have another drink?

TRIGORIN.   Haven't you had enough?

MASHA.   Fiddlesticks! [*She fills a glass*] Don't look at me with that expression on your face. Women drink oftener than you imagine, but most of them do it in secret, and not openly, as I do. They do indeed, and it is always either vodka or brandy. [*They touch glasses*] To your good health! You are so easy to get on with that I am sorry to see you go. [*They drink.*]

TRIGORIN.   And I am sorry to leave.

MASHA.   You should ask her to stay.

TRIGORIN.   She would not do that now. Her son has been behaving outrageously. First he attempted suicide, and now I hear he is

148

going to challenge me to a duel, though what his provocation may be I can't imagine. He is always sulking and sneering and preaching about a new form of art, as if the field of art were not large enough to accommodate both old and new without the necessity of jostling.

MASHA. It is jealousy. However, that is none of my business. [*Pause.* JACOB *walks through the room carrying a trunk;* NINA *comes in and stands by the window*] That school-teacher of mine is none too clever, but he is very good, poor man, and he loves me dearly, and I am sorry for him. However, let me say good-bye and wish you a pleasant journey. Remember me kindly in your thoughts. [*She shakes hands with him*] Thanks for your goodwill. Send me your books, and be sure to write something in them; nothing formal, but simply this: "To Masha, who, forgetful of her origin, for some unknown reason is living in this world." Good-bye. [*She goes out.*]

NINA [*holding out her closed hand to* TRIGORIN]. Is it odd or even?

TRIGORIN. Even.

NINA [*with a sigh*]. No, it is odd. I had only one pea in my hand. I wanted to see whether I was to become an actress or not. If only some one would advise me what to do!

TRIGORIN. One cannot give advice in a case like this [*pause*].

NINA. We shall soon part, perhaps never to meet again. I should like you to accept this little medallion as a remembrance of me. I have had your initials engraved on it, and on this side is the name of one of your books: "Days and Nights."

TRIGORIN. How sweet of you! [*He kisses the medallion*] It is a lovely present.

NINA. Think of me sometimes.

TRIGORIN. I shall never forget you. I shall always remember you as I saw you that bright day—do you recall it?—a week ago, when you wore your light dress, and we talked together, and the white sea gull lay on the bench beside us.

NINA [*lost in thought*]. Yes, the sea gull. [*Pause*] I beg you to let me see you alone for two minutes before you go.

[*She goes out to the left. At the same moment* ARKADINA *comes in from the right, followed by* SORIN *in a long coat, with his orders on his breast, and by* JACOB, *who is busy packing.*]

ARKADINA. Stay here at home, you poor old man. How could you pay visits with that rheumatism of yours? [*To* TRIGORIN] Who left the room just now, was it Nina?

TRIGORIN. Yes.

ARKADINA. I beg your pardon; I am afraid we interrupted you.

[*She sits down*] I think everything is packed. I am absolutely exhausted.

TRIGORIN [*reading the inscription on the medallion*]. "Days and Nights, page 121, lines 11 and 12."

JACOB [*clearing the table*]. Shall I pack your fishing-rods, too, sir?

TRIGORIN. Yes, I shall need them, but you can give my books away.

JACOB. Very well, sir.

TRIGORIN [*to himself*]. Page 121, lines 11 and 12. [*To* ARKADINA] Have we my books here in the house?

ARKADINA. Yes, they are in my brother's library, in the corner cupboard.

TRIGORIN. Page 121— [*He goes out.*]

SORIN. You are going away, and I shall be lonely without you.

ARKADINA. What would you do in town?

SORIN. Oh, nothing in particular, but somehow—[*He laughs*] They are soon to lay the corner-stone of the new court-house here. How I should like to leap out of this minnow-pond, if but for an hour or two! I am tired of lying here like an old cigarette stump. I have ordered the carriage for one o'clock. We can go away together.

ARKADINA [*after a pause*]. No, you must stay here. Don't be lonely, and don't catch cold. Keep an eye on my boy. Take good care of him; guide him along the proper paths. [*Pause*] I am going away, and so shall never find out why Constantine shot himself, but I think the chief reason was jealousy, and the sooner I take Trigorin away, the better.

SORIN. There were—how shall I explain it to you?—other reasons besides jealousy for his act. Here is a clever young chap living in the depths of the country, without money or position, with no future ahead of him, and with nothing to do. He is ashamed and afraid of being so idle. I am devoted to him and he is fond of me, but nevertheless he feels that he is useless here, that he is little more than a dependant in this house. It is the pride in him.

ARKADINA. He is a misery to me! [*Thoughtfully*] He might possibly enter the army.

SORIN [*gives a whistle, and then speaks with hesitation*]. It seems to me that the best thing for him would be if you were to let him have a little money. For one thing, he ought to be allowed to dress like a human being. See how he looks! Wearing the same little old coat that he has had for three years, and he doesn't even possess an overcoat! [*Laughing*] And it wouldn't hurt the youngster to sow a few wild oats; let him go abroad, say, for a time. It wouldn't cost much.

ARKADINA. Yes, but— However, I think I might manage about

his clothes, but I couldn't let him go abroad. And no, I don't think I can let him have his clothes even, now. [*Decidedly*] I have no money at present.

[SORIN *laughs.*]

ARKADINA.   I haven't indeed.

SORIN [*whistles*].   Very well. Forgive me, darling; don't be angry. You are a noble, generous woman!

ARKADINA [*weeping*].   I really haven't the money.

SORIN.   If I had any money of course I should let him have some myself, but I haven't even a penny. The farm manager takes my pension from me and puts it all into the farm or into cattle or bees, and in that way it is always lost for ever. The bees die, the cows die, they never let me have a horse.

ARKADINA.   Of course I have some money, but I am an actress and my expenses for dress alone are enough to bankrupt me.

SORIN.   You are a dear, and I am very fond of you, indeed I am. But something is the matter with me again. [*He staggers*] I feel giddy. [*He leans against the table*] I feel faint, and all.

ARKADINA [*frightened*].   Peter! [*She tries to support him*] Peter! dearest! [*She calls*] Help! Help!

[TREPLIEFF *and* MEDVIEDENKO *come in;* TREPLIEFF *has a bandage around his head.*]

ARKADINA.   He is fainting!

SORIN.   I am all right. [*He smiles and drinks some water*] It is all over now.

TREPLIEFF [*to his mother*].   Don't be frightened, mother, these attacks are not dangerous; my uncle often has them now. [*To his uncle*] You must go and lie down, Uncle.

SORIN.   Yes, I think I shall, for a few minutes. I am going to Moscow all the same, but I shall lie down a bit before I start. [*He goes out leaning on his cane.*]

MEDVIEDENKO [*giving him his arm*].   Do you know this riddle? On four legs in the morning; on two legs at noon; and on three legs in the evening?

SORIN [*laughing*].   Yes, exactly, and on one's back at night. Thank you, I can walk alone.

MEDVIEDENKO.   Dear me, what formality! [*He and* SORIN *go out.*]

ARKADINA.   He gave me a dreadful fright.

TREPLIEFF.   It is not good for him to live in the country. Mother, if you would only untie your purse-strings for once, and lend him a thousand rubles! He could then spend a whole year in town.

ARKADINA.   I have no money. I am an actress and not a banker.
[*Pause*]

TREPLIEFF.   Please change my bandage for me, mother, you do it so gently.

[ARKADINA *goes to the cupboard and takes out a box of bandages and a bottle of iodoform.*]

ARKADINA.   The doctor is late.

TREPLIEFF.   Yes, he promised to be here at nine, and now it is noon already.

ARKADINA.   Sit down. [*She takes the bandage off his head*] You look as if you had a turban on. A stranger that was in the kitchen yesterday asked to what nationality you belonged. Your wound is almost healed. [*She kisses his head*] You won't be up to any more of these silly tricks again, will you, when I am gone?

TREPLIEFF.   No, mother. I did that in a moment of insane despair, when I had lost all control over myself. It will never happen again. [*He kisses her hand*] Your touch is golden. I remember when you were still acting at the State Theater, long ago, when I was still a little chap, there was a fight one day in our court, and a poor washerwoman was almost beaten to death. She was picked up unconscious, and you nursed her till she was well, and bathed her children in the washtubs. Have you forgotten it?

ARKADINA.   Yes, entirely. [*She puts on a new bandage.*]

TREPLIEFF.   Two ballet dancers lived in the same house, and they used to come and drink coffee with you.

ARKADINA.   I remember that.

TREPLIEFF.   They were very pious. [*Pause*] I love you again, these last few days, as tenderly and trustingly as I did as a child. I have no one left me now but you. Why, why do you let yourself be controlled by that man?

ARKADINA.   You don't understand him, Constantine. He has a wonderfully noble personality.

TREPLIEFF.   Nevertheless, when he has been told that I wish to challenge him to a duel his nobility does not prevent him from playing the coward. He is about to beat an ignominious retreat.

ARKADINA.   What nonsense! I have asked him myself to go.

TREPLIEFF.   A noble personality indeed! Here we are almost quarrelling over him, and he is probably in the garden laughing at us at this very moment, or else enlightening Nina's mind and trying to persuade her into thinking him a man of genius.

ARKADINA.   You enjoy saying unpleasant things to me. I have the greatest respect for that man, and I must ask you not to speak ill of him in my presence.

TREPLIEFF.   I have no respect for him at all. You want me to think him a genius, as you do, but I refuse to lie: his books make me sick.

ARKADINA.   You envy him. There is nothing left for people with no talent and mighty pretensions to do but to criticize those who are really gifted. I hope you enjoy the consolation it brings.

TREPLIEFF [*with irony*].   Those who are really gifted, indeed! [*Angrily*] I am cleverer than any of you, if it comes to that! [*He tears the bandage off his head*] You are the slaves of convention, you have seized the upper hand and now lay down as law everything that you do; all else you strangle and trample on. I refuse to accept your point of view, yours and his, I refuse!

ARKADINA.   That is the talk of a decadent.

TREPLIEFF.   Go back to your beloved stage and act the miserable ditch-water plays you so much admire!

ARKADINA.   I never acted in a play like that in my life. You couldn't write even the trashiest music-hall farce, you idle good-for-nothing!

TREPLIEFF.   Miser!

ARKADINA.   Rag bag!

[TREPLIEFF *sits down and begins to cry softly.*]

ARKADINA [*walking up and down in great excitement*].   Don't cry! You mustn't cry! [*She bursts into tears*] You really mustn't. [*She kisses his forehead, his cheeks, his head*] My darling child, forgive me. Forgive your wicked mother.

TREPLIEFF [*embracing her*].   Oh, if you could only know what it is to have lost everything under heaven! She does not love me. I see I shall never be able to write. Every hope has deserted me.

ARKADINA.   Don't despair. This will all pass. He is going away to-day, and she will love you once more. [*She wipes away his tears*] Stop crying. We have made peace again.

TREPLIEFF [*kissing her hand*].   Yes, mother.

ARKADINA [*tenderly*].   Make your peace with him, too. Don't fight with him. You surely won't fight?

TREPLIEFF.   I won't, but you must not insist on my seeing him again, mother, I couldn't stand it. [TRIGORIN *comes in.*] There he is; I am going. [*He quickly puts the medicines away in the cupboard*] The doctor will attend to my head.

TRIGORIN [*looking through the pages of a book*].   Page 121, lines 11 and 12; here it is. [*He reads*] "If at any time you should have need of my life, come and take it."

[TREPLIEFF *picks up the bandage off the floor and goes out.*]

ARKADINA [*looking at her watch*].   The carriage will soon be here.

TRIGORIN [*to himself*].   If at any time you should have need of my life, come and take it.

ARKADINA.   I hope your things are all packed.

TRIGORIN [*impatiently*].   Yes, yes. [*In deep thought*] Why do I hear a note of sadness that wrings my heart in this cry of a pure soul? If at any time you should have need of my life, come and take it. [*To* ARKADINA] Let us stay here one more day!

[ARKADINA *shakes her head.*]

TRIGORIN.   Do let us stay!

ARKADINA.   I know, dearest, what keeps you here, but you must control yourself. Be sober; your emotions have intoxicated you a little.

TRIGORIN.   You must be sober, too. Be sensible; look upon what has happened as a true friend would. [*Taking her hand*] You are capable of self-sacrifice. Be a friend to me and release me!

ARKADINA [*in deep excitement*].   Are you so much in love?

TRIGORIN.   I am irresistibly impelled toward her. It may be that this is just what I need.

ARKADINA.   What, the love of a country girl? Oh, how little you know yourself!

TRIGORIN.   People sometimes walk in their sleep, and so I feel as if I were asleep, and dreaming of her as I stand here talking to you. My imagination is shaken by the sweetest and most glorious visions. Release me!

ARKADINA [*shuddering*].   No, no! I am only an ordinary woman; you must not say such things to me. Do not torment me, Boris; you frighten me.

TRIGORIN.   You could be an extraordinary woman if you only would. Love alone can bring happiness on earth, love the enchanting, the poetical love of youth, that sweeps away the sorrows of the world. I had no time for it when I was young and struggling with want and laying siege to the literary fortress, but now at last this love has come to me. I see it beckoning; why should I fly?

ARKADINA [*with anger*].   You are mad!

TRIGORIN.   Release me.

ARKADINA.   You have all conspired together to torture me today. [*She weeps.*]

TRIGORIN [*clutching his head desperately*].   She doesn't understand me! She won't understand me!

ARKADINA.   Am I then so old and ugly already that you can talk to me like this without any shame about another woman? [*She embraces and kisses him*] Oh, you have lost your senses! My splendid, my glorious friend, my love for you is the last chapter of my life. [*She falls on her knees*] You are my pride, my joy, my light. [*She embraces his knees*] I could never endure it should you desert me, if only for an hour; I should go mad. Oh, my wonder, my marvel, my king!

TRIGORIN.   Some one might come in. [*He helps her to rise.*]

ARKADINA.   Let them come! I am not ashamed of my love. [*She kisses his hands*] My jewel! My despair! You want to do a foolish thing, but I don't want you to do it. I shan't let you do it! [*She laughs*] You are mine, you are mine! This forehead is mine, these eyes are mine, this silky hair is mine. All your being is mine. You are so clever, so wise, the first of all living writers; you are the only hope of your country. You are so fresh, so simple, so deeply humorous. You can bring out every feature of a man or of a landscape in a single line, and your characters live and breathe. Do you think that these words are but the incense of flattery? Do you think I am not speaking the truth? Come, look into my eyes; look deep; do you find lies there? No, you see that I alone know how to treasure you. I alone tell you the truth. Oh, my very dear, you will go with me? You will? You will not forsake me?

TRIGORIN.   I have no will of my own; I never had. I am too indolent, too submissive, too phlegmatic, to have any. Is it possible that women like that? Take me. Take me away with you, but do not let me stir a step from your side.

ARKADINA [*to herself*].   Now he is mine! [*Carelessly, as if nothing unusual had happened*] Of course you must stay here if you really want to. I shall go, and you can follow in a week's time. Yes, really, why should you hurry away?

TRIGORIN.   Let us go together.

ARKADINA.   As you like. Let us go together then. [*Pause.* TRIGORIN *writes something in his note-book*] What are you writing?

TRIGORIN.   A happy expression I heard this morning: "A grove of maiden pines." It may be useful. [*He yawns*] So we are really off again, condemned once more to railway carriages, to stations and restaurants, to Hamburger steaks and endless arguments!

[SHAMRAEFF *comes in.*]

SHAMRAEFF.   I am sorry to have to inform you that your carriage is at the door. It is time to start, honored madam, the train leaves at two-five. Would you be kind enough, madam, to remember to inquire for me where Suzdaltzeff the actor is now? Is he still alive, I wonder? Is he well? He and I have had many a jolly time together. He was inimitable in "The Stolen Mail." A tragedian called Izmailoff was in the same company, I remember, who was also quite remarkable. Don't hurry, madam, you still have five minutes. They were both of them conspirators once, in the same melodrama, and one night when in the course of the play they were suddenly discovered, instead of saying "We have been trapped!" Izmailoff cried out: "We have been rapped!" [*He laughs*] Rapped!

[*While he has been talking* JACOB *has been busy with the trunks, and the maid has brought* ARKADINA *her hat, coat, parasol, and gloves. The cook looks hesitatingly through the door on the right, and finally comes into the room.* PAULINA *comes in.* MEDVIEDENKO *comes in.*]

PAULINA [*presenting* ARKADINA *with a little basket*].   Here are some plums for the journey. They are very sweet ones. You may want to nibble something good on the way.

ARKADINA.   You are very kind, Paulina.

PAULINA.   Good-bye, my dearie. If things have not been quite as you could have wished, please forgive us. [*She weeps.*]

ARKADINA.   It has been delightful, delightful. You mustn't cry.

[SORIN *comes in through the door on the left, dressed in a long coat with a cape, and carrying his hat and cane. He crosses the room.*]

SORIN.   Come, sister, it is time to start, unless you want to miss the train. I am going to get into the carriage. [*He goes out.*]

MEDVIEDENKO.   I shall walk quickly to the station and see you off there. [*He goes out.*]

ARKADINA.   Good-bye, all! We shall meet again next summer if we live. [*The maid servant,* JACOB, *and the cook kiss her hand*] Don't forget me. [*She gives the cook a ruble*] There is a ruble for all three of you.

THE COOK.   Thank you, mistress; a pleasant journey to you.

JACOB.   God bless you, mistress.

SHAMRAEFF.   Send us a line to cheer us up. [*To* TRIGORIN] Good-bye, sir.

ARKADINA.   Where is Constantine? Tell him I am starting. I must say good-bye to him. [*To* JACOB] I gave the cook a ruble for all three of you.

[*All go out through the door on the right. The stage remains empty. Sounds of farewell are heard. The maid comes running back to fetch the basket of plums which has been forgotten.* TRIGORIN *comes back.*]

TRIGORIN.   I had forgotten my cane. I think I left it on the terrace. [*He goes toward the door on the right and meets* NINA, *who comes in at that moment*] Is that you? We are off.

NINA.   I knew we should meet again. [*With emotion*] I have come to an irrevocable decision, the die is cast: I am going on the stage. I am deserting my father and abandoning everything. I am beginning life anew. I am going, as you are, to Moscow. We shall meet there.

TRIGORIN [*glancing about him*].   Go to the Hotel Slavianski Bazar. Let me know as soon as you get there. I shall be at the Grosholski House in Moltchanofka Street. I must go now. [*Pause*]

NINA.   Just one more minute!

TRIGORIN [*in a low voice*].   You are so beautiful! What bliss to think that I shall see you again so soon! [*She sinks on his breast*] I shall see those glorious eyes again, that wonderful, ineffably tender smile, those gentle features with their expression of angelic purity! My darling! [*A prolonged kiss.*]

CURTAIN.

Two years elapse between the third and fourth acts.

ACT IV

The sitting-room in SORIN's *house, which has been converted into a writing-room for* TREPLIEFF. *To the right and left are doors leading into inner rooms, and in the center is a glass door opening onto a terrace. Besides the usual furniture of a sitting-room there is a writing-desk in the right-hand corner of the room. There is a Turkish divan near the door on the left, and shelves full of books stand against the walls. Books are lying scattered about on the window-sills and chairs. It is evening. The room is dimly lighted by a shaded lamp on a table. The wind moans in the tree tops and whistles down the chimney. The watchman in the garden is heard sounding his rattle.* MEDVIEDENKO *and* MASHA *come in.*

MASHA [*calling* TREPLIEFF]. Mr. Constantine, where are you? [*Looking about her*] There is no one here. His old uncle is forever asking for Constantine, and can't live without him for an instant.

MEDVIEDENKO. He dreads being left alone. [*Listening to the wind*] This is a wild night. We have had this storm for two days.

MASHA [*turning up the lamp*]. The waves on the lake are enormous.

MEDVIEDENKO. It is very dark in the garden. Do you know, I think that old theater ought to be knocked down. It is still standing there, naked and hideous as a skeleton, with the curtain flapping in the wind. I thought I heard a voice weeping in it as I passed there last night.

MASHA. What an idea! [*Pause*]

MEDVIEDENKO. Come home with me, Masha.

MASHA [*shaking her head*]. I shall spend the night here.

MEDVIEDENKO [*imploringly*]. Do come, Masha. The baby must be hungry.

MASHA. Nonsense, Matriona will feed it. [*Pause*]

MEDVIEDENKO. It is a pity to leave him three nights without his mother.

MASHA. You are getting too tiresome. You used sometimes to talk of other things besides home and the baby, home and the baby. That is all I ever hear from you now.

MEDVIEDENKO.   Come home, Masha.

MASHA.   You can go home if you want to.

MEDVIEDENKO.   Your father won't give me a horse.

MASHA.   Yes, he will; ask him.

MEDVIEDENKO.   I think I shall. Are you coming home to-morrow?

MASHA.   Yes, yes, to-morrow.

[*She takes snuff.* TREPLIEFF *and* PAULINA *come in.* TREPLIEFF *is carrying some pillows and a blanket, and* PAULINA *is carrying sheets and pillow cases. They lay them on the divan, and* TREPLIEFF *goes and sits down at his desk.*]

MASHA.   Who is that for, mother?

PAULINA.   Mr. Sorin asked to sleep in Constantine's room to-night.

MASHA.   Let me make the bed.

[*She makes the bed.* PAULINA *goes up to the desk and looks at the manuscripts lying on it. Pause*]

MEDVIEDENKO.   Well, I am going. Good-bye, Masha. [*He kisses his wife's hand*] Good-bye, mother. [*He tries to kiss his mother-in-law's hand.*]

PAULINA [*crossly*].   Be off, in God's name!

[TREPLIEFF *shakes hands with him in silence, and* MEDVIEDENKO *goes out.*]

PAULINA [*looking at the manuscripts*].   No one ever dreamed, Constantine, that you would one day turn into a real author. The magazines pay you well for your stories. [*She strokes his hair.*] You have grown handsome, too. Dear, kind Constantine, be a little nicer to my Masha.

MASHA [*still making the bed*].   Leave him alone, mother.

PAULINA.   She is a sweet child. [*Pause*] A woman, Constantine, asks only for kind looks. I know that from experience.

[TREPLIEFF *gets up from his desk and goes out without a word.*]

MASHA.   There now! You have vexed him. I told you not to bother him.

PAULINA.   I am sorry for you, Masha.

MASHA.   Much I need your pity!

PAULINA.   My heart aches for you, Masha. I see how things are, and understand.

MASHA.   You see what doesn't exist. Hopeless love is only found in novels. It is a trifle; all one has to do is to keep a tight rein on oneself, and keep one's head clear. Love must be plucked out the moment it springs up in the heart. My husband has been promised a school in another district, and when we have once left this place I shall forget it all. I shall tear my passion out by the roots. [*The notes of a melancholy waltz are heard in the distance.*]

PAULINA.   Constantine is playing. That means he is sad.

[MASHA *silently waltzes a few turns to the music.*]

MASHA.   The great thing, mother, is not to have him continually in sight. If my Simon could only get his remove I should forget it all in a month or two. It is a trifle.

[DORN *and* MEDVIEDENKO *come in through the door on the left, wheeling* SORIN *in an arm-chair.*]

MEDVIEDENKO.   I have six mouths to feed now, and flour is at seventy kopecks.

DORN.   A hard riddle to solve!

MEDVIEDENKO.   It is easy for you to make light of it. You are rich enough to scatter money to your chickens, if you wanted to.

DORN.   You think I am rich? My friend, after practicing for thirty years, during which I could not call my soul my own for one minute of the night or day, I succeeded at last in scraping together one thousand rubles, all of which went, not long ago, in a trip which I took abroad. I haven't a penny.

MASHA [*to her husband*].   So you didn't go home after all?

MEDVIEDENKO [*apologetically*].   How can I go home when they won't give me a horse?

MASHA [*under her breath, with bitter anger*].   Would I might never see your face again!

[SORIN *in his chair is wheeled to the left-hand side of the room.* PAULINA, MASHA, *and* DORN *sit down beside him.* MEDVIEDENKO *stands sadly aside.*]

DORN.   What a lot of changes you have made here! You have turned this sitting-room into a library.

MASHA.   Constantine likes to work in this room, because from it he can step out into the garden to meditate whenever he feels like it. [*The watchman's rattle is heard.*]

SORIN.   Where is my sister?

DORN.   She has gone to the station to meet Trigorin. She will soon be back.

SORIN.   I must be dangerously ill if you had to send for my sister.

[*He falls silent for a moment*] A nice business this is! Here I am dangerously ill, and you won't even give me any medicine.

DORN.   What shall I prescribe for you? Camomile tea? Soda?
Quinine?

SORIN.   Don't inflict any of your discussions on me again. [*He
nods toward the sofa*] Is that bed for me?

PAULINA.   Yes, for you, sir.

SORIN.   Thank you.

DORN [*sings*].   "The moon swims in the sky to-night."

SORIN.   I am going to give Constantine an idea for a story. It shall
be called "The Man Who Wished—*L'Homme qui a voulu*." When I
was young, I wished to become an author; I failed. I wished to be an
orator; I speak abominably, [*Exciting himself*] with my eternal "and all,
and all," dragging each sentence on and on until I sometimes break
out into a sweat all over. I wished to marry, and I didn't; I wished to
live in the city, and here I am ending my days in the country, and
all.

DORN.   You wished to become State Councillor, and—you are
one!

SORIN [*laughing*].   I didn't try for that, it came of its own accord.

DORN.   Come, you must admit that it is petty to cavil at life at
sixty-two years of age.

SORIN.   You are pig-headed! Can't you see I want to live?

DORN.   That is futile. Nature has commanded that every life shall
come to an end.

SORIN.   You speak like a man who is satiated with life. Your
thirst for it is quenched, and so you are calm and indifferent, but even
you dread death.

DORN.   The fear of death is an animal passion which must be
overcome. Only those who believe in a future life and tremble for
sins committed, can logically fear death; but you, for one thing, don't
believe in a future life, and for another, you haven't committed any
sins. You have served as a Councillor for twenty-five years, that is
all.

SORIN [*laughing*].   Twenty-eight years!

[TREPLIEFF *comes in and sits down on a stool at* SORIN's *feet*. MASHA
    fixes her eyes on his face and never once tears them away.]

DORN.   We are keeping Constantine from his work.

TREPLIEFF.   No matter. [*Pause*]

MEDVIEDENKO.   Of all the cities you visited when you were
abroad, Doctor, which one did you like the best?

DORN.   Genoa.

TREPLIEFF.   Why Genoa?

DORN.   Because there is such a splendid crowd in its streets. When you leave the hotel in the evening, and throw yourself into the heart of that throng, and move with it without aim or object, swept along, hither and thither, their life seems to be yours, their soul flows into you, and you begin to believe at last in a great world spirit, like the one in your play that Nina Zarietchnaya acted. By the way, where is Nina now? Is she well?

TREPLIEFF.   I believe so.

DORN.   I hear she has led rather a strange life; what happened?

TREPLIEFF.   It is a long story, Doctor.

DORN.   Tell it shortly. [*Pause*]

TREPLIEFF.   She ran away from home and joined Trigorin; you know that?

DORN.   Yes.

TREPLIEFF.   She had a child that died. Trigorin soon tired of her and returned to his former ties, as might have been expected. He had never broken them, indeed, but out of weakness of character had always vacillated between the two. As far as I can make out from what I have heard, Nina's domestic life has not been altogether a success.

DORN.   What about her acting?

TREPLIEFF.   I believe she made an even worse failure of that. She made her debut on the stage of the Summer Theater in Moscow, and afterward made a tour of the country towns. At that time I never let her out of my sight, and wherever she went I followed. She always attempted great and difficult parts, but her delivery was harsh and monotonous, and her gestures heavy and crude. She shrieked and died well at times, but those were but moments.

DORN.   Then she really has a talent for acting?

TREPLIEFF.   I never could make out. I believe she has. I saw her, but she refused to see me, and her servant would never admit me to her rooms. I appreciated her feelings, and did not insist upon a meeting. [*Pause*] What more can I tell you? She sometimes writes to me now that I have come home, such clever, sympathetic letters, full of warm feeling. She never complains, but I can tell that she is profoundly unhappy; not a line but speaks to me of an aching, breaking nerve. She has one strange fancy; she always signs herself "The Sea Gull." The miller in "Rusalka" called himself "The Crow," and so she repeats in all her letters that she is a sea gull. She is here now.

DORN.   What do you mean by "here?"

TREPLIEFF.   In the village, at the inn. She has been there for five days. I should have gone to see her, but Masha here went, and she refuses to see any one. Some one told me she had been seen wandering in the fields a mile from here yesterday evening.

MEDVIEDENKO.   Yes, I saw her. She was walking away from here in the direction of the village. I asked her why she had not been to see us. She said she would come.

TREPLIEFF.   But she won't. [*Pause*] Her father and stepmother have disowned her. They have even put watchmen all around their estate to keep her away. [*He goes with the doctor toward the desk*] How easy it is, Doctor, to be a philosopher on paper, and how difficult in real life!

SORIN.   She was a beautiful girl. Even the State Councillor himself was in love with her for a time.

DORN.   You old Lovelace, you!

[SHAMRAEFF's *laugh is heard.*]

PAULINA.   They are coming back from the station.

TREPLIEFF.   Yes, I hear my mother's voice.

[ARKADINA *and* TRIGORIN *come in, followed by* SHAMRAEFF.]

SHAMRAEFF.   We all grow old and wither, my lady, while you alone, with your light dress, your gay spirits, and your grace, keep the secret of eternal youth.

ARKADINA.   You are still trying to turn my head, you tiresome old man.

TRIGORIN [*to* SORIN].   How do you do, Peter? What, still ill? How silly of you! [*With evident pleasure, as he catches sight of* MASHA] How are you, Miss Masha?

MASHA.   So you recognized me? [*She shakes hands with him.*]

TRIGORIN.   Did you marry him?

MASHA.   Long ago.

TRIGORIN.   You are happy now? [*He bows to* DORN *and* MEDVIEDENKO, *and then goes hesitatingly toward* TREPLIEFF] Your mother says you have forgotten the past and are no longer angry with me.

[TREPLIEFF *gives him his hand.*]

ARKADINA [*to her son*].   Here is a magazine that Boris has brought you with your latest story in it.

TREPLIEFF [*to* TRIGORIN, *as he takes the magazine*].   Many thanks; you are very kind.

TRIGORIN.   Your admirers all send you their regards. Every one in Moscow and St. Petersburg is interested in you, and all ply me with questions about you. They ask me what you look like, how old you are, whether you are fair or dark. For some reason they all think that you are no longer young, and no one knows who you are, as you always write under an assumed name. You are as great a mystery as the Man in the Iron Mask.

TREPLIEFF.   Do you expect to be here long?

TRIGORIN.   No, I must go back to Moscow to-morrow. I am finishing another novel, and have promised something to a magazine besides. In fact, it is the same old business.

[*During their conversation* ARKADINA *and* PAULINA *have put up a card-table in the center of the room;* SHAMRAEFF *lights the candles and arranges the chairs, then fetches a box of lotto from the cupboard.*]

TRIGORIN.   The weather has given me a rough welcome. The wind is frightful. If it goes down by morning I shall go fishing in the lake, and shall have a look at the garden and the spot—do you remember?—where your play was given. I remember the piece very well, but should like to see again where the scene was laid.

MASHA [*to her father*]   Father, do please let my husband have a horse. He ought to go home.

SHAMRAEFF [*angrily*].   A horse to go home with! [*Sternly*] You know the horses have just been to the station. I can't send them out again.

MASHA.   But there are other horses. [*Seeing that her father remains silent*] You are impossible!

MEDVIEDENKO.   I shall go on foot, Masha.

PAULINA [*with a sigh*].   On foot in this weather? [*She takes a seat at the card-table*] Shall we begin?

MEDVIEDENKO.   It is only six miles. Good-bye. [*He kisses his wife's hand*] Good-bye, mother. [*His mother-in-law gives him her hand unwillingly*] I should not have troubled you all, but the baby— [*He bows to every one*] Good-bye. [*He goes out with an apologetic air.*]

SHAMRAEFF.   He will get there all right, he is not a major-general.

PAULINA.   Come, let us begin. Don't let us waste time, we shall soon be called to supper.

[SHAMRAEFF, MASHA, *and* DORN *sit down at the card-table.*]

ARKADINA [*to* TRIGORIN].   When the long autumn evenings descend on us we while away the time here by playing lotto. Look at this old set; we used it when our mother played with us as children. Don't you want to take a hand in the game with us until supper time? [*She and* TRIGORIN *sit down at the table*] It is a monotonous game, but it is all right when one gets used to it. [*She deals three cards to each of the players.*]

TREPLIEFF [*looking through the pages of the magazine*].   He has read his own story, and hasn't even cut the pages of mine. [*He lays the magazine on his desk and goes toward the door on the right, stopping as he passes his mother to give her a kiss.*]

ARKADINA.   Won't you play, Constantine?

TREPLIEFF.   No, excuse me please, I don't feel like it. I am going to take a turn through the rooms. [*He goes out.*]

MASHA.   Are you all ready? I shall begin: twenty-two.

ARKADINA.   Here it is.

MASHA.   Three.

DORN.   Right.

MASHA.   Have you put down three? Eight. Eighty-one. Ten.

SHAMRAEFF.   Don't go so fast.

ARKADINA.   Could you believe it? I am still dazed by the reception they gave me in Kharkoff.

MASHA.   Thirty-four. [*The notes of a melancholy waltz are heard.*]

ARKADINA.   The students gave me an ovation; they sent me three baskets of flowers, a wreath, and this thing here. [*She unclasps a brooch from her breast and lays it on the table.*]

SHAMRAEFF.   There is something worth while!

MASHA.   Fifty.

DORN.   Fifty, did you say?

ARKADINA. I wore a perfectly magnificent dress; I am no fool when it comes to clothes.

PAULINA.   Constantine is playing again; the poor boy is sad.

SHAMRAEFF.   He has been severely criticized in the papers.

MASHA.   Seventy-seven.

ARKADINA.   They want to attract attention to him.

TRIGORIN.   He doesn't seem able to make a success, he can't somehow strike the right note. There is an odd vagueness about his writings that sometimes verges on delirium. He has never created a single living character.

MASHA.   Eleven.

ARKADINA.   Are you bored, Peter? [*Pause*] He is asleep.

DORN.   The Councillor is taking a nap.

MASHA.   Seven. Ninety.

TRIGORIN.   Do you think I should write if I lived in such a place as this, on the shore of this lake? Never! I should overcome my passion, and give my life up to the catching of fish.

MASHA.   Twenty-eight.

TRIGORIN.   And if I caught a perch or a bass, what bliss it would be!

DORN.   I have great faith in Constantine. I know there is something in him. He thinks in images; his stories are vivid and full of color, and always affect me deeply. It is only a pity that he has no definite object in view. He creates impressions, and nothing more, and one cannot go far on impressions alone. Are you glad, madam, that you have an author for a son?

ARKADINA.   Just think, I have never read anything of his; I never have time.

MASHA.   Twenty-six.

[TREPLIEFF *comes in quietly and sits down at his table.*]

SHAMRAEFF [*to* TRIGORIN].   We have something here that belongs to you, sir.

TRIGORIN.   What is it?

SHAMRAEFF.   You told me to have the sea gull stuffed that Mr. Constantine killed some time ago.

TRIGORIN.   Did I? [*Thoughtfully*] I don't remember.

MASHA.   Sixty-one. One.

[TREPLIEFF *throws open the window and stands listening.*]

TREPLIEFF.   How dark the night is! I wonder what makes me so restless.

ARKADINA.   Shut the window, Constantine, there is a draught here.

[TREPLIEFF *shuts the window.*]

MASHA.   Ninety-eight.

TRIGORIN.   See, my card is full.

ARKADINA [*gaily*].   Bravo! Bravo!

SHAMRAEFF.   Bravo!

ARKADINA.   Wherever he goes and whatever he does, that man always has good luck. [*She gets up*] And now, come to supper. Our renowned guest did not have any dinner to-day. We can continue our game later. [*To her son*] Come, Constantine, leave your writing and come to supper.

TREPLIEFF.   I don't want anything to eat, mother; I am not hungry.

ARKADINA.   As you please. [*She wakes* SORIN] Come to supper, Peter. [*She takes* SHAMRAEFF's *arm*] Let me tell you about my reception in Kharkoff.

[PAULINA *blows out the candles on the table, then she and* DORN *roll* SORIN'*s chair out of the room, and all go out through the door on the left, except* TREPLIEFF, *who is left alone.* TREPLIEFF *prepares to write. He runs his eye over what he has already written.*]

TREPLIEFF.   I have talked a great deal about new forms of art, but I feel myself gradually slipping into the beaten track. [*He reads*] "The placard cried it from the wall—a pale face in a frame of dusky hair"— cried—frame—that is stupid. [*He scratches out what he has written*] I shall begin again from the place where my hero is wakened by the noise of the rain, but what follows must go. This description of a moonlight night is long and stilted. Trigorin has worked out a process of his own, and descriptions are easy for him. He writes that the neck of a broken bottle lying on the bank glittered in the moonlight, and that the shadows lay black under the mill-wheel. There you have a moon-light night before your eyes, but I speak of the shimmering light, the twinkling stars, the distant sounds of a piano melting into the still and scented air, and the result is abominable. [*Pause*] The conviction is gradually forcing itself upon me that good literature is not a question of forms new or old, but of ideas that must pour freely from the au-thor's heart, without his bothering his head about any forms whatso-ever. [*A knock is heard at the window nearest the table*] What was that? [*He looks out of the window*] I can't see anything. [*He opens the glass door and looks out into the garden*] I heard some one run down the steps. [*He calls*] Who is there? [*He goes out, and is heard walking quickly along the terrace. In a few minutes he comes back with* NINA ZARIETCHNAYA] Oh, Nina, Nina!

[NINA *lays her head on* TREPLIEFF'*s breast and stifles her sobs.*]

TREPLIEFF [*deeply moved*].   Nina, Nina! It is you—you! I felt you would come; all day my heart has been aching for you. [*He takes off her hat and cloak*] My darling, my beloved has come back to me! We mustn't cry, we mustn't cry.

NINA.   There is some one here.

TREPLIEFF.   No one is here.

NINA.   Lock the door, some one might come.

TREPLIEFF.   No one will come in.

NINA.   I know your mother is here. Lock the door.

[TREPLIEFF *locks the door on the right and comes back to* NINA.]

TREPLIEFF.   There is no lock on that one. I shall put a chair against it. [*He puts an arm-chair against the door*] Don't be frightened, no one shall come in.

NINA [*gazing intently into his face*]. Let me look at you. [*She looks about her*] It is warm and comfortable in here. This used to be a sitting-room. Have I changed much?

TREPLIEFF. Yes, you have grown thinner, and your eyes are larger than they were. Nina, it seems so strange to see you! Why didn't you let me go to you? Why didn't you come sooner to me? You have been here nearly a week, I know. I have been several times each day to where you live, and have stood like a beggar beneath your window.

NINA. I was afraid you might hate me. I dream every night that you look at me without recognising me. I have been wandering about on the shores of the lake ever since I came back. I have often been near your house, but I have never had the courage to come in. Let us sit down. [*They sit down*] Let us sit down and talk our hearts out. It is so quiet and warm in here. Do you hear the wind whistling outside? As Turgenieff says, "Happy is he who can sit at night under the roof of his home, who has a warm corner in which to take refuge." I am a sea gull—and yet—no. [*She passes her hand across her forehead*] What was I saying? Oh, yes, Turgenieff. He says, "and God help all houseless wanderers." [*She sobs.*]

TREPLIEFF. Nina! You are crying again, Nina!

NINA. It is all right. I shall feel better after this. I have not cried for two years. I went into the garden last night to see if our old theater were still standing. I see it is. I wept there for the first time in two years, and my heart grew lighter, and my soul saw more clearly again. See, I am not crying now. [*She takes his hand in hers*] So you are an author now, and I am an actress. We have both been sucked into the whirlpool. My life used to be as happy as a child's; I used to wake singing in the morning; I loved you and dreamt of fame, and what is the reality? To-morrow morning early I must start for Eltz by train in a third-class carriage, with a lot of peasants, and at Eltz the educated trades-people will pursue me with compliments. It is a rough life.

TREPLIEFF. Why are you going to Eltz?

NINA. I have accepted an engagement there for the winter. It is time for me to go.

TREPLIEFF. Nina, I have cursed you, and hated you, and torn up your photograph, and yet I have known every minute of my life that my heart and soul were yours for ever. To cease from loving you is beyond my power. I have suffered continually from the time I lost you and began to write, and my life has been almost unendurable. My youth was suddenly plucked from me then, and I seem now to have lived in this world for ninety years. I have called out to you, I have kissed the ground you walked on, wherever I looked I have seen your face before my eyes, and the smile that had illumined for me the best years of my life.

NINA [*despairingly*].   Why, why does he talk to me like this?

TREPLIEFF.   I am quite alone, unwarmed by any attachment. I am as cold as if I were living in a cave. Whatever I write is dry and gloomy and harsh. Stay here, Nina, I beseech you, or else let me go away with you.

[NINA *quickly puts on her coat and hat.*]

TREPLIEFF.   Nina, why do you do that? For God's sake, Nina! [*He watches her as she dresses. Pause*]

NINA.   My carriage is at the gate. Do not come out to see me off. I shall find the way alone. [*Weeping*] Let me have some water.

[TREPLIEFF *hands her a glass of water.*]

TREPLIEFF.   Where are you going?

NINA.   Back to the village. Is your mother here?

TREPLIEFF.   Yes, my uncle fell ill on Thursday, and we telegraphed for her to come.

NINA.   Why do you say that you have kissed the ground I walked on? You should kill me rather. [*She bends over the table*] I am so tired. If I could only rest—rest. [*She raises her head*] I am a sea gull—no—no, I am an actress. [*She hears* ARKADINA *and* TRIGORIN *laughing in the distance, runs to the door on the left and looks through the keyhole*] He is there too. [*She goes back to* TREPLIEFF] Ah, well—no matter. He does not believe in the theater; he used to laugh at my dreams, so that little by little I became down-hearted and ceased to believe in it too. Then came all the cares of love, the continual anxiety about my little one, so that I soon grew trivial and spiritless, and played my parts without meaning. I never knew what to do with my hands, and I could not walk properly or control my voice. You cannot imagine the state of mind of one who knows as he goes through a play how terribly badly he is acting. I am a sea gull—no—no, that is not what I meant to say. Do you remember how you shot a seagull once? A man chanced to pass that way and destroyed it out of idleness. That is an idea of a short story, but it is not what I meant to say. [*She passes her hand across her forehead*] What was I saying? Oh, yes, the stage. I have changed now. Now I am a real actress. I act with joy, with exaltation, I am intoxicated by it, and feel that I am superb. I have been walking and walking, and thinking and thinking, ever since I have been here, and I feel the strength of my spirit growing in me every day. I know now, I understand at last, Constantine, that for us, whether we write or act, it is not the honor and glory of which I have dreamt that is important, it is the strength to endure. One must know how to bear one's cross, and one must have faith. I believe, and so do not suffer so much, and when I think of my calling I do not fear life.

TREPLIEFF [*sadly*].   You have found your way, you know where you are going, but I am still groping in a chaos of phantoms and dreams, not knowing whom and what end I am serving by it all. I do not believe in anything, and I do not know what my calling is.

NINA [*listening*].   Hush! I must go. Good-bye. When I have become a famous actress you must come and see me. Will you promise to come? But now— [*She takes his hand*] it is late. I can hardly stand. I am fainting. I am hungry.

TREPLIEFF.   Stay, and let me bring you some supper.

NINA.   No, no—and don't come out, I can find the way alone. My carriage is not far away. So she brought him back with her? However, what difference can that make to me? Don't tell Trigorin anything when you see him. I love him—I love him even more than I used to. It is an idea for a short story. I love him—I love him passionately—I love him to despair. Have you forgotten, Constantine, how pleasant the old times were? What a gay, bright, gentle, pure life we led? How a feeling as sweet and tender as a flower blossomed in our hearts? Do you remember, [*She recites*] "All men and beasts, lions, eagles, and quails, horned stags, geese, spiders, silent fish that inhabit the waves, starfish from the sea, and creatures invisible to the eye—in one word, life—all, all life, completing the dreary round set before it, has died out at last. A thousand years have passed since the earth last bore a living creature on its breast, and the unhappy moon now lights her lamp in vain. No longer are the cries of storks heard in the meadows, or the drone of beetles in the groves of limes——"

[*She embraces* TREPLIEFF *impetuously and runs out onto the terrace.*]

TREPLIEFF [*after a pause*].   It would be a pity if she were seen in the garden. My mother would be distressed.

[*He stands for several minutes tearing up his manuscripts and throwing them under the table, then unlocks the door on the right and goes out.*]

DORN [*trying to force open the door on the left*].   Odd! This door seems to be locked. [*He comes in and puts the chair back in its former place*] This is like a hurdle race.

[ARKADINA *and* PAULINA *come in, followed by* JACOB *carrying some bottles; then come* MASHA, SHAMRAEFF, *and* TRIGORIN.]

ARKADINA.   Put the claret and the beer here, on the table, so that we can drink while we are playing. Sit down, friends.

PAULINA.   And bring the tea at once.

[*She lights the candles and takes her seat at the card-table.* SHAMRAEFF *leads* TRIGORIN *to the cupboard.*]

SHAMRAEFF.   Here is the stuffed sea gull I was telling you about. [*He takes the sea gull out of the cupboard*] You told me to have it done.

TRIGORIN [*looking at the bird*].   I don't remember a thing about it, not a thing. [*A shot is heard. Every one jumps.*]

ARKADINA [*frightened*].   What was that?

DORN.   Nothing at all; probably one of my medicine bottles has blown up. Don't worry. [*He goes out through the door on the right, and comes back in a few moments*] It is as I thought, a flask of ether has exploded. [*He sings*] "Spellbound once more I stand before thee."

ARKADINA [*sitting down at the table*].   Heavens! I was really frightened. That noise reminded me of— [*She covers her face with her hands*] Everything is black before my eyes.

DORN [*looking through the pages of a magazine, to* TRIGORIN].   There was an article from America in this magazine about two months ago that I wanted to ask you about, among other things. [*He leads* TRIGORIN *to the front of the stage*] I am very much interested in this question. [*He lowers his voice and whispers*] You must take Madame Arkadina away from here; what I wanted to say was, that Constantine has shot himself.

CURTAIN.

UNCLE VANYA

Characters

ALEXANDER SEREBRAKOV, *a retired professor*

HELENA, *his wife, twenty-seven years old*

SONIA, *his daughter by a former marriage*

MME. VOITSKAYA, *widow of a privy councillor, and mother of Serebrakov's first wife*

IVAN (VANYA) VOITSKI, *her son*

MICHAEL ASTROV, *a doctor*

ILIA (WAFFLES) TELEGIN, *an impoverished landowner*

MARINA, *an old nurse*

A WORKMAN

The scene is SEREBRAKOV'*s country place.*

ACT I

A country house on a terrace. In front of it is a garden. In an avenue of trees, under an old poplar, stands a table set for tea, with a samovar, etc. Some benches and chairs stand near the table. On one of them is lying a guitar. A hammock is hung near the table. It is three o'clock in the afternoon of a cloudy day.

MARINA, *a quiet, gray-haired, little old woman, is sitting at the table knitting a stocking.*

ASTROV *is walking up and down near her.*

MARINA [*pouring some tea into a glass*].   Take a little tea, my son.

ASTROV [*takes the glass from her unwillingly*].   Somehow, I don't seem to want any.

MARINA.   Then will you have a little vodka instead?

ASTROV.   No, I don't drink vodka every day, and besides, it is too hot now. [*Pause*] Tell me, nurse, how long have we known each other?

MARINA [*thoughtfully*].   Let me see, how long is it? Lord—help me to remember. You first came here, into our parts—let me think— when was it? Sonia's mother was still alive—it was two winters before she died; that was eleven years ago— [*thoughtfully*] perhaps more.

ASTROV.   Have I changed much since then?

MARINA.   Oh, yes. You were handsome and young then, and now you are an old man and not handsome any more. You drink, too.

ASTROV.   Yes, ten years have made me another man. And why? Because I am overworked. Nurse, I am on my feet from dawn till dusk. I know no rest; at night I tremble under my blankets for fear of being dragged out to visit someone who is sick; I have toiled without repose or a day's freedom since I have known you; could I help growing old? And then, existence is tedious, anyway; it is a senseless, dirty business, this life, and goes heavily. Every one about here is silly, and after living with them for two or three years one grows silly oneself. It is inevitable. [*Twisting his moustache*] See what a long moustache

I have grown. A foolish, long moustache. Yes, I am as silly as the rest, nurse, but not as stupid; no, I have not grown stupid. Thank God, my brain is not addled yet, though my feelings have grown numb. I ask nothing, I need nothing, I love no one, unless it is yourself alone. [*He kisses her head*] I had a nurse just like you when I was a child.

MARINA.   Don't you want a bite of something to eat?

ASTROV.   No. During the third week of Lent I went to the epidemic at Malitskoi. It was eruptive typhoid. The peasants were all lying side by side in their huts, and the calves and pigs were running about the floor among the sick. Such dirt there was, and smoke! Unspeakable! I slaved among those people all day, not a crumb passed my lips, but when I got home there was still no rest for me; a switchman was carried in from the railroad; I laid him on the operating table and he went and died in my arms under chloroform, and then my feelings that should have been deadened awoke again, my conscience tortured me as if I had killed the man. I sat down and closed my eyes—like this—and thought: will our descendants two hundred years from now, for whom we are breaking the road, remember to give us a kind word? No, nurse, they will forget.

MARINA.   Man is forgetful, but God remembers.

ASTROV.   Thank you for that. You have spoken the truth.

[*Enter* VOITSKI *from the house. He has been asleep after dinner and looks rather dishevelled. He sits down on the bench and straightens his collar.*]

VOITSKI.   H'm. Yes. [*Pause*] Yes.

ASTROV.   Have you been asleep?

VOITSKI.   Yes, very much so. [*He yawns*] Ever since the professor and his wife have come, our daily life seems to have jumped the track. I sleep at the wrong time, drink wine, and eat all sorts of messes for luncheon and dinner. It isn't wholesome. Sonia and I used to work together and never had an idle moment, but now Sonia works alone and I only eat and drink and sleep. Something is wrong.

MARINA [*shaking her head*].   Such a confusion in the house! The professor gets up at twelve, the samovar is kept boiling all the morning, and everything has to wait for him. Before they came we used to have dinner at one o'clock, like everybody else, but now we have it at seven. The professor sits up all night writing and reading, and suddenly, at two o'clock, there goes the bell! Heavens, what is that? The professor wants some tea! Wake the servants, light the samovar! Lord, what disorder!

ASTROV.   Will they be here long?

VOITSKI.   A hundred years! The professor has decided to make his home here.

MARINA. Look at this now! The samovar has been on the table for two hours, and they are all out walking!

VOITSKI. All right, don't get excited; here they come.

[*Voices are heard approaching.* SEREBRAKOV, HELENA, SONIA, *and* TELEGIN *come in from the depths of the garden, returning from their walk.*]

SEREBRAKOV. Superb! Superb! What beautiful views!

TELEGIN. They are wonderful, your Excellency.

SONIA. To-morrow we shall go into the woods, shall we, papa?

VOITSKI. Ladies and gentlemen, tea is ready.

SEREBRAKOV. Won't you please be good enough to send my tea into the library? I still have some work to finish.

SONIA. I am sure you will love the woods.

[HELENA, SEREBRAKOV, *and* SONIA *go into the house.* TELEGIN *sits down at the table beside* MARINA.]

VOITSKI. There goes our learned scholar on a hot, sultry day like this, in his overcoat and goloshes and carrying an umbrella!

ASTROV. He is trying to take good care of his health.

VOITSKI. How lovely she is! How lovely! I have never in my life seen a more beautiful woman.

TELEGIN. Do you know, Marina, that as I walk in the fields or in the shady garden, as I look at this table here, my heart swells with unbounded happiness. The weather is enchanting, the birds are singing, we are all living in peace and contentment—what more could the soul desire? [*Takes a glass of tea.*]

VOITSKI [*dreaming*]. Such eyes—a glorious woman!

ASTROV. Come, Ivan, tell us something.

VOITSKI [*indolently*]. What shall I tell you?

ASTROV. Haven't you any news for us?

VOITSKI. No, it is all stale. I am just the same as usual, or perhaps worse, because I have become lazy. I don't do anything now but croak like an old raven. My mother, the old magpie, is still chattering about the emancipation of woman, with one eye on her grave and the other on her learned books, in which she is always looking for the dawn of a new life.

ASTROV. And the professor?

VOITSKI. The professor sits in his library from morning till night, as usual:

> Straining the mind, wrinkling the brow,
> We write, write, write,
> Without respite
> Or hope of praise in the future or now.

Poor paper! He ought to write his autobiography; he would make a really splendid subject for a book! Imagine it, the life of a retired professor, as stale as a piece of hardtack, tortured by gout, headaches, and rheumatism, his liver bursting with jealousy and envy, living on the estate of his first wife, although he hates it, because he can't afford to live in town. He is everlastingly whining about his hard lot, though, as a matter of fact, he is extraordinarily lucky. He is the son of a common deacon and has attained the professor's chair, become the son-in-law of a senator, is called "your Excellency," and so on. But I'll tell you something; the man has been writing on art for twenty-five years, and he doesn't know the very first thing about it. For twenty-five years he has been chewing on other men's thoughts about realism, naturalism, and all such foolishness; for twenty-five years he has been reading and writing things that clever men have long known and stupid ones are not interested in; for twenty-five years he has been making his imaginary mountains out of molehills. And just think of the man's self-conceit and presumption all this time! For twenty-five years he has been masquerading in false clothes and has now retired, absolutely unknown to any living soul; and yet see him stalking across the earth like a demi-god!

ASTROV.   I believe you envy him.

VOITSKI.   Yes, I do. Look at the success he has had with women! Don Juan himself was not more favored. His first wife, who was my sister, was a beautiful, gentle being, as pure as the blue heaven there above us, noble, great-hearted, with more admirers than he has pupils, and she loved him as only beings of angelic purity can love those who are as pure and beautiful as themselves. His mother-in-law, my mother, adores him to this day, and he still inspires a sort of worshipful awe in her. His second wife is, as you see, a brilliant beauty; she married him in his old age and has surrendered all the glory of her beauty and freedom to him. Why? What for?

ASTROV.   Is she faithful to him?

VOITSKI.   Yes, unfortunately she is.

ASTROV.   Why unfortunately?

VOITSKI.   Because such fidelity is false and unnatural, root and branch. It sounds well, but there is no logic in it. It is thought immoral for a woman to deceive an old husband whom she hates, but quite moral for her to strangle her poor youth in her breast and banish every vital desire from her heart.

TELEGIN [*in a tearful voice*].   Vanya, I don't like to hear you talk so. Listen, Vanya; every one who betrays husband or wife is faithless, and could also betray his country.

VOITSKI [*crossly*].   Turn off the tap, Waffles.

TELEGIN. No, allow me, Vanya. My wife ran away with a lover on the day after our wedding, because my exterior was unprepossessing. I have never failed in my duty since then. I love her and am true to her to this day. I help her all I can and have given my fortune to educate the daughter of herself and her lover. I have forfeited my happiness, but I have kept my pride. And she? Her youth has fled, her beauty has faded according to the laws of nature, and her lover is dead. What has she kept?

[HELENA and SONIA come in; after them comes MME. VOITSKAYA carrying a book. She sits down and begins to read. Some one hands her a glass of tea, which she drinks without looking up.]

SONIA [hurriedly, to the nurse]. There are some peasants waiting out there. Go and see what they want. I shall pour the tea. [Pours out some glasses of tea.]

[MARINA goes out. HELENA takes a glass and sits drinking in the hammock.]

ASTROV. I have come to see your husband. You wrote me that he had rheumatism and I know not what else, and that he was very ill, but he appears to be as lively as a cricket.

HELENA. He had a fit of the blues yesterday evening and complained of pains in his legs, but he seems all right again to-day.

ASTROV. And I galloped over here twenty miles at break-neck speed! No matter, though, it is not the first time. Once here, however, I am going to stay until to-morrow, and at any rate sleep *quantum satis*.

SONIA. Oh, splendid! You so seldom spend the night with us. Have you had dinner yet?

ASTROV. No.

SONIA. Good. So you will have it with us. We dine at seven now. [Drinks her tea] This tea is cold!

TELEGIN. Yes, the samovar has grown cold.

HELENA. Don't mind, Monsieur Ivan, we will drink cold tea, then.

TELEGIN. I beg your pardon, my name is not Ivan, but Ilia, ma'am—Ilia Telegin, or Waffles, as I am sometimes called on account of my pock-marked face. I am Sonia's godfather, and his Excellency, your husband, knows me very well. I now live with you, ma'am, on this estate, and perhaps you will be so good as to notice that I dine with you every day.

SONIA. He is our great help, our right-hand man. [Tenderly] Dear godfather, let me pour you some tea.

MME. VOITSKAYA.   Oh! Oh!

SONIA.   What is it, grandmother?

MME. VOITSKAYA.   I forgot to tell Alexander—I have lost my memory—I received a letter to-day from Paul Alexevitch in Kharkoff. He has sent me a new pamphlet.

ASTROV.   Is it interesting?

MME. VOITSKAYA.   Yes, but strange. He refutes the very theories which he defended seven years ago. It is appalling!

VOITSKI.   There is nothing appalling about it. Drink your tea, mamma.

MME. VOITSKAYA.   It seems you never want to listen to what I have to say. Pardon me, Jean, but you have changed so in the last year that I hardly know you. You used to be a man of settled convictions and had an illuminating personality—

VOITSKI.   Oh, yes. I had an illuminating personality, which illuminated no one. [*Pause*] I had an illuminating personality! You couldn't say anything more biting. I am forty-seven years old. Until last year I endeavoured, as you do now, to blind my eyes by your pedantry to the truths of life. But now— Oh, if you only knew! If you knew how I lie awake at night, heartsick and angry, to think how stupidly I have wasted my time when I might have been winning from life everything which my old age now forbids.

SONIA.   Uncle Vanya, how dreary!

MME. VOITSKAYA [*to her son*].   You speak as if your former convictions were somehow to blame, but you yourself, not they, were at fault. You have forgotten that a conviction, in itself, is nothing but a dead letter. You should have done something.

VOITSKI.   Done something! Not every man is capable of being a writer *perpetuum mobile* like your Herr Professor.

MME. VOITSKAYA.   What do you mean by that?

SONIA [*imploringly*].   Mother! Uncle Vanya! I entreat you!

VOITSKI.   I am silent. I apologize and am silent. [*Pause*]

HELENA.   What a fine day! Not too hot. [*Pause*]

VOITSKI.   A fine day to hang oneself.

[TELEGIN *tunes the guitar.* MARINA *appears near the house, calling the chickens.*]

MARINA.   Chick, chick, chick!

SONIA.   What did the peasants want, nurse?

MARINA.   The same old thing, the same old nonsense. Chick, chick, chick!

SONIA.   Why are you calling the chickens?

MARINA.   The speckled hen has disappeared with her chicks. I am afraid the crows have got her.

[TELEGIN *plays a polka. All listen in silence. Enter the* WORKMAN.]

WORKMAN.   Is the doctor here? [*To* ASTROV] Excuse me, sir, but I have been sent to fetch you.

ASTROV.   Where are you from?

WORKMAN.   The factory.

ASTROV [*annoyed*].   Thank you. There is nothing for it, then, but to go. [*Looking around him for his cap*] Damn it, this is annoying!

SONIA.   Yes, it is too bad, really. You must come back to dinner from the factory.

ASTROV.   No, I won't be able to do that. It will be too late. Now where, where— [*To the* WORKMAN] Look here, my man, get me a glass of vodka, will you? [*The* WORKMAN *goes out.*] Where—where— [*Finds his cap*] One of the characters in Ostroff's plays is a man with a long moustache and short wits, like me. However, let me bid you good-bye, ladies and gentlemen. [*To* HELENA] I should be really delighted if you would come to see me some day with Miss Sonia. My estate is small, but if you are interested in such things I would like to show you a nursery and seed-bed whose like you will not find within a thousand miles of here. My place is surrounded by government forests. The forester is old and always ailing, so I superintend almost all the work myself.

HELENA.   I have always heard that you were very fond of the woods. Of course one can do a great deal of good by helping to preserve them, but does not that work interfere with your real calling?

ASTROV.   God alone knows what a man's real calling is.

HELENA.   And do you find it interesting?

ASTROV.   Yes, very.

VOITSKI [*sarcastically*].   Oh, extremely!

HELENA.   You are still young, not over thirty-six or seven, I should say, and I suspect that the woods do not interest you as much as you say they do. I should think you would find them monotonous.

SONIA.   No, the work is thrilling. Dr. Astrov watches over the old woods and sets out new plantations every year, and he has already received a diploma and a bronze medal. If you will listen to what he can tell you, you will agree with him entirely. He says that forests are the ornaments of the earth, that they teach mankind to understand beauty and attune his mind to lofty sentiments. Forests temper a stern climate, and in countries where the climate is milder, less strength is wasted in the battle with nature, and the people are kind and gentle.

The inhabitants of such countries are handsome, tractable, sensitive, graceful in speech and gesture. Their philosophy is joyous, art and science blossom among them, their treatment of women is full of exquisite nobility—

VOITSKI [*laughing*].   Bravo! Bravo! All that is very pretty, but it is also unconvincing. So, my friend [*To* ASTROV] you must let me go on burning firewood in my stoves and building my sheds of planks.

ASTROV.   You can burn peat in your stoves and build your sheds of stone. Oh, I don't object, of course, to cutting wood from necessity, but why destroy the forests? The woods of Russia are trembling under the blows of the axe. Millions of trees have perished. The homes of the wild animals and birds have been desolated; the rivers are shrinking, and many beautiful landscapes are gone forever. And why? Because men are too lazy and stupid to stoop down and pick up their fuel from the ground. [*To* HELENA] Am I not right, Madame? Who but a stupid barbarian could burn so much beauty in his stove and destroy that which he cannot make? Man is endowed with reason and the power to create, so that he may increase that which has been given him, but until now he has not created, but demolished. The forests are disappearing, the rivers are running dry, the game is exterminated, the climate is spoiled, and the earth becomes poorer and uglier every day. [*To* VOITSKI] I read irony in your eye; you do not take what I am saying seriously, and—and—after all, it may very well be nonsense. But when I pass peasant-forests that I have preserved from the axe, or hear the rustling of the young plantations set out with my own hands, I feel as if I had had some small share in improving the climate, and that if mankind is happy a thousand years from now I will have been a little bit responsible for their happiness. When I plant a little birch tree and then see it budding into young green and swaying in the wind, my heart swells with pride and I— [*Sees the* WORKMAN, *who is bringing him a glass of vodka on a tray*] however— [*He drinks*] I must be off. Probably it is all nonsense, anyway. Good-bye.

[*He goes toward the house.* SONIA *takes his arm and goes with him.*]

SONIA.   When are you coming to see us again?
ASTROV.   I can't say.
SONIA.   In a month?

[ASTROV *and* SONIA *go into the house.* HELENA *and* VOITSKI *walk over to the terrace.*]

HELENA.   You have behaved shockingly again. Ivan, what sense was there in teasing your mother and talking about *perpetuum mobile*?

And at breakfast you quarreled with Alexander again. Really, your behavior is too petty.

VOITSKI.   But if I hate him?

HELENA.   You hate Alexander without reason; he is like everyone else, and no worse than you are.

VOITSKI.   If you could only see your face, your gestures! Oh, how tedious your life must be.

HELENA.   It is tedious, yes, and dreary! You all abuse my husband and look on me with compassion; you think, "Poor woman, she is married to an old man." How well I understand your compassion! As Astrov said just now, see how you thoughtlessly destroy the forests, so that there will soon be none left. So you also destroy mankind, and soon fidelity and purity and self-sacrifice will have vanished with the woods. Why cannot you look calmly at a woman unless she is yours? Because, the doctor was right, you are all possessed by a devil of destruction; you have no mercy on the woods or the birds or on women or on one another.

VOITSKI.   I don't like your philosophy.

HELENA.   That doctor has a sensitive, weary face— an interesting face. Sonia evidently likes him, and she is in love with him, and I can understand it. This is the third time he has been here since I have come, and I have not had a real talk with him yet or made much of him. He thinks I am disagreeable. Do you know, Ivan, the reason you and I are such friends? I think it is because we are both lonely and unfortunate. Yes, unfortunate. Don't look at me in that way, I don't like it.

VOITSKI.   How can I look at you otherwise when I love you? You are my joy, my life, and my youth. I know that my chances of being loved in return are infinitely small, do not exist, but I ask nothing of you. Only let me look at you, listen to your voice—

HELENA.   Hush, someone will overhear you.

[*They go toward the house.*]

VOITSKI [*following her*].   Let me speak to you of my love, do not drive me away, and this alone will be my greatest happiness!

HELENA.   Ah! This is agony!

[TELEGIN *strikes the strings of his guitar and plays a polka.* MME. VOITSKAYA *writes something on the leaves of her pamphlet.*]

CURTAIN.

ACT II

The dining room of SEREBRAKOV'S *house. It is night. The tapping of the* WATCHMAN'S *rattle is heard in the garden.* SEREBRAKOV *is dozing in an armchair by an open window and* HELENA *is sitting beside him, also half asleep.*

SEREBRAKOV [*rousing himself*].   Who is here? Is it you, Sonia?
HELENA.   It is I.
SEREBRAKOV.   Oh, it is you, Nelly. This pain is intolerable.
HELENA.   Your shawl has slipped down. [*She wraps up his legs in the shawl*] Let me shut the window.
SEREBRAKOV.   No, leave it open; I am suffocating. I dreamt just now that my left leg belonged to some one else, and it hurt so that I woke. I don't believe this is gout, it is more like rheumatism. What time is it?
HELENA.   Half past twelve. [*Pause*]
SEREBRAKOV.   I want you to look for Batushka's works in the library to-morrow. I think we have him.
HELENA.   What is that?
SEREBRAKOV.   Look for Batushka to-morrow morning; we used to have him, I remember. Why do I find it so hard to breathe?
HELENA.   You are tired; this is the second night you have had no sleep.
SEREBRAKOV.   They say that Turgenieff got angina of the heart from gout. I am afraid I am getting angina too. Oh, damn this horrible, accursed old age! Ever since I have been old I have been hateful to myself, and I am sure, hateful to you all as well.
HELENA.   You speak as if we were to blame for your being old.
SEREBRAKOV.   I am more hateful to you than to anyone.

[HELENA *gets up and walks away from him, sitting down at a distance.*]

SEREBRAKOV.   You are quite right, of course. I am not an idiot; I can understand you. You are young and healthy and beautiful, and longing for life, and I am an old dotard, almost a dead man already.

184

Don't I know it? Of course I see that it is foolish for me to live so long, but wait! I shall soon set you all free. My life cannot drag on much longer.

HELENA.   You are overtaxing my powers of endurance. Be quiet, for God's sake!

SEREBRAKOV.   It appears that, thanks to me, everybody's power of endurance is being overtaxed; everybody is miserable, only I am blissfully triumphant. Oh, yes, of course!

HELENA.   Be quiet! You are torturing me.

SEREBRAKOV.   I torture everybody. Of course.

HELENA [weeping].   This is unbearable! Tell me, what is it you want me to do?

SEREBRAKOV.   Nothing.

HELENA.   Then be quiet, please.

SEREBRAKOV.   It is funny that everybody listens to Ivan and his old idiot of a mother, but the moment I open my lips you all begin to feel ill-treated. You can't even stand the sound of my voice. Even if I am hateful, even if I am a selfish tyrant, haven't I the right to be one at my age? Haven't I deserved it? Haven't I, I ask you, the right to be respected, now that I am old?

HELENA.   No one is disputing your rights. [The window slams in the wind] The wind is rising, I must shut the window. [She shuts it] We shall have rain in a moment. Your rights have never been questioned by anybody.

[The WATCHMAN in the garden sounds his rattle.]

SEREBRAKOV.   I have spent my life working in the interests of learning. I am used to my library and the lecture hall and to the esteem and admiration of my colleagues. Now I suddenly find myself plunged in this wilderness, condemned to see the same stupid people from morning till night and listen to their futile conversation. I want to live; I long for success and fame and the stir of the world, and here I am in exile! Oh, it is dreadful to spend every moment grieving for the lost past, to see the success of others and sit here with nothing to do but to fear death. I cannot stand it! It is more than I can bear. And you will not even forgive me for being old!

HELENA.   Wait, have patience; I shall be old myself in four or five years.

[SONIA comes in.]

SONIA.   Father, you sent for Dr. Astrov, and now when he comes you refuse to see him. It is not nice to give a man so much trouble for nothing.

SEREBRAKOV.   What do I care about your Astrov? He understands medicine about as well as I understand astronomy.

SONIA.   We can't send for the whole medical faculty, can we, to treat your gout?

SEREBRAKOV.   I won't talk to that madman!

SONIA.   Do as you please. It's all the same to me. [*She sits down.*]

SEREBRAKOV.   What time is it?

HELENA.   One o'clock.

SEREBRAKOV.   It is stifling in here. Sonia, hand me that bottle on the table.

SONIA.   Here it is. [*She hands him a bottle of medicine.*]

SEREBRAKOV [*crossly*].   No, not that one! Can't you understand me? Can't I ask you to do a thing?

SONIA.   Please don't be captious with me. Some people may like it, but you must spare me, if you please, because I don't. Besides, I haven't the time; we are cutting the hay to-morrow and I must get up early.

[VOITSKI *comes in dressed in a long gown and carrying a candle.*]

VOITSKI.   A thunderstorm is coming up. [*The lightning flashes*] There it is! Go to bed, Helena and Sonia. I have come to take your place.

SEREBRAKOV [*frightened*] No, no, no! Don't leave me alone with him! Oh, don't. He will begin to lecture me.

VOITSKI.   But you must give them a little rest. They have not slept for two nights.

SEREBRAKOV.   Then let them go to bed, but you go away too! Thank you. I implore you to go. For the sake of our former friendship do not protest against going. We will talk some other time—

VOITSKI.   Our former friendship! Our former—

SONIA.   Hush, Uncle Vanya!

SEREBRAKOV [*to his wife*].   My darling, don't leave me alone with him. He will begin to lecture me.

VOITSKI.   This is ridiculous.

[MARINA *comes in carrying a candle.*]

SONIA.   You must go to bed, nurse, it is late.

MARINA.   I haven't cleared away the tea things. Can't go to bed yet.

SEREBRAKOV.   No one can go to bed. They are all worn out, only I enjoy perfect happiness.

MARINA [*goes up to* SEREBRAKOV *and speaks tenderly*].   What's the matter, master? Does it hurt? My own legs are aching too, oh, so badly. [*Arranges his shawl about his legs*] You have had this illness such a long time. Sonia's dead mother used to stay awake with you too, and wear herself out for you. She loved you dearly. [*Pause*] Old people want to be pitied as much as young ones, but nobody cares about them somehow. [*She kisses* SEREBRAKOV*'s shoulder*] Come, master, let me give you some linden-tea and warm your poor feet for you. I shall pray to God for you.

SEREBRAKOV [*touched*].   Let us go, Marina.

MARINA.   My own feet are aching so badly, oh, so badly! [*She and* SONIA *lead* SEREBRAKOV *out*] Sonia's mother used to wear herself out with sorrow and weeping. You were still little and foolish then, Sonia. Come, come, master.

[SEREBRAKOV, SONIA *and* MARINA *go out.*]

HELENA.   I am absolutely exhausted by him, and can hardly stand.

VOITSKI.   You are exhausted by him, and I am exhausted by my own self. I have not slept for three nights.

HELENA.   Something is wrong in this house. Your mother hates everything but her pamphlets and the professor; the professor is vexed, he won't trust me, and fears you; Sonia is angry with her father, and with me, and hasn't spoken to me for two weeks; I am at the end of my strength, and have come near bursting into tears at least twenty times to-day. Something is wrong in this house.

VOITSKI.   Leave speculating alone.

HELENA.   You are cultured and intelligent, Ivan, and you surely understand that the world is not destroyed by villains and conflagrations, but by hate and malice and all this spiteful tattling. It is your duty to make peace, and not to growl at everything.

VOITSKI.   Help me first to make peace with myself. My darling! [*Seizes her hand.*]

HELENA.   Let go! [*She drags her hand away*] Go away!

VOITSKI.   Soon the rain will be over, and all nature will sigh and awake refreshed. Only I am not refreshed by the storm. Day and night the thought haunts me like a fiend, that my life is lost forever. My past does not count, because I frittered it away on trifles, and the present has so terribly miscarried! What shall I do with my life and my love? What is to become of them? This wonderful feeling of mine will be wasted and lost as a ray of sunlight is lost that falls into a dark chasm, and my life will go with it.

HELENA.   I am, as it were, benumbed when you speak to me of your love, and I don't know how to answer you. Forgive me, I have nothing to say to you. [*She tries to go out*] Good-night!

VOITSKI [*barring the way*].   If you only knew how I am tortured by the thought that beside me in this house is another life that is being lost forever—it is yours! What are you waiting for? What accursed philosophy stands in your way? Oh, understand, understand—

HELENA [*looking at him intently*].   Ivan, you are drunk!

VOITSKI.   Perhaps. Perhaps.

HELENA.   Where is the doctor?

VOITSKI.   In there, spending the night with me. Perhaps I am drunk, perhaps I am; nothing is impossible.

HELENA.   Have you just been drinking together? Why do you do that?

VOITSKI.   Because in that way I get a taste of life. Let me do it, Helena!

HELENA.   You never used to drink, and you never used to talk so much. Go to bed, I am tired of you.

VOITSKI [*falling on his knees before her*].   My sweetheart, my beautiful one—

HELENA [*angrily*].   Leave me alone! Really, this has become too disagreeable.

[HELENA *goes out. Pause*]

VOITSKI [*alone*].   She is gone! I met her first ten years ago, at her sister's house, when she was seventeen and I was thirty-seven. Why did I not fall in love with her then and propose to her? It would have been so easy! And now she would have been my wife. Yes, we would both have been waked to-night by the thunderstorm, and she would have been frightened, but I would have held her in my arms and whispered: "Don't be afraid! I am here." Oh, enchanting dream, so sweet that I laugh to think of it. [*He laughs*] But my God! My head reels! Why am I so old? Why won't she understand me? I hate all that rhetoric of hers, that morality of indolence, that absurd talk about the destruction of the world— [*Pause*] Oh, how I have been deceived! For years I have worshipped that miserable gout-ridden professor. Sonia and I have squeezed this estate dry for his sake. We have bartered our butter and curds and peas like misers, and have never kept a morsel for ourselves, so that we could scrape enough pennies together to send to him. I was proud of him and of his learning; I received all his words and writings as inspired, and now? Now he has retired, and what is the total of his life? A blank! He is absolutely unknown, and his fame has burst like a soap-bubble. I have been deceived; I see that now, basely deceived.

[ASTROV *comes in. He has his coat on, but is without his waistcoat or collar, and is slightly drunk.* TELEGIN *follows him, carrying a guitar.*]

ASTROV.   Play!
TELEGIN.   But everyone is asleep.
ASTROV.   Play!

[TELEGIN *begins to play softly.*]

ASTROV.   Are you alone here? No women about? [*Sings with his arms akimbo.*]

> The hut is cold, the fire is dead;
> Where shall the master lay his head?

The thunderstorm woke me. It was a heavy shower. What time is it?

VOITSKI.   The devil only knows.
ASTROV.   I thought I heard Helena's voice.
VOITSKI.   She was here a moment ago.
ASTROV.   What a beautiful woman! [*Looking at the medicine bottles on the table*] Medicine, is it? What a variety we have; prescriptions from Moscow, from Kharkoff, from Tula! Why, he has been pestering all the towns of Russia with his gout! Is he ill, or simply shamming?
VOITSKI.   He is really ill.
ASTROV.   What is the matter with you to-night? You seem sad. Is it because you are sorry for the professor?
VOITSKI.   Leave me alone.
ASTROV.   Or in love with the professor's wife?
VOITSKI.   She is my friend.
ASTROV.   Already?
VOITSKI.   What do you mean by "already"?
ASTROV.   A woman can only become a man's friend after having first been his acquaintance and then his beloved—then she becomes his friend.
VOITSKI.   What vulgar philosophy!
ASTROV.   What do you mean? Yes, I must confess I am getting vulgar, but then, you see, I am drunk. I usually only drink like this once a month. At such times my audacity and temerity know no bounds. I feel capable of anything. I attempt the most difficult operations and do them magnificently. The most brilliant plans for the future take shape in my head. I am no longer a poor fool of a doctor, but mankind's greatest benefactor. I evolve my own system of phi-

losophy and all of you seem to crawl at my feet like so many insects or microbes. [*To* TELEGIN] Play, Waffles!

TELEGIN.   My dear boy, I would with all my heart, but do listen to reason; everybody in the house is asleep.

ASTROV.   Play!

[TELEGIN *plays softly.*]

ASTROV.   I want a drink. Come, we still have some brandy left. And then, as soon as it is day, you will come home with me. [*He sees* SONIA, *who comes in at that moment.*]

ASTROV.   I beg your pardon, I have no collar on. [*He goes out quickly, followed by* TELEGIN.]

SONIA. Uncle Vanya, you and the doctor have been drinking! The good fellows have been getting together! It is all very well for him, he has always done it, but why do you follow his example? It looks dreadfully at your age.

VOITSKI.   Age has nothing to do with it. When real life is wanting one must create an illusion. It is better than nothing.

SONIA.   Our hay is all cut and rotting in these daily rains, and here you are busy creating illusions! You have given up the farm altogether. I have done all the work alone until I am at the end of my strength— [*Frightened*] Uncle! Your eyes are full of tears!

VOITSKI.   Tears? Nonsense, there are no tears in my eyes. You looked at me then just as your dead mother used to, my darling—[*He eagerly kisses her face and hands*] My sister, my dearest sister, where are you now? Ah, if you only knew, if you only knew!

SONIA.   If she only knew what, Uncle?

VOITSKI.   My heart is bursting. It is awful. No matter, though. I must go. [*He goes out.*]

SONIA [*knocks at the door*].   Dr. Astrov! Are you awake? Please come here for a minute.

ASTROV [*behind the door*].   In a moment. [*He appears in a few seconds. He has put on his collar and waistcoat.*]

ASTROV.   What do you want?

SONIA.   Drink as much as you please yourself, if you don't find it revolting, but I implore you not to let my uncle do it. It is bad for him.

ASTROV.   Very well; we won't drink any more. I am going home at once. That is settled. It will be dawn by the time the horses are harnessed.

SONIA.   It is still raining; wait till morning.

ASTROV.   The storm is blowing over. This is only the edge of it. I must go. And please don't ask me to come and see your father any-

more. I tell him he has gout, and he says it is rheumatism. I tell him
to lie down, and he sits up. To-day he refused to see me at all.

SONIA.   He has been spoilt. [*She looks in the sideboard*] Won't you
have a bite to eat?

ASTROV.   Yes, please. I believe I will.

SONIA.   I love to eat at night. I am sure we shall find something
in here. They say that he has made a great many conquests in his life,
and that the women have spoiled him. Here is some cheese for you.

[*They stand eating by the sideboard.*]

ASTROV.   I haven't eaten anything to-day. Your father has a very
difficult nature. [*He takes a bottle out of the sideboard*] May I? [*He pours
himself a glass of vodka*] We are alone here, and I can speak frankly. Do
you know, I could not stand living in this house for even a month?
This atmosphere would stifle me. There is your father, entirely absorbed in his books, and his gout; there is your Uncle Vanya with his
hypochondria, your grandmother, and finally, your step-mother—

SONIA.   What about her?

ASTROV.   A human being should be entirely beautiful: the face,
the clothes, the mind, the thoughts. Your step-mother is, of course,
beautiful to look at, but don't you see? She does nothing but sleep
and eat and walk and bewitch us, and that is all. She has no responsi-
bilities, everything is done for her—am I not right? And an idle life
can never be a pure one. [*Pause*] However, I may be judging her too
severely. Like your Uncle Vanya, I am discontented, and so we are
both grumblers.

SONIA.   Aren't you satisfied with life?

ASTROV.   I like life as life, but I hate and despise it in a little
Russian country village, and as far as my own personal life goes— by
heaven! There is absolutely no redeeming feature about it. Haven't
you noticed if you are riding through a dark wood at night and see a
little light shining ahead, how you forget your fatigue and the darkness and the sharp twigs that whip your face? I work, that you
know—as no one else in the country works. Fate beats me on without rest; at times I suffer unendurably and I see no light ahead. I have
no hope; I do not like people. It is long since I have loved anyone.

SONIA.   You love no one?

ASTROV.   Not a soul. I only feel a sort of tenderness for your old
nurse for old-times' sake. The peasants are all alike; they are stupid
and live in dirt, and the educated people are hard to get along with.
One gets tired of them. All our good friends are petty and shallow
and see no farther than their own noses; in one word, they are dull.
Those that have brains are hysterical, devoured with a mania for self-

analysis. They whine, they hate, they pick faults everywhere with unhealthy sharpness. They sneak up to me sideways, look at me out of a corner of the eye, and say: "That man is a lunatic," "That man is a wind-bag." Or, if they don't know what else to label me with, they say I am strange. I like the woods; that is strange. I don't eat meat; that is strange, too. Simple, natural relations between man and man or man and nature do not exist. [*He tries to go out;* SONIA *prevents him.*]

SONIA. I beg you, I implore you, not to drink any more!

ASTROV. Why not?

SONIA. It is so unworthy of you. You are well-bred, your voice is sweet, you are even—more than any one I know—handsome. Why do you want to resemble the common people that drink and play cards? Oh, don't, I beg you! You always say that people do not create anything, but only destroy what heaven has given them. Why, oh, why, do you destroy yourself? Oh, don't, I implore you not to! I entreat you!

ASTROV [*gives her his hand*]. I won't drink any more.

SONIA. Promise me.

ASTROV. I give you my word of honor.

SONIA [*squeezing his hand*]. Thank you.

ASTROV. I have done with it. You see, I am perfectly sober again, and so I shall stay till the end of my life. [*He looks at his watch*] But, as I was saying, life holds nothing for me; my race is run. I am old, I am tired, I am trivial; my sensibilities are dead. I could never attach myself to anyone again. I love no one, and never shall! Beauty alone has the power to touch me still. I am deeply moved by it. Helena could turn my head in a day if she wanted to, but that is not love, that is not affection— [*He shudders and covers his face with his hands.*]

SONIA. What is it?

ASTROV. Nothing. During Lent one of my patients died under chloroform.

SONIA. It is time to forget that. [*Pause*] Tell me, doctor, if I had a friend or a younger sister, and if you knew that she, well—loved you, what would you do?

ASTROV [*shrugging his shoulders*]. I don't know. I don't think I would do anything. I would make her understand that I could not return her love—however, my mind is not bothered about those things now. I must start at once if I am ever to get off. Good-bye, my dear girl. At this rate we shall stand here talking till morning. [*He shakes hands with her*] I shall go out through the sitting-room, because I am afraid your uncle might detain me. [*He goes out.*]

SONIA [*alone*].   Not a word! His heart and soul are still locked from me, and yet for some reason I am strangely happy. I wonder why? [*She laughs with pleasure*] I told him that he was well-bred and handsome and that his voice was sweet. Was that a mistake? I can still feel his voice vibrating in the air; it caresses me. [*Wringing her hands*] Oh! how terrible it is to be plain! I am plain, I know it. As I came out of church last Sunday I overheard a woman say, "She is a dear, noble girl, but what a pity she is so ugly!" So ugly!

[HELENA *comes in and throws open the window.*]

HELENA.   The storm is over. What delicious air! [*Pause*] Where is the doctor?

SONIA.   He has gone. [*Pause*]

HELENA.   Sonia!

SONIA.   Yes?

HELENA.   How much longer are you going to sulk at me? We have not hurt each other. Why not be friends? We have had enough of this.

SONIA.   I myself— [*She embraces* HELENA] Let us make peace.

HELENA.   With all my heart. [*They are both moved.*]

SONIA.   Has papa gone to bed?

HELENA.   No, he is sitting up in the drawing-room. Heaven knows what reason you and I had for not speaking to each other for weeks. [*Sees the open sideboard*] Who left the sideboard open?

SONIA.   Dr. Astrov has just had supper.

HELENA.   There is some wine. Let us seal our friendship.

SONIA.   Yes, let us.

HELENA.   Out of one glass. [*She fills a wine-glass*] So, we are friends, are we?

SONIA.   Yes. [*They drink and kiss each other*] I have long wanted to make friends, but somehow, I was ashamed to. [*She weeps.*]

HELENA.   Why are you crying?

SONIA.   I don't know. It is nothing.

HELENA.   There, there, don't cry. [*She weeps*] Silly! Now I am crying too. [*Pause*] You are angry with me because I seem to have married your father for his money, but don't believe the gossip you hear. I swear to you I married him for love. I was fascinated by his fame and learning. I know now that it was not real love, but it seemed real at the time. I am innocent, and yet your clever, suspicious eyes have been punishing me for an imaginary crime ever since my marriage.

SONIA.   Peace, peace! Let us forget the past.

HELENA.   You must not look so at people. It is not becoming to you. You must trust people, or life becomes impossible.

SONIA. Tell me truly, as a friend, are you happy?

HELENA. Truly, no.

SONIA. I knew it. One more question: do you wish your husband were young?

HELENA. What a child you are! Of course I do. Go on, ask something else.

SONIA. Do you like the doctor?

HELENA. Yes, very much indeed.

SONIA [*laughing*]. I have a stupid face, haven't I? He has just gone out, and his voice is still in my ears; I hear his step; I see his face in the dark window. Let me say all I have in my heart! But no, I cannot speak of it so loudly. I am ashamed. Come to my room and let me tell you there. I seem foolish to you, don't I? Talk to me of him.

HELENA. What can I say?

SONIA. He is clever. He can do everything. He can cure the sick, and plant woods.

HELENA. It is not a question of medicine and woods, my dear, he is a man of genius. Do you know what that means? It means he is brave, profound, and of clear insight. He plants a tree and his mind travels a thousand years into the future, and he sees visions of the happiness of the human race. People like him are rare and should be loved. What if he does drink and act roughly at times? A man of genius cannot be a saint in Russia. There he lives, cut off from the world by cold and storm and endless roads of bottomless mud, surrounded by a rough people who are crushed by poverty and disease, his life one continuous struggle, with never a day's respite; how can a man live like that for forty years and keep himself sober and unspotted? [*Kissing* SONIA] I wish you happiness with all my heart; you deserve it. [*She gets up*] As for me, I am a worthless, futile woman. I have always been futile; in music, in love, in my husband's house—in a word, in everything. When you come to think of it, Sonia, I am really very, very unhappy. [*Walks excitedly up and down*] Happiness can never exist for me in this world. Never. Why do you laugh?

SONIA [*laughing and covering her face with her hands*] I am so happy, so happy!

HELENA. I want to hear music. I might play a little.

SONIA. Oh, do, do! [*She embraces her*] I could not possibly go to sleep now. Do play!

HELENA. Yes, I will. Your father is still awake. Music irritates him when he is ill, but if he says I may, then I shall play a little. Go, Sonia, and ask him.

SONIA. Very well.

[*She goes out. The* WATCHMAN*'s rattle is heard in the garden.*]

HELENA.   It is long since I have heard music. And now, I shall sit and play, and weep like a fool. [*Speaking out of the window*] Is that you rattling out there, Ephim?

VOICE OF THE WATCHMAN.   It is I.

HELENA.   Don't make such a noise. Your master is ill.

VOICE OF THE WATCHMAN.—I am going away this minute. [*Whistles a tune.*]

SONIA [*comes back*].   He says, no.

CURTAIN.

ACT III

The drawing room of SEREBRAKOV's *house. There are three doors: one to the right, one to the left, and one in the center of the room.* VOITSKI *and* SONIA *are sitting down.* HELENA *is walking up and down, absorbed in thought.*

VOITSKI.   We were asked by the professor to be here at one o'clock. [*Looks at his watch*] It is now a quarter to one. It seems he has some communication to make to the world.

HELENA.   Probably a matter of business.

VOITSKI.   He never had any business. He writes twaddle, grumbles, and eats his heart out with jealousy; that's all he does.

SONIA [*reproachfully*].   Uncle!

VOITSKI.   All right. I beg your pardon. [*He points to* HELENA] Look at her. Wandering up and down from sheer idleness. A sweet picture, really.

HELENA.   I wonder you are not bored, droning on in the same key from morning till night. [*Despairingly*] I am dying of this tedium. What shall I do?

SONIA [*shrugging her shoulders*].   There is plenty to do if you would.

HELENA.   For instance?

SONIA.   You could help run this place, teach the children, care for the sick—isn't that enough? Before you and papa came, Uncle Vanya and I used to go to market ourselves to deal in flour.

HELENA.   I don't know anything about such things, and besides, they don't interest me. It is only in novels that women go out and teach and heal the peasants; how can I suddenly begin to do it?

SONIA.   How can you live here and not do it? Wait awhile, you will get used to it all. [*Embraces her*] Don't be sad, dearest. [*Laughing*] You feel miserable and restless, and can't seem to fit into this life, and your restlessness is catching. Look at Uncle Vanya, he does nothing now but haunt you like a shadow, and I have left my work to-day to

196

come here and talk with you. I am getting lazy, and don't want to go on with it. Dr. Astrov hardly ever used to come here; it was all we could do to persuade him to visit us once a month, and now he has abandoned his forestry and his practice, and comes every day. You must be a witch.

VOITSKI.   Why should you languish here? Come, my dearest, my beauty, be sensible! The blood of a nixey runs in your veins. Oh, won't you let yourself be one? Give your nature the reins for once in your life; fall head over ears in love with some other water sprite and plunge down head first into a deep pool, so that the Herr Professor and all of us may have our hands free again.

HELENA [*angrily*].   Leave me alone! How cruel you are! [*She tries to go out.*]

VOITSKI [*preventing her*].   There, there, my beauty, I apologize. [*He kisses her hand*] Forgive me.

HELENA.   Confess that you would try the patience of an angel.

VOITSKI.   As a peace offering I am going to fetch some flowers which I picked for you this morning: some autumn roses, beautiful, sorrowful roses. [*He goes out.*]

SONIA.   Autumn roses, beautiful, sorrowful roses!

[*She and* HELENA *stand looking out of the window.*]

HELENA.   September already! How shall we live through the long winter here? [*Pause*] Where is the doctor?

SONIA.   He is writing in Uncle Vanya's room. I am glad Uncle Vanya has gone out, I want to talk to you about something.

HELENA.   About what?

SONIA.   About what? [*She lays her head on* HELENA*'s breast.*]

HELENA [*stroking her hair*].   There, there, that will do. Don't, Sonia.

SONIA.   I am ugly!

HELENA.   You have lovely hair.

SONIA.   Don't say that! [*She turns to look at herself in the glass*] No, when a woman is ugly they always say she has beautiful hair or eyes. I have loved him now for six years, I have loved him more than one loves one's mother. I seem to hear him beside me every moment of the day. I feel the pressure of his hand on mine. If I look up, I seem to see him coming, and as you see, I run to you to talk of him. He is here every day now, but he never looks at me, he does not notice my presence. It is agony. I have absolutely no hope, no, no hope. Oh, my God! Give me strength to endure. I prayed all last night. I often go up to him and speak to him and look into his eyes. My pride is gone. I am not mistress of myself. Yesterday I told Uncle Vanya. I couldn't control myself, and all the servants know it. Every one knows that I love him.

HELENA. Does he?

SONIA. No, he never notices me.

HELENA [*thoughtfully*]. He is a strange man. Listen, Sonia, will you allow me to speak to him? I shall be careful, only hint. [*Pause*] Really, to be in uncertainty all these years! Let me do it!

[SONIA *nods an affirmative.*]

HELENA. Splendid! It will be easy to find out whether he loves you or not. Don't be ashamed, sweetheart, don't worry. I shall be careful; he will not notice a thing. We only want to find out whether it is yes or no, don't we? [*Pause*] And if it is no, then he must keep away from here, is that so?

[SONIA *nods.*]

HELENA. It will be easier not to see him anymore. We won't put off the examination an instant. He said he had a sketch to show me. Go and tell him at once that I want to see him.

SONIA [*in great excitement*]. Will you tell me the whole truth?

HELENA. Of course I will. I am sure that no matter what it is, it will be easier for you to bear than this uncertainty. Trust me, dearest.

SONIA. Yes, yes. I shall say that you want to see his sketch. [*She starts out, but stops near the door and looks back*] No, it is better not to know—and yet—there may be hope.

HELENA. What do you say?

SONIA. Nothing. [*She goes out.*]

HELENA [*alone*]. There is no greater sorrow than to know another's secret when you cannot help them. [*In deep thought*] He is obviously not in love with her, but why shouldn't he marry her? She is not pretty, but she is so clever and pure and good, she would make a splendid wife for a country doctor of his years. [*Pause*] I can understand how the poor child feels. She lives here in this desperate loneliness with no one around her except these colorless shadows that go mooning about talking nonsense and knowing nothing except that they eat, drink, and sleep. Among them appears from time to time this Dr. Astrov, so different, so handsome, so interesting, so charming. It is like seeing the moon rise on a dark night. Oh, to surrender oneself to his embrace! To lose oneself in his arms! I am a little in love with him myself! Yes, I am lonely without him, and when I think of him I smile. That Uncle Vanya says I have the blood of a nixey in my veins: "Give rein to your nature for once in your life!" Perhaps it is

right that I should. Oh, to be free as a bird, to fly away from all your
sleepy faces and your talk and forget that you have existed at all! But
I am a coward, I am afraid; my conscience torments me. He comes
here every day now. I can guess why, and feel guilty already; I should
like to fall on my knees at Sonia's feet and beg her forgiveness, and
weep.

[ASTROV *comes in carrying a portfolio.*]

ASTROV.   How do you do? [*Shakes hands with her*] Do you want
to see my sketch?

HELENA.   Yes, you promised to show me what you had been
doing. Have you time now?

ASTROV.   Of course I have! [*He lays the portfolio on the table, takes
out the sketch and fastens it to the table with thumbtacks.*] Where were you
born?

HELENA [*helping him*].   In St. Petersburg.

ASTROV.   And educated?

HELENA.   At the Conservatory there.

ASTROV.   You don't find this life very interesting, I dare say?

HELENA.   Oh, why not? It is true I don't know the country very
well, but I have read a great deal about it.

ASTROV.   I have my own desk there in Ivan's room. When I am
absolutely too exhausted to go on I drop everything and rush over
here to forget myself in this work for an hour or two. Ivan and Miss
Sonia sit rattling at their counting boards, the cricket chirps, and I sit
beside them and paint, feeling warm and peaceful. But I don't permit
myself this luxury very often, only once a month. [*Pointing to the picture*] Look there! That is a map of our region as it was fifty years ago.
The green tints, both dark and light, represent forests. Half the map,
as you see, is covered with it. Where the green is striped with red the
forests were inhabited by elk and wild goats. Here, on this lake, lived
great flocks of swans and geese and ducks; as the old folks say, there
was a power of birds of every kind. Now they have vanished like a
cloud. Beside the hamlets and villages, you see, I have dotted down
here and there the various settlements, farms, hermit's caves, and
water-mills. This district carried a great many cattle and horses, as you
can see by the quantity of blue paint. For instance, see how thickly it
lies in this part; there were great herds of them here, an average of
three horses to every house. [*Pause*] Now, look lower down. This is
the region as it was twenty-five years ago. Only a third of the map is
green now with forests. There are no goats left and no elk. The blue
paint is lighter, and so on, and so on. Now we come to the third part;
our region as it appears to-day. We still see spots of green, but not

much. The elk, the swans, the black-cock have disappeared. It is, on the whole, the picture of a regular and slow decline which it will evidently only take about ten or fifteen more years to complete. You may perhaps object that it is the march of progress, that the old order must give place to the new, and you might be right if roads had been run through these ruined woods, or if factories and schools had taken their place. The people then would have become better educated and healthier and richer, but as it is, we have nothing of the sort. We have the same swamps and mosquitoes; the same disease and want; the typhoid, the diphtheria, the burning villages. We are confronted by the degradation of our country, brought on by the fierce struggle for existence of the human race. It is the consequence of the ignorance and unconsciousness of starving, shivering, sick humanity that, to save its children, instinctively snatches at everything that can warm it and still its hunger. So it destroys everything it can lay its hands on, without a thought for the morrow. And almost everything has gone, and nothing has been created to take its place. [*Coldly*] But I see by your face that I am not interesting you.

HELENA.   I know so little about such things!

ASTROV.   There is nothing to know. It simply isn't interesting, that's all.

HELENA.   Frankly, my thoughts were elsewhere. Forgive me! I want to submit you to a little examination, but I am embarrassed and don't know how to begin.

ASTROV.   An examination?

HELENA.   Yes, but quite an innocent one. Sit down. [*They sit down*] It is about a certain young girl I know. Let us discuss it like honest people, like friends, and then forget what has passed between us, shall we?

ASTROV.   Very well.

HELENA.   It is about my step-daughter, Sonia. Do you like her?

ASTROV.   Yes, I respect her.

HELENA.   Do you like her—as a woman?

ASTROV [*slowly*].   No.

HELENA.   One more word, and that will be the last. You have not noticed anything?

ASTROV.   No, nothing.

HELENA [*taking his hand*].   You do not love her. I see that in your eyes. She is suffering. You must realize that, and not come here any more.

ASTROV.   My sun has set, yes, and then I haven't the time. [*Shrugging his shoulders*] Where shall I find time for such things? [*He is embarrassed.*]

HELENA.   Bah! What an unpleasant conversation! I am as out of breath as if I had been running three miles uphill. Thank heaven, that is over! Now let us forget everything as if nothing had been said. You are sensible. You understand. [*Pause*] I am actually blushing.

ASTROV.   If you had spoken a month ago I might perhaps have considered it, but now— [*He shrugs his shoulders*] Of course, if she is suffering—but I cannot understand why you had to put me through this examination. [*He searches her face with his eyes, and shakes his finger at her*] Oho, you are wily!

HELENA.   What does this mean?

ASTROV [*laughing*].   You are a wily one! I admit that Sonia is suffering, but what does this examination of yours mean? [*He prevents her from retorting, and goes on quickly*] Please don't put on such a look of surprise; you know perfectly well why I come here every day. Yes, you know perfectly why and for whose sake I come! Oh, my sweet tigress! Don't look at me in that way; I am an old bird!

HELENA [*perplexed*].   A tigress? I don't understand you.

ASTROV.   Beautiful, sleek tigress, you must have your victims! For a whole month I have done nothing but seek you eagerly. I have thrown over everything for you, and you love to see it. Now then, I am sure you knew all this without putting me through your examination. [*Crossing his arms and bowing his head*] I surrender. Here you have me—now, eat me.

HELENA.   You have gone mad!

ASTROV.   You are afraid!

HELENA.   I am a better and stronger woman than you think me. Good-bye. [*She tries to leave the room.*]

ASTROV.   Why good-bye? Don't say good-bye, don't waste words. Oh, how lovely you are—what hands! [*He kisses her hands.*]

HELENA.   Enough of this! [*She frees her hands*] Leave the room! You have forgotten yourself.

ASTROV.   Tell me, tell me, where can we meet to-morrow? [*He puts his arm around her*] Don't you see that we must meet, that it is inevitable?

[*He kisses her.* VOITSKI *comes in carrying a bunch of roses, and stops in the doorway.*]

HELENA [*without seeing* VOITSKI].   Have pity! Leave me! [*Lays her head on* ASTROV's *shoulder*] Don't! [*She tries to break away from him.*]

ASTROV [*holding her by the waist*].   Be in the forest tomorrow at two o'clock. Will you? Will you?

HELENA [*sees* VOITSKI].   Let me go! [*Goes to the window, deeply embarrassed*] This is appalling!

VOITSKI [*throws the flowers on a chair, and speaks in great excitement, wiping his face with his handkerchief*] Nothing—yes, yes, nothing.

ASTROV.   The weather is fine to-day, my dear Ivan; the morning was overcast and looked like rain, but now the sun is shining again. Honestly, we have had a very fine autumn, and the wheat is looking fairly well. [*Puts his map back into the portfolio*] But the days are growing short. [*He goes out.*]

HELENA [*goes quickly up to* VOITSKI].   You must do your best; you must use all your power to get my husband and myself away from here to-day! Do you hear? I say, this very day!

VOITSKI [*wiping his face*].   Oh! Ah! Oh! All right! I—Helena, I saw everything!

HELENA [*in great agitation*].   Do you hear me? I must leave here this very day.

[SEREBRAKOV, SONIA, MARINA, *and* TELEGIN *come in.*]

TELEGIN.   I am not very well myself, your Excellency. I have been limping for two days, and my head—

SEREBRAKOV.   Where are the others? I hate this house. It is a regular labyrinth. Everyone is always scattered through the twenty-six enormous rooms; one never can find a soul. [*Rings*] Ask my wife and Madame Voitskaya to come here!

HELENA.   I am here already.

SEREBRAKOV.   Please, all of you, sit down.

SONIA [*goes up to* HELENA *and asks anxiously*] What did he say?

HELENA.   I'll tell you later.

SONIA.   You are moved. [*Looking quickly and inquiringly into her face*] I understand; he said he would not come here anymore. [*Pause*] Tell me, did he?

[HELENA *nods.*]

SEREBRAKOV [*to* TELEGIN].   One can, after all, become reconciled to being an invalid, but not to this country life. The ways of it stick in my throat and I feel exactly as if I had been whirled off the earth and landed on a strange planet. Please be seated, ladies and gentlemen. Sonia! [SONIA *does not hear. She is standing with her head bowed sadly forward on her breast*] Sonia! [*Pause*] She does not hear me. [*To* MARINA] Sit down too, nurse.

[MARINA *sits down and begins to knit her stocking.*]

I crave your indulgence, ladies and gentlemen; hang your ears, if I may say so, on the peg of attention. [*He laughs.*]

VOITSKI [*agitated*]. Perhaps you do not need me—may I be excused?

SEREBRAKOV. No, you are needed now more than anyone.

VOITSKI. What is it you want of me?

SEREBRAKOV. You—but what are you angry about? If it is anything I have done, I ask you to forgive me.

VOITSKI. Oh, drop that and come to business; what do you want?

[MME. VOITSKAYA *comes in.*]

SEREBRAKOV. Here is mother. Ladies and gentlemen, I shall begin. I have asked you to assemble here, my friends, in order to discuss a very important matter. I want to ask you for your assistance and advice, and knowing your unfailing amiability I think I can count on both. I am a bookworm and a scholar, and am unfamiliar with practical affairs. I cannot, I find, dispense with the help of well-informed people such as you, Ivan, and you, Telegin, and you, mother. The truth is, *manet omnes una nox,* that is to say, our lives are in the hands of God, and as I am old and ill, I realize that the time has come for me to dispose of my property in regard to the interests of my family. My life is nearly over, and I am not thinking of myself, but I have a young wife and daughter. [*Pause*] I cannot continue to live in the country; we were not made for country life, and yet we cannot afford to live in town on the income derived from this estate. We might sell the woods, but that would be an expedient we could not resort to every year. We must find some means of guaranteeing to ourselves a certain more or less fixed yearly income. With this object in view, a plan has occurred to me which I now have the honor of presenting to you for your consideration. I shall only give you a rough outline, avoiding all details. Our estate does not pay on an average more than two percent on the money invested in it. I propose to sell it. If we then invest our capital in bonds, it will earn us four to five percent, and we should probably have a surplus over of several thousand rubles, with which we could buy a summer cottage in Finland—

VOITSKI. Hold on! Repeat what you just said; I don't think I heard you quite right.

SEREBRAKOV. I said we would invest the money in bonds and buy a cottage in Finland with the surplus.

VOITSKI. No, not Finland—you said something else.

SEREBRAKOV. I propose to sell this place.

VOITSKI. Aha! That was it! So you are going to sell the place?

Splendid. The idea is a rich one. And what do you propose to do with my old mother and me and with Sonia here?

SEREBRAKOV. That will be decided in due time. We can't do everything at once.

VOITSKI. Wait! It is clear that until this moment I have never had a grain of sense in my head. I have always been stupid enough to think that the estate belonged to Sonia. My father bought it as a wedding present for my sister, and I foolishly imagined that as our laws were made for Russians and not Turks, my sister's estate would come down to her child.

SEREBRAKOV. Of course it is Sonia's. Has anyone denied it? I don't want to sell it without Sonia's consent; on the contrary, what I am doing is for Sonia's good.

VOITSKI. This is absolutely incomprehensible. Either I have gone mad or—or—

MME. VOITSKAYA. Jean, don't contradict Alexander. Trust to him; he knows better than we do what is right and what is wrong.

VOITSKI. I shan't. Give me some water. [*He drinks*] Go ahead! Say anything you please—anything!

SEREBRAKOV. I can't imagine why you are so upset. I don't pretend that my scheme is an ideal one, and if you all object to it I shall not insist. [*Pause*]

TELEGIN [*with embarrassment*]. I not only nourish feelings of respect toward learning, your Excellency, but I am also drawn to it by family ties. My brother Gregory's wife's brother, whom you may know; his name is Constantine Lakedemonoff, and he used to be a magistrate—

VOITSKI. Stop, Waffles. This is business; wait a bit, we will talk of that later. [*To* SEREBRAKOV] There now, ask him what he thinks; this estate was bought from his uncle.

SEREBRAKOV. Ah! Why should I ask questions? What good would it do?

VOITSKI. The price was ninety-five thousand rubles. My father paid seventy and left a debt of twenty-five. Now listen! This place could never have been bought had I not renounced my inheritance in favor of my sister, whom I deeply loved—and what is more, I worked for ten years like an ox, and paid off the debt.

SEREBRAKOV. I regret ever having started this conversation.

VOITSKI. Thanks entirely to my own personal efforts, the place is entirely clear of debts, and now, when I have grown old, you want to throw me out, neck and crop!

SEREBRAKOV. I can't imagine what you are driving at.

VOITSKI. For twenty-five years I have managed this place, and have sent you the returns from it like the most honest of servants, and you have never given me one single word of thanks for my work, not one—neither in my youth nor now. You allowed me a meager salary of five hundred rubles a year, a beggar's pittance, and have never even thought of adding a ruble to it.

SEREBRAKOV.   What did I know about such things, Ivan? I am not a practical man and don't understand them. You might have helped yourself to all you wanted.

VOITSKI.   Yes, why did I not steal? Don't you all despise me for not stealing, when it would have been only justice? And I should not now have been a beggar!

MME. VOITSKAYA [*sternly*].   Jean!

TELEGIN [*agitated*].   Vanya, old man, don't talk in that way. Why spoil such pleasant relations? [*He embraces him*] Do stop!

VOITSKI.   For twenty-five years I have been sitting here with my mother like a mole in a burrow. Our every thought and hope was yours and yours only. By day we talked with pride of you and your work, and spoke your name with veneration; our nights we wasted reading the books and papers which my soul now loathes.

TELEGIN.   Don't, Vanya, don't. I can't stand it.

SEREBRAKOV [*wrathfully*].   What under heaven do you want, anyway?

VOITSKI.   We used to think of you as almost superhuman, but now the scales have fallen from my eyes and I see you as you are! You write on art without knowing anything about it. Those books of yours, which I used to admire, are not worth one copper kopeck. You are a hoax!

SEREBRAKOV.   Can't anyone make him stop? I am going!

HELENA.   Ivan, I command you to stop this instant! Do you hear me?

VOITSKI.   I refuse! [SEREBRAKOV *tries to get out of the room, but* VOITSKI *bars the door*] Wait! I have not done yet! You have wrecked my life. I have never lived. My best years have gone for nothing, have been ruined, thanks to you. You are my most bitter enemy!

TELEGIN.   I can't stand it; I can't stand it. I am going. [*He goes out in great excitement.*]

SEREBRAKOV.   But what do you want? What earthly right have you to use such language to me? Ruination! If this estate is yours, then take it, and let me be ruined!

HELENA.   I am going away out of this hell this minute. [*Shrieks*] This is too much!

VOITSKI.   My life has been a failure. I am clever and brave and strong. If I had lived a normal life I might have become another

Schopenhauer or Dostoevski. I am losing my head! I am going crazy! Mother, I am in despair! Oh, mother!

MME. VOITSKAYA [*sternly*].   Listen, Alexander!

[SONIA *falls on her knees beside the nurse and nestles against her.*]

SONIA.   Oh, nurse, nurse!

VOITSKI.   Mother! What shall I do? But no, don't speak! I know what to do. [*To* SEREBRAKOV] And you will understand me! [*He goes out through the door in the center of the room and* MME. VOITSKAYA *follows him.*]

SEREBRAKOV.   Tell me, what on earth is the matter? Take this lunatic out of my sight! I cannot possibly live under the same roof with him. His room [*He points to the center door*] is almost next door to mine. Let him take himself off into the village or into the wing of the house, or I shall leave here at once. I cannot stay in the same house with him.

HELENA [*to her husband*].   We are leaving to-day; we must get ready at once for our departure.

SEREBRAKOV.   What a perfectly dreadful man!

SONIA [*on her knees beside the nurse and turning to her father. She speaks with emotion*].   You must be kind to us, papa. Uncle Vanya and I are so unhappy! [*Controlling her despair*] Have pity on us. Remember how Uncle Vanya and Granny used to copy and translate your books for you every night—every, every night. Uncle Vanya has toiled without rest; he would never spend a penny on us, we sent it all to you. We have not eaten the bread of idleness. I am not saying this as I should like to, but you must understand us, papa, you must be merciful to us.

HELENA [*very excited, to her husband*].   For heaven's sake, Alexander, go and have a talk with him—explain!

SEREBRAKOV.   Very well, I shall have a talk with him, but I won't apologize for a thing. I am not angry with him, but you must confess that his behavior has been strange, to say the least. Excuse me, I shall go to him. [*He goes out through the center door.*]

HELENA.   Be gentle with him; try to quiet him. [*She follows him out.*]

SONIA [*nestling nearer to* MARINA].   Nurse, oh, nurse!

MARINA.   It's all right, my baby. When the geese have cackled they will be still again. First they cackle and then they stop.

SONIA.   Nurse!

MARINA.   You are trembling all over, as if you were freezing. There, there, little orphan baby, God is merciful. A little linden tea, and it will all pass away. Don't cry, my sweetest. [*Looking angrily at the door in the center of the room*] See, the geese have all gone now. The devil take them!

[*A shot is heard.* HELENA *screams behind the scenes.* SONIA *shudders.*]

MARINA.   Bang! What's that?

SEREBRAKOV [*comes in reeling with terror*].   Hold him! Hold him! He has gone mad!

[HELENA *and* VOITSKI *are seen struggling in the doorway.*]

HELENA [*trying to wrest the revolver from him*].   Give it to me; give it to me, I tell you!

VOITSKI.   Let me go, Helena, let me go! [*He frees himself and rushes in, looking everywhere for* SEREBRAKOV] Where is he? Ah, there he is! [*He shoots at him. Pause*] I didn't get him? I missed again? [*Furiously*] Damnation! Damnation! To hell with him!

[*He flings the revolver on the floor, and drops helpless into a chair.* SEREBRAKOV *stands as if stupefied.* HELENA *leans against the wall, almost fainting.*]

HELENA.   Take me away! Take me away! I can't stay here—I can't!

VOITSKI [*in despair*].   Oh, what shall I do? What shall I do?

SONIA [*softly*].   Oh, nurse, nurse!

CURTAIN.

ACT IV

VOITSKI's *bedroom, which is also his office. A table stands near the window; on it are ledgers, letter scales, and papers of every description. Nearby stands a smaller table belonging to* ASTROV, *with his paints and drawing materials. On the wall hangs a cage containing a starling. There is also a map of Africa on the wall, obviously of no use to anybody. There is a large sofa covered with buckram. A door to the left leads into an inner room; one to the right leads into the front hall, and before this door lies a mat for the peasants with their muddy boots to stand on. It is an autumn evening. The silence is profound.* TELEGIN *and* MARINA *are sitting facing one another, winding wool.*

TELEGIN. Be quick, Marina, or we shall be called away to say good-bye before you have finished. The carriage has already been ordered.

MARINA [*trying to wind more quickly*]. I am a little tired.

TELEGIN. They are going to Kharkov to live.

MARINA. They do well to go.

TELEGIN. They have been frightened. The professor's wife won't stay here an hour longer. "If we are going at all, let's be off," says she, "we shall go to Kharkov and look about us, and then we can send for our things." They are travelling light. It seems, Marina, that fate has decreed for them not to live here.

MARINA. And quite rightly. What a storm they have just raised! It was shameful!

TELEGIN. It was indeed. The scene was worthy of the brush of Aibazofski.

MARINA. I wish I'd never laid eyes on them. [*Pause*] Now we shall have things as they were again: tea at eight, dinner at one, and supper in the evening; everything in order as decent folks, as Christians like to have it. [*Sighs*] It is a long time since I have eaten noodles.

TELEGIN. Yes, we haven't had noodles for ages. [*Pause*] Not for ages. As I was going through the village this morning, Marina, one of the shop-keepers called after me, "Hi! you hanger-on!" I felt it bitterly.

MARINA.   Don't pay the least attention to them, master; we are all dependants on God. You and Sonia and all of us. Everyone must work, no one can sit idle. Where is Sonia?

TELEGIN.   In the garden with the doctor, looking for Ivan. They fear he may lay violent hands on himself.

MARINA.   Where is his pistol?

TELEGIN [whispers].   I hid it in the cellar.

[VOITSKI and ASTROV come in.]

VOITSKI.   Leave me alone! [To MARINA and TELEGIN] Go away! Go away and leave me to myself, if but for an hour. I won't have you watching me like this!

TELEGIN.   Yes, yes, Vanya. [He goes out on tiptoe.]

MARINA.   The gander cackles; ho! ho! ho! [She gathers up her wool and goes out.]

VOITSKI.   Leave me by myself!

ASTROV.   I would, with the greatest pleasure. I ought to have gone long ago, but I shan't leave you until you have returned what you took from me.

VOITSKI.   I took nothing from you.

ASTROV.   I am not jesting, don't detain me, I really must go.

VOITSKI.   I took nothing of yours.

ASTROV.   You didn't? Very well, I shall have to wait a little longer, and then you will have to forgive me if I resort to force. We shall have to bind you and search you. I mean what I say.

VOITSKI.   Do as you please. [Pause] Oh, to make such a fool of myself! To shoot twice and miss him both times! I shall never forgive myself.

ASTROV.   When the impulse came to shoot, it would have been as well had you put a bullet through your own head.

VOITSKI [shrugging his shoulders].   Strange! I attempted murder, and am not going to be arrested or brought to trial. That means they think me mad. [With a bitter laugh] Me! I am mad, and those who hide their worthlessness, their dullness, their crying heartlessness behind a professor's mask, are sane! Those who marry old men and then deceive them under the noses of all, are sane! I saw you kiss her; I saw you in each other's arms!

ASTROV.   Yes, sir, I did kiss her; so there. [He puts his thumb to his nose.]

VOITSKI [his eyes on the door].   No, it is the earth that is mad, because she still bears us on her breast.

ASTROV.   That is nonsense.

VOITSKI.   Well? Am I not a madman, and therefore irresponsible? Haven't I the right to talk nonsense?

ASTROV.   This is a farce! You are not mad; you are simply a ridiculous fool. I used to think every fool was out of his senses, but now I see that lack of sense is a man's normal state, and you are perfectly normal.

VOITSKI [*covers his face with his hands*].   Oh! If you knew how ashamed I am! These piercing pangs of shame are like nothing on earth. [*In an agonized voice*] I can't endure them! [*He leans against the table*] What can I do? What can I do?

ASTROV.   Nothing.

VOITSKI.   You must tell me something! Oh, my God! I am forty-seven years old. I may live to sixty; I still have thirteen years before me; an eternity! How shall I be able to endure life for thirteen years? What shall I do? How can I fill them? Oh, don't you see? [*He presses* ASTROV*'s hand convulsively*] Don't you see, if only I could live the rest of my life in some new way! If I could only wake some still, bright morning and feel that life had begun again; that the past was forgotten and had vanished like smoke. [*He weeps*] Oh, to begin life anew! Tell me, tell me how to begin.

ASTROV [*crossly*].   What nonsense! What sort of a new life can you and I look forward to? We can have no hope.

VOITSKI.   None?

ASTROV.   None. Of that I am convinced.

VOITSKI.   Tell me what to do. [*He puts his hand to his heart*] I feel such a burning pain here.

ASTROV [*shouts angrily*].   Stop! [*Then, more gently*] It may be that posterity, which will despise us for our blind and stupid lives, will find some road to happiness; but we—you and I—have but one hope, the hope that we may be visited by visions, perhaps by pleasant ones, as we lie resting in our graves. [*Sighing*] Yes, brother, there were only two respectable, intelligent men in this district, you and I. Ten years or so of this life of ours, this miserable life, have sucked us under, and we have become as contemptible and petty as the rest. But don't try to talk me out of my purpose! Give me what you took from me, will you?

VOITSKI.   I took nothing from you.

ASTROV.   You took a little bottle of morphine out of my medicine case. [*Pause*] Listen! If you are positively determined to make an end to yourself, go into the woods and shoot yourself there. Give up the morphine, or there will be a lot of talk and guesswork; people will think I gave it to you. I don't fancy having to perform a postmortem on you. Do you think I should find it interesting?

[SONIA *comes in.*]

VOITSKI.   Leave me alone.

ASTROV [*to* SONIA].   Sonia, your uncle has stolen a bottle of morphine out of my medicine case and won't give it up. Tell him that his behavior is—well, unwise. I haven't time, I must be going.

SONIA.   Uncle Vanya, did you take the morphine?

ASTROV.   Yes, he took it. [*Pause*] I am absolutely sure.

SONIA.   Give it up! Why do you want to frighten us? [*Tenderly*] Give it up, Uncle Vanya! My misfortune is perhaps even greater than yours, but I am not plunged in despair. I endure my sorrow, and shall endure it until my life comes to a natural end. You must endure yours, too. [*Pause*] Give it up! Dear, darling Uncle Vanya. Give it up! [*She weeps*] You are so good, I am sure you will have pity on us and give it up. You must endure your sorrow, Uncle Vanya; you must endure it.

[VOITSKI *takes a bottle from the drawer of the table and hands it to* ASTROV.]

VOITSKI.   There it is! [*To* SONIA] And now, we must get to work at once; we must do something, or else I shall not be able to endure it.

SONIA.   Yes, yes, to work! As soon as we have seen them off we shall go to work. [*She nervously straightens out the papers on the table*] Everything is in a muddle!

ASTROV [*putting the bottle in his case, which he straps together*] Now I can be off.

[HELENA *comes in.*]

HELENA.   Are you here, Ivan? We are starting in a moment. Go to Alexander, he wants to speak to you.

SONIA.   Go, Uncle Vanya. [*She takes* VOITSKI's *arm*] Come, you and papa must make peace; that is absolutely necessary.

[SONIA *and* VOITSKI *go out.*]

HELENA.   I am going away. [*She gives* ASTROV *her hand*] Goodbye.

ASTROV.   So soon?

HELENA.   The carriage is waiting.

ASTROV.   Good-bye.

HELENA.   You promised me you would go away yourself to-day.

ASTROV.   I have not forgotten. I am going at once. [*Pause*] Were you frightened? Was it so terrible?

HELENA.   Yes.

ASTROV.   Couldn't you stay? Couldn't you? To-morrow—in the forest—

HELENA.   No. It is all settled, and that is why I can look you so bravely in the face. Our departure is fixed. One thing I must ask of you: don't think too badly of me; I would like you to respect me.

ASTROV.   Ah! [*With an impatient gesture*] Stay, I implore you! Confess that there is nothing for you to do in this world. You have no object in life; there is nothing to occupy your attention, and sooner or later your feelings must master you. It is inevitable. It would be better if it happened not in Kharkov or in Kursk, but here, in nature's lap. It would then at least be poetical, even beautiful. Here you have the forests, the houses half in ruins that Turgenev writes of.

HELENA.   How comical you are! I am angry with you and yet I shall always remember you with pleasure. You are interesting and original. You and I will never meet again, and so I shall tell you— why should I conceal it?—that I am just a little in love with you. Come, one more last pressure of our hands, and then let us part good friends. Let us not bear each other any ill will.

ASTROV [*pressing her hand*].   Yes, go. [*Thoughtfully*] You seem to be sincere and good, and yet there is something strangely disquieting about all your personality. No sooner did you arrive here with your husband than everyone whom you found busy and actively creating something was forced to drop his work and give himself up for the whole summer to your husband's gout and yourself. You and he have infected us with your idleness. I have been swept off my feet; I have not put my hand to a thing for weeks, during which sickness has been running its course unchecked among the people, and the peasants have been pasturing their cattle in my woods and young plantations. Go where you will, you and your husband will always carry destruction in your train. I am joking, of course, and yet I am strangely sure that had you stayed here we should have been overtaken by the most immense desolation. I would have gone to my ruin, and you—you would not have prospered. So go! *E finita la comedia!*

HELENA [*snatching a pencil off* ASTROV's *table, and hiding it with a quick movement*] I shall take this pencil for memory!

ASTROV.   How strange it is. We meet, and then suddenly it seems that we must part forever. That is the way in this world. As long as we are alone, before Uncle Vanya comes in with a bouquet—allow me—to kiss you good-bye—may I? [*He kisses her on the cheek*] So! Splendid!

HELENA.   I wish you every happiness. [*She glances about her*] For once in my life, I shall, and scorn the consequences! [*She kisses him impetuously, and they quickly part*] I must go.

ASTROV.   Yes, go. If the carriage is there, then start at once. [*They stand listening.*] E finita!

[VOITSKI, SEREBRAKOV, MME. VOITSKAYA *with her book,* TELEGIN, *and* SONIA *come in.*]

SEREBRAKOV [*to* VOITSKI].   Shame on him who bears malice for the past. I have gone through so much in the last few hours that I feel capable of writing a whole treatise on the conduct of life for the instruction of posterity. I gladly accept your apology, and myself ask your forgiveness. [*He kisses* VOITSKI *three times.*]

[HELENA *embraces* SONIA.]

SEREBRAKOV [*kissing* MME. VOITSKAYA*'s hand*].   Mother!

MME. VOITSKAYA [*kissing him*].   Have your picture taken, Alexander, and send me one. You know how dear you are to me.

TELEGIN.   Good-bye, your Excellency. Don't forget us.

SEREBRAKOV [*kissing his daughter*].   Good-bye, good-bye all. [*Shaking hands with* ASTROV] Many thanks for your pleasant company. I have a deep regard for your opinions and your enthusiasm, but let me, as an old man, give one word of advice at parting: do something, my friend! Work! Do something! [*They all bow*] Good luck to you all. [*He goes out followed by* MME. VOITSKAYA *and* SONIA.]

VOITSKI [*kissing* HELENA*'s hand fervently*].   Good-bye—forgive me. I shall never see you again!

HELENA [*touched*].   Good-bye, dear boy. [*She lightly kisses his head as he bends over her hand, and goes out.*]

ASTROV.   Tell them to bring my carriage around too, Waffles.

TELEGIN.   All right, old man.

[ASTROV *and* VOITSKI *are left behind alone.* ASTROV *collects his paints and drawing materials on the table and packs them away in a box.*]

ASTROV.   Why don't you go to see them off?

VOITSKI.   Let them go! I—I can't go out there. I feel too sad. I must go to work on something at once. To work! To work! [*He rummages through his papers on the table.*]

[Pause. *The tinkling of bells is heard as the horses trot away.*]

ASTROV. They have gone! The professor, I suppose, is glad to go. He couldn't be tempted back now by a fortune.

[MARINA *comes in.*]

MARINA. They have gone. [*She sits down in an arm-chair and knits her stocking.*]

[SONIA *comes in wiping her eyes.*]

SONIA. They have gone. God be with them. [*To her uncle*] And now, Uncle Vanya, let us do something!
VOITSKI. To work! To work!
SONIA. It is long, long, since you and I have sat together at this table. [*She lights a lamp on the table*] No ink! [*She takes the inkstand to the cupboard and fills it from an ink-bottle*] How sad it is to see them go!

[MME. VOITSKAYA *comes in slowly.*]

MME. VOITSKAYA. They have gone. [*She sits down and at once becomes absorbed in her book.*]

[SONIA *sits down at the table and looks through an account book.*]

SONIA. First, Uncle Vanya, let us write up the accounts. They are in a dreadful state. Come, begin. You take one and I will take the other.
VOITSKI. In account with—

[*They sit silently writing.*]

MARINA [*yawning*]. The sand-man has come.
ASTROV. How still it is. Their pens scratch, the cricket sings; it is so warm and comfortable. I hate to go.

[*The tinkling of bells is heard.*]

ASTROV. My carriage has come. There now remains but to say good-bye to you, my friends, and to my table here, and then—away! [*He puts the map into the portfolio.*]
MARINA. Don't hurry away; sit a little longer with us.
ASTROV. Impossible.
VOITSKI [*writing*]. And carry forward from the old debt two seventy-five—

[WORKMAN *comes in.*]

WORKMAN. Your carriage is waiting, sir.

ASTROV. All right. [*He hands* WORKMAN *his medicine-case, portfolio, and box*] Look out, don't crush the portfolio!

WORKMAN. Very well, sir.

SONIA. When shall we see you again?

ASTROV. Hardly before next summer. Probably not this winter, though, of course, if anything should happen you will let me know. [*He shakes hands with them*] Thank you for your kindness, for your hospitality, for everything! [*He goes up to* MARINA *and kisses her head*] Good-bye, old nurse!

MARINA. Are you going without your tea?

ASTROV. I don't want any, nurse.

MARINA. Won't you have a drop of vodka?

ASTROV [*hesitatingly*]. Yes, I might.

[MARINA *goes out.*]

ASTROV [*after a pause*]. My off-wheeler has gone lame for some reason. I noticed it yesterday when Peter was taking him to water.

VOITSKI. You should have him re-shod.

ASTROV. I shall have to go around by the blacksmith's on my way home. It can't be avoided. [*He stands looking up at the map of Africa hanging on the wall*] I suppose it is roasting hot in Africa now.

VOITSKI. Yes, I suppose it is.

[MARINA *comes back carrying a tray on which are a glass of vodka and a piece of bread.*]

MARINA. Help yourself.

[ASTROV *drinks.*]

MARINA. To your good health! [*She bows deeply*] Eat your bread with it.

ASTROV. No, I like it so. And now, good-bye. [*To* MARINA] You needn't come out to see me off, nurse. [*He goes out.*]

[SONIA *follows him with a candle to light him to the carriage.* MARINA *sits down in her armchair.*]

VOITSKI [*writing*]. On the 2d of February, twenty pounds of butter; on the 16th, twenty pounds of butter again. Buckwheat flour—

[*Pause. Bells are heard tinkling.*]

MARINA. He has gone. [*Pause*]

[SONIA *comes in and sets the candlestick on the table.*]

SONIA. He has gone.

VOITSKI [*adding and writing*].   Total, fifteen—twenty-five—

[SONIA *sits down and begins to write.*]

MARINA [*yawning*].   Oh, ho! The Lord have mercy.

[TELEGIN *comes in on tiptoe, sits down near the door, and begins to tune his guitar.*]

VOITSKI [*to* SONIA, *stroking her hair*].   Oh, my child, I am so miserable; if you only knew how miserable I am!

SONIA.   What can we do? We must live our lives. [*Pause*] Yes, we shall live, Uncle Vanya. We shall live through the long procession of days before us, and through the long evenings; we shall patiently bear the trials that fate imposes on us; we shall work for others without rest, both now and when we are old; and when our last hour comes we shall meet it humbly, and there, beyond the grave, we shall say that we have suffered and wept, that our life was bitter, and God will have pity on us. Ah, then, dear, dear Uncle, we shall see that bright and beautiful life; we shall rejoice and look back upon our sorrow here; a tender smile—and—we shall rest. I have faith, Uncle, fervent, passionate faith. [SONIA *kneels down before her uncle and lays her head on his hands. She speaks in a weary voice*] We shall rest. [TELEGIN *plays softly on the guitar*] We shall rest. We shall hear the angels. We shall see heaven shining like a jewel. We shall see all evil and all our pain sink away in the great compassion that shall enfold the world. Our life will be as peaceful and tender and sweet as a caress. I have faith; I have faith. [*She wipes away her tears*] My poor, poor Uncle Vanya, you are crying! [*Weeping*] You have never known what happiness was, but wait, Uncle Vanya, wait! We shall rest. [*She embraces him*] We shall rest. [*The* WATCHMAN's *rattle is heard in the garden;* TELEGIN *plays softly;* MME. VOITSKAYA *writes something on the margin of her pamphlet;* MARINA *knits her stocking*] We shall rest.

CURTAIN.

THE THREE SISTERS

Characters

ANDREY SERGEYEVICH PROZOROV
NATALIA IVANOVNA [NATASHA], *his fiancée, later his wife*
OLGA ⎫
MASHA [MARYA] ⎬ *his sisters*
IRINA ⎭
FYODOR ILYICH KULYGIN, *high school teacher, married to* MASHA
ALEXANDER IGNATYEVICH VERSHININ, *lieutenant-colonel in charge of a battery*
NIKOLAI LVOVICH TUZENBAKH, *baron, lieutenant in the army*
VASSILI VASSILYEVICH SOLYONI, *captain*
IVAN ROMANOVICH CHEBUTYKIN, *army doctor*
ALEXEY PETROVICH FEDOTIK, *second lieutenant*
VLADIMIR KARLOVICH RODÉ, *second lieutenant*
FERAPONT, *door-keeper at local council offices, an old man*
ANFISA, *nurse, 80 years old*

The action takes place in a provincial town.

ACT I

In PROZOROV's *house. A sitting-room with pillars; behind is seen a large dining-room. It is midday, the sun is shining brightly outside. In the dining-room the table is being laid for lunch.*

OLGA, *in the regulation blue dress of a teacher at a girl's high school, is walking about correcting exercise books;* MASHA, *in a black dress, with a hat on her knees, sits and reads a book;* IRINA, *in white, stands about, with a thoughtful expression.*

OLGA.   A year since father died last May the fifth, on your name-day, Irina. It was very cold then, and snowing. I thought I would never live, and you were in a dead faint. And now a year has gone by and it does not affect us, and you are wearing a white dress and look happy. [*Clock strikes twelve.*] And the clock struck just the same way then. [*Pause*] I remember that there was music at the funeral, and they fired a volley in the cemetery. A general in command but few people present. Rain and snow.

IRINA.   Why recall it?

[BARON TUZENBAKH, CHEBUTYKIN *and* SOLYONI *appear by the table in the dining-room, behind the pillars.*]

OLGA.   It's so warm to-day that we can keep the windows open, though the birches are not yet in flower. Father was put in command of a brigade, and he rode out of Moscow with us eleven years ago. I remember perfectly that it was early in May and all Moscow was blooming. It was warm too, everything in sunshine. Eleven years, and I remember everything as if we rode out only yesterday. Oh God! When I awoke this morning and saw all the light and the spring, I was homesick.

CHEBUTYKIN.   Will you take a bet on it?

TUZENBAKH.   Don't be foolish.

[MASHA, *lost in a reverie over her book, whistles softly.*]

OLGA.   Don't whistle, Masha. How can you! [*Pause*] I'm always

219

having headaches from having to go to the High School every day and then teach till evening. Strange thoughts come to me, as if I were aged. And really, during these four years I have been feeling as if every day had been drained from me. And only one desire grows and gains in strength. . . .

IRINA.   To go away to Moscow. To sell the house, leave all and go to Moscow. . . .

OLGA.   Yes! To Moscow, and as soon as possible.

[CHEBUTYKIN *and* TUZENBAKH *laugh.*]

IRINA.   I expect Andrey will become a professor, but still, he won't want to live here. Only poor Masha must go on living here.

OLGA.   Masha can come to Moscow every summer.

[MASHA *is whistling gently.*]

IRINA.   Everything will be arranged, please God. [*Looks out of window.*] It's nice out to-day. I don't know why I'm so happy: I remembered this morning that it was my name-day, and I suddenly felt glad and remembered my childhood, when mother was still with us. What beautiful thoughts I had, what thoughts!

OLGA.   You're all radiance to-day, I've never seen you look so lovely. And Masha is pretty, too. Andrey wouldn't be bad-looking, if he wasn't so stout; it does spoil his appearance. But I've grown old and very thin, I suppose it's because I get angry with the girls at school. To-day I'm free. I'm at home. I haven't got a headache, and I feel younger than I was yesterday. I'm only twenty-eight. . . . All's well, God is everywhere, but it seems to me that if only I were married and could stay at home all day, it would be even better. [*Pause*] I should love my husband.

TUZENBAKH [*to* SOLYONI].   I'm tired of listening to the rot you talk. [*Entering the sitting-room.*] I forgot to say that Vershinin, our new lieutenant-colonel of artillery, is coming to see us to-day. [*Sits down to the piano.*]

OLGA.   That's good. I'm glad.

IRINA.   Is he old?

TUZENBAKH.   Oh, no. Forty or forty-five, at the very outside. [*Plays softly.*] He seems rather a good sort. He's certainly no fool, only he likes to hear himself speak.

IRINA.   Is he interesting?

TUZENBAKH.   Oh, he's all right, but there's his wife, his mother-in-law, and two daughters. This is his second wife. He pays calls and tells everybody that he's got a wife and two daughters. He'll tell you so here. The wife isn't all there, she does her hair like a flapper and gushes extremely. She talks philosophy and tries to commit suicide every now and again, apparently in order to annoy her husband. I should have left her long ago, but he bears up patiently, and just grumbles.

SOLYONI [*enters with* CHEBUTYKIN *from the dining-room*]. With one hand I can only lift fifty-four pounds, but with both hands I can lift 180, or even 200 pounds. From this I conclude that two men are not twice as strong as one, but three times, perhaps even more. . . .

CHEBUTYKIN [*reads a newspaper as he walks*]. If your hair is coming out . . . take an ounce of naphthaline and half a bottle of spirit . . . dissolve and use daily. . . . [*Makes a note in his pocket diary.*] When found make a note of! Not that I want it though. . . . [*Crosses it out.*] It doesn't matter.

IRINA. Ivan Romanovich, dear Ivan Romanovich!

CHEBUTYKIN. What does my own little girl want?

IRINA. Ivan Romanovich, dear Ivan Romanovich! I feel as if I were sailing under the broad blue sky with great white birds around me. Why is that? Why?

CHEBUTYKIN [*kisses her hands, tenderly*]. My white bird. . . .

IRINA. When I woke up to-day and got up and dressed myself, I suddenly began to feel as if everything in this life was open to me, and that I knew how I must live. Dear Ivan Romanovich, I know everything. A man must work, toil in the sweat of his brow, whoever he may be, for that is the meaning and object of his life, his happiness, his enthusiasm. How fine it is to be a workman who gets up at daybreak and breaks stones in the street, or a shepherd, or a schoolmaster, who teaches children, or an engine-driver on the railway. . . . My God, let alone a man, it's better to be an ox, or just a horse, so long as it can work, than a young woman who wakes up at twelve o'clock, has her coffee in bed, and then spends two hours dressing. . . . Oh it's awful! Sometimes when it's hot, your thirst can be just as tiresome as my need for work. And if I don't get up early in future and work, Ivan Romanovich, then you may refuse me your friendship.

CHEBUTYKIN [*tenderly*]. I'll refuse, I'll refuse. . . .

OLGA. Father used to make us get up at seven. Now Irina wakes at seven and lies and meditates about something till nine at least. And she looks so serious! [*Laughs*]

IRINA. You're so used to seeing me as a little girl that it seems queer to you when my face is serious. I'm twenty!

TUZENBAKH. How well I can understand that craving for work, oh God! I've never worked once in my life. I was born in Petersburg, a chilly, lazy place, in a family which never knew what work or worry meant. I remember that when I used to come home from my regiment, a footman used to have to pull off my boots while I fidgeted and my mother looked on in adoration and wondered why other people didn't see me in the same light. They shielded me from work; but only just in time! A new age is dawning, the people are marching on us all, a powerful, health-giving storm is gathering, it is drawing near, soon it will be upon us and it will drive away laziness, indifference, the prejudice against labor, and rotten dullness from our society. I shall work, and in twenty-five or thirty years, every man will have to work. Every one!

CHEBUTYKIN. I shan't work.

TUZENBAKH. You don't matter.

SOLYONI. In twenty-five years' time, we shall all be dead, thank the Lord. In two or three years' time apoplexy will carry you off, or else I'll blow your brains out, my pet. [*Takes a scent-bottle out of his pocket and sprinkles his chest and hands.*]

CHEBUTYKIN [*laughs*]. It's quite true, I never have worked. After I came down from the university I never stirred a finger or opened a book, I just read the papers. . . . [*Takes another newspaper out of his pocket.*] Here we are. . . . I've learnt from the papers that there used to be one, Dobrolyubov, for instance, but what he wrote—I don't know. . . . God only knows. . . . [*Somebody is heard tapping on the floor from below.*] There . . . They're calling me downstairs, somebody's come to see me. I'll be back in a minute . . . won't be long. . . . [*Exit hurriedly, scratching his beard.*]

IRINA. He's up to something.

TUZENBAKH. Yes, he looked so pleased as he went out that I'm pretty certain he'll bring you a present in a moment.

IRINA. How unpleasant!

OLGA. Yes, it's awful. He's always doing silly things.

MASHA. "There stands a green oak by the sea.
　　　　And a chain of bright gold is around it . . .
　　　　And a chain of bright gold is around it. . . ."[1]

[*Gets up and sings softly.*]

OLGA. You're not very bright to-day, Masha. [MASHA *sings, putting on her hat.*] Where are you off to?

MASHA. Home.

IRINA. That's odd. . . .

TUZENBAKH. On a name-day, too!

MASHA. It doesn't matter. I'll come in the evening. Good-bye, dear. [*Kisses* IRINA.] Many happy returns, though I've said it before.

---

[1]The opening of Pushkin's *Ruslan and Lyudmila*.

In the old days when father was alive, every time we had a name-day, thirty or forty officers used to come, and there was lots of noise and fun, and to-day there's only a man and a half, and it's quiet as a desert . . . I'm off . . . I've got the hump to-day, and am not at all cheerful, so don't you mind me. [*Laughs through her tears.*] We'll have a talk later on, but good-bye for the present, my dear; I'll go somewhere.

IRINA [*displeased*]. You are queer. . . .

OLGA [*crying*]. I understand you, Masha.

SOLYONI. When a man talks philosophy, well, it is philosophy or at any rate sophistry; but when a woman, or two women, talk philosophy—it's all my eye.

MASHA. What do you mean by that, you very awful man?

SOLYONI. Oh, nothing. You came down on me before I could say . . . help! [*Pause*]

MASHA [*angry, to* OLGA]. Don't cry!

[*Enter* ANFISA *and* FERAPONT *with a cake.*]

ANFISA. This way, my dear. Come in, your feet are clean. [*To* IRINA] From the District Council, from Mikhail Ivanich Protopopov . . . a cake.

IRINA. Thank you. Please thank him. [*Takes the cake.*]

FERAPONT. What?

IRINA [*louder*]. Please thank him.

OLGA. Give him a pie, nurse. Ferapont, go, she'll give you a pie.

FERAPONT. What?

ANFISA. Come on, gran'fer, Ferapont Spiridonich. Come on. [*Exeunt*]

MASHA. I don't like this Mikhail Potapich or Ivanich, Protopopov. We oughtn't to invite him here.

IRINA. I never asked him.

MASHA. That's all right.

[*Enter* CHEBUTYKIN *followed by a soldier with a silver samovar; there is a rumble of dissatisfied surprise.*]

OLGA [*covers her face with her hands*]. A samovar! That's awful! [*Exit into the dining-room, to the table.*]

IRINA. My dear Ivan Romanovich, what are you doing!

TUZENBAKH [*laughs*]. I told you so!

MASHA. Ivan Romanovich, you are simply shameless!

CHEBUTYKIN. My dear good girl, you are the only thing, and the dearest thing, I have in the world. I'll soon be sixty. I'm an old man, a lonely worthless old man. The only good thing in me is my love for

you, and if it hadn't been for that, I would have been dead long ago.
. . . [*To* IRINA] My dear little girl, I've known you since the day of
your birth, I've carried you in my arms . . . I loved your dead
mother. . . .

MASHA. But your presents are so expensive!

CHEBUTYKIN [*angrily, through his tears*]. Expensive presents. . . .
You really are! . . . [*To the orderly*] Take the samovar in there. . . .
[*Teasing*] Expensive presents!

[*The orderly goes into the dining-room with the samovar.*]

ANFISA [*enters and crosses stage*]. My dear, there's a strange Colonel
come! He's taken off his coat already. Children, he's coming here.
Irina darling, you'll be a nice and polite little girl, won't you. . . .
Should have lunched a long time ago. . . . Oh, Lord. . . . [*Exit*]

TUZENBAKH. It must be Vershinin. [*Enter* VERSHININ.]
Lieutenant-Colonel Vershinin!

VERSHININ [*to* MASHA *and* IRINA]. I have the honor to introduce
myself, my name is Vershinin. I am very glad indeed to be able to
come at last. How you've grown! Oh! Oh!

IRINA. Please sit down. We're very glad you've come.

VERSHININ [*gaily*]. I am glad, very glad! But there are three sisters, surely. I remember—three little girls. I forget your faces, but
your father, Colonel Prozorov, used to have three little girls. I remember that perfectly, I saw them with my own eyes. How time
does fly! Oh, dear, how it flies!

TUZENBAKH. Alexander Ignatyevich comes from Moscow.

IRINA. From Moscow? Are you from Moscow?

VERSHININ. Yes, that's so. Your father used to be in charge of a
battery there, and I was an officer in the same brigade. [*To* MASHA] I
seem to remember your face a little.

MASHA. I don't remember you.

IRINA. Olga! Olga! [*Shouts into the dining-room.*] Olga! Come
along! [OLGA *enters from the dining-room.*] Lieutenant-Colonel Vershinin
comes from Moscow, as it happens.

VERSHININ. I take it that you are Olga Sergeyevna, the eldest,
and that you are Marya . . . and you are Irina, the youngest. . . .

OLGA. So you come from Moscow?

VERSHININ. Yes. I went to school in Moscow and began my
service there; I was there for a long time until at last I got my battery
and moved over here, as you see. I don't really remember you, I only
remember that there used to be three sisters. I remember your father
well; I have only to shut my eyes to see him as he was. I used to come
to your house in Moscow. . . .

OLGA.   I used to think I remembered everybody, but . . .

VERSHININ.   My name is Alexander Ignatyevich.

IRINA.   Alexander Ignatyevich, you've come from Moscow. That is really a surprise!

OLGA.   We are going to live there, you see.

IRINA.   We think we may be there this autumn. It's our native town, we were born there. In Old Basmanni Road. . . . [*They both laugh for joy.*]

MASHA.   We've unexpectedly met a fellow countryman. [*Briskly*] I remember: Do you remember, Olga, they used to speak at home of a "lovelorn Major." You were only a Lieutenant then, and in love with somebody, but for some reason they always called you a Major for fun.

VERSHININ [*laughs*].   That's it . . . the lovelorn Major, that's got it!

MASHA.   You only wore moustaches then. You have grown older! [*Through her tears.*] You have grown older!

VERSHININ.   Yes, when they used to call me the lovelorn Major, I was young and in love. I've grown out of both now.

OLGA.   But you haven't a single white hair yet. You're older, but you're not yet old.

VERSHININ.   I'm forty-two, anyway. Have you been away from Moscow long?

IRINA.   Eleven years. What are you crying for, Masha, you little fool. . . . [*Crying*] And I'm crying too.

MASHA.   It's all right. And where did you live?

VERSHININ.   Old Basmanni Road.

OLGA.   Same as we.

VERSHININ.   Once I used to live in German Street. That was when the Red Barracks were my headquarters. There's an ugly bridge in between, where the water rushes underneath. One gets melancholy when one is alone there. [*Pause*] Here the river is so wide and fine! It's a splendid river!

OLGA.   Yes, but it's so cold. It's very cold here, and the midges. . . .

VERSHININ.   What are you saying! Here you've got such a fine healthy Russian climate. You've a forest, a river . . . and birches. Dear, modest birches, I like them more than any other tree. It's good to live here. Only it's odd that the railway station should be thirteen miles away . . . Nobody knows why.

SOLYONI.   I know why. [*All look at him.*] Because if it was near it wouldn't be far off, and if it's far off, it can't be near. [*An awkward pause*]

TUZENBAKH.   Funny man.

OLGA.   Now I know who you are. I remember.

VERSHININ.   I used to know your mother.

CHEBUTYKIN.   She was a good woman, rest her soul.

IRINA.   Mother is buried in Moscow.

OLGA.   At the Novo-Devichi Cemetery.

MASHA.   Do you know, I'm beginning to forget her face. We'll be forgotten in just the same way.

VERSHININ.   Yes, they'll forget us. It's our fate, it can't be helped. A time will come when everything that seems serious, significant, or very important to us will be forgotten, or considered trivial. [*Pause*] And the curious thing is that we can't possibly find out what will come to be regarded as great and important, and what will be feeble, or silly. Didn't the discoveries of Copernicus, or Columbus, say, seem unnecessary and ludicrous at first, while wasn't it thought that some rubbish written by a fool, held all the truth? And it may so happen that our present existence, with which we are so satisfied, will in time appear strange, inconvenient, stupid, unclean, perhaps even sinful. . . .

TUZENBAKH.   Who knows? But on the other hand, they may call our life noble and honor its memory. We've abolished torture and capital punishment, we live in security, but how much suffering there is still!

SOLYONI [*in a feeble voice*].   There, there. . . . The Baron will go without his dinner if you only let him talk philosophy.

TUZENBAKH.   Vassili Vassilyevich, kindly leave me alone. [*Changes his chair.*] You're very dull, you know.

SOLYONI [*feebly*].   There, there, there.

TUZENBAKH [*to* VERSHININ].   The sufferings we see to-day—there are so many of them!—still indicate a certain moral improvement in society.

VERSHININ.   Yes, yes, of course.

CHEBUTYKIN.   You said just now, Baron, that they may call our life noble; but we are very petty. . . . [*Stands up*] See how little I am. [*Violin played behind.*]

MASHA.   That's Andrey playing—our brother.

IRINA.   He's the learned member of the family. I expect he will be a professor some day. Father was a soldier, but his son chose an academic career for himself.

MASHA.   That was father's wish.

OLGA.   We ragged him to-day. We think he's a little in love.

IRINA.   To a local lady. She will probably come here to-day.

MASHA.   You should see the way she dresses! Quite prettily, quite fashionably, too, but so badly! Some queer bright yellow skirt with a wretched little fringe and a red bodice. And such a complexion! Andrey isn't in love. After all he has taste, he's simply making fun of us. I heard yesterday that she was going to marry Protopopov, the chairman of the Local Council. That would do her nicely. . . . [*At the side door*] Andrey, come here! Just for a minute, dear! [*Enter* ANDREY.]

OLGA.   My brother, Andrey Sergeyevich.

VERSHININ.   My name is Vershinin.

ANDREY.   Mine is Prozorov. [*Wipes his perspiring hands.*] You've come to take charge of the battery?

OLGA.   Just think, Alexander Ignatyevich comes from Moscow.

ANDREY.   That's all right. Now my little sisters won't give you any rest.

VERSHININ.   I've already managed to bore your sisters.

IRINA.   Just look what a nice little photograph frame Andrey gave me to-day. [*Shows it.*] He made it himself.

VERSHININ [*looks at the frame and does not know what to say*].   Yes. . . . It's a thing that . . .

IRINA.   And he made that frame there, on the piano as well. [ANDREY *waves his hand and walks away.*]

OLGA.   He's got a degree, and plays the violin, and cuts all sorts of things out of wood, and is really a domestic Admirable Crichton. Don't go away, Andrey! He's got into a habit of always going away. Come here!

[MASHA *and* IRINA *take his arms and laughingly lead him back.*]

MASHA.   Come on, come on!

ANDREY.   Please leave me alone.

MASHA.   You are funny. Alexander Ignatyevich used to be called the lovelorn Major, but he never minded.

VERSHININ.   Not in the least.

MASHA.   I'd like to call you a lovelorn fiddler!

IRINA.   Or the lovelorn professor!

OLGA.   He's in love! little Andrey is in love!

IRINA [*applauds*].   Bravo! Bravo! Encore! Little Andrey is in love.

CHEBUTYKIN [*goes up behind* ANDREY *and takes him around the waist with both arms*].   Nature only brought us into the world that we should love!

[*Roars with laughter, then sits down and reads a newspaper which he takes out of his pocket*]

ANDREY.   That's enough, quite enough. . . . [*Wipes his face.*] I couldn't sleep all night and now I can't quite find my feet, so to

speak. I read until four o'clock, then tried to sleep, but nothing happened. I thought about one thing and another, and then it dawned
and the sun crawled into my bedroom. This summer, while I'm here,
I want to translate a book from the English. . . .

VERSHININ.   Do you read English?

ANDREY.   Yes; father, rest his soul, educated us almost violently.
It may seem funny and silly, but it's nevertheless true, that after his
death I began to fill out and get rounder, as if my body had had some
great pressure taken off it. Thanks to father, my sisters and I know
French, German, and English, and Irina knows Italian as well. But we
paid dearly for it all!

MASHA.   A knowledge of three languages is an unnecessary luxury
in this town. It isn't even a luxury but a sort of useless extra, like a
sixth finger. We know a lot too much.

VERSHININ.   Well, I say! [*Laughs*] You know a lot too much! I
don't think there can really be a town so dull and stupid as to have
no place for a clever, cultured person. Let us suppose even that among
the hundred thousand inhabitants of this backward and uneducated
town, there are only three persons like yourself. It stands to reason
that you won't be able to conquer that dark mob around you; little
by little as you grow older you will be bound to give way and lose
yourselves in this crowd of a hundred thousand human beings; their
life will suck you up in itself; but still, you won't disappear having
influenced nobody; later on, others like you will come, perhaps six of
them, then twelve, and so on, until at last your sort will be in the
majority. In two or three hundred years' time life on this earth will
be unimaginably beautiful and wonderful. Mankind needs such a life,
and if it is not ours to-day then we must look ahead for it, wait, think,
prepare for it. We must see and know more than our fathers and
grandfathers saw and knew. [*Laughs*] And you complain that you
know too much.

MASHA [*takes off her hat*].   I'll stay to lunch.

IRINA [*sighs*].   Yes, all that ought to be written down.

[ANDREY *has gone out quietly.*]

TUZENBAKH.   You say that many years later on, life on this earth
will be beautiful and wonderful. That's true. But to share in it now,
even though at a distance, we must prepare by work. . . .

VERSHININ [*gets up*].   Yes. What a lot of flowers you have. [*Looks
round.*] It's a beautiful flat. I envy you! I've spent my whole life in
rooms with two chairs, one sofa, and fires which always smoke. I've
never had flowers like these in my life. . . . [*Rubs his hands.*] Well,
well!

TUZENBAKH.   Yes, we must work. You are probably thinking to yourself: the German lets himself go. But I assure you I'm a Russian, I can't even speak German. My father belonged to the Orthodox Church. . . . [*Pause*]

VERSHININ [*walks about the stage*].   I often wonder: suppose we could begin life over again, knowing what we were doing? Suppose we could use one life, already ended, as a sort of rough draft for another? I think that every one of us would try, more than anything else, not to repeat himself, at the very least he would rearrange his manner of life, he would make sure of rooms like these, with flowers and light . . . I have a wife and two daughters, my wife's health is delicate and so on and so on, and if I had to begin life all over again I would not marry . . . No, no!

[*Enter KULYGIN in a regulation jacket.*]

KULYGIN [*going up to IRINA*].   Dear sister, allow me to congratulate you on the day sacred to your good angel and to wish you, sincerely and from the bottom of my heart, good health and all that one can wish for a girl of your years. And then let me offer you this book as a present. [*Gives it to her.*] It is the history of our High School during the last fifty years, written by myself. The book is worthless, and written because I had nothing to do, but read it all the same. Good day, gentlemen! [*To VERSHININ*] My name is Kulygin, I am a master of the local High School. [*To IRINA*] In this book you will find a list of all those who have taken a full course at our High School during these fifty years. *Feci quod potui, faciant meliora potentes.*[1] [*Kisses MASHA.*]

IRINA.   But you gave me one of these at Easter.

KULYGIN [*laughs*].   I couldn't have, surely! You'd better give it back to me in that case, or else give it to the Colonel. Take it, Colonel. You'll read it some day when you're bored.

VERSHININ.   Thank you. [*Prepares to go.*] I am extremely happy to have made the acquaintance of . . .

OLGA.   Must you go? No, not yet?

IRINA.   You'll stop and have lunch with us. Please do.

OLGA.   Yes, please!

VERSHININ [*bows*].   I seem to have dropped in on your name-day. Forgive me, I didn't know, and I didn't offer you my congratulations. . . .

[*Goes with OLGA into the dining-room.*]

---

[1] I did what I could, let those who can do better.

KULYGIN. To-day is Sunday, the day of rest, so let us rest and rejoice, each in a manner compatible with his age and disposition. The carpets will have to be taken up for the summer and put away till winter . . . Persian powder or naphthaline. . . . The Romans were healthy because they knew both how to work and how to rest, they had *mens sana in corpore sano.*[1] Their life ran along certain recognized patterns. Our director says: "The chief thing about each life is its pattern. Whoever loses his pattern is lost himself"—and it's just the same in our daily life. [*Takes* MASHA *by the waist, laughing.*] Masha loves me. My wife loves me. And you ought to put the window curtains away with the carpets. . . . I'm feeling awfully pleased with life to-day. Masha, we've got to be at the director's at four. They're getting up a walk for the pedagogues and their families.

MASHA. I shan't go.

KULYGIN [*hurt*]. My dear Masha, why not?

MASHA. I'll tell you later. . . . [*Angrily*] All right, I'll go, only please stand back. . . . [*Steps away.*]

KULYGIN. And then we're to spend the evening at the director's. In spite of his ill-health that man tries, above everything else, to be sociable. A splendid, illuminating personality. A wonderful man. After yesterday's committee he said to me: "I'm tired, Fyodor Ilyich, I'm tired!" [*Looks at the clock, then at his watch.*] Your clock is seven minutes fast. "Yes," he said, "I'm tired." [*Violin played off.*]

OLGA. Let's go and have lunch! There's to be a master-piece of baking!

KULYGIN. Oh my dear Olga, my dear. Yesterday I was working till eleven o'clock at night, and got awfully tired. To-day I'm quite happy. [*Goes into dining-room.*] My dear . . .

CHEBUTYKIN [*puts his paper into his pocket, and combs his beard*]. A pie? Splendid!

MASHA [*severely to* CHEBUTYKIN]. Only mind; you're not to drink anything to-day. Do you hear? It's bad for you.

CHEBUTYKIN. Oh, that's all right. I haven't been drunk for two years. And it's all the same, anyway!

MASHA. You're not to dare to drink, all the same. [*Angrily, but so that her husband should not hear.*] Another dull evening at the director's, confound it!

TUZENBAKH. I shouldn't go if I were you. . . . It's quite simple.

CHEBUTYKIN. Don't go.

MASHA. Yes, "don't go. . . ." It's a cursed, unbearable life. . . . [*Goes into dining-room.*]

---

[1] Sound minds in sound bodies.

CHEBUTYKIN [*follows her*].   It's not so bad.

SOLYONI [*going into the dining-room*].   There, there, there. . . .

TUZENBAKH.   Vassili Vassilyevich, that's enough. Be quiet!

SOLYONI.   There, there, there. . . .

KULYGIN [*gaily*].   Your health, Colonel! I'm a pedagogue and not quite at home here. I'm Masha's husband. . . . She's a good sort, a very good sort. . . .

VERSHININ.   I'll have some of this black vodka. . . . [*Drinks*] Your health! [*To* OLGA] I'm very comfortable here!

[*Only* IRINA *and* TUZENBAKH *are now left in the sitting-room.*]

IRINA.   Masha's out of sorts to-day. She married when she was eighteen, when he seemed to her the wisest of men. And now it's different. He's the kindest man, but not the wisest.

OLGA [*impatiently*].   Andrey, when are you coming?

ANDREY [*off*].   One minute. [*Enters and goes to the table.*]

TUZENBAKH.   What are you thinking about?

IRINA.   I don't like this Solyoni of yours and I'm afraid of him. He only says silly things.

TUZENBAKH.   He's a queer man. I'm sorry for him, though he vexes me. I think he's shy. When there are just two of us he's quite all right and very good company; when other people are about he's rough and hectoring. Don't let's go in, let them have their meal without us. Let me stay with you. What are you thinking of? [*Pause*] You're twenty. I'm not yet thirty. How many years are there left to us, with their long, long lines of days, filled with my love for you. . . .

IRINA.   Nikolai Lvovich, don't speak to me of love.

TUZENBAKH [*does not hear*].   I've a great thirst for life, struggle, and work, and this thirst has united with my love for you, Irina, and you're so beautiful, and life seems so beautiful to me! What are you thinking about?

IRINA.   You say that life is beautiful. Yes, if only it seems so! The life of us three hasn't been beautiful yet; it has been stifling us as if it was weeds . . . I'm crying. I oughtn't. . . . [*Dries her tears, smiles.*] We must work, work. That is why we are unhappy and look at the world so sadly; we don't know what work is. Our parents despised work. . . .

[*Enter* NATALIA IVANOVNA; *she wears a pink dress and a green sash.*]

NATASHA.   They're already at lunch . . . I'm late . . . [*Carefully examines herself in a mirror, and puts herself straight*] I think my hair's done all right. . . . [*Sees* IRINA.] Dear Irina Sergeyevna, I congratulate you! [*Kisses her firmly and at length.*] You've so many visitors, I'm really ashamed. . . . How do you do, Baron!

OLGA [*enters from dining-room*]. Here's Natalia Ivanovna. How are you, dear! [*They kiss.*]

NATASHA. Happy returns. I'm awfully shy, you've so many people here.

OLGA. All our friends. [*Frightened, in an undertone.*] You're wearing a green sash! My dear, you shouldn't!

NATASHA. Is it a sign of anything?

OLGA. No, it simply doesn't go well . . . and it looks so queer.

NATASHA [*in a tearful voice*]. Yes? But it isn't really green, it's too dull for that. [*Goes into dining-room with* OLGA.]

[*They have all sat down to lunch in the dining-room, the sitting-room is empty.*]

KULYGIN. I wish you a nice *fiancé*, Irina. It's quite time you married.

CHEBUTYKIN. Natalia Ivanovna, I wish you the same.

KULYGIN. Natalia Ivanovna has a *fiancé* already.

MASHA [*raps with her fork on a plate*]. Let's all get drunk and make life purple for once!

KULYGIN. You've lost three good conduct marks.

VERSHININ. This is a nice drink. What's it made of?

SOLYONI. Blackbeetles.

IRINA [*tearfully*]. Phoo! How disgusting!

OLGA. There is to be roast turkey and a sweet apple pie for dinner. Thank goodness I can spend all day and the evening at home. You'll come in the evening, ladies and gentlemen. . . .

VERSHININ. And please may I come in the evening!

IRINA. Please do.

NATASHA. They don't stand on ceremony here.

CHEBUTYKIN. Nature only brought us into the world that we should love! [*Laughs*]

ANDREY [*angrily*]. Please don't! Aren't you tired of it?

[*Enter* FEDOTIK *and* RODÉ *with a large basket of flowers.*]

FEDOTIK. They're lunching already.

RODÉ [*loudly and thickly*]. Lunching? Yes, so they are. . . .

FEDOTIK. Wait a minute! [*Takes a photograph.*] That's one. No, just a moment. . . . [*Takes another.*] That's two. Now we're ready!

[*They take the basket and go into the dining-room, where they have a noisy reception.*]

Rodé [*loudly*].   Congratulations and best wishes! Lovely weather to-day, simply perfect. Was out walking with the High School students all the morning. I take their drills.

Fedotik.   You may move, Irina Sergeyevna! [*Takes a photograph.*] You look well to-day. [*Takes a humming-top out of his pocket.*] Here's a humming-top, by the way. It's got a lovely note!

Irina.   How awfully nice!

Masha.   "There stands a green oak by the sea.
                     And a chain of bright gold is around it . . .
                     And a chain of bright gold is around it. . . ."

[*tearfully*] What am I saying that for? I've had those words running in my head all day. . . .

Kulygin.   There are thirteen at table!

Rodé [*aloud*].   Surely you don't believe in that superstition? [*Laughter*]

Kulygin.   If there are thirteen at table then it means there are lovers present. It isn't you, Ivan Romanovich, hang it all. . . . [*Laughter*]

Chebutykin.   I'm a hardened sinner, but I really don't see why Natalia Ivanovna should blush. . . .

[*Loud laughter;* Natasha *runs out into the sitting-room, followed by* Andrey.]

Andrey.   Don't pay any attention to them! Wait . . . do stop, please. . . .

Natasha.   I'm shy . . . I don't know what's the matter with me and they're all laughing at me. It wasn't nice of me to leave the table like that, but I can't . . . I can't. [*Covers her face with her hands.*]

Andrey.   My dear, I beg you. I implore you not to excite yourself. I assure you they're only joking, they're kind people. My dear, good girl, they're all kind and sincere people, and they like both you and me. Come here to the window, they can't see us here. . . . [*Looks round.*]

Natasha.   I'm so unaccustomed to meeting people!

Andrey.   Oh your youth, your splendid, beautiful youth! My darling, don't be so excited! Believe me, believe me . . . I'm so happy, my soul is full of love, of ecstasy. . . . They don't see us! They can't! Why, why or when did I fall in love with you—Oh, I can't understand anything. My dear, my pure darling, be my wife! I love you, love you . . . as never before. . . . [*They kiss.*]

[*Two officers come in and, seeing the lovers kiss, stop in astonishment.*]

CURTAIN.

ACT II

Scene as before. It is 8 P.M. Somebody is heard playing a concertina outside in the street. There is no fire. NATALIA IVANOVNA enters in indoor dress carrying a candle; she stops by the door which leads into ANDREY's room.

NATASHA. What are you doing, Andrey? Are you reading? It's nothing, only I. . . . [*She opens another door, and looks in, then closes it.*] Isn't there any fire. . . .

ANDREY [*enters with book in hand*]. What are you doing, Natasha?

NATASHA. I was looking to see if there wasn't a fire. It's Shrovetide, and the servant is simply beside herself; I must look out that something doesn't happen. When I came through the dining-room yesterday midnight, there was a candle burning. I couldn't get her to tell me who had lighted it. [*Puts down her candle*] What's the time?

ANDREY [*looks at his watch*]. A quarter past eight.

NATASHA. And Olga and Irina aren't in yet. The poor things are still at work. Olga at the teacher's council, Irina at the telegraph of-fice. . . . [*Sighs*] I said to your sister this morning, "Irina, darling, you must take care of yourself." But she pays no attention. Did you say it was a quarter past eight? I am afraid little Bobby is quite ill. Why is he so cold? He was feverish yesterday, but to-day he is quite cold. . . . I am so frightened!

ANDREY. It's all right, Natasha. The boy is well.

NATASHA. Still, I think we ought to put him on a diet. I am so afraid. And the entertainers were to be here after nine; they had bet-ter not come, Andrey.

ANDREY. I don't know. After all, they were asked.

NATASHA. This morning, when the little boy woke up and saw me he suddenly smiled; that means he knew me. "Good morning, Bobby!" I said, "good morning, darling." And he laughed. Children

234

understand, they understand very well. So I'll tell them, Andrey dear, not to receive the entertainers.

ANDREY [*hesitatingly*].   But what about my sisters? This is their flat.

NATASHA.   They'll do as I want them. They are so kind. . . . [*Going*] I ordered sour milk for supper. The doctor says you must eat sour milk and nothing else, or you won't get thin. [*Stops*] Bobby is so cold. I'm afraid his room is too cold for him. It would be nice to put him into another room till the warm weather comes. Irina's room, for instance, is just right for a child: it's dry and has the sun all day. I must tell her, she can share Olga's room. . . . It isn't as if she was at home in the daytime, she only sleeps here. . . . [*Pause*] Andrey, darling, why are you so silent?

ANDREY.   I was just thinking. . . . There is really nothing to say. . . .

NATASHA.   Yes . . . there was something I wanted to tell you . . . Oh, yes. Ferapont has come from the Council offices, he wants to see you.

ANDREY [*yawns*].   Call him here.

[NATASHA *goes out;* ANDREY *reads his book, stooping over the candle she has left behind.* FERAPONT *enters; he wears a tattered old coat with the collar up. His ears are muffled.*]

ANDREY.   Good morning, grandfather. What have you to say?

FERAPONT.   The Chairman sends a book and some documents or other. Here. . . . [*Hands him a book and a packet.*]

ANDREY.   Thank you. It's all right. Why couldn't you come earlier? It's past eight now.

FERAPONT.   What?

ANDREY [*louder*].   I say you've come late, it's past eight.

FERAPONT.   Yes, yes. I came when it was still light, but they wouldn't let me in. They said you were busy. Well, what was I to do? If you're busy, you're busy, and I'm in no hurry. [*He thinks that* ANDREY *is asking him something.*] What?

ANDREY.   Nothing. [*Looks through the book.*] To-morrow's Friday. I'm not supposed to go to work, but I'll come—all the same . . . and do some work. It's dull at home. . . . [*Pause*] Oh, my dear old man, how strangely life changes, and how it deceives! To-day, out of sheer boredom, I took up this book—old university lectures, and I couldn't help laughing. My God, I'm secretary of the local district council, the council which has Protopopov for its chairman, yes, I'm secretary, and the summit of my ambitions is—to become a member of the council! I to be a member of the local district council, I, who dream every night that I'm a professor of Moscow University, a famous scholar of whom all Russia is proud!

FERAPONT. I can't tell . . . I'm hard of hearing. . . .

ANDREY. If you weren't, I don't suppose I should talk to you. I've got to talk to somebody, and my wife doesn't understand me, and I'm a bit afraid of my sisters—I don't know why unless it is that they may make fun of me and make me feel ashamed . . . I don't drink, I don't like public-houses, but how I should like to be sitting just now in Tyestov's place in Moscow, or at the Great Moscow, old fellow!

FERAPONT. Moscow? That's where a contractor was once telling that some merchants or other were eating pancakes; one ate forty pancakes and he went and died, he was saying. Either forty or fifty, I forget which.

ANDREY. In Moscow you can sit in an enormous restaurant where you don't know anybody and where nobody knows you, and you don't feel all the same that you're a stranger. And here you know everybody and everybody knows you, and you, and you're a stranger . . . and a lonely stranger.

FERAPONT. What? And the same contractor was telling—perhaps he was lying—that there was a cable stretching right across Moscow.

ANDREY. What for?

FERAPONT. I can't tell. The contractor said so.

ANDREY. Rubbish. [*He reads.*] Were you ever in Moscow?

FERAPONT [*after a pause*]. No, God did not lead me there. [*Pause*] Shall I go?

ANDREY. You may go. Good-bye. [FERAPONT *goes.*] Good-bye. [*Reads*] You can come to-morrow and fetch these documents. . . . Go along. . . . [*Pause*] He's gone. [*A ring*] Yes, yes. . . . [*Stretches himself and slowly goes into his own room.*]

[*Behind the scene the nurse is singing a lullaby to the child.* MASHA *and* VERSHININ *come in. While they talk, a maidservant lights candles and a lamp.*]

MASHA. I don't know. [*Pause*] I don't know. Of course, habit counts for a great deal. After father's death, for instance, it took us a long time to get used to the absence of orderlies. But, apart from habit, it seems to me in all fairness that, however it may be in other towns, the best and most-educated people are army men.

VERSHININ. I'm thirsty. I should like some tea.

MASHA [*glancing at her watch*]. They'll bring some soon. I was given in marriage when I was eighteen, and I was afraid of my husband because he was a teacher and I'd only just left school. He then seemed to me frightfully wise and learned and important. And now, unfortunately, that has changed.

VERSHININ.   Yes . . . yes.

MASHA.   I don't speak of my husband, I've grown used to him, but civilians in general are so often coarse, impolite, uneducated. Their rudeness offends me, it angers me. I suffer when I see that a man isn't quite sufficiently refined, or delicate, or polite. I simply suffer agonies when I happen to be among schoolmasters, my husband's colleagues.

VERSHININ.   Yes . . . It seems to me that civilians and army men are equally interesting, in this town, at any rate. It's all the same! If you listen to a member of the local intelligentsia, whether to civilian or military, he will tell you that he's sick of his wife, sick of his house, sick of his estate, sick of his horses. . . . We Russians are extremely gifted in the direction of thinking on an exalted plane, but, tell me, why do we aim so low in real life? Why?

MASHA.   Why?

VERSHININ.   Why is a Russian sick of his children, sick of his wife? And why are his wife and children sick of him?

MASHA.   You're a little downhearted to-day.

VERSHININ.   Perhaps I am. I haven't had any dinner, I've had nothing since the morning. My daughter is a little unwell, and when my girls are ill, I get very anxious and my conscience tortures me because they have such a mother. Oh, if you had seen her to-day! What a trivial personality! We began quarrelling at seven in the morning and at nine I slammed the door and went out. [*Pause*] I never speak of her, it's strange that I bear my complaints to you alone. [*Kisses her hand.*] Don't be angry with me. I haven't anybody but you, nobody at all. . . . [*Pause*]

MASHA.   What a noise in the oven! Just before father's death there was a noise in the pipe, just like that.

VERSHININ.   Are you superstitious?

MASHA.   Yes.

VERSHININ.   That's strange. [*Kisses her hand.*] You are a splendid, wonderful woman. Splendid, wonderful! It is dark here, but I see your sparkling eyes.

MASHA [*sits on another chair*].   There is more light here.

VERSHININ.   I love you, love you, love you . . . I love your eyes, your movements, I dream of them. . . . Splendid, wonderful woman!

MASHA [*laughing*].   When you talk to me like that, I laugh; I don't know why, for I'm afraid. Don't repeat it, please. . . . [*In an under-*

tone.] No, go on, it's all the same to me. . . . [*Covers her face with her hands.*] Somebody's coming, let's talk about something else. . . .

[IRINA *and* TUZENBAKH *come in through the dining-room.*]

TUZENBAKH. My surname is really triple. I am called Baron Tuzenbakh-Krone-Altschauer, but I am Russian and Orthodox, the same as you. There is very little German left in me, unless perhaps it is the patience and the obstinacy with which I bore you. I see you home every night.

IRINA. How tired I am!

TUZENBAKH. And I'll come to the telegraph office to see you home every day for ten or twenty years, until you drive me away. [*He sees* MASHA *and* VERSHININ; *joyfully.*] Is that you? How do you do.

IRINA. Well, I am home at last. [*To* MASHA.] A lady came to-day to telegraph to her brother in Saratov that her son died to-day, and she couldn't remember the address anyhow. So she sent the telegram without an address, just to Saratov. She was crying. And for some reason or other I was rude to her. "I've no time," I said. It was so stupid. Are the entertainers coming to-night?

MASHA. Yes.

IRINA [*sitting down in an armchair*]. I want rest. I am tired.

TUZENBAKH [*smiling*]. When you come home from your work you seem so young, and so unfortunate. . . . [*Pause*]

IRINA. I am tired. No, I don't like the telegraph office, I don't like it.

MASHA. You've grown thinner. . . . [*Whistles a little.*] And you look younger, and your face has become like a boy's.

TUZENBAKH. That's the way she does her hair.

IRINA. I must find another job, this one won't do for me. What I wanted, what I hoped to get, just that is lacking here. Labor without poetry, without ideas. . . . [*A knock on the door*] The doctor is knocking. [*To* TUZENBAKH.] Will you knock, dear. I can't . . . I'm tired. . . . [TUZENBAKH *knocks.*] He'll come in a minute. Something ought to be done. Yesterday the doctor and Andrey played cards at the club and lost money. Andrey seems to have lost 200 rubles.

MASHA [*with indifference*]. What can we do now?

IRINA. He lost money a fortnight ago, he lost money in December. Perhaps if he lost everything we should go away from this town. Oh, my God. I dream of Moscow every night. I'm just like a lunatic. [*Laughs*] We go there in June, and before June there's still . . . February, March, April, May . . . nearly half a year!

MASHA. Only Natasha mustn't get to know of these losses.

IRINA. I expect it will be all the same to her.

[CHEBUTYKIN, *who has only just got out of bed—he was resting after dinner—comes into the dining-room and combs his beard. He then sits by the table and takes a newspaper from his pocket.*]

MASHA.   Here he is. . . . Has he paid his rent?

IRINA [*laughs*].   No. He's been here eight months and hasn't paid a kopeck. Seems to have forgotten.

MASHA [*laughs*].   What dignity in his pose! [*They all laugh. Pause*]

IRINA.   Why are you so silent, Alexander Ignatyevich?

VERSHININ.   I don't know. I want some tea. Half my life for a tumbler of tea. I haven't had anything since morning.

CHEBUTYKIN.   Irina Sergeyevna!

IRINA.   What is it?

CHEBUTYKIN.   Please come here, *Venez ici.* [IRINA *goes and sits by the table.*] I can't do without you. [IRINA *begins to play patience.*]

VERSHININ.   Well, if we can't have any tea, let's philosophize, at any rate.

TUZENBAKH.   Yes, let's. About what?

VERSHININ.   About what? Let us meditate . . . about life as it will be after our time; for example, in two or three hundred years.

TUZENBAKH.   Well? After our time people will fly about in balloons, the cut of one's coat will change, perhaps they'll discover a sixth sense and develop it, but life will remain the same, laborious, mysterious, and happy. And in a thousand years' time, people will still be sighing: "Life is hard!"—and at the same time they'll be just as afraid of death, and unwilling to meet it, as we are.

VERSHININ [*thoughtfully*].   How can I put it? It seems to me that everything on earth must change, little by little, and is already changing under our very eyes. After two or three hundred years, after a thousand—the actual time doesn't matter—a new and happy age will begin. We, of course, shall not take part in it, but we live and work and even suffer to-day that it should come. We create it—and in that one object is our destiny, if you like, our happiness.

[MASHA *laughs softly.*]

TUZENBAKH.   What is it?

MASHA.   I don't know. I've been laughing all day, ever since morning.

VERSHININ.   I finished my education at the same point as you, I have not studied at universities; I read a lot, but I cannot choose my books and perhaps what I read is not at all what I should, but the longer I live, the more I want to know. My hair is turning white, I am nearly an old man now, but I know so little, oh, so little! But I think I know the things that matter most, and that are most real. I know them well. And I wish I could make you understand that there is no happiness for us, that there should not and cannot be. . . . We must only work and work, and happiness is only for our distant posterity. [*Pause*] If not for me, then for the descendants of my descendants.

[FEDOTIK *and* RODÉ *come into the dining-room; they sit and sing softly, strumming on a guitar.*]

TUZENBAKH.   According to you, one should not even think about happiness! But suppose I am happy!

VERSHININ.   No.

TUZENBAKH [*moves his hands and laughs*].   We do not seem to understand each other. How can I convince you? [MASHA *laughs quietly,* TUZENBAKH *continues, pointing at her.*] Yes, laugh! [*To* VERSHININ.] Not only after two or three centuries, but in a million years, life will still be as it was; life does not change, it remains for ever, following its own laws which do not concern us, or which, at any rate, you will never find out. Migrant birds, cranes for example, fly and fly, and whatever thoughts, high or low, enter their heads, they will still fly and not know why or where. They fly and will continue to fly, whatever philosophers come to life among them; they may philosophize as much as they like, only they will fly. . . .

MASHA.   Still, is there a meaning?

TUZENBAKH.   A meaning. . . . Now the snow is falling. What meaning? [*Pause*]

MASHA.   It seems to me that a man must have faith, or must search for a faith, or his life will be empty, empty. . . . To live and not know why the cranes fly, why babies are born, why are stars in the sky. . . . Either you must know why you live, or everything is trivial, not worth a straw. [*Pause*]

VERSHININ.   Still, I am sorry that my youth has gone.

MASHA.   Gogol says: life in this world is a dull matter, my masters!

TUZENBAKH.   And I say it's difficult to argue with you, my masters! Hang it all.

CHEBUTYKIN [*reading*].   Balzac was married at Berdichev. [IRINA *is singing softly.*] That's worth making note of. [*He makes a note.*] Balzac was married at Berdichev. [*Goes on reading.*]

IRINA [*laying out cards, thoughtfully*].   Balzac was married at Berdichev.

TUZENBAKH.   The die is cast. I've handed in my resignation, Marya Sergeyevna.

MASHA.   So I heard. I don't see what good it is; I don't like civilians.

TUZENBAKH.   Never mind. . . . [*Gets up.*] I'm not handsome; what use am I as a soldier? Well, it makes no difference . . . I shall work. If only just once in my life I could work so that I could come home in the evening, fall exhausted on my bed, and go to sleep at once. [*Going into the dining-room.*] Workmen, I suppose, do sleep soundly!

FEDOTIK [*to* IRINA].   I bought some colored pencils for you at Pizhikov's in the Moscow Road, just now. And here is a little knife.

IRINA.   You have got into the habit of behaving to me as if I am a little girl, but I am grown up. [*Takes the pencils and the knife, then, with joy.*] How lovely!

FEDOTIK.   And I bought myself a knife . . . look at it . . . one blade, another, a third, an ear-scoop, scissors, nail-cleaners. . . .

RODÉ [*loudly*].   Doctor, how old are you?

CHEBUTYKIN.   I? Thirty-two. [*Laughter.*]

FEDOTIK.   I'll show you another kind of patience. . . . [*Lays out cards.*]

[*A samovar is brought in;* ANFISA *attends to it; a little later* NATASHA *enters and helps by the table;* SOLYONI *arrives and, after greetings, sits by the table.*]

VERSHININ.   What a wind!

MASHA.   Yes. I'm tired of winter. I've already forgotten what summer's like.

IRINA.   It's coming out I see. We're going to Moscow.

FEDOTIK.   No, it won't come out. Look, the eight was on the two of spades. [*Laughs*] That means you won't go to Moscow.

CHEBUTYKIN [*reading paper*].   Tsitsigar. Smallpox is raging here.

ANFISA [*coming up to* MASHA].   Masha, have some tea, little mother. [*To* VERSHININ.] Please have some, sir . . . excuse me, but I've forgotten your name. . . .

MASHA.   Bring some here, nurse. I shan't go over there.

IRINA.   Nurse!

ANFISA.   Coming, coming!

NATASHA [*to* SOLYONI].   Children at the breast understand perfectly. I said "Good morning, Bobby; good morning, dear!" And he looked at me in quite an unusual way. You think it's only the mother in me that is speaking; I assure you that isn't so! He's a wonderful child.

SOLYONI.   If he was my child I'd roast him on a frying-pan and eat him.

[*Takes his tumbler into the drawing-room and sits in a corner.*]

NATASHA [*covers her face in her hands*].   Vulgar, ill-bred man!

MASHA.   He's lucky who doesn't notice whether it's winter now, or summer. I think that if I were in Moscow, I shouldn't mind about the weather.

VERSHININ.   A few days ago I was reading the prison diary of a French minister. He had been sentenced on account of the Panama scandal. With what joy, what delight, he speaks of the birds he saw through the prison windows, which he had never noticed while he was a minister. Now, of course, that he is at liberty, he notices birds no more than he did before. When you go to live in Moscow you'll not notice it, in just the same way. There can be no happiness for us, it only exists in our wishes.

TUZENBAKH [*takes cardboard box from the table*].   Where are the pastries?

IRINA.   Solyoni has eaten them.

TUZENBAKH.   All of them?

ANFISA [*serving tea*].   There's a letter for you.

VERSHININ.   For me? [*Takes the letter.*] From my daughter. [*Reads*] Yes, of course . . . I will go quietly. Excuse me, Marya Sergeyevna. I shan't have any tea. [*Stands up, excited.*] That eternal story. . . .

MASHA.   What is it? Is it a secret?

VERSHININ [*quietly*].   My wife has poisoned herself again. I must go. I'll go out quietly. It's all awfully unpleasant. [*Kisses* MASHA'*s hand.*] My dear, my splendid, good woman . . . I'll go this way, quietly. [*Exit*]

ANFISA.   Where has he gone? And I'd served tea. . . . What a man!

MASHA [*angrily*].   Be quiet! You bother so one can't have a moment's peace. . . . [*Goes to the table with her cup.*] I'm tired of you, old woman!

ANFISA.   My dear! Why are you offended!

ANDREY'S VOICE.   Anfisa!

ANFISA [*mocking*].   Anfisa! He sits there and . . . [*Exit*]

MASHA [*in the dining-room, by the table angrily*].   Let me sit down! [*Disturbs the cards on the table.*] Here you are, spreading your cards out. Have some tea!

IRINA.   You are cross, Masha.

MASHA.   If I am cross, then don't talk to me. Don't touch me!

CHEBUTYKIN.   Don't touch her, don't touch her. . . .

MASHA.   You're sixty, but you're like a boy, always up to some beastly nonsense.

NATASHA [*sighs*].   Dear Masha, why use such expressions? With
your beautiful exterior you would be simply fascinating in good society, I tell you so directly, if it wasn't for your words. *Je vous prie,
pardonnez-moi, Marie, mais vous avez des manières un peu grossières.*[1]

TUZENBAKH [*restraining his laughter*].   Give me . . . give me . . .
there's some cognac, I think.

NATASHA.   *Il parait, que mon Bobick déjà ne dort pas,*[2] he has awakened. He isn't well to-day. I'll go to him, excuse me. . . . [*Exit*]

IRINA.   Where has Alexander Ignatyevich gone?

MASHA.   Home. Something extraordinary has happened to his
wife again.

TUZENBAKH [*goes to* SOLYONI *with a cognac-flask in his hands*].   You
go on sitting by yourself, thinking of something—goodness knows
what. Come and let's make peace. Let's have some cognac. [*They
drink.*] I expect I'll have to play the piano all night, some rubbish most
likely . . . well, so be it!

SOLYONI.   Why make peace? I haven't quarrelled with you.

TUZENBAKH.   You always make me feel as if something has taken
place between us. You've a strange character, you must admit.

SOLYONI [*declaims*].   "I am strange, but who is not? Don't be
angry, Aleko!"[3]

TUZENBAKH.   And what has Aleko to do with it? [*Pause*]

SOLYONI.   When I'm with one other man I behave just like
everybody else, but in company I'm dull and shy and . . . talk all manner of rubbish. But I'm more honest and more honorable than very,
very many people. And I can prove it.

TUZENBAKH.   I often get angry with you, you always fasten on to
me in company, but I like you all the same. I'm going to drink my
fill to-night, whatever happens. Drink, now!

SOLYONI.   Let's drink. [*They drink.*] I never had anything against
you, Baron. But my character is like Lermontov's.[4] [*In a low voice.*] I
even rather resemble Lermontov, they say. . . .

[*Takes a scent-bottle from his pocket, and scents his hands.*]

TUZENBAKH.   I've sent in my resignation. Basta! I've been thinking about it for five years, and at last made up my mind. I shall
work.

---

[1] I beg your pardon, Marya, but your manners are a little coarse.
[2] It seems my Bobick is no longer sleeping.
[3] From Pushkin's poem *The Gypsies*.
[4] The great Byronic Russian author, 1814–1841.

SOLYONI [*declaims*]. "Do not be angry, Aleko . . . forget, forget, thy dreams of yore. . . ."

[*While he is speaking* ANDREY *enters quietly with a book, and sits by the table.*]

TUZENBAKH. I shall work.

CHEBUTYKIN [*going with* IRINA *into the dining-room*]. And the food was also real Caucasian onion soup, and, for a roast some chekhartma.

SOLYONI. Cheremsha isn't meat at all, but a plant something like an onion.

CHEBUTYKIN. No, my angel. Chekhartma isn't onion, but roast mutton.

SOLYONI. And I tell you, cheremsha—is a sort of onion.

CHEBUTYKIN. And I tell you, chekhartma—is mutton.

SOLYONI. And I tell you, cheremsha—is a sort of onion.

CHEBUTYKIN. What's the use of arguing! You've never been in the Caucasus, and never ate any chekhartma.

SOLYONI. I never ate it, because I hate it. It smells like garlic.

ANDREY [*imploring*]. Please, please! I ask you!

TUZENBAKH. When are the entertainers coming?

IRINA. They promised for about nine; that is, quite soon.

TUZENBAKH [*embraces* ANDREY]. "Oh my house, my house, my new-built house."

ANDREY [*dances and sings*]. "Newly-built of maple-wood."

CHEBUTYKIN [*dances*]. "Its walls are like a sieve!"

[*Laughter*]

TUZENBAKH [*kisses* ANDREY]. Hang it all, let's drink. Andrey, old boy, let's drink with you. And I'll go with you, Andrey, to the University of Moscow.

SOLYONI. Which one? There are two universities in Moscow.

ANDREY. There's one university in Moscow.

SOLYONI. Two, I tell you.

ANDREY. Don't care if there are three. So much the better.

SOLYONI. There are two universities in Moscow! [*There are murmurs and "hushes."*] There are two universities in Moscow, the old one and the new one. And if you don't like to listen, if my words annoy you, then I need not speak. I can even go into another room. . . . [*Exit*]

TUZENBAKH. Bravo, bravo! [*Laughs*] Come on, now. I'm going to play. Funny man, Solyoni. . . . [*Goes to the piano and plays a waltz.*]

MASHA [*dancing solo*].   The Baron's drunk, the Baron's drunk, the Baron's drunk!

[NATASHA *comes in.*]

NATASHA [*To* CHEBUTYKIN].   Ivan Romanovich! [*Says something to* CHEBUTYKIN, *then goes out quietly.*]

[CHEBUTYKIN *touches* TUZENBAKH *on the shoulder and whispers something to him.*]

IRINA.   What is it?

CHEBUTYKIN.   Time for us to go. Good-bye.

TUZENBAKH.   Good-night. It's time we went.

IRINA.   But really the entertainers?

ANDREY [*in confusion*].   There won't be any entertainers. You see, dear, Natasha says that Bobby isn't quite well, and so. . . . In a word, I don't care, and it's absolutely all one to me.

IRINA [*shrugging her shoulders*].   Bobby ill!

MASHA.   What is she thinking of! Well, if they are sent home, I suppose they must go. [*To* IRINA] Bobby's all right, it's she herself. . . . Here! [*Taps her forehead.*] Little bourgeoise!

[ANDREY *goes to his room through the right-hand door.* CHEBUTYKIN *follows him. In the dining-room they are saying good-bye.*]

FEDOTIK.   What a shame! I was expecting to spend the evening here, but of course, if the little baby is ill . . . I'll bring him some toys to-morrow.

RODÉ [*loudly*].   I slept late after dinner to-day because I thought I was going to dance all night. It's only nine o'clock now!

MASHA.   Let's go into the street, we can talk there. Then we can settle things.

[*Good-byes and good nights are heard.* TUZENBAKH'S *merry laughter is heard. All go out.* ANFISA *and the maid clear the table, and put out the lights. The nurse sings.* ANDREY, *wearing an overcoat and a hat, and* CHEBUTYKIN *enter silently.*]

CHEBUTYKIN.   I never managed to get married because my life flashed by like lightning, and because I was madly in love with your mother, who was married.

ANDREY.   One shouldn't marry. One shouldn't, because it's dull.

CHEBUTYKIN.   So there I am, in my loneliness. Say what you will, loneliness is a terrible thing, old fellow. . . . Though really . . . of course, it absolutely doesn't matter!

ANDREY. Let's be quicker.

CHEBUTYKIN. What are you in such a hurry for? We shall be in time.

ANDREY. I'm afraid my wife may stop me.

CHEBUTYKIN. Ah!

ANDREY. I shan't play to-night, I shall only sit and look on. I don't feel very well. . . . What am I to do for my asthma, Ivan Romanovich?

CHEBUTYKIN. Don't ask me! I don't remember, old fellow, I don't know.

ANDREY. Let's go through the kitchen. [*They go out.*]

[*A bell rings, then a second time; voices and laughter are heard.*]

IRINA [*enters*]. What's that?

ANFISA [*whispers*]. The entertainers! [*bell*]

IRINA. Tell them there's nobody at home, nurse. They must excuse us.

[ANFISA *goes out.* IRINA *walks about the room deep in thought; she is excited.* SOLYONI *enters.*]

SOLYONI [*in surprise*]. There's nobody here. . . . Where are they all?

IRINA. They've gone home.

SOLYONI. How strange. Are you here alone?

IRINA. Yes, alone. [*Pause*] Good-bye.

SOLYONI. Just now I behaved tactlessly, with insufficient reserve. But you are not like all the others, you are noble and pure, you can see the truth. . . . You alone can understand me. I love you deeply, beyond measure, I love you.

IRINA. Good-bye! Go away.

SOLYONI. I cannot live without you. [*Follows her.*] Oh, my happiness! [*Through his tears.*] Oh, joy! Wonderful, marvelous, glorious eyes, such as I have never seen before. . . .

IRINA [*coldly*]. Stop it, Vassili Vassilyevich!

SOLYONI. This is the first time I speak to you of love, and it is as if I am no longer on the earth, but on another planet. [*Wipes his forehead.*] Well, never mind. I can't make you love me by force, of course . . . but I don't intend to have any more-favored rivals. . . . No . . . I swear to you by all the saints, I shall kill my rival. . . . Oh, beautiful one!

[NATASHA *enters with a candle; she looks in through one door, then*

*through another, and goes past the door leading to her husband's
room.*]

NATASHA.   Here's Andrey. Let him go on reading. Excuse me,
Vassili Vassilyevich, I did not know you were here; I am engaged in
domesticities.

SOLYONI.   It's all the same to me. Good-bye! [*Exit*]

NATASHA.   You're so tired, my poor dear girl! [*kisses* IRINA] If
you only went to bed earlier.

IRINA.   Is Bobby asleep?

NATASHA.   Yes, but restlessly. By the way, dear, I wanted to tell
you, but either you weren't at home, or I was busy . . . I think
Bobby's present nursery is cold and damp. And your room would be
so nice for the child. My dear, darling girl, do change over to Olga's
for a bit!

IRINA [*not understanding*].   Where?

[*The bells of a troika are heard as it drives up to the house.*]

NATASHA.   You and Olga can share a room, for the time being,
and Bobby can have yours. He's such a darling; to-day I said to him,
"Bobby, you're mine! Mine." And he looked at me with his dear
little eyes. [*A bell rings.*] It must be Olga. How late she is! [*The maid
enters and whispers to* NATASHA.] Protopopov? What a queer man to
do such a thing. Protopopov's come and wants me to go for a drive
with him in his troika. [*Laughs*] How funny these men are. . . . [*A bell
rings.*] Somebody has come. Suppose I did go and have half an hour's
drive. . . . [*to the maid*] Say I shan't be long. [*Bell rings.*] Somebody's
ringing, it must be Olga. [*Exit*]

[*The maid runs out;* IRINA *sits deep in thought;* KULYGIN *and* OLGA
enter, followed by VERSHININ.]

KULYGIN.   Well, there you are. And you said there was going to
be a party.

VERSHININ.   It's queer; I went away not long ago, half an hour
ago, and they were expecting entertainers.

IRINA.   They've all gone.

KULYGIN.   Has Masha gone too? Where has she gone? And
what's Protopopov waiting for downstairs in his troika? Whom is he
expecting?

IRINA.   Don't ask questions . . . I'm tired.

KULYGIN.   Oh, you're all whimsies. . . .

OLGA.   My committee meeting is only just over. I'm tired out.

Our chairwoman is ill, so I had to take her place. My head, my head is aching. . . . [*Sits*] Andrey lost 200 rubles at cards yesterday . . . the whole town is talking about it. . . .

KULYGIN. Yes, my meeting tired me too. [*Sits*]

VERSHININ. My wife took it into her head to frighten me just now by nearly poisoning herself. It's all right now, and I'm glad; I can rest now. . . . But perhaps we ought to go away? Well, my best wishes, Fyodor Ilyich, let's go somewhere together! I can't, I absolutely can't stop at home. . . . Come on!

KULYGIN. I'm tired. I won't go. [*Gets up*] I'm tired. Has my wife gone home?

IRINA. I suppose so.

KULYGIN [*kisses* IRINA'*s hand*]. Good-bye, I'm going to rest all day to-morrow and the day after. Best wishes! [*Going*] I should like some tea. I was looking forward to spending the whole evening in pleasant company and—*o, fallacem hominum spem!*[1] . . . Accusative case after an interjection. . . .

VERSHININ. Then I'll go somewhere by myself. [*Exit with* KULYGIN, *whistling.*]

OLGA. I've such a headache . . . Andrey has been losing money. . . . The whole town is talking. . . . I'll go and lie down. [*Going*] I'm free to-morrow. . . . Oh, my God, what a mercy! I'm free to-morrow, I'm free the day after. . . . Oh my head, my head. . . . [*Exit*]

IRINA [*alone*]. They've all gone. Nobody's left.

[*A concertina is being played in the street. The nurse sings.*]

NATASHA [*in fur coat and cap, steps across the dining-room, followed by the maid*]. I'll be back in half an hour. I'm only going for a little drive. [*Exit*]

IRINA [*alone in her misery*]. To Moscow! Moscow! Moscow!

CURTAIN.

---

[1] O delusive hope of man!

ACT III

The room shared by OLGA *and* IRINA. *Beds, screened off, on the right and left. It is past 2* A.M. *Behind the stage a fire-alarm is ringing; it has apparently been going for some time. Nobody in the house has gone to bed yet.* MASHA *is lying on a sofa dressed, as usual, in black. Enter* OLGA *and* ANFISA.

ANFISA.   Now they are downstairs, sitting under the stairs. I said to them, "Won't you come up," I said, "You can't go on like this," and they simply cried, "We don't know where father is." They said, "He may be burnt up by now." What an idea! And in the yard there are some people . . . also undressed.

OLGA [*takes a dress out of the cupboard*].   Take this gray dress. . . . And this . . . and the blouse as well. . . . Take the skirt, too, nurse. . . . My God! How awful it is! The whole of the Kirsanovsky Road seems to have burned down. Take this . . . and this. . . . [*Throws clothes into her hands.*] The poor Vershinins are so frightened. . . . Their house was nearly burnt. They ought to come here for the night. . . . They shouldn't be allowed to go home. . . . Poor Fedotik is completely burnt out, there's nothing left. . . .

ANFISA.   Couldn't you call Ferapont, Olga dear? I can hardly manage. . . .

OLGA [*rings*].   They'll never answer. [*at the door*] Come here, whoever there is! [*Through the open door can be seen a window, red with flame: a fire-engine is heard passing the house.*] How awful this is. And how I'm sick of it! [FERAPONT *enters.*] Take these things down. . . . The Kolotilin girls are down below . . . and let them have them. This too. . . .

FERAPONT.   Yes'm. In the year twelve Moscow was burning too. Oh, my God! The Frenchmen were surprised.

OLGA.   Go on, go on. . . .

FERAPONT.   Yes'm. [*Exit*]

OLGA.   Nurse, dear, let them have everything. We don't want anything. Give it all to them, nurse. . . . I'm tired, I can hardly keep

249

on my legs. . . . The Vershinins mustn't be allowed to go home. . . .
The girls can sleep in the drawing-room, and Alexander Ignatyevich
can go downstairs to the Baron's flat . . . Fedotik can go there, too,
or else into our dining-room. . . . The doctor is drunk, beastly drunk,
as if on purpose, so nobody can go to him. Vershinin's wife, too, may
go into the drawing-room.

ANFISA [*tired*].   Olga, dear girl, don't dismiss me! Don't dismiss
me!

OLGA.   You're talking nonsense, nurse. Nobody is dismissing
you.

ANFISA [*puts* OLGA's *head against her bosom*].   My dear, precious
girl, I'm working, I'm toiling away . . . I'm growing weak, and they'll
all say go away! And where shall I go? Where? I'm eighty. Eighty-one
years old. . . .

OLGA.   You sit down, nurse dear. . . . You're tired, poor dear. . . .
[*Makes her sit down.*] Rest, dear. You're so pale!

[NATASHA *comes in.*]

NATASHA.   They are saying that a committee to assist the sufferers
from the fire must be formed at once. What do you think of that? It's
a beautiful idea. Of course the poor ought to be helped, it's the duty
of the rich. Bobby and little Sophy are sleeping, sleeping as if nothing
at all was the matter. There's such a lot of people here, the place is
full of them, wherever you go. There's influenza in the town now.
I'm afraid the children may catch it.

OLGA [*not attending*].   In this room we can't see the fire, it's quiet
here. . . .

NATASHA.   Yes . . . I suppose I'm all untidy. [*Before the looking-
glass*] They say I'm growing stout . . . it isn't true! Certainly it isn't!
Masha's asleep; the poor thing is tired out. . . . [*Coldly, to* ANFISA.]
Don't dare to be seated in my presence! Get up! Out of this! [*Exit*
ANFISA; *pause.*] I don't understand what makes you keep on that old
woman!

OLGA [*confusedly*].   Excuse me, I don't understand either. . . .

NATASHA.   She's no good here. She comes from the country, she
ought to live there. . . . Spoiling her, I call it! I like order in the
house! We don't want any unnecessary people here. [*Strokes her
cheek.*] You're tired, poor thing! Our head mistress is tired! And when
my little Sophie grows up and goes to school I shall be so afraid of
you.

OLGA.   I shan't be head mistress.

NATASHA.   They'll appoint you, Olga. It's settled.

OLGA.   I'll refuse the post. I can't . . . I'm not strong enough. . . .

[*drinks water*] You were so rude to nurse just now . . . I'm sorry. I can't stand it . . . everything seems dark in front of me. . . .

NATASHA [*excited*].   Forgive me, Olga, forgive me . . . I didn't want to annoy you.

[MASHA *gets up, takes a pillow and goes out angrily.*]

OLGA.   Remember, dear . . . we have been brought up, in an unusual way, perhaps, but I can't bear this. Such behavior has a bad effect on me, I get ill . . . I simply lose heart!

NATASHA.   Forgive me, forgive me. . . . [*kisses her*]

OLGA.   Even the least bit of rudeness, the slightest impoliteness, upsets me.

NATASHA.   I often say too much, it's true, but you must agree, dear, that she could just as well live in the country.

OLGA.   She has been with us for thirty years.

NATASHA.   But she can't do any work now. Either I don't understand, or you don't want to understand me. She's no good for work, she can only sleep or sit about.

OLGA.   And let her sit about.

NATASHA [*surprised*].   What do you mean? She's only a servant. [*crying*] I don't understand you, Olga. I've got a nurse, a wet-nurse, we've a cook, a housemaid . . . what do we want that old woman for as well? What good is she? [*fire-alarm behind the stage*]

OLGA.   I've grown ten years older to-night.

NATASHA.   We must come to an agreement, Olga. Your place is the school, mine—the home. You devote yourself to teaching, I, to the household. And if I talk about servants, then I do know what I am talking about; I do know what I am talking about. . . . And to-morrow there's to be no more of that old thief, that old hag . . . [*stamping*] That witch! And don't you dare to annoy me! Don't you dare! [*stopping short*] Really, if you don't move downstairs, we shall always be quarrelling. This is awful.

[*Enter* KULYGIN.]

KULYGIN.   Where's Masha? It's time we went home. The fire seems to be going down. [*stretches himself*] Only one block has burnt down, but there was such a wind that it seemed at first the whole town was going to burn. [*sits*] I'm tired out. My dear Olga . . . I often think that if it hadn't been for Masha, I should have married you. You are awfully nice. . . . I am absolutely tired out. [*listens*]

OLGA.   What is it?

KULYGIN.   The doctor, of course, has been drinking hard; he's terribly drunk. He might have done it on purpose! [*gets up*] He seems

to be coming here. . . . Do you hear him? Yes, here. . . . [*laughs*]
What a man . . . really . . . I'll hide myself. [*Goes to the cupboard and
stands in the corner.*] What a rogue.

OLGA.　He hadn't touched a drop for two years, and now he suddenly goes and gets drunk. . . . [*Retires with* NATASHA *to the back of the
room.*]

[CHEBUTYKIN *enters; apparently sober, he stops, looks round, then goes
to the wash-stand and begins to wash his hands.*]

CHEBUTYKIN [*angrily*].　Devil take them all . . . take them all. . . .
They think I'm a doctor and can cure everything, and I know absolutely nothing. I've forgotten all I ever knew, I remember nothing,
absolutely nothing. [OLGA *and* NATASHA *go out, unnoticed by him.*]
Devil take it. Last Wednesday I attended a woman in Zasip—and she
died, and it's my fault that she died. Yes . . . I used to know a certain
amount five-and-twenty years ago, but I don't remember anything
now. Nothing. Perhaps I'm not really a man, and am only pretending that I've got arms and legs and a head; perhaps I don't exist at
all, and only imagine that I walk, and eat, and sleep. [*cries*] Oh, if
only I didn't exist! [*Stops crying; angrily*] The devil only knows. . . .
Day before yesterday they were talking in the club; they said,
Shakespeare, Voltaire . . . I'd never read, never read at all, and I put
on an expression as if I had read. And so did the others. Oh, how
beastly! How petty! And then I remembered the woman I killed on
Wednesday . . . and I couldn't get her out of my mind, and everything in my mind became crooked, nasty, wretched. . . . So I went
and drank. . . .

[IRINA, VERSHININ *and* TUZENBAKH *enter;* TUZENBAKH *is wearing
new and fashionable civilian clothes.*]

IRINA.　Let's sit down here. Nobody will come in here.

VERSHININ.　The whole town would have been destroyed if it
hadn't been for the soldiers. Good men! [*Rubs his hands appreciatively.*]
Splendid people! Oh, what a fine lot!

KULYGIN [*coming up to him*].　What's the time?

TUZENBAKH.　It's past three now. It's dawning.

IRINA.　They are all sitting in the dining-room, nobody is going.
And that Solyoni of yours is sitting there. . . . [*To* CHEBUTYKIN]
Hadn't you better be going to sleep, doctor?

CHEBUTYKIN.　It's all right . . . thank you. . . . [*combs his beard*]

KULYGIN [*laughs*].　Speaking's a bit difficult, eh, Ivan Romanovich!

[*pats him on the shoulder*] Good man! *In vino veritas,*[1] the ancients used to say.

TUZENBAKH.   They keep on asking me to get up a concert in aid of the sufferers.

IRINA.   As if one could do anything. . . .

TUZENBAKH.   It might be arranged, if necessary. In my opinion Marya Sergeyevna is an excellent pianist.

KULYGIN.   Yes, excellent!

IRINA.   She's forgotten everything. She hasn't played for three years . . . or four.

TUZENBAKH.   In this town absolutely nobody understands music, not a soul except myself, but I do understand it, and assure you on my word of honor that Marya Sergeyevna plays excellently, almost with genius.

KULYGIN.   You are right, Baron, I'm awfully fond of Masha. She's very fine.

TUZENBAKH.   To be able to play so admirably and to realize at the same time that nobody, nobody can understand you!

KULYGIN [*sighs*].   Yes. . . . But will it be quite all right for her to take part in a concert? [*pause*] You see, I don't know anything about it. Perhaps it will even be all to the good. Although I must admit that our Director is a good man, a very good man even, a very clever man, still he has such views. . . . Of course it isn't his business but still if you wish it, perhaps I'd better talk to him.

[CHEBUTYKIN *takes a porcelain clock into his hands and examines it.*]

VERSHININ.   I got so dirty while the fire was on, I don't look like anybody on earth. [*pause*] Yesterday I happened to hear, casually, that they want to transfer our brigade to some distant place. Some said to Poland, others, to Chita.

TUZENBAKH.   I heard so, too. Well, if it is so, the town will be quite empty.

IRINA.   And we'll go away, too!

CHEBUTYKIN [*drops the clock which breaks to pieces*].   To smithereens!

[*A pause; everybody is pained and confused.*]

KULYGIN [*gathering up the pieces*].   To smash such a valuable object—oh, Ivan Romanovich, Ivan Romanovich! A very bad mark for your misbehavior!

---

[1]In wine there is truth.

IRINA.   That clock used to belong to our mother.

CHEBUTYKIN.   Perhaps. . . . To your mother, your mother. Perhaps I didn't break it; it only looks as if I broke it. Perhaps we only think that we exist, when really we don't. I don't know anything, nobody knows anything. [*at the door*] What are you looking at? Natasha has a little romance with Protopopov, and you don't see it. . . . There you sit and see nothing, and Natasha has a little romance with Protopopov. . . . [*sings*] Won't you please accept this date? . . . [*exit*]

VERSHININ.   Yes. [*laughs*] How strange everything really is! [*pause*] When the fire broke out, I hurried off home; when I get there I see the house is whole, uninjured, and in no danger, but my two girls are standing by the door in just their underclothes, their mother isn't there, the crowd is excited, horses and dogs are running about, and the girls' faces are so agitated, terrified, beseeching, and I don't know what else. My heart was pained when I saw those faces. My God, I thought, what these girls will have to put up with if they live long! I caught them up and ran, and still kept on thinking the one thing: what they will have to live through in this world! [*fire-alarm; a pause*] I come here and find their mother shouting and angry. [MASHA *enters with a pillow and sits on the sofa.*] And when my girls were standing by the door in just their underclothes, and the street was red from the fire, there was a dreadful noise, and I thought that something of the sort used to happen many years ago when an enemy made a sudden attack, and looted, and burned. . . . And at the same time what a difference there really is between the present and the past! And when a little more time has gone by, in two or three hundred years perhaps, people will look at our present life with just the same fear, and the same contempt, and the whole past will seem clumsy and dull, and very uncomfortable, and strange. Oh, indeed, what a life there will be, what a life! [*laughs*] Forgive me, I've dropped into philosophy again. Please let me continue. I do awfully want to philosophize, it's just how I feel at present. [*pause*] As if they are all asleep. As I was saying: what a life there will be! Only just imagine. . . . There are only three persons like yourselves in the town just now, but in future generations there will be more and more, and still more, and the time will come when everything will change and become as you would have it, people will live as you do, and then you too will go out of date; people will be born who are better than you. . . . [*laughs*] Yes, to-day I am quite exceptionally in the vein. I am devilishly keen on living. [*sings*]

> "The power of love all ages know,
>   From its assaults great good does grow."

[*laughs*]

MASHA.   Trum-tum-tum . . .
VERSHININ.   Tum-tum . . .
MASHA.   Tra-ra-ra?
VERSHININ.   Tra-ta-ta.

[*Enter* FEDOTIK.]

FEDOTIK [*dancing*].   I'm burnt out, I'm burnt out! Down to the
ground! [*laughter*]
IRINA.   I don't see anything funny about it. Is everything burnt?
FEDOTIK [*laughs*].   Absolutely. Nothing left at all. The guitar's
burnt, and the photographs are burnt, and all my correspondence. . . .
And I was going to make you a present of a notebook, and that's
burnt too.

[SOLYONI *comes in.*]

IRINA.   No, you can't come here, Vassili Vassilyevich. Please go
away.
SOLYONI.   Why can the Baron come here and I can't?
VERSHININ.   We really must go. How's the fire?
SOLYONI.   They say it's going down. No, I absolutely don't see
why the Baron can, and I can't? [*scents his hands*]
VERSHININ.   Trum-tum-tum.
MASHA.   Trum-tum.
VERSHININ [*laughs to* SOLYONI].   Let's go into the dining-room.
SOLYONI.   Very well, we'll make a note of it. "If I should try to
make this clear, the geese would be annoyed, I fear." [*looks at*
TUZENBAKH] There, there, there. . . .

[*Goes out with* VERSHININ *and* FEDOTIK.]

IRINA.   How Solyoni smelt of tobacco . . . [*in surprise*] The
Baron's asleep! Baron! Baron!
TUZENBAKH [*waking*].   I am tired, I must say. . . . The brickworks.
. . . No, I'm not wandering, I mean it; I'm going to start work soon
at the brickworks . . . I've already talked it over. [*tenderly, to* IRINA]
You're so pale, and beautiful, and charming. . . . Your paleness seems
to shine through the dark air as if it was a light. . . . You are sad,
displeased with life. . . . Oh, come with me, let's go and work
together!
MASHA.   Nikolai Lvovich, go away from here.
TUZENBAKH [*laughs*].   Are you here? I didn't see you. [*kisses*
IRINA*'s hand*] Good-bye, I'll go . . . I look at you now and I remember, as if it was long ago, your name-day, when you, cheerfully and

merrily, were talking about the joys of labor. . . . And how happy life seemed to me, then! What has happened to it now? [*kisses her hand*] There are tears in your eyes. Go to bed now; it is already day . . . the morning begins. . . . If only I was allowed to give my life for you!

MASHA.   Nikolai Lvovich, go away! What business . . .

TUZENBAKH.   I'm off. [*exit*]

MASHA [*lies down*].   Are you asleep, Fyodor?

KULYGIN.   Eh?

MASHA.   Shouldn't you go home?

KULYGIN.   My dear Masha, my darling Masha. . . .

IRINA.   She's tired out. You might let her rest, Fydia.

KULYGIN.   I'll go at once. My wife's a good, splendid . . . I love you, my only one. . . .

MASHA [*angrily*].   *Amo, amas, amat, amamus, amatis, amant.*[1]

KULYGIN [*laughs*].   No, she really is wonderful. I've been your husband seven years, and it seems as if I was only married yesterday. On my word. No, you really are a wonderful woman. I'm satisfied, I'm satisfied, I'm satisfied!

MASHA.   I'm bored, I'm bored, I'm bored. . . . [*sits up*] But I can't get it out of my head. . . . It's simply disgraceful. It has been gnawing away at me . . . I can't keep silent. I mean about Andrey. . . . He has mortgaged this house with the bank, and his wife has got all the money; but the house doesn't belong to him alone, but to the four of us! He ought to know that, if he's an honorable man.

KULYGIN.   What's the use, Masha? Andrey is in debt all round; well, let him do as he pleases.

MASHA.   It's disgraceful, anyway. [*lies down*]

KULYGIN.   You and I are not poor. I work, take my classes, give private lessons . . . I am a plain, honest man . . . *Omnia mea mecum porto,*[2] as they say.

MASHA.   I don't want anything, but the unfairness of it disgusts me. [*pause*] You go, Fyodor.

KULYGIN [*kisses her*].   You're tired, just rest for half an hour, and I'll sit and wait for you. Sleep. . . . [*going*] I'm satisfied, I'm satisfied, I'm satisfied. [*exit*]

IRINA.   Yes, really, our Andrey has grown smaller; how he's snuffed out and aged with that woman! He used to want to be a professor, and yesterday he was boasting that at last he had been made a member of the district council. He is a member, and Protopopov is chairman. . . . The whole town talks and laughs

---

[1]Latin conjugation of *to love*.
[2]All that I own I carry with me.

about it, and he alone knows and sees nothing. . . . And now everybody's gone to look at the fire, but he sits alone in his room and pays no attention, only just plays on his fiddle. [*nervily*] Oh, it's awful, awful, awful. [*weeps*] I can't, I can't bear it any longer! . . . I can't, I can't! . . . [OLGA *comes in and clears up at her little table.* IRINA *is sobbing loudly.*] Throw me out, throw me out, I can't bear any more!

OLGA [*alarmed*].   What is it, what is it? Dear!

IRINA [*sobbing*].   Where? Where has everything gone? Where is it all? Oh my God, my God! I've forgotten everything, everything . . . I don't remember what is the Italian for window or, well, for ceiling . . . I forget everything, every day I forget it, and life passes and will never return, and we'll never go away to Moscow . . . I see that we'll never go. . . .

OLGA.   Dear, dear. . . .

IRINA [*controlling herself*].   Oh, I am unhappy . . . I can't work, I shan't work. Enough, enough! I used to be a telegraphist, now I work at the town council offices, and I have nothing but hate and contempt for all they give me to do . . . I am already twenty-three, I have already been at work for a long while, and my brain has dried up, and I've grown thinner, plainer, older, and there is no relief of any sort, and time goes and it seems all the while as if I am going away from the real, the beautiful life, further and further away, down some precipice. I'm in despair and I can't understand how it is that I am still alive, that I haven't killed myself.

OLGA.   Don't cry, dear girl, don't cry . . . I suffer, too.

IRINA.   I'm not crying, not crying. . . . Enough. . . . Look, I'm not crying any more. Enough . . . enough!

OLGA.   Dear, I tell you as a sister and a friend, if you want my advice, marry the Baron. [IRINA *cries softly.*] You respect him, you think highly of him. . . . It is true that he is not handsome, but he is so honorable and clean . . . people don't marry from love, but in order to do one's duty. I think so, at any rate, and I'd marry without being in love. Whoever he was, I should marry him, so long as he was a decent man. Even if he was old. . . .

IRINA.   I was always waiting until we should be settled in Moscow, there I should meet my true love; I used to think about him, and love him. . . . But it's all turned out to be nonsense, all nonsense. . . .

OLGA [*embraces her sister*].   My dear, beautiful sister, I understand everything; when Baron Nikolai Lvovich left the army and came in evening dress, he seemed so bad-looking to me that I even started crying. . . . He asked, "What are you crying for?" How could I tell him! But if God brought him to marry you, I should be happy. That would be different, quite different.

[NATASHA *with a candle walks across the stage from right to left without saying anything.*]

MASHA [*sitting up*].   She walks as if she's set something on fire.

OLGA.   Masha, you're silly, you're the silliest of the family. Please forgive me for saying so. [*pause*]

MASHA.   I want to make a confession, dear sisters. My soul is in pain. I will confess to you, and never again to anybody . . . I'll tell you this minute. [*softly*] It's my secret but you must know everything . . . I can't be silent. . . . [*pause*] I love, I love . . . I love that man. . . . You saw him only just now. . . . Why don't I say it . . . in one word? I love Vershinin.

OLGA [*goes behind her screen*].   Stop that, I don't hear you in any case.

MASHA.   What am I to do? [*takes her head in her hands*] First he seemed queer to me, then I was sorry for him . . . then I fell in love with him . . . fell in love with his voice, his words, his misfortunes, his two daughters.

OLGA [*behind the screen*].   I'm not listening. You may talk any nonsense you like, it will be all the same. I shan't hear.

MASHA.   Oh, Olga, you are foolish. I am in love—that means that is to be my fate. It means that is to be my lot. . . . And he loves me. . . . It is all awful. Yes; it isn't good, is it? [*Takes* IRINA'*s hand and draws her to her.*] Oh, my dear. . . . How are we going to live through our lives, what is to become of us. . . . When you read a novel it all seems so old and easy, but when you fall in love yourself, then you learn that nobody knows anything, and each must decide for himself. . . . My dear ones, my sisters . . . I've confessed, now I shall keep silence. . . . Like the lunatics in Gogol's story, I'm going to be silent . . . silent. . . .

[ANDREY *enters, followed by* FERAPONT.]

ANDREY [*angrily*].   What do you want? I don't understand.

FERAPONT [*at the door, impatiently*].   I've already told you ten times, Andrey Sergeyevich.

ANDREY.   In the first place I'm not Andrey Sergeyevich, but sir.

FERAPONT.   The firemen, sir, ask if they can go across your garden to the river. Else they go right round, right round; it's a nuisance.

ANDREY.   All right. Tell them it's all right. [*Exit* FERAPONT] I'm tired of them. Where is Olga? [OLGA *comes out from behind the screen.*]

I came to you for the key of the cupboard. I lost my own. You've got a little key. [OLGA *gives him the key;* IRINA *goes behind her screen; pause.*] What a huge fire! It's going down now. Hang it all, that Ferapont made me so angry that I talked nonsense to him. . . . Sir, indeed. . . . [*pause*] Why are you so silent, Olga? [*pause*] It's time you stopped all that nonsense and behaved as if you were properly alive. . . . You are here, Masha. Irina is here, well, since we're all here, let's come to a complete understanding, once and for all. What have you against me? What is it?

OLGA.   Please don't, Andrey dear. We'll talk to-morrow. [*excited*] What an awful night!

ANDREY [*much confused*].   Don't excite yourself. I ask you in perfect calmness; what have you against me? Tell me straight.

VERSHININ'S VOICE.   Trum-tum-tum!

MASHA [*stands; loudly*].   Tra-ta-ta! [*to* OLGA] Good-bye, Olga, God bless you. [*Goes behind screen and kisses* IRINA.] Sleep well. . . . Good-bye, Andrey. Go away now, they're tired . . . you can explain to-morrow. . . . [*exit*]

ANDREY.   I'll only say this and go. Just now. . . . In the first place, you've got something against Natasha, my wife; I've noticed it since the very day of my marriage. Natasha is a beautiful and honest creature, straight and honorable—that's my opinion. I love and respect my wife; understand it, I respect her, and I insist that others should respect her too. I repeat, she's an honest and honorable person, and all your disapproval is simply silly. . . . [*pause*] In the second place, you seem to be annoyed because I am not a professor, and I am not engaged in study. But I work for the zemstvo,[1] I am a member of the district council, and I consider my service as worthy and as high as the service of science. I am a member of the district council, and I am proud of it, if you want to know. . . . [*pause*] In the third place, I have still this to say . . . that I have mortgaged the house without obtaining your permission. . . . For that I am to blame, and ask to be forgiven. My debts led me into doing it . . . thirty-five thousand . . . I do not play at cards any more, I stopped long ago, but the chief thing I have to say in my defense is that you girls receive a pension, and I don't . . . my wages, so to speak. . . . [*pause*]

KULYGIN [*at the door*].   Is Masha there? [*excitedly*] Where is she? It's queer. . . . [*exit*]

ANDREY.   They don't hear. Natasha is a splendid, honest person. [*walks about in silence, then stops*] When I married I thought we should

---

[1]Local council.

be happy . . . all of us. . . . But, my God. . . . [*weeps*] My dear, dear
sisters, don't believe me, don't believe me. . . . [*exit*]

[*Fire-alarm. The stage is clear.*]

IRINA [*behind her screen*].   Olga, who's knocking on the floor?
OLGA.   It's doctor Ivan Romanovich. He's drunk.
IRINA.   What a restless night! [*pause*] Olga! [*looks out*] Did you
hear? They are taking the brigade away from us; it's going to be trans-
ferred to some place far away.
OLGA.   It's only a rumor.
IRINA.   Then we shall be left alone. . . . Olga!
OLGA.   Well?
IRINA.   My dear, darling sister, I esteem, I highly value the Baron,
he's a splendid man; I'll marry him, I'll consent, only let's go to
Moscow! I implore you, let's go! There's nothing better than Moscow
on earth! Let's go, Olga, let's go!

CURTAIN.

ACT IV

The old garden at the house of the PROZOROVS. *There is a long avenue of firs, at the end of which the river can be seen. There is a forest on the far side of the river. On the right is the terrace of the house: bottles and tumblers are on a table here; it is evident that champagne has just been drunk. It is midday. Every now and again passers-by walk across the garden, from the road to the river; five soldiers go past rapidly. CHEBUTYKIN, in a comfortable frame of mind which does not desert him throughout the act, sits in an armchair in the garden, waiting to be called. He wears a peaked cap and has a stick. IRINA, KULYGIN with a cross hanging from his neck and without his moustaches, and TUZEN-BAKH are standing on the terrace seeing off* FEDOTIK *and* RODÉ, *who are coming down into the garden; both officers are in service uniform.*

TUZENBAKH [*exchanges kisses with* FEDOTIK]. You're a good sort, we got on so well together. [*exchanges kisses with* RODÉ] Once again. . . . Good-bye, old man!

IRINA. Au revoir!

FEDOTIK. It isn't au revoir, it's good-bye; we'll never meet again!

KULYGIN. Who knows! [*wipes his eyes; smiles*] Here, I've started crying!

IRINA. We'll meet again sometime.

FEDOTIK. After ten years—or fifteen? We'll hardly know one another then; we'll say, "How do you do?" coldly. . . . [*takes a snap-shot*] Keep still. . . . Once more, for the last time.

RODÉ [*embracing* TUZENBAKH]. We shan't meet again. . . . [*kisses* IRINA's *hand*] Thank you for everything, for everything!

FEDOTIK [*grieved*]. Don't be in such a hurry!

TUZENBAKH. We shall meet again, if God wills it. Write to us. Be sure to write.

RODÉ [*looking round the garden*]. Good-bye, trees! [*shouts*] Yo-ho! [*pause*] Good-bye, echo!

KULYGIN. Best wishes. Go and get yourselves wives there in

261

Poland. . . . Your Polish wife will clasp you and call you "kochanku!"[1] [*laughs*]

FEDOTIK [*looking at the time*]. There's less than an hour left. Solyoni is the only one of our battery who is going on the barge; the rest of us are going with the main body. Three batteries are leaving to-day, another three to-morrow and then the town will be quiet and peaceful.

TUZENBAKH. And terribly dull.

RODÉ. And where is Marya Sergeyevna?

KULYGIN. Masha is in the garden.

FEDOTIK. We'd like to say good-bye to her.

RODÉ. Good-bye, I must go, or else I'll start weeping. [*Quickly embraces* KULYGIN *and* TUZENBAKH, *and kisses* IRINA'*s hand.*] We've been so happy here. . . .

FEDOTIK [*to* KULYGIN]. Here's a keepsake for you . . . a note-book with a pencil. . . . We'll go to the river from here. . . . [*They go aside and both look round.*]

RODÉ [*shouts*]. Yo-ho!

KULYGIN [*shouts*]. Good-bye.

[*At the back of the stage* FEDOTIK *and* RODÉ *meet* MASHA; *they say good-bye and go out with her.*]

IRINA. They've gone. . . . [*sits on the bottom step of the terrace*]

CHEBUTYKIN. And they forgot to say good-bye to me.

IRINA. But why is that?

CHEBUTYKIN. I just forgot, somehow. Though I'll soon see them again, I'm going to-morrow. Yes . . . just one day left. I shall be retired in a year, then I'll come here again and finish my life near you. I've only one year before I get my pension. . . . [*puts one news-paper into his pocket and takes another out*] I'll come here to you and change my life radically . . . I'll be so quiet . . . so agree . . . agreeable, respectable. . . .

IRINA. Yes, you ought to change your life, dear man, somehow or other.

CHEBUTYKIN. Yes, I feel it. [*sings softly*] "Tarara-boom-deay. . . ."

KULYGIN. We won't reform Ivan Romanovich! We won't re-form him!

CHEBUTYKIN. If only I was apprenticed to you! Then I'd re-form.

---

[1]"Sweetheart" in Polish.

IRINA. Fyodor has shaved his moustache! I can't bear to look at him.

KULYGIN. Well, what about it?

CHEBUTYKIN. I could tell you what your face looks like now, but it wouldn't be polite.

KULYGIN. Well! It's the custom, it's *modus vivendi*. Our Director is clean-shaven, and so I too, when I received my inspectorship, had my moustaches removed. Nobody likes it, but it's all one to me. I'm satisfied. Whether I've got moustaches or not, I'm satisfied. . . . [*sits*]

[*At the back of the stage* ANDREY *is wheeling a perambulator containing a sleeping infant.*]

IRINA. Ivan Romanovich, be a darling. I'm awfully worried. You were out on the boulevard last night; tell me, what happened?

CHEBUTYKIN. What happened? Nothing. Quite a trifling matter. [*reads paper*] Of no importance!

KULYGIN. They say that Solyoni and the Baron met yesterday on the boulevard near the theater. . . .

TUZENBAKH. Stop! What right. . . . [*waves his hand and goes into the house*]

KULYGIN. Near the theater . . . Solyoni started behaving offensively to the Baron, who lost his temper and said something nasty. . . .

CHEBUTYKIN. I don't know. It's all bunkum.

KULYGIN. At some seminary or other a master wrote "bunkum" on an essay, and the student couldn't make the letters out—thought it was a Latin word "luckum." [*laughs*] Awfully funny, that. They say that Solyoni is in love with Irina and hates the Baron. . . . That's quite natural. Irina is a very nice girl. She's even like Masha, she's so thoughtful. . . . Only, Irina, your character is gentler. Though Masha's character, too, is a very good one. I'm very fond of Masha.

[*Shouts of "Yo-ho!" are heard behind the stage.*]

IRINA [*shudders*]. Everything seems to frighten me today. [*pause*] I've got everything ready, and I send my things off after dinner. The Baron and I will be married to-morrow, and to-morrow we go away to the brickworks, and the next day I go to school, and the new life begins. God will help me! When I took my examination for the teacher's post, I actually wept for joy and gratitude. . . . [*pause*] The cart will be here in a minute for my things. . . .

KULYGIN. Somehow or other, all this doesn't seem at all serious. As if it was all ideas, and nothing really serious. Still, with all my soul I wish you happiness.

CHEBUTYKIN [*with deep feeling*]. My splendid . . . my dear, precious girl. . . . You've gone on far ahead, I won't catch up with you. I'm left behind like a migrant bird grown old, and unable to fly. Fly, my dear, fly, and God be with you! [*pause*] It's a pity you shaved your moustaches, Fyodor Ilyich.

KULYGIN. Oh, drop it! [*sighs*] To-day the soldiers will be gone, and everything will go on as in the old days. Say what you will, Masha is a good, honest woman. I love her very much, and thank my fate for her. People have such different fates. There's a Kosirev who works in the excise department here. He was at school with me; he was expelled from the fifth class of the High School for being entirely unable to understand *ut consecutivum*.[1] He's awfully hard up now and in very poor health, and when I meet him I say to him, "How do you do, *ut consecutivum*." "Yes," he says, "precisely *consecutivum* . . ." and coughs. But I've been successful all my life, I'm happy, and I even have a Stanislaus Cross, of the second class, and now I myself teach others that *ut consecutivum*. Of course, I'm a clever man, much cleverer than many, but happiness doesn't only lie in that. . . .

[*"The Maiden's Prayer" is being played on the piano in the house.*]

IRINA. To-morrow night I shan't hear that "Maiden's Prayer" any more, and I shan't be meeting Protopopov. . . . [*pause*] Protopopov is sitting there in the drawing-room; and he came to-day. . . .

KULYGIN. Hasn't the head-mistress come yet?

IRINA. No. She has been sent for. If you only knew how difficult it is for me to live alone, without Olga. . . . She lives at the High School; she, a head-mistress, busy all day with her affairs and I'm alone, bored, with nothing to do, and hate the room I live in. . . . I've made up my mind; if I can't live in Moscow, then it must come to this. It's fate. It can't be helped. It's all the will of God, that's the truth. Nikolai Lvovich made me a proposal. . . . Well? I thought it over and made up my mind. He's a good man . . . it's quite remarkable how good he is. . . . And suddenly my soul put out wings, I became happy, and light-hearted, and once again the desire for work, work, came over me. . . . Only something happened yesterday, some secret dread has been hanging over me. . . .

CHEBUTYKIN. Luckum. Rubbish.

NATASHA [*at the window*]. The head-mistress.

KULYGIN. The head-mistress has come. Let's go.

[*Exit with* IRINA *into the house.*]

---

[1] A Latin grammatical term.

CHEBUTYKIN. "It is my washing day. . . . Tara-ra . . . boom-deay."

[MASHA *approaches,* ANDREY *is wheeling a perambulator at the back.*]

MASHA.   Here you are, sitting here, doing nothing.

CHEBUTYKIN.   What then?

MASHA [*sits*].   Nothing. . . . [*pause*] Did you love my mother?

CHEBUTYKIN.   Very much.

MASHA.   And did she love you?

CHEBUTYKIN [*after a pause*].   I don't remember that.

MASHA.   Is my man here? When our cook Martha used to ask about her gendarme, she used to say my man. Is he here?

CHEBUTYKIN.   Not yet.

MASHA.   When you take your happiness in little bits, in snatches, and then lose it, as I have done, you gradually get coarser, more bitter. [*points to her bosom*] I'm boiling in here. . . . [*Looks at* ANDREY *with the perambulator.*] There's our brother Andrey. . . . All our hopes in him have gone. There was once a great bell, a thousand persons were hoisting it, much money and labor had been spent on it, when it suddenly fell and was broken. Suddenly, for no particular reason. . . . Andrey is like that. . . .

ANDREY.   When are they going to stop making such a noise in the house? It's awful.

CHEBUTYKIN.   They won't be much longer. [*looks at his watch*] My watch is very old-fashioned, it strikes the hours. . . . [*winds the watch and makes it strike*] The first, second, and fifth batteries are to leave at one o'clock precisely. [*pause*] And I go to-morrow.

ANDREY.   For good?

CHEBUTYKIN.   I don't know. Perhaps I'll return in a year. The devil only knows . . . it's all one. . . .

[*Somewhere a harp and violin are being played.*]

ANDREY.   The town will grow empty. It will be as if they put a cover over it. [*pause*] Something happened yesterday by the theater. The whole town knows of it, but I don't.

CHEBUTYKIN.   Nothing. A silly little affair. Solyoni started irritating the Baron, who lost his temper and insulted him, and so at last Solyoni had to challenge him. [*looks at his watch*] It's about time, I think. . . . At half-past twelve, in the public wood, that one you can see from here across the river. . . . Piff-paff. [*laughs*] Solyoni thinks he's Lermontov, and even writes verses. That's all very well, but this is his third duel.

MASHA.   Whose?

CHEBUTYKIN. Solyoni's.

MASHA. And the Baron?

CHEBUTYKIN. What about the Baron? [*pause*]

MASHA. Everything's all muddled up in my head. . . . But I say it ought not to be allowed. He might wound the Baron or even kill him.

CHEBUTYKIN. The Baron is a good man, but one Baron more or less—what difference does it make? It's all the same! [*Beyond the garden somebody shouts "Co-ee! Hallo!"*] You wait. That's Skvortsov shouting; one of the seconds. He's in a boat. [*pause*]

ANDREY. In my opinion it's simply immoral to fight in a duel, or to be present, even in the quality of a doctor.

CHEBUTYKIN. It only seems so. . . . We don't exist, there's nothing on earth, we don't really live, it only seems that we live. Does it matter, anyway!

MASHA. You talk and talk the whole day long. . . . [*going*] You live in a climate like this, where it might snow any moment, and there you talk. . . . [*stops*] I won't go into the house, I can't go there. . . . Tell me when Vershinin comes . . . [*goes along the avenue*] The migrant birds are already on the wing. . . . [*looks up*] Swans or geese. My dear, happy things. . . . [*exit*]

ANDREY. Our house will be empty. The officers will go away, you are going, my sister is getting married, and I alone will remain in the house.

CHEBUTYKIN. And your wife?

[FERAPONT *enters with some documents.*]

ANDREY. A wife's a wife. She's honest, well-bred, yes, and kind, but with all that there is still something about her that degenerates her into a petty, blind, even in some respects misshapen animal. In any case, she isn't a man. I tell you as a friend, as the only man to whom I can lay bare my soul. I love Natasha, it's true, but sometimes she seems extraordinarily vulgar, and then I lose myself and can't understand why I love her so much, or, at any rate, used to love her. . . .

CHEBUTYKIN [*rises*]. I'm going away to-morrow, old chap, and perhaps we'll never meet again, so here's my advice. Put on your cap, take a stick in your hand, go . . . go on and on, without looking round. And the farther you go, the better.

[SOLYONI *goes across the back of the stage with two officers; he catches sight of* CHEBUTYKIN, *and turns to him; the officers go on.*]

SOLYONI. Doctor, it's time. It's half-past twelve already. [*Shakes hands with* ANDREY.]

CHEBUTYKIN. Half a minute. I'm tired of the lot of you. [*to* ANDREY] If anybody asks for me, say I'll be back soon. . . . [*sighs*] Oh, oh, oh!

SOLYONI. "He didn't have the time to sigh. The bear sat on him heavily." [*goes up to him*] What are you groaning about, old man?

CHEBUTYKIN. Stop it!

SOLYONI. How's your health?

CHEBUTYKIN [*angry*]. Mind your own business.

SOLYONI. The old man is unnecessarily excited. I won't go far, I'll only just bring him down like a snipe. [*Takes out his scent-bottle and scents his hands.*] I've poured out a whole bottle of scent to-day and they still smell . . . of a dead body. [*pause*] Yes. . . . You remember the poem.

> "But he, the rebel seeks the storm,
> As if the storm will bring him rest . . ."?

CHEBUTYKIN. Yes.

> "He didn't have the time to sigh,
> The bear sat on him heavily."

[*Exit with* SOLYONI. *Shouts are heard.* ANDREY *and* FERAPONT *come in.*]

FERAPONT. Documents to sign. . . .

ANDREY [*irritated*]. Go away! Leave me! Please! [*goes away with the perambulator*]

FERAPONT. That's what documents are for, to be signed. [*retires to back of stage*]

[*Enter* IRINA, *with* TUZENBAKH *in a straw hat;* KULYGIN *walks across the stage, shouting "Co-ee, Masha, co-ee!"*]

TUZENBAKH. He seems to be the only man in the town who is glad that the soldiers are going.

IRINA. One can understand that. [*pause*] The town will be empty.

TUZENBAKH. My dear, I shall return soon.

IRINA. Where are you going?

TUZENBAKH. I must go into the town and then . . . see the others off.

IRINA. It's not true . . . Nikolai, why are you so absent-minded to-day? [*pause*] What took place by the theater yesterday?

TUZENBAKH [*making a movement of impatience*]. In an hour's time I shall return and be with you again. [*kisses her hands*] My darling . . . [*looking her closely in the face*] it's five years now since I fell in love with you, and still I can't get used to it, and you seem to me to grow more and more beautiful. What lovely, wonderful hair! What eyes! I'm going to take you away to-morrow. We shall work, we shall be rich, my dreams will come true. You will be happy. There's only one thing, one thing only: you don't love me!

IRINA.   It isn't in my power! I shall be your wife, I shall be true to you, and obedient to you, but I can't love you. What can I do! [*cries*] I have never been in love in my life. Oh, I used to think so much of love, I have been thinking about it for so long by day and by night, but my soul is like an expensive piano which is locked and the key lost. [*pause*] You seem so unhappy.

TUZENBAKH.   I didn't sleep all night. There is nothing in my life so awful as to be able to frighten me, only that lost key torments my soul and does not let me sleep. Say something to me. [*pause*] Say something to me. . . .

IRINA.   What can I say, what?

TUZENBAKH.   Anything.

IRINA.   Don't! don't! [*pause*]

TUZENBAKH.   It is curious how silly trivial little things, sometimes for no apparent reason, become significant. At first you laugh at these things, you think they are of no importance, you go on and you feel that you haven't got the strength to stop yourself. Oh don't let's talk about it! I am happy. It is as if for the first time in my life I see these firs, maples, beeches, and they all look at me inquisitively and wait. What beautiful trees and how beautiful, when one comes to think of it, life must be near them! [*a shout of Co-ee! in the distance*] It's time I went. . . . There's a tree which has dried up but it still sways in the breeze with the others. And so it seems to me that if I die, I shall still take part in life in one way or another. Good-bye, dear. . . . [*kisses her hands*] The papers which you gave me are on my table under the calendar.

IRINA.   I am coming with you.

TUZENBAKH [*nervously*].   No, no! [*he goes quickly and stops in the avenue*] Irina!

IRINA.   What is it?

TUZENBAKH [*not knowing what to say*].   I haven't had any coffee to-day. Tell them to make me some. . . . [*he goes out quickly*]

[IRINA *stands deep in thought. Then she goes to the back of the stage and sits on a swing.* ANDREY *comes in with the perambulator and* FERAPONT *also appears.*]

FERAPONT.   Andrey Sergeyevich, it isn't as if the documents were mine, they are the government's. I didn't make them.

ANDREY. Oh, what has become of my past and where is it? I used to be young, happy, clever, I used to be able to think and frame clever ideas, the present and the future seemed to me full of hope. Why do we, almost before we have begun to live, become dull, gray, uninteresting, lazy, apathetic, useless, unhappy? . . . This town has already been in existence for two hundred years and it has a hundred thousand inhabitants, not one of whom is in any way different from the others. There has never been, now or at any other time, a single leader of men, a single scholar, an artist, a man of even the slightest eminence who might arouse envy or a passionate desire to be imitated. They only eat, drink, sleep, and then they die . . . more people are born and also eat, drink, sleep, and so as not to go silly from boredom, they try to make life many-sided with their beastly backbiting, vodka, cards, and litigation. The wives deceive their husbands, and the husbands lie, and pretend they see nothing and hear nothing, and the evil influence irresistibly oppresses the children and the divine spark in them is extinguished, and they become just as pitiful corpses and just as much like one another as their fathers and mothers. . . . [angrily to FERAPONT] What do you want?

FERAPONT. What? Documents want signing.

ANDREY. I'm tired of you.

FERAPONT [handing him papers]. The hall-porter from the law courts was saying just now that in the winter there were two hundred degrees of frost in Petersburg.

ANDREY. The present is beastly, but when I think of the future, how good it is! I feel so light, so free; there is a light in the distance, I see freedom. I see myself and my children freeing ourselves from vanities, from kvass, from goose baked with cabbage, from after-dinner naps, from base idleness. . . .

FERAPONT. He was saying that two thousand people were frozen to death. The people were frightened, he said. In Petersburg or Moscow, I don't remember which.

ANDREY [overcome by a tender emotion]. My dear sisters, my beautiful sisters! [crying] Masha, my sister. . . .

NATASHA [at the window]. Who's talking so loudly out here? Is that you, Andrey? You'll wake little Sophie. Il ne faut pas faire du bruit, la Sophie est dormie déjà. Vous êtes un ours.[1] [angrily] If you want to talk, then give the perambulator and the baby to somebody else. Ferapont, take the perambulator!

FERAPONT. Yes'm. [takes the perambulator]

ANDREY [confused]. I'm speaking quietly.

---

[1]You mustn't make noise, Sophie is already asleep. You are a bear.

NATASHA [*at the window, nursing her boy*].   Bobby! Naughty Bobby! Bad little Bobby!

ANDREY [*looking through the papers*].   All right, I'll look them over and sign if necessary, and you can take them back to the offices. . . .

[*Goes into house reading papers;* FERAPONT *takes the perambulator to the back of the garden.*]

NATASHA [*at the window*].   Bobby, what's your mother's name? Dear, dear! And who's this? That's Aunt Olga. Say to your aunt, "How do you do, Olga!"

[*Two wandering musicians, a man and a girl, are playing on a violin and a harp.* VERSHININ, OLGA, *and* ANFISA *come out of the house and listen for a minute in silence;* IRINA *comes up to them.*]

OLGA.   Our garden might be a public thoroughfare, from the way people walk and ride across it. Nurse, give those musicians something!

ANFISA [*gives money to the musicians*].   Go away with God's blessing on you. [*the musicians bow and go away*] A bitter sort of people. You don't play on a full stomach. [*to* IRINA] How do you do, Irisha! [*kisses her*] Well, little girl, here I am, still alive! Still alive! In the High School, together with little Olga, in her official apartments . . . so the Lord has appointed for my old age. Sinful woman that I am, I've never lived like that in my life before. . . . A large flat, government property, and I've a whole room and bed to myself. All government property. I wake up at nights and, oh God, and Holy Mother, there isn't a happier person than I!

VERSHININ [*looks at his watch*].   We are going soon, Olga Sergeyevna. It's time for me to go. [*pause*] I wish you every . . . every . . . Where's Marya Sergeyevna?

IRINA.   She's somewhere in the garden. I'll go and look for her.

VERSHININ.   If you'll be so kind. I haven't time.

ANFISA.   I'll go and look, too. [*shouts*] Little Masha, co-ee! [*goes out with* IRINA *down into the garden*] Co-ee, co-ee!

VERSHININ.   Everything comes to an end. And so we, too, must part [*looks at his watch*] The town gave us a sort of farewell breakfast, we had champagne to drink and the mayor made a speech, and I ate and listened, but my soul was here all the time. . . . [*looks round the garden*] I'm so used to you now.

OLGA.   Shall we ever meet again?

VERSHININ.   Probably not. [*pause*] My wife and both my daughters will stay here another two months. If anything happens, or if anything has to be done . . .

OLGA.   Yes, yes, of course. You need not worry. [*pause*] To-morrow there won't be a single soldier left in the town, it will all be a memory, and, of course, for us a new life will begin. . . . [*pause*] None of our plans are coming right. I didn't want to be a head-mistress, but they made me one, all the same. It means there's no chance of Moscow. . . .

VERSHININ.   Well . . . thank you for everything. Forgive me if I've . . . I've said such an awful lot—forgive me for that too, don't think badly of me.

OLGA [*wipes her eyes*].   Why isn't Masha coming? . . .

VERSHININ.   What else can I say in parting? Can I philosophize about anything? [*laughs*] Life is heavy. To many of us it seems dull and hopeless, but still, it must be acknowledged that it is getting lighter and clearer, and it seems that the time is not far off when it will be quite clear. [*looks at his watch*] It's time I went! Mankind used to be absorbed in wars, and all its existence was filled with campaigns, at-tacks, defeats, now we've outlived all that, leaving after us a great waste place, which there is nothing to fill with at present; but man-kind is looking for something, and will certainly find it. Oh, if it only happened more quickly! [*pause*] If only education could be added to industry, and industry to education! [*looks at his watch*] It's time I went. . . .

OLGA.   Here she comes.

[*Enter* MASHA.]

VERSHININ.   I came to say good-bye.

[OLGA *steps aside a little, so as not to be in their way.*]

MASHA [*looking him in the face*].   Good-bye. . . . [*prolonged kiss*]

OLGA.   Don't, don't. [MASHA *is crying bitterly.*]

VERSHININ.   Write to me. . . . Don't forget! Let me go. . . . It's time. Take her, Olga Sergeyevna. . . . it's time . . . I'm late . . .

[*He kisses* OLGA's *hand in evident emotion, then embraces* MASHA *once more and goes out quickly.*]

OLGA.   Don't, Masha! Stop, dear. . . . [KULYGIN *enters*]

KULYGIN [*confused*].   Never mind, let her cry, let her. . . . My dear Masha, my good Masha. . . . You're my wife, and I'm happy, what-ever happens . . . I'm not complaining, I don't reproach you at all. . . . Olga is a witness to it. . . . Let's begin to live again as we used to, and not by a single word, or hint . . .

MASHA [*restraining her sobs*].

> "There stands a green oak by the sea.
> And a chain of bright gold is around it. . . .
> And a chain of bright gold is around it. . . ."

I'm going off my head. . . . "There stands . . . a green oak . . . by the sea." . . .

OLGA.　Don't, Masha, don't . . . give her some water. . . .

MASHA.　I'm not crying any more. . . .

KULYGIN.　She's not crying any more . . . she's a good . . . [*a shot is heard from a distance*]

MASHA.　　"There stands a green oak by the sea.
> And a chain of bright gold is around it. . . .
> An oak of green gold. . . ."

I'm mixing it up. . . . [*drinks some water*] Life is dull . . . I don't want anything more now . . . I'll be all right in a moment. . . . It doesn't matter. . . . What do those lines mean? Why do they run in my head? My thoughts are all tangled.

[IRINA *enters.*]

OLGA.　Be quiet, Masha. There's a good girl. . . . Let's go in.

MASHA [*angrily*].　I shan't go in there. [*sobs, but controls herself at once*] I'm not going to go into the house, I won't go. . . .

IRINA.　Let's sit here together and say nothing. I'm going away to-morrow. . . . [*pause*]

KULYGIN.　Yesterday I took away these whiskers and this beard from a boy in the third class. . . . [*he puts on the whiskers and beard*] Don't I look like the German master? . . . [*laughs*] Don't I? The boys are amusing.

MASHA.　You really do look like that German of yours.

OLGA [*laughs*].　Yes. [MASHA *weeps*]

IRINA.　Don't, Masha!

KULYGIN.　It's a very good likeness. . . .

[*Enter* NATASHA.]

NATASHA [*to the maid*].　What? Mikhail Ivanich Protopopov will sit with little Sophie, and Andrey Sergeyevich can take little Bobby out. Children are such a bother. . . . [*to* IRINA] Irina, it's such a pity you're going away to-morrow. Do stop just another week. [*Sees* KULYGIN *and screams; he laughs and takes off his beard and whiskers.*] How you frightened me! [*to* IRINA] I've grown used to you and do you think it will be easy for me to part from you? I'm going to have Andrey and his violin put into your room—let him fiddle away in there!—and we'll put little Sophie into his room. The beautiful, lovely child! What a little girlie! To-day she looked at me with such pretty eyes and said "Mamma!"

KULYGIN.   A beautiful child, it's quite true.

NATASHA.   That means I shall have the place to myself to-morrow. [*sighs*] In the first place I shall have that avenue of fir-trees cut down, then that maple. It's so ugly at night. . . . [*to* IRINA] That belt doesn't suit you at all, dear. . . . It's an error of taste. And I'll give orders to have lots and lots of little flowers planted here, and they'll smell. . . . [*severely*] Why is there a fork lying about here on the seat? [*going towards the house, to the maid*] Why is there a fork lying about here on the seat, I say? [*shouts*] Don't you dare to answer me!

KULYGIN.   Temper! temper!

[*A march is played off; they all listen.*]

OLGA.   They're going.

[CHEBUTYKIN *comes in.*]

MASHA.   They're going. Well, well. . . . *Bon voyage!* [*to her husband*] We must be going home. . . . Where's my coat and hat?

KULYGIN.   I took them in . . . I'll bring them, in a moment.

OLGA.   Yes, now we can all go home. It's time.

CHEBUTYKIN.   Olga Sergeyevna!

OLGA.   What is it? [*pause*] What is it?

CHEBUTYKIN.   Nothing . . . I don't know how to tell you. . . . [*whispers to her*]

OLGA [*frightened*].   It can't be true!

CHEBUTYKIN.   Yes . . . such a story . . . I'm tired out, exhausted, I won't say any more. . . . [*sadly*] Still, it's all the same!

MASHA.   What's happened?

OLGA [*embraces* IRINA].   This is a terrible day . . . I don't know how to tell you, dear. . . .

IRINA.   What is it? Tell me quickly, what is it? For God's sake! [*cries*]

CHEBUTYKIN.   The Baron was killed in the duel just now.

IRINA [*cries softly*].   I knew it, I knew it. . . .

CHEBUTYKIN [*sits on a bench at the back of the stage*].   I'm tired. . . . [*takes a paper from his pocket*] Let 'em cry. . . . [*sings softly*] "Tarara-boom-deay, it is my washing day. . . ." Isn't it all the same!

[*The three sisters are standing, pressing against one another.*]

MASHA.   Oh, how the music plays! They are leaving us, one has quite left us, quite and for ever. We remain alone, to begin our life over again. We must live . . . we must live. . . .

IRINA [*puts her head on* OLGA's *bosom*].   There will come a time when everybody will know why, for what purpose, there is all this suffering, and there will be no more mysteries. But now we must live . . . we must work, just work! To-morrow, I'll go away alone, and I'll teach and give my whole life to those who, perhaps, need it. It's autumn now, soon it will be winter, the snow will cover everything, and I shall be working, working. . . .

OLGA [*embraces both her sisters*].   The bands are playing so gaily, so bravely, and one does so want to live! Oh, my God! Time will pass on, and we shall depart for ever, we shall be forgotten; they will forget our faces, voices, and even how many there were of us, but our sufferings will turn into joy for those who will live after us, happiness and peace will reign on earth, and people will remember with kindly words, and bless those who are living now. Oh dear sisters, our life is not yet at an end. Let us live. The music is so gay, so joyful, and it seems that in a little while we shall know why we are living, why we are suffering. . . . If we could only know, if we could only know!

[*The music has been growing softer and softer;* KULYGIN, *smiling happily, brings out the hat and coat;* ANDREY *wheels out the perambulator in which* BOBBY *is sitting.*]

CHEBUTYKIN [*sings softly*].   "Tara . . . ra-boom-deay. . . . It is my washing-day." [*reads a paper*] It's all the same! It's all the same!

OLGA.   If only we could know, if only we could know!

CURTAIN.

THE CHERRY ORCHARD

Characters

YERMOLAI ALEXEYITCH LOPAKHIN, *a wealthy neighbor*

DUNYASHA (AVDOTYA FYODOROVNA KOZOYEDOV), *a maidservant*

SIMEON PANTELEYITCH EPHIKHODOF, *a clerk*

FIRS NIKOLAYEVITCH, *an old servant*

ANYA, *younger daughter of* MADAME RANEVSKY

MADAME LYUBOF (LYUBA) ANDREYEVNA RANEVSKY, *joint owner of the estate, sister of* GAYEF

BARBARA (VARVARA MIKHAILOVNA), *elderly daughter of* MADAME RANEVSKY

LEONID (LENYA) ANDREYITCH GAYEF, *joint owner of the estate, brother of* MADAME RANEVSKY

CHARLOTTE IVANOVNA, ANYA'*s governess*

SIMEONOF-PISHTCHIK, *a neighboring landowner*

YASHA, *a manservant*

PETER TROPHIMOF, *a tutor*

STATIONMASTER

POSTMASTER (silent role)

ACT I

A room which is still called the nursery. One door leads to ANYA'S *room. Dawn, the sun will soon rise. It is already May, the cherry trees are in blossom, but it is cold in the garden and there is a morning frost. The windows are closed.*

Enter DUNYASHA *with a candle, and* LOPAKHIN *with a book in his hand.*

LOPAKHIN.   Here's the train, thank heaven. What is the time?

DUNYASHA.   Near two. [*putting the candle out*] It is light already.

LOPAKHIN.   How late is the train? Two hours at least. [*yawning and stretching*] A fine mess I have made of it. I came to meet them at the station and then I went and fell asleep, as I sat in my chair. What trouble! Why did you not rouse me?

DUNYASHA.   I thought that you had gone. [*she listens*] I think they are coming.

LOPAKHIN [*listening*].   No; they have got to get the baggage and the rest. [*pause*] Madame Ranevsky has been five years abroad. I wonder what she is like now. What a fine character she is! So easy and simple. I remember when I was only fifteen my old father (he used to keep a shop here in the village then) struck me in the face with his fist and my nose bled. We were out in the courtyard, and he had been drinking. Madame Ranevsky, I remember it like yesterday, still a slender young girl, brought me to the wash-hand stand, here, in this very room, in the nursery. "Don't cry, little peasant," she said, "it'll be all right for your wedding." [*pause*] "Little peasant!" . . . My father, it is true, was a peasant, and here am I in a white waistcoat and brown boots; a silk purse out of a sow's ear; just turned rich, with plenty of money, but still a peasant of the peasants. [*turning over the pages of the book*] Here's this book that I was reading without any attention and fell asleep.

DUNYASHA.   The dogs never slept all night, they knew that their master and mistress were coming.

LOPAKHIN.   What's the matter with you, Dunyasha? You're all . . .

277

DUNYASHA.   My hands are trembling, I feel quite faint.

LOPAKHIN.   You are too refined, Dunyasha, that's what it is. You dress yourself like a young lady, and look at your hair! You ought not to do it; you ought to remember your place.

[*Enter* EPHIKHODOF *with a nosegay. He is dressed in a short jacket and brightly polished boots which squeak noisily. As he comes in he drops the nosegay.*]

EPHIKHODOF [*picking it up*].   The gardener has sent this; he says it is to go in the dining-room. [*handing it to* DUNYASHA]

LOPAKHIN.   And bring me some kvass.

DUNYASHA.   Yes, sir.

[*Exit* DUNYASHA.]

EPHIKHODOF.   There's a frost this morning, three degrees, and the cherry trees all in blossom. I can't say I think much of our climate; [*sighing*] that is impossible. Our climate is not adapted to contribute; and I should like to add, with your permission, that only two days ago I bought myself a new pair of boots, and I venture to assure you they do squeak beyond all bearing. What am I to grease them with?

LOPAKHIN.   Get out; I'm tired of you.

EPHIKHODOF.   Every day some misfortune happens to me; but do I grumble? No; I am used to it; I can afford to smile. [*enter* DUNYASHA, *and hands a glass of kvass to* LOPAKHIN] I must be going. [*he knocks against a chair, which falls to the ground*] There you are! [*in a voice of triumph*] You see, if I may venture on the expression, the sort of incidents *inter alia*. It really is astonishing!

[*Exit* EPHIKHODOF.]

DUNYASHA.   To tell you the truth, Yermolai Alexeyitch, Ephikhodof has made me a proposal.

LOPAKHIN.   Hmph!

DUNYASHA.   I hardly know what to do. He is such a well-behaved young man, only so often when he talks one doesn't know what he means. It is all so nice and full of good feeling, but you can't make out what it means. I fancy I am rather fond of him. He adores me passionately. He is a most unfortunate man; every day something seems to happen to him. They call him "Twenty-two misfortunes," that's his nickname.

LOPAKHIN [*listening*].   There, surely that is them coming!

DUNYASHA.   They're coming! Oh, what is the matter with me? I am all turning cold.

LOPAKHIN.   Yes, there they are, and no mistake. Let's go and meet them. Will she know me again, I wonder? It is five years since we met.

DUNYASHA.   I am going to faint! . . . I am going to faint!

[*Two carriages are heard driving up to the house.* LOPAKHIN *and* DUNYASHA *exeunt quickly. The stage remains empty. A hubbub begins in the neighboring rooms.* FIRS *walks hastily across the stage, leaning on a walking-stick. He has been to meet them at the station. He is wearing an old-fashioned livery and a tall hat; he mumbles something to himself but not a word is audible. The noise behind the scenes grows louder and louder. A voice says: "Let's go this way." Enter* MADAME RANEVSKY, ANYA, CHARLOTTE, *leading a little dog on a chain, all dressed in travelling dresses;* BARBARA *in greatcoat with a kerchief over her head,* GAYEF, SIMEONOF-PISHTCHIK, LOPAKHIN, DUNYASHA, *carrying parcel and umbrella, servants with luggage, all cross the stage.*]

ANYA.   Come through this way. Do you remember what room this is, mamma?

MADAME RANEVSKY [*joyfully through her tears*].   The nursery.

BARBARA.   How cold it is. My hands are simply frozen. [*to* MADAME RANEVSKY] Your two rooms, the white room and the violet room, are just the same as they were, mamma.

MADAME RANEVSKY.   My nursery, my dear, beautiful nursery! This is where I used to sleep when I was a little girl. [*crying*] I am like a little girl still. [*kissing* GAYEF *and* BARBARA *and then* GAYEF *again*] Barbara has not altered a bit, she is just like a nun, and I knew Dunyasha at once. [*kissing* DUNYASHA]

GAYEF.   Your train was two hours late. What do you think of that? There's punctuality for you!

CHARLOTTE [*to* SIMEONOF-PISHTCHIK].   My little dog eats nuts.

PISHTCHIK [*astonished*].   You don't say so! Well, I never!

[*Exeunt all but* ANYA *and* DUNYASHA.]

DUNYASHA.   At last you've come!

[*She takes off* ANYA's *overcoat and hat.*]

ANYA.   I have not slept for four nights on the journey. I am frozen to death.

DUNYASHA.   It was Lent when you went away. There was snow on the ground, it was freezing; but now! Oh, my dear! [*laughing and kissing her*] How I have waited for you, my joy, my light! Oh, I must tell you something at once, I cannot wait another minute.

ANYA [*without interest*].   What, again?

DUNYASHA. Ephikhodof, the clerk, proposed to me in Easter week.

ANYA. Same old story. . . . [*putting her hair straight*] All my hairpins have dropped out. [*she is very tired, staggering with fatigue*]

DUNYASHA. I hardly know what to think of it. He loves me! oh, how he loves me!

ANYA [*looking into her bedroom, affectionately*]. My room, my windows, just as if I had never gone away! I am at home again! When I wake up in the morning I shall run out into the garden. . . . Oh, if only I could get to sleep! I have not slept the whole journey from Paris, I was so nervous and anxious.

DUNYASHA. Monsieur Trophimof arrived the day before yesterday.

ANYA [*joyfully*]. Peter?

DUNYASHA. He is sleeping outside in the bath-house; he is living there. He was afraid he might be in the way. [*looking at her watch*] I'd like to go and wake him, only Mamzelle Barbara told me not to. "Mind you don't wake him," she said.

[*Enter BARBARA with bunch of keys hanging from her girdle.*]

BARBARA. Dunyasha, go and get some coffee, quick. Mamma wants some coffee.

DUNYASHA. In a minute.

[*Exit DUNYASHA.*]

BARBARA. Well, thank heaven, you have come. Here you are at home again. [*caressing her*] My little darling is back! My pretty one is back!

ANYA. What I've had to go through!

BARBARA. I can believe you.

ANYA. I left here in Holy Week. How cold it was! Charlotte would talk the whole way and keep doing conjuring tricks. What on earth made you tie Charlotte round my neck?

BARBARA. Well, you couldn't travel alone, my pet. At seventeen!

ANYA. When we got to Paris, it was so cold! there was snow on the ground. I can't talk French a bit. Mamma was on the fifth floor of a big house. When I arrived there were a lot of Frenchmen with her, and ladies, and an old Catholic priest with a book, and it was very uncomfortable and full of tobacco smoke. I suddenly felt so sorry for mamma, oh, so sorry! I took her head in my arms and squeezed it and could not let it go, and then mamma kept kissing me and crying.

BARBARA [*crying*]. Don't go on, don't go on!

ANYA.   She's sold her villa near Mentone already. She's nothing left, absolutely nothing; and I hadn't a farthing either. We only just managed to get home. And mamma won't understand! We get out at a station to have some dinner, and she asks for all the most expensive things and gives the waiters a florin each for a tip; and Charlotte does the same. And Yasha wanted his portion too. It was too awful! Yasha is mamma's new manservant. We have brought him back with us.

BARBARA.   I've seen the rascal.

ANYA.   Come, tell me all about everything! Has the interest on the mortgage been paid?

BARBARA.   How could it be?

ANYA.   Oh dear! Oh dear!

BARBARA.   The property will be sold in August.

ANYA.   Oh dear! Oh dear!

LOPAKHIN [*looking in at the door and mooing like a cow*].   Moo-o. [*he goes away again*]

BARBARA [*laughing through her tears and shaking her fist at the door*].   Oh, I should like to give him one!

ANYA [*embracing* BARBARA *softly*].   Barbara, has he proposed to you? [BARBARA *shakes her head*] And yet I am sure he loves you. Why don't you come to an understanding? What are you waiting for?

BARBARA.   I don't think anything will come of it. He has so much to do; he can't be bothered with me; he hardly takes any notice. Confound the man, I can't bear to see him! Everyone talks about our marriage; everyone congratulates me, but, as a matter of fact, there is nothing in it; it's all a dream [*changing her tone*] You've got on a brooch like a bee.

ANYA [*sadly*].   Mamma bought it for me. [*going into her room, talking gaily, like a child*] When I was in Paris, I went up in a balloon!

BARBARA.   How glad I am you are back, my little pet! my pretty one! [DUNYASHA *has already returned with a coffee-pot and begins to prepare the coffee*] [*standing by the door*] I trudge about all day looking after things, and I think and think. What are we to do? If only we could marry you to some rich man it would be a load off my mind. I would go into a retreat, and then to Kief, to Moscow; I would tramp about from one holy place to another, always tramping and tramping. What bliss!

ANYA.   The birds are singing in the garden. What time is it now?

BARBARA.   It must be past two. It is time to go to bed, my darling. [*following* ANYA *into her room*] What bliss!

[*Enter* YASHA *with a shawl and a travelling bag.*]

YASHA [*crossing the stage, delicately*].   May I pass this way, mademoiselle?

DUNYASHA.   One would hardly know you, Yasha. How you've changed abroad!

YASHA.   Ahem! and who may you be?

DUNYASHA.   When you left here I was a little thing like that. [*indicating with her hand*] My name is Dunyasha, Theodore Kozoyedof's daughter. Don't you remember me?

YASHA.   Ahem! you little cucumber! [*He looks round cautiously, then embraces her. She screams and drops a saucer. Exit* YASHA, *hastily.*]

BARBARA [*in the doorway, crossly*].   What's all this?

DUNYASHA [*crying*].   I've broken a saucer.

BARBARA.   Well, it brings luck.

[*Enter* ANYA *from her room.*]

ANYA.   We must tell mamma that Peter's here.

BARBARA.   I've told them not to wake him.

ANYA [*thoughtfully*].   It's just six years since papa died. And only a month afterwards poor little Grisha was drowned in the river; my pretty little brother, only seven years old! It was too much for mamma; she ran away, ran away without looking back. [*shuddering*] How well I can understand her, if only she knew! [*pause*] Peter Trophimof was Grisha's tutor; he might remind her.

[*Enter* FIRS *in long coat and white waistcoat.*]

FIRS [*going over to the coffee-pot, anxiously*].   My mistress is going to take coffee here. [*putting on white gloves*] Is the coffee ready? [*sternly, to* DUNYASHA] Here, girl, where's the cream?

DUNYASHA.   Oh dear! Oh dear!

[*Exit* DUNYASHA, *hastily.*]

FIRS [*bustling about the coffee-pot*].   Ah, you . . . job-lot! [*mumbling to himself*] She's come back from Paris. The master went to Paris once in a post-chaise. [*laughing*]

BARBARA.   What is it, Firs?

FIRS.   I beg your pardon? [*joyfully*] My mistress has come home; at last I've seen her. Now I'm ready to die.

[*He cries with joy. Enter* MADAME RANEVSKY, LOPAKHIN, GAYEF *and*
    PISHTCHIK; PISHTCHIK *in Russian breeches and coat of fine cloth.*
    GAYEF *as he enters makes gestures as if playing billiards.*]

MADAME RANEVSKY.   What was the expression? Let me see. "I'll put the red in the corner pocket; double into the middle——"

GAYEF.   I'll chip the red in the right-hand top. Once upon a time. Lyuba, when we were children, we used to sleep here side by side in two little cots, and now I'm fifty-one, and can't bring myself to believe it.

LOPAKHIN.   Yes; time flies.

GAYEF.   Who's that?

LOPAKHIN.   Time flies. I say.

GAYEF.   There's a smell of patchouli!

ANYA.   I am going to bed. Good-night, mamma. [*kissing her mother*]

MADAME RANEVSKY.   My beloved little girl! [*kissing her hands*] Are you glad you're home again? I can't come to my right senses.

ANYA.   Good-night, uncle.

GAYEF [*kissing her face and hands*].   God bless you, little Anya. How like your mother you are! [*to* MADAME RANEVSKY] You were just such another girl at her age, Lyuba.

[ANYA *shakes hands with* LOPAKHIN *and* SIMEONOF-PISHTCHIK *and exit, shutting her bedroom door behind her.*]

MADAME RANEVSKY.   She's very, very tired.

PISHTCHIK.   It must have been a long journey.

BARBARA [*to* LOPAKHIN *and* PISHTCHIK].   Well, gentlemen, it's past two; time you were off.

MADAME RANEVSKY [*laughing*].   You haven't changed a bit, Barbara! [*drawing her to herself and kissing her*] I'll just finish my coffee, then we'll all go. [FIRS *puts a footstool under her feet*] Thank you, friend, I'm used to my coffee. I drink it day and night. Thank you, you dear old man. [*kissing* FIRS]

BARBARA.   I'll go and see if they've got all the luggage. [*exit* BARBARA]

MADAME RANEVSKY.   Can it be me that's sitting here? [*laughing*] I want to jump and wave my arms about [*pausing and covering her face*] Surely I must be dreaming! God knows I love my country. I love it tenderly. I couldn't see out of the window from the train, I was crying so. [*crying*] However, I must drink my coffee. Thank you, Firs; thank you, dear old man. I'm so glad to find you still alive.

FIRS.   The day before yesterday.

GAYEF.   He's hard of hearing.

LOPAKHIN.   I've got to be off for Kharkof by the five o'clock train. Such a nuisance! I wanted to stay and look at you and talk to you. You're as splendid as you always were.

PISHTCHIK [*sighing heavily*].   Handsomer than ever and dressed like a Parisian . . . perish my waggon and all its wheels!

LOPAKHIN.   Your brother, Leonid Andreyitch, says I'm a snob, a money-grubber. He can say what he likes. I don't care a hang. Only I want you to believe in me as you used to; I want your wonderful, touching eyes to look at me as they used to. Merciful God in heaven! My father was your father's serf, and your grandfather's serf before him; but you, you did so much for me in the old days that I've forgotten everything, and I love you like a sister—more than a sister.

MADAME RANEVSKY.   I can't sit still! I can't do it! [*jumping up and walking about in great agitation*] This happiness is more than I can bear. Laugh at me! I am a fool! [*kissing a cupboard*] My darling old cupboard! [*caressing a table*] My dear little table!

GAYEF.   Nurse is dead since you went away.

MADAME RANEVSKY [*sitting down and drinking coffee*].   Yes, Heaven rest her soul. They wrote and told me.

GAYEF.   And Anastasi is dead. Squint-eyed Peter has left us and works in the town at the Police Inspector's now. [*He takes out a box of sugar candy from his pocket, and begins to eat it.*]

PISHTCHIK.   My daughter Dashenka sent her compliments.

LOPAKHIN.   I long to say something charming and delightful to you. [*Looking at his watch*] I'm just off; there's no time to talk. Well, yes, I'll put it in two or three words. You know that your cherry orchard is going to be sold to pay the mortgage: the sale is fixed for the twenty-second of August; but don't you be uneasy, my dear lady; sleep peacefully; there's a way out of it. This is my plan. Listen to me carefully. Your property is only fifteen miles from the town; the railway runs close beside it; and if only you will cut up the cherry orchard and the land along the river into building lots and let it off on lease for villas, you will get at least two thousand five hundred pounds a year out of it.

GAYEF.   Come, come! What rubbish you're talking!

MADAME RANEVSKY.   I don't quite understand what you mean, Yermolai Alexeyitch.

LOPAKHIN.   You will get a pound a year at least for every acre from the tenants, and if you advertise the thing at once, I am ready to bet whatever you like, by the autumn you won't have a clod of that earth left on your hands. It'll all be snapped up. In two words, I congratulate you; you are saved. It's a first-class site, with a good deep river. Only of course you will have to put it in order and clear the ground; you will have to pull down all the old buildings—this house, for instance, which is no longer fit for anything; you'll have to cut down the cherry orchard. . . .

MADAME RANEVSKY.   Cut down the cherry orchard! Excuse me, but you don't know what you're talking about. If there is one thing that's interesting, remarkable in fact, in the whole province, it's our cherry orchard.

LOPAKHIN.   There's nothing remarkable about the orchard except that it's a very big one. It only bears once every two years, and then you don't know what to do with the fruit. Nobody wants to buy it.

GAYEF.   Our cherry orchard is mentioned in Andreyevsky's Encyclopaedia.

LOPAKHIN [*looking at his watch*].   If we don't make up our minds or think of any way, on the twenty-second of August the cherry orchard and the whole property will be sold by auction. Come, make up your mind! There's no other way out of it, I swear—absolutely none.

FIRS.   In the old days, forty or fifty years ago, they used to dry the cherries and soak 'em and pickle 'em, and make jam of 'em; and the dried cherries . . .

GAYEF.   Shut up, Firs.

FIRS.   The dried cherries used to be sent in waggons to Moscow and Kharkof. A heap of money! The dried cherries were soft and juicy and sweet and sweet-smelling then. They knew some way in those days.

MADAME RANEVSKY.   And why don't they do it now?

FIRS.   They've forgotten. Nobody remembers how to do it.

PISHTCHIK [*to* MADAME RANEVSKY].   What about Paris? How did you get on? Did you eat frogs?

MADAME RANEVSKY.   Crocodiles.

PISHTCHIK.   You don't say so! Well, I never!

LOPAKHIN.   Until a little while ago there was nothing but gentry and peasants in the villages; but now villa residents have made their appearance. All the towns, even the little ones, are surrounded by villas now. In another twenty years the villa resident will have multiplied like anything. At present he only sits and drinks tea on his verandah, but it is quite likely that he will soon take to cultivating his three acres of land, and then your old cherry orchard will become fruitful, rich and happy. . . .

GAYEF [*angry*].   What gibberish!

[*Enter* BARBARA *and* YASHA.]

BARBARA [*taking out a key and noisily unlocking an old-fashioned cupboard*].   There are two telegrams for you, mamma. Here they are.

MADAME RANEVSKY [*tearing them up without reading them*].   They're from Paris. I've done with Paris.

GAYEF.   Do you know how old this cupboard is, Lyuba? A week ago I pulled out the bottom drawer and saw a date burnt in it. That cupboard was made exactly a hundred years ago. What do you think of that, eh? We might celebrate its jubilee. It's only an inanimate thing, but for all that it's a historic cupboard.

PISHTCHIK [*astonished*].   A hundred years? Well, I never!

GAYEF [*touching the cupboard*].   Yes, it's a wonderful thing. . . . Beloved and venerable cupboard; honor and glory to your existence, which for more than a hundred years has been directed to the noble ideals of justice and virtue. Your silent summons to profitable labor has never weakened in all these hundred years. [*crying*] You have upheld the courage of succeeding generations of our human kind; you have upheld faith in a better future and cherished in us ideals of goodness and social consciousness. [*pause*]

LOPAKHIN.   Yes. . . .

MADAME RANEVSKY.   You haven't changed, Leonid.

GAYEF [*embarrassed*].   Off the white in the corner, chip the red in the middle pocket!

LOPAKHIN [*looking at his watch*].   Well, I must be off.

YASHA [*handing a box to* MADAME RANEVSKY].   Perhaps you'll take your pills now.

PISHTCHIK.   You oughtn't to take medicine, dear lady. It does you neither good nor harm. Give them here, my friend. [*he empties all the pills into the palm of his hand, blows on them, puts them in his mouth and swallows them down with a draught of kvass*] There!

MADAME RANEVSKY [*alarmed*].   Have you gone off your head?

PISHTCHIK.   I've taken all the pills.

LOPAKHIN.   Greedy fellow! [*everyone laughs*]

FIRS [*mumbling*].   They were here in Easter week and finished off a gallon of pickled gherkins.

MADAME RANEVSKY.   What's he talking about?

BARBARA.   He's been mumbling like that these three years. We've got used to it.

YASHA.   Advancing age.

[CHARLOTTE *crosses in a white frock, very thin, tightly laced, with a lorgnette at her waist.*]

LOPAKHIN.   Excuse me, Charlotte Ivanovna, I've not paid my respects to you yet. [*he prepares to kiss her hand*]

CHARLOTTE [*drawing her hand away*].   If one allows you to kiss one's hand, you will want to kiss one's elbow next, and then one's shoulder.

LOPAKHIN.   I'm having no luck today. [*all laugh*] Charlotte Ivanovna, do us a conjuring trick.

MADAME RANEVSKY.   Charlotte, do do us a conjuring trick.

CHARLOTTE.   No, thank you. I'm going to bed. [*exit*]

LOPAKHIN.   We shall meet again in three weeks. [*kissing* MADAME RANEVSKY'*s hand*] Meanwhile, good-bye. I must be off. [*to* GAYEF] So-long. [*kissing* PISHTCHIK] Ta-ta. [*shaking hands with* BARBARA, *then with* FIRS *and* YASHA] I hate having to go. [*to* MADAME RANEVSKY] If you make up your mind about the villas, let me know, and I'll raise you five thousand pounds at once. Think it over seriously.

BARBARA [*angrily*].   For heaven's sake do go!

LOPAKHIN.   I'm going, I'm going. [*exit*]

GAYEF.   Snob! . . . However, *pardon!* Barbara's going to marry him; he's Barbara's young man.

BARBARA.   You talk too much, uncle.

MADAME RANEVSKY.   Why, Barbara, I shall be very glad. He's a nice man.

PISHTCHIK.   Not a doubt about it. . . . A most worthy individual. My Dashenka, she says . . . oh, she says . . . lots of things. [*snoring and waking up again at once*] By the by, dear lady, can you lend me twenty-five pounds? I've got to pay the interest on my mortgage to-morrow.

BARBARA [*alarmed*].   We can't! we can't!

MADAME RANEVSKY.   It really is a fact that I haven't any money.

PISHTCHIK.   I'll find it somewhere. [*laughing*] I never lose hope. Last time I thought: "Now I really am done for, I'm a ruined man," when behold, they ran a railway over my land and paid me compensation. And so it'll be again; something will happen, if not today, then to-morrow. Dashenka may win the twenty-thousand-pound prize; she's got a ticket in the lottery.

MADAME RANEVSKY.   The coffee's finished. Let's go to bed.

FIRS [*brushing* GAYEF'*s clothes, admonishingly*].   You've put on the wrong trousers again. Whatever am I to do with you?

BARBARA [*softly*].   Anya is asleep. [*she opens the window quietly*] The suns's up already; it isn't cold now. Look, mamma, how lovely the trees are. Heavens! what a sweet air! The starlings are singing!

GAYEF [*opening the other window*].   The orchard is all white. You've not forgotten it, Lyuba? This long avenue going straight on, straight on, like a ribbon between the trees? It shines like silver on moonlight nights. Do you remember? You've not forgotten?

MADAME RANEVSKY [*looking out into the garden*].   Oh, my childhood, my pure and happy childhood! I used to sleep in this nursery. I used to look out from here into the garden. Happiness awoke with me every morning! and the orchard was just the same then as it is now; nothing is altered. [*laughing with joy*] It is all white, all white!

Oh, my cherry orchard! After the dark and stormy autumn and the frosts of winter you are young again and full of happiness; the angels of heaven have not abandoned you. Oh! if only I could free my neck and shoulders from the stone that weighs them down! If only I could forget my past!

GAYEF. Yes; and this orchard will be sold to pay our debts, however impossible it may seem. . . .

MADAME RANEVSKY. Look! There's mamma walking in the orchard . . . in a white frock! [*laughing with joy*] There she is!

GAYEF. Where?

BARBARA. Heaven help you!

MADAME RANEVSKY. There's no one there, really. It only looked like it; there on the right where the path turns down to the summerhouse; there's a white tree that leans over and looks like a woman. [*enter* TROPHIMOF *in a shabby student uniform and spectacles*] What a wonderful orchard, with its white masses of blossom and the blue sky above!

TROPHIMOF. Lyubof Andreyevna! [*she looks round at him*] I only want to say, "How do you do," and go away at once. [*kissing her hand eagerly*] I was told to wait till the morning, but I hadn't the patience.

[MADAME RANEVSKY *looks at him in astonishment.*]

BARBARA [*crying*]. This is Peter Trophimof.

TROPHIMOF. Peter Trophimof; I was Grisha's tutor, you know. Have I really altered so much?

[MADAME RANEVSKY *embraces him and cries softly.*]

GAYEF. Come, come, that's enough, Lyuba!

BARBARA [*crying*]. I told you to wait till to-morrow, you know, Peter.

MADAME RANEVSKY. My little Grisha! My little boy! Grisha . . . my son. . . .

BARBARA. It can't be helped, mamma. It was the will of God.

TROPHIMOF [*gently, crying*]. There, there!

MADAME RANEVSKY [*crying*]. He was drowned. My little boy was drowned. Why? What was the use of that, my dear? [*in a softer voice*] Anya's asleep in there, and I am speaking so loud, and making a noise. . . . But tell me, Peter, why have you grown so ugly? Why have you grown so old?

TROPHIMOF. An old woman in the train called me a "moldy gentleman."

MADAME RANEVSKY. You were quite a boy then, a dear little

student, and now your hair's going and you wear spectacles. Are you really still a student? [*going towards the door*]

TROPHIMOF.　Yes, I expect I shall be a perpetual student.

MADAME RANEVSKY [*kissing her brother and then* BARBARA].　Well, go to bed. You've grown old too, Leonid.

PISHTCHIK [*following her*].　Yes, yes; time for bed. Oh, oh, my gout! I'll stay the night here. Don't forget, Lyubof Andreyevna, my angel, to-morrow morning . . . twenty-five.

GAYEF.　He's still on the same string.

PISHTCHIK.　Twenty-five . . . to pay the interest on my mortgage.

MADAME RANEVSKY.　I haven't any money, my friend.

PISHTCHIK.　I'll pay you back, dear lady. It's a trifling sum.

MADAME RANEVSKY.　Well, well, Leonid will give it to you. Let him have it, Leonid.

GAYEF [*ironical*].　I'll give it him right enough! Hold your pocket wide!

MADAME RANEVSKY.　It can't be helped. . . . He needs it. He'll pay it back.

[*Exeunt* MADAME RANEVSKY, TROPHIMOF, PISHTCHIK *and* FIRS.
GAYEF, BARBARA *and* YASHA *remain.*]

GAYEF.　My sister hasn't lost her old habit of scattering the money. [*to* YASHA] Go away, my lad! You smell of chicken.

YASHA [*laughing*].　You're just the same as you always were, Leonid Andreyevitch!

GAYEF.　Who's that? [*to* BARBARA] What does he say?

BARBARA [*to* YASHA].　Your mother's come up from the village. She's been waiting for you since yesterday in the servants' hall. She wants to see you.

YASHA.　What a nuisance she is!

BARBARA.　You wicked, unnatural son!

YASHA.　Well, what do I want with her? She might just as well have waited till to-morrow. [*exit*]

BARBARA.　Mamma is just like she used to be; she hasn't changed a bit. If she had her way, she'd give away everything she has.

GAYEF.　Yes. [*pause*] If people recommend very many cures for an illness, that means that the illness is incurable. I think and think, I batter my brains; I know of many remedies, very many, and that means really that there is none. How nice it would be to get a fortune left one by somebody! How nice it would be if Anya could marry a very rich man! How nice it would be to go to Yaroslav and try my luck with my aunt the Countess. My aunt is very, very rich, you know.

BARBARA [*crying softly*].   If only God would help us!

GAYEF.   Don't howl! My aunt is very rich, but she does not like us. In the first place, my sister married a solicitor, not a nobleman. [ANYA *appears in the doorway*] She married a man who was not a nobleman, and it's no good pretending that she has led a virtuous life. She's a dear, kind, charming creature, and I love her very much, but whatever mitigating circumstances one may find for her, there's no getting round it that she's a sinful woman. You can see it in her every gesture.

BARBARA [*whispering*].   Anya is standing in the door!

GAYEF.   Who's that? [*pause*] It's very odd, something's got into my right eye. I can't see properly out of it. Last Thursday when I was down at the District Court . . .

[ANYA *comes down.*]

BARBARA.   Why aren't you asleep, Anya?

ANYA.   I can't sleep. It's no good trying.

GAYEF.   My little pet! [*kissing* ANYA'*s hands and face*] My little girl! [*crying*] You're not my niece; you're my angel; you're my everything. Trust me, trust me. . . .

ANYA.   I do trust you, uncle. Everyone loves you, everyone respects you; but dear, dear uncle, you ought to hold your tongue, only to hold your tongue. What were you saying just now about mamma? about your own sister? What was the good of saying that?

GAYEF.   Yes, yes. [*covering his face with her hand*] You're quite right; it was awful of me! Lord, Lord! save me from myself! And a little while ago I made a speech over a cupboard. What a stupid thing to do! As soon as I had done it, I knew it was stupid.

BARBARA.   Yes, really, uncle. You ought to hold your tongue. Say nothing; that's all that's wanted.

ANYA.   If only you would hold your tongue, you'd be so much happier!

GAYEF.   I will! I will! [*kissing* ANYA'*s and* BARBARA'*s hands*] I'll hold my tongue. But there's one thing I must say; it's business. Last Thursday, when I was down at the District Court, a lot of us were there together, we began to talk about this and that, one thing and another, and it seems I could arrange a loan on note of hand to pay the interest into the bank.

BARBARA.   If only Heaven would help us!

GAYEF.   I'll go on Tuesday and talk it over again. [*to* BARBARA] Don't howl! [*to* ANYA] Your mamma shall have a talk with Lopakhin.

Of course he won't refuse her. And as soon as you are rested you must go to see your grandmother, the Countess, at Yaroslav. We'll operate from three points, and the trick is done. We'll pay the interest, I'm certain of it. [*taking sugar candy*] I swear on my honor, or whatever you will, the property shall not be sold. [*excitedly*] I swear by my hope of eternal happiness! There's my hand on it. Call me a base, dishonorable man if I let it go to auction. I swear by my whole being.

ANYA [*calm again and happy*].   What a dear you are, uncle, and how clever! [*embraces him*] Now I'm easy again. I'm easy again! I'm happy!

[*Enter* FIRS.]

FIRS [*reproachfully*].   Leonid Andreyevitch, have you no fear of God? When are you going to bed?

GAYEF.   I'm just off—just off. You get along, Firs. I'll undress myself all right. Come, children, bye-bye! Details to-morrow, but now let's go to bed. [*kissing* ANYA *and* BARBARA] I'm a good Liberal, a man of the eighties. People abuse the eighties, but I think that I may say I've suffered something for my convictions in my time. It's not for nothing that the peasants love me. We ought to know the peasants; we ought to know with what . . .

ANYA.   You're at it again, uncle!

BARBARA.   Why don't you hold your tongue, uncle?

FIRS [*angrily*].   Leonid Andreyevitch!

GAYEF.   I'm coming; I'm coming. Now go to bed. Off two cushions in the middle pocket! I start another life! . . . [*exit, with* FIRS *hobbling after him*]

ANYA.   Now my mind is at rest. I don't want to go to Yaroslav; I don't like grandmamma; but my mind is at rest, thanks to Uncle Leonid. [*she sits down*]

BARBARA.   Time for bed. I'm off. Whilst you were away there's been a scandal. You know that nobody lives in the old servants' quarters except the old people. Ephim, Pauline, Evstigney and old Karp. Well, they took to having in all sorts of queer fish to sleep there with them. I didn't say a word. But at last I heard they had spread a report that I had given orders that they were to have nothing but peas to eat; out of stinginess, you understand? It was all Evstigney's doing. "Very well," I said to myself, "you wait a bit." So I sent for Evstigney. [*yawning*] He comes. "Now then, Evstigney." I said, "you old imbecile, how do you dare . . ." [*looking at* ANYA] Anya, Anya! [*pause*] She's asleep. [*taking* ANYA*'s arm*] Let's go to bed. Come along. [*leading her away*] Sleep on, my little one! Come along; come along! [*they go* *towards* ANYA's *room. In the distance beyond the orchard a shepherd plays his pipe.* TROPHIMOF *crosses the stage and, seeing* BARBARA *and* ANYA, *stops*] 'Sh! She's asleep, she's asleep! Come along, my love.

ANYA [*drowsily*].   I'm so tired! Listen to the bells! Uncle, dear uncle! Mamma! Uncle!

BARBARA.   Come along, my love! Come along.

[*Exeunt* BARBARA *and* ANYA *to the bedroom.*]

TROPHIMOF [*with emotion*].   My sunshine! My spring!

CURTAIN.

ACT II

In the open fields; an old crooked half-ruined shrine. Near it a well; big stones, apparently old tombstones; an old bench. Road to the estate beyond. On one side rise dark poplar trees. Beyond them begins the cherry orchard. In the distance a row of telegraph poles, and, far away on the horizon, the dim outlines of a big town, visible only in fine, clear weather. It is near sunset.

CHARLOTTE, YASHA *and* DUNYASHA *sit on the bench.* EPHIKHODOF *stands by them and plays on a guitar; they meditate.* CHARLOTTE *wears an old peaked cap. She has taken a gun from off her shoulders and is mending the buckle of the strap.*

CHARLOTTE [*thoughtfully*]. I have no proper passport. I don't know how old I am; I always feel I am still young. When I was a little girl my father and mother used to go about from one country fair to another, giving performances, and very good ones too. I used to do the *salto mortale* and all sorts of tricks. When papa and mamma died an old German lady adopted me and educated me. Good! When I grew up I became a governess. But where I come from and who I am, I haven't a notion. Who my parents were—very likely they weren't married—I don't know. [*taking a cucumber from her pocket and beginning to eat it*] I don't know anything about it. [*pause*] I long to talk so, and I have no one to talk to, I have no friends or relations.

EPHIKHODOF [*playing on the guitar and singing*].

> "What is the noisy world to me?
> Oh, what are friends and foes?"

How sweet it is to play upon a mandoline!

DUNYASHA. That's a guitar, not a mandoline. [*she looks at herself in a hand-glass and powders her face*]

EPHIKHODOF. For the madman who loves, it is a mandoline. [*singing*] "Oh, that my heart were cheered
> By the warmth of requited love."

[YASHA *joins in.*]

293

CHARLOTTE. How badly these people do sing! Foo! Like jackals howling!

DUNYASHA [*to* YASHA]. What happiness it must be to live abroad!

YASHA. Of course it is; I quite agree with you. [*he yawns and lights a cigar*]

EPHIKHODOF. It stands to reason. Everything abroad has attained a certain culmination.

YASHA. That's right.

EPHIKHODOF. I am a man of cultivation; I have studied various remarkable books, but I cannot fathom the direction of my preferences; do I want to live or do I want to shoot myself, so to speak? But in order to be ready for all contingencies, I always carry a revolver in my pocket. Here it is. [*showing revolver*]

CHARLOTTE. That's done. I'm off. [*slinging the rifle over her shoulder*] You're a clever fellow, Ephikhodof, and very alarming. Women must fall madly in love with you. Brrr! [*going*] These clever people are all so stupid; I have no one to talk to. I am always alone, always alone; I have no friends or relations, and who I am, or why I exist, is a mystery. [*exit slowly*]

EPHIKHODOF. Strictly speaking, without touching upon other matters, I must protest *inter alia* that destiny treats me with the utmost rigor, as a tempest might treat a small ship. If I labor under a misapprehension, how is it that when I woke up this morning, behold, so to speak, I perceived sitting on my chest a spider of praeternatural dimensions, like that [*indicating with both hands*]? And if I go to take a draught of kvass, I am sure to find something of the most indelicate character, in the nature of a cockroach. [*pause*] Have you read Buckle? [*pause; to* DUNYASHA] I should like to trouble you, Avdotya Fyodorovna, for a momentary interview.

DUNYASHA. Talk away.

EPHIKHODOF. I should prefer to conduct it *tête-à-tête*. [*sighing*]

DUNYASHA [*confused*]. Very well, only first please fetch me my cloak. It's by the cupboard. It's rather damp here.

EPHIKHODOF. Very well, mademoiselle. I will go and fetch it, mademoiselle. Now I know what to do with my revolver. [*takes his guitar and exit, playing*]

YASHA. Twenty-two misfortunes! Between you and me, he's a stupid fellow. [*yawning*]

DUNYASHA. Heaven help him, he'll shoot himself! [*pause*] I have grown so nervous, I am always in a twitter. I was quite a little girl when they took me into the household, and now I have got quite disused to common life, and my hands are as white as white, like a lady's. I have grown so refined, so delicate and genteel, I am afraid of everything. I'm always frightened. And if you deceive me, Yasha, I don't know what will happen to my nerves.

YASHA [*kissing her*].   You little cucumber! Of course every girl ought to behave herself properly; there's nothing I dislike as much as when girls aren't proper in their behavior.

DUNYASHA.   I've fallen dreadfully in love with you. You're so educated; you can talk about anything! [*pause*]

YASHA [*yawning*].   Yes. . . . The way I look at it is this; if a girl falls in love with anybody, then I call her immoral. [*pause*] How pleasant it is to smoke one's cigar in the open air. [*listening*] There's someone coming. It's the missis and the rest of 'em. . . . [DUNYASHA *embraces him hastily*] Go towards the house as if you'd just been for a bathe. Go by this path or else they'll meet you and think that I've been walking out with you. I can't stand that sort of thing.

DUNYASHA [*coughing softly*].   Your cigar has given me a headache. [*exit*]

[YASHA *remains sitting by the shrine. Enter* MADAME RANEVSKY, GAYEF *and* LOPAKHIN.]

LOPAKHIN.   You must make up your minds once and for all. Time waits for no man. The question is perfectly simple. Are you going to let off the land for villas or not? Answer in one word; yes or no. Only one word!

MADAME RANEVSKY.   Who's smoking horrible cigars here? [*she sits down*]

GAYEF.   How handy it is now they've built that railway. [*sitting*] We've been into town for lunch and back again. . . . Red in the middle! I must just go up to the house and have a game.

MADAME RANEVSKY.   There's no hurry.

LOPAKHIN.   Only one word—yes or no! [*entreatingly*] Come, answer the question!

GAYEF [*yawning*].   Who's that?

MADAME RANEVSKY [*looking into her purse*].   I had a lot of money yesterday but there's hardly any left now. Poor Barbara tries to save money by feeding us all on milk soup; the old people in the kitchen get nothing but peas, and yet I go squandering aimlessly. . . . [*dropping her purse and scattering gold coins; vexed*] There, I've dropped it all!

YASHA.   Allow me, I'll pick it up. [*collecting the coins*]

MADAME RANEVSKY.   Yes, please do, Yasha! Whatever made me go into town for lunch? I hate your horrid restaurant with the organ and the tablecloths all smelling of soap. Why do you drink so much, Leonid? Why do you eat so much? Why do you talk so much? You talked too much at the restaurant again, and most unsuitably, about the seventies, and the decadents. And to whom? Fancy talking about decadents to the waiters!

LOPAKHIN.   Quite true.

GAYEF [*with a gesture*].   I'm incorrigible, that's plain. [*irritably to* YASHA] What do you keep dodging about in front of me for?

YASHA [*laughing*].   I can't hear your voice without laughing.

GAYEF [*to* MADAME RANEVSKY].   Either he or I . . .

MADAME RANEVSKY.   Go away, Yasha; run along.

YASHA [*handing* MADAME RANEVSKY *her purse*].   I'll go at once. [*restraining his laughter with difficulty*] This very minute. [*exit*]

LOPAKHIN.   Deriganof, the millionaire, wants to buy your property. They say he'll come to the auction himself.

MADAME RANEVSKY.   How did you hear?

LOPAKHIN.   I was told so in town.

GAYEF.   Our aunt at Yaroslav has promised to send something; but I don't know when, or how much.

LOPAKHIN.   How much will she send? Ten thousand pounds? Twenty thousand pounds?

MADAME RANEVSKY.   Oh, come . . . A thousand or fifteen hundred at the most.

LOPAKHIN.   Excuse me, but in all my life I never met anybody so frivolous as you two, so crazy and unbusinesslike! I tell you in plain Russian your property is going to be sold, and you don't seem to understand what I say.

MADAME RANEVSKY.   Well, what are we to do? Tell us what you want us to do.

LOPAKHIN.   Don't I tell you every day? Every day I say the same thing over and over again. You must lease off the cherry orchard and the rest of the estate for villas; you must do it at once, this very moment; the auction will be on you in two twos! Try and understand. Once you make up your mind there are to be villas, you can get all the money you want, and you're saved.

MADAME RANEVSKY.   Villas and villa residents, oh, please, . . . it's so vulgar!

GAYEF.   I quite agree with you.

LOPAKHIN.   I shall either cry, or scream, or faint. I can't stand it! You'll be the death of me. [*to* GAYEF] You're an old woman!

GAYEF.   Who's that?

LOPAKHIN.   You're an old woman! [*going*]

MADAME RANEVSKY [*frightened*].   No, don't go. Stay here, there's a dear! Perhaps we shall think of some way.

LOPAKHIN.   What's the good of thinking!

MADAME RANEVSKY.   Please don't go; I want you. At any rate it's gayer when you're here. [*pause*] I keep expecting something to happen, as if the house were going to tumble down about our ears.

GAYEF [*in deep abstraction*].   Off the cushion on the corner; double into the middle pocket. . . .

MADAME RANEVSKY.   We have been very, very sinful!

LOPAKHIN.   You! What sins have you committed?

GAYEF [*eating candy*].   They say I've devoured all my substance in sugar candy. [*laughing*]

MADAME RANEVSKY.   Oh, the sins that I have committed . . . I've always squandered money at random like a madwoman; I married a man who made nothing but debts. My husband drank himself to death on champagne; he was a fearful drinker. Then for my sins I fell in love and went off with another man; and immediately—that was my first punishment—a blow full on the head . . . here, in this very river . . . my little boy was drowned; and I went abroad, right, right away, never to come back any more, never to see this river again. . . . I shut my eyes and ran, like a mad thing, and *he* came after me, pitiless and cruel. I bought a villa at Mentone, because he fell ill there, and for three years I knew no rest day or night; the sick man tormented and wore down my soul. Then, last year, when my villa was sold to pay my debts, I went off to Paris, and he came and robbed me of everything, left me and took up with another woman, and I tried to poison myself. . . . It was all so stupid, so humiliating. . . . Then suddenly I longed to be back in Russia, in my own country, with my little girl. . . . [*wiping away her tears*] Lord, Lord, be merciful to me; forgive my sins! Do not punish me any more! [*taking a telegram from her pocket*] I got this to-day from Paris. . . . He asks to be forgiven, begs me to go back. . . . [*tearing up the telegram*] Isn't that music that I hear? [*listening*]

GAYEF.   That's our famous Jewish band. You remember? Four fiddles, a flute and a double bass.

MADAME RANEVSKY.   Does it still exist? We must make them come up some time; we'll have a dance.

LOPAKHIN [*listening*].   I don't hear anything. [*singing softly*]

> "The Germans for a fee will turn
> A Russ into a Frenchman."

[*laughing*] I saw a very funny piece at the theater last night; awfully funny!

MADAME RANEVSKY.   It probably wasn't a bit funny. You people ought to go and see plays; you ought to try to see yourselves; to see what a dull life you lead, and how much too much you talk.

LOPAKHIN.   Quite right. To tell the honest truth, our life's an imbecile affair. [*pause*] My papa was a peasant, an idiot; he understood nothing; he taught me nothing; all he did was to beat me when he was drunk, with a walking-stick. As a matter of fact I'm just as big a blockhead and idiot as he was. I never did any lessons; my handwriting's abominable; I write so badly I'm ashamed before people; like a pig.

MADAME RANEVSKY.   You ought to get married.

LOPAKHIN.   Yes, that's true.

MADAME RANEVSKY.   Why not marry Barbara? She's a nice girl.

LOPAKHIN.   Yes.

MADAME RANEVSKY.   She's a nice straightforward creature; works all day; and what's most important, she loves you. You've been fond of her for a long time.

LOPAKHIN.   Well, why not? I'm quite willing. She's a very nice girl. [*pause*]

GAYEF.   I've been offered a place in a bank. Six hundred pounds a year. Do you hear?

MADAME RANEVSKY.   You in a bank! Stay where you are.

[*Enter* FIRS *carrying an overcoat.*]

FIRS [*to* GAYEF].   Put this on, please, master; it's getting damp.

GAYEF [*putting on the coat*].   What a plague you are, Firs!

FIRS.   What's the use. . . . You went off and never told me. [*examining his clothes*]

MADAME RANEVSKY.   How old you've got, Firs!

FIRS.   I beg your pardon?

LOPAKHIN.   She says how old you've got!

FIRS.   I've been alive a long time. When they found me a wife, your father wasn't even born yet. [*laughing*] And when the Liberation came I was already chief valet. But I wouldn't have any Liberation then; I stayed with the master. [*pause*] I remember how happy everybody was, but why they were happy they didn't know themselves.

LOPAKHIN.   It was fine before then. Anyway they used to flog 'em.

FIRS [*mishearing him*].   I should think so! The peasants minded the masters, and the masters minded the peasants, but now it's all higgledy-piggledy; you can't make head or tail of it.

GAYEF.   Shut up, Firs. I must go into town again to-morrow. I've been promised an introduction to a general who'll lend money on a bill.

LOPAKHIN.   You'll do no good. You won't even pay the interest; set your mind at ease about that.

MADAME RANEVSKY [*to* LOPAKHIN].   He's only talking nonsense. There's no such general at all.

[*Enter* TROPHIMOF, ANYA *and* BARBARA.]

GAYEF.   Here come the others.

ANYA.   Here's the mamma.

MADAME RANEVSKY [*tenderly*].   Come along, come along, . . . my little ones. . . . [*embracing* ANYA *and* BARBARA] If only you knew how much I love you both! Sit beside me . . . there, like that. [*everyone sits*]

LOPAKHIN.   The Perpetual Student's always among the girls.

TROPHIMOF.   It's no affair of yours.

LOPAKHIN.   He's nearly fifty and still a student.

TROPHIMOF.   Stop your idiotic jokes!

LOPAKHIN.   What are you losing your temper for, silly?

TROPHIMOF.   Why can't you leave me alone?

LOPAKHIN [*laughing*].   I should like to know what your opinion is of me?

TROPHIMOF.   My opinion of you, Yermolai Alexeyitch, is this. You're a rich man; you'll soon be a millionaire. Just as a beast of prey which devours everything that comes in its way is necessary for the conversion of matter, so you are necessary too.

[*All laugh.*]

BARBARA.   Tell us something about the planets, Peter, instead.

MADAME RANEVSKY.   No. Let's go on with the conversation we were having yesterday.

TROPHIMOF.   What about?

GAYEF.   About the proud man.

TROPHIMOF.   We had a long talk yesterday, but we didn't come to any conclusion. There is something mystical in the proud man in the sense in which you use the words. You may be right from your point of view, but, if we look at it simple-mindedly, what room is there for pride? Is there any sense in it, when man is so poorly constructed from the physiological point of view, when the vast majority of us are so gross and stupid and profoundly unhappy? We must give up admiring ourselves. The only thing to do is to work.

GAYEF.   We shall die all the same.

TROPHIMOF.   Who knows? And what does it mean, to die? Perhaps man has a hundred senses, and when he dies only the five senses that we know perish with him, and the other ninety-five remain alive.

MADAME RANEVSKY.   How clever you are, Peter.

LOPAKHIN [*ironically*]. Oh, extraordinary!

TROPHIMOF. Mankind marches forward, perfecting its strength. Everything that is unattainable for us now will one day be near and clear; but we must work; we must help with all our force those who seek for truth. At present only a few men work in Russia. The vast majority of the educated people that I know seek after nothing, do nothing, and are as yet incapable of work. They call themselves the "Intelligentsia," they say "thou" and "thee" to the servants, they treat the peasants like animals, learn nothing, read nothing serious, do absolutely nothing, only talk about science, and understand little or nothing about art. They are all serious; they all have solemn faces; they only discuss important subjects; they philosophize; but meanwhile the vast majority of us, ninety-nine percent., live like savages; at the least thing they curse and punch people's heads; they eat like beasts and sleep in dirt and bad air; there are bugs everywhere, evil smells, damp and moral degradation. . . . It's plain that all our clever conversations are only meant to distract our own attention and other people's. Show me where those crèches are, that they're always talking so much about; or those reading-rooms. They are only things people write about in novels; they don't really exist at all. Nothing exists but dirt, vulgarity and Asiatic ways. I am afraid of solemn faces; I dislike them; I am afraid of solemn conversations. Let us rather hold our tongues.

LOPAKHIN. Do you know, I get up at five every morning, I work from morning till night; I am always handling my own money or other people's, and I see the sort of men there are about me. One only has to begin to do anything to see how few honest and decent people there are. Sometimes, as I lie awake in bed, I think: "O Lord, you have given us mighty forests, boundless fields and immeasurable horizons, and we, living in their midst, ought really to be giants."

MADAME RANEVSKY. Oh dear, you want giants! They are all very well in fairy stories; but in real life they are rather alarming. [EPHIKHODOF *passes at the back of the scene, playing on his guitar; pensively*] There goes Ephikhodof.

ANYA [*pensively*]. There goes Ephikhodof.

GAYEF. The sun has set.

TROPHIMOF. Yes.

GAYEF [*as if declaiming, but not loud*]. O Nature, wonderful Nature, you glow with eternal light; beautiful and indifferent, you whom we call our mother, uniting in yourself both life and death, you animate and you destroy. . . .

BARBARA [*entreatingly*]. Uncle!

ANYA. You're at it again, uncle!

TROPHIMOF.   You'd far better double the red into the middle pocket.

GAYEF.   I'll hold my tongue! I'll hold my tongue!

[*They all sit pensively. Silence reigns, broken only by the mumbling of old* FIRS. *Suddenly a distant sound is heard as if from the sky, the sound of a string breaking, dying away, melancholy.*]

MADAME RANEVSKY.   What's that?

LOPAKHIN.   I don't know. It's a lifting–tub given way somewhere away in the mines. It must be a long way off.

GAYEF.   Perhaps it's some sort of bird . . . a heron, or something.

TROPHIMOF.   Or an owl. . . .

MADAME RANEVSKY [*shuddering*].   There's something uncanny about it!

FIRS.   The same thing happened before the great misfortune: the owl screeched and the samovar kept humming.

GAYEF.   What great misfortune?

FIRS.   The Liberation. [*pause*]

MADAME RANEVSKY.   Come, everyone, let's go in; it's getting late. [*to* ANYA] You've tears in your eyes. What is it, little one? [*embracing her*]

ANYA.   Nothing, mamma. I'm all right.

TROPHIMOF.   There's someone coming.

[*A Tramp appears in a torn white-peaked cap and overcoat. He is slightly drunk.*]

TRAMP.   Excuse me, but can I go through this way straight to the station?

GAYEF.   Certainly. Follow this path.

TRAMP.   I am uncommonly obliged to you, sir. [*coughing*] We're having lovely weather. [*declaiming*] "Brother, my suffering brother" . . . "Come forth to the Volga. Who moans?" . . . [*to* BARBARA] Mademoiselle, please spare a sixpence for a hungry fellow–countryman.

[BARBARA, *frightened, screams.*]

LOPAKHIN [*angrily*].   There's a decency for even indecency to observe.

MADAME RANEVSKY.   Take this; here you are. [*fumbling in her purse*] I haven't any silver. . . . Never mind, take this sovereign.

TRAMP.   I am uncommonly obliged to you, madam.

[*Exit* TRAMP. *Laughter.*]

BARBARA [*frightened*]. I'm going! I'm going! Oh, mamma, there's nothing for the servants to eat at home, and you've gone and given this man a sovereign.

MADAME RANEVSKY. What's to be done with your stupid old mother? I'll give you up everything I have when I get back. Yermolai Alexeyitch, lend me some more money.

LOPAKHIN. Very good.

MADAME RANEVSKY. Come along, everyone; it's time to go in. We've settled all about your marriage between us, Barbara. I wish you joy.

BARBARA [*through her tears*]. You mustn't joke about such things, mamma.

LOPAKHIN. Amelia, get thee to a nunnery, go!

GAYEF. My hands are all trembling; it's ages since I had a game of billiards.

LOPAKHIN. Amelia, nymphlet, in thine orisons remember me.

MADAME RANEVSKY. Come along. It's nearly supper-time.

BARBARA. How he frightened me! My heart is simply throbbing.

LOPAKHIN. Allow me to remind you, the cherry orchard is to be sold on the twenty-second of August. Bear that in mind; bear that in mind!

[*Exeunt omnes except* TROPHIMOF *and* ANYA.]

ANYA [*laughing*]. Many thanks to the Tramp for frightening Barbara; at last we are alone.

TROPHIMOF. Barbara's afraid we shall go and fall in love with each other. Day after day she never leaves us alone. With her narrow mind she cannot understand that we are above love. To avoid everything petty, everything illusory, everything that prevents one from being free and happy, that is the whole meaning and purpose of our life. Forward! We march on irresistibly towards that bright star which burns far, far before us! Forward! Don't tarry, comrades!

ANYA [*clasping her hands*]. What beautiful things you say! [*pause*] Isn't it enchanting here to-day!

TROPHIMOF. Yes, it's wonderful weather.

ANYA. What have you done to me, Peter? Why is it that I no longer love the cherry orchard as I did? I used to love it so tenderly; I thought there was no better place on earth than our garden.

TROPHIMOF. All Russia is our garden. The earth is great and beautiful; it is full of wonderful places. [*pause*] Think, Anya, your grandfather, your great-grandfather and all your ancestors were serf-owners, owners of living souls. Do not human spirits look out at you from every tree in the orchard, from every leaf and every stem? Do you not hear human voices? . . . Oh! it is terrible. Your orchard frightens me. When I walk through it in the evening or at night, the rugged bark on the trees glows with a dim light, and the cherry trees seem to see all that happened a hundred and two hundred years ago in painful and oppressive dreams. Well, well, we have fallen at least two hundred years behind the times. We have achieved nothing at all as yet; we have not made up our minds how we stand with the past; we only philosophize, complain of boredom, or drink vodka. It is so plain that, before we can live in the present, we must first redeem the past, and have done with it; and it is only by suffering that we can redeem it, only by strenuous, unremitting toil. Understand that, Anya.

ANYA.   The house we live in has long since ceased to be our house; and I shall go away, I give you my word.

TROPHIMOF.   If you have the household keys, throw them in the well and go away. Be free, be free as the wind.

ANYA [*enthusiastically*].   How beautifully you put it!

TROPHIMOF.   Believe what I say, Anya; believe what I say. I'm not thirty yet; I am still young, still a student; but what I have been through! I am hungry as the winter; I am sick, anxious, poor as a beggar. Fate has tossed me hither and thither; I have been every-where, everywhere. But wherever I have been, every minute, day and night, my soul has been full of mysterious anticipations. I feel the approach of happiness; Anya; I see it coming. . . .

ANYA [*pensively*].   The moon is rising.

[EPHIKHODOF *is heard still playing the same sad tune on his guitar. The moon rises. Somewhere beyond the poplar trees,* BARBARA *is heard calling for* ANYA: "*Anya, where are you?*"]

TROPHIMOF.   Yes, the moon is rising. [*pause*] There it is, there is happiness; it is coming towards us, nearer and nearer; I can hear the sound of its footsteps. . . . And if we do not see it, if we do not know it, what does it matter? Others will see it.

BARBARA [*without*].   Anya? Where are you?

TROPHIMOF.   There's Barbara again! [*angrily*] It really is too bad!

ANYA.   Never mind. Let us go down to the river. It's lovely there.

TROPHIMOF.   Come on!

[*Exeunt* ANYA *and* TROPHIMOF.]

BARBARA [*without*].   Anya! Anya!

CURTAIN.

ACT III

A sitting-room separated by an arch from a big drawing-room behind. Chandelier lighted. The Jewish band mentioned in Act II is heard playing on the landing. Evening. In the drawing-room they are dancing the grand rond. SIMEONOF–PISHTCHIK *is heard crying: "Promenade à une paire!"*

The dancers come down into the sitting-room. The first pair consists of PISHTCHIK *and* CHARLOTTE; *the second of* TROPHIMOF *and* MADAME RANEVSKY; *the third of* ANYA *and the* POST OFFICE OFFICIAL; *the fourth of* BARBARA *and the* STATION-MASTER, *etc., etc.* BARBARA *is crying softly and wipes away the tears as she dances. In the last pair comes* DUNYASHA. *They cross the sitting-room.*

PISHTCHIK.   Grand rond, balancez. . . . Les cavaliers à genou et remerciez vos dames.

[FIRS *in evening dress carries seltzer water across on a tray.* PISHTCHIK *and* TROPHIMOF *come down into the sitting-room.*]

PISHTCHIK.   I am a full-blooded man; I've had two strokes already; it's hard work dancing, but, as the saying goes: "If you run with the pack, bark or no, but anyway wag your tail." I'm as strong as a horse. My old father, who was fond of his joke, rest his soul, used to say, talking of our pedigree, that the ancient stock of the Simeonof-Pishtchiks was descended from that very horse that Caligula made a senator. . . . [*sitting*] But the worst of it is, I've got no money. A hungry dog believes in nothing but meat. [*snoring and waking up again at once*] I'm just the same. . . . It's nothing but money, money, with me.

TROPHIMOF.   Yes, it's quite true, there is something horselike about your build.

PISHTCHIK.   Well, well . . . a horse is a jolly creature . . . you can sell a horse.

[*A sound of billiards being played in the next room.* BARBARA *appears in the drawing-room beyond the arch.*]

TROPHIMOF [*teasing her*].   Madame Lopakhin!   Madame Lopakhin!

BARBARA [*angrily*].   Moldy gentleman!

TROPHIMOF.   Yes, I'm a moldy gentleman, and I'm proud of it.

BARBARA [*bitterly*].   We've hired the band, but where's the money to pay for it? [*exit*]

TROPHIMOF [*to* PISHTCHIK].   If the energy which you have spent in the course of your whole life in looking for money to pay the interest on your loans had been diverted to some other purpose, you would have had enough of it, I dare say, to turn the world upside down.

PISHTCHIK.   Nietzsche, the philosopher, a very remarkable man, very famous, a man of gigantic intellect, says in his works that it's quite right to forge banknotes.

TROPHIMOF.   What, have you read Nietzsche?

PISHTCHIK.   Well . . . Dashenka told me. . . . But I'm in such a hole, I'd forge 'em for two-pence. I've got to pay thirty-one pounds the day after to-morrow. . . . I've got thirteen pounds already. [*feeling his pockets; alarmed*] My money's gone! I've lost my money! [*crying*] Where's my money got to? [*joyfully*] Here it is, inside the lining. . . . It's thrown me all in a perspiration.

[*Enter* MADAME RANEVSKY *and* CHARLOTTE.]

MADAME RANEVSKY [*humming a lezginka*].   Why is Leonid so long? What can he be doing in the town? [*to* DUNYASHA] Dunyasha, ask the musicians if they'll have some tea.

TROPHIMOF.   The sale did not come off, in all probability.

MADAME RANEVSKY.   It was a stupid day for the musicians to come; it was a stupid day to have this dance. . . . Well, well, it doesn't matter. . . . [*she sits down and sings softly to herself*]

CHARLOTTE [*giving* PISHTCHIK *a pack of cards*].   Here is a pack of cards. Think of any card you like.

PISHTCHIK.   I've thought of one.

CHARLOTTE.   Now shuffle the pack. That's all right. Give them here, O most worthy Mr. Pishtchik. Ein, zwei, drei! Now look and you'll find it in your side pocket.

PISHTCHIK [*taking a card from his side pocket*].   The Eight of Spades. You're perfectly right. [*astonished*] Well, I never!

CHARLOTTE [*holding the pack on the palm of her hand, to* TROPHIMOF].   Say quickly, what's the top card?

TROPHIMOF.   Well, say the Queen of Spades.

CHARLOTTE.   Right! [*to* PISHTCHIK] Now then, what's the top card?

PISHTCHIK.　　Ace of Hearts.

CHARLOTTE.　　Right! [*she claps her hands; the pack of cards disappears*]
What a beautiful day we've been having.

[*A mysterious female* VOICE *answers her as if from under the floor:* "Yes,
　indeed, a charming day, mademoiselle."]

CHARLOTTE.　　You are my beautiful ideal.

THE VOICE.　　"I think you also ferry peautiful, mademoiselle."

STATION-MASTER [*applauding*].　　Bravo, Miss Ventriloquist!

PISHTCHIK [*astonished*].　　Well, I never! Bewitching Charlotte
Ivanovna, I'm head over ears in love with you.

CHARLOTTE.　　In love! [*shrugging her shoulders*] Are you capable of
love? Guter Mensch, aber schlechter Musikant!

TROPHIMOF [*slapping* PISHTCHIK *on the shoulder*].　　You old horse!

CHARLOTTE.　　Now attention, please; one more trick. [*taking a
shawl from a chair*] Now here's a shawl, and a very pretty shawl; I'm
going to sell this very pretty shawl. [*shaking it*] Who'll buy? who'll
buy?

PISHTCHIK [*astonished*].　　Well, I never!

CHARLOTTE.　　Ein, zwei, drei! [*she lifts the shawl quickly; behind it
stands* ANYA, *who drops a curtsy, runs to her mother, kisses her, then runs
up into the drawing-room amid general applause*]

MADAME RANEVSKY [*applauding*].　　Bravo! bravo!

CHARLOTTE.　　Once more. Ein, zwei, drei! [*she lifts up the shawl;
behind it stands* BARBARA, *bowing*]

PISHTCHIK [*astonished*].　　Well, I never!

CHARLOTTE.　　That's all. [*she throws the shawl over* PISHTCHIK,
makes a curtsy and runs up into the drawing-room]

PISHTCHIK [*hurrying after her*].　　You little rascal . . . there's a girl for
you, there's a girl. . . . [*exit*]

MADAME RANEVSKY.　　And still no sign of Leonid. What he's
doing in the town so long, I can't understand. It must be all over by
now; the property's sold; or the auction never came off; why does he
keep me in suspense so long?

BARBARA [*trying to soothe her*].　　Uncle has bought it, I am sure of
that.

TROPHIMOF [*mockingly*].　　Of course he has!

BARBARA.　　Grannie sent him a power of attorney to buy it in her
name and transfer the mortgage. She's done it for Anya's sake. I'm
perfectly sure that Heaven will help us and uncle will buy it.

MADAME RANEVSKY.　　Your Yaroslav grannie sent fifteen hundred
pounds to buy the property in her name—she doesn't trust us—but

it wouldn't be enough even to pay the interest. [*covering her face with her hands*] My fate is being decided to-day, my fate. . . .

TROPHIMOF [*teasing* BARBARA].   Madame Lopakhin!

BARBARA [*angrily*].   Perpetual Student! He's been sent down twice from the University.

MADAME RANEVSKY.   Why do you get angry, Barbara? He calls you Madame Lopakhin for fun. Why not? You can marry Lopakhin if you like; he's a nice, interesting man; you needn't if you don't; nobody wants to force you, my pet.

BARBARA.   I take it very seriously, mamma, I must confess. He's a nice man and I like him.

MADAME RANEVSKY.   Then marry him. There's no good putting it off that I can see.

BARBARA.   But, mamma, I can't propose to him myself. For two whole years everybody's been talking about him to me, everyone; but he either says nothing or makes a joke of it. I quite understand. He's making money; he's always busy; he can't be bothered with me. If I only had some money, even a little, even ten pounds, I would give everything up and go right away. I would go into a nunnery.

TROPHIMOF [*mockingly*].   What bliss!

BARBARA [*to* TROPHIMOF].   A student ought to be intelligent. [*in a gentler voice, crying*] How ugly you've grown, Peter; how old you've grown! [*she stops crying; to* MADAME RANEVSKY] But I can't live without work, mamma. I must have something to do every minute of the day.

[*Enter* YASHA.]

YASHA [*trying not to laugh*].   Ephikhodof has broken a billiard cue. [*exit*]

BARBARA.   What's Ephikhodof doing here? Who gave him leave to play billiards? I don't understand these people. [*exit*]

MADAME RANEVSKY.   Don't tease her, Peter. Don't you see that she's unhappy enough already?

TROPHIMOF.   I wish she wouldn't be so fussy, always meddling in other people's affairs. The whole summer she's given me and Anya no peace; she is afraid we'll work up a romance between us. What business is it of hers? I'm sure I never gave her any grounds; I'm not likely to be so commonplace. We are above love!

MADAME RANEVSKY.   Then I suppose I must be beneath love. [*deeply agitated*] Why doesn't Leonid come? Oh, if only I knew whether the property's sold or not! It seems such an impossible disaster, that I don't know what to think. . . . I'm bewildered. . . . I shall

burst out screaming, I shall do something idiotic. Save me, Peter; say
something to me, say something. . . .

TROPHIMOF.   Whether the property is sold to-day or whether it's
not sold, surely it's all one? It's all over with it long ago; there's no
turning back, the path is overgrown. Be calm, dear Lyubof
Andreyevna. You mustn't deceive yourself any longer; for once you
must look the truth straight in the face.

MADAME RANEVSKY.   What truth? You can see what's truth, and
what's untruth, but I seem to have lost the power of vision; I see
nothing. You settle every important question so boldly; but tell me,
Peter, isn't that because you're young, because you have never solved
any question of your own as yet by suffering? You look boldly ahead;
isn't it only that you don't see or divine anything terrible in the future; because life is still hidden from your young eyes? You are
bolder, honester, deeper than we are, but reflect, show me just a finger's breadth of consideration, take pity on me. Don't you see? I was
born here, my father and mother lived here, and my grandfather; I
love this house; without the cherry orchard my life has no meaning
for me, and if it *must* be sold, then for heaven's sake sell me too! [*embracing* TROPHIMOF *and kissing him on the forehead*] My little boy was
drowned here. [*crying*] Be gentle with me, dear, kind Peter.

TROPHIMOF.   You know I sympathize with all my heart.

MADAME RANEVSKY.   Yes, yes, but you ought to say it somehow
differently. [*taking out her handkerchief and dropping a telegram*] I am so
wretched to-day, you can't imagine! All this noise jars on me, my
heart jumps at every sound. I tremble all over; but I can't shut myself
up; I am afraid of the silence when I'm alone. Don't be hard on me,
Peter; I love you like a son. I would gladly let Anya marry you, I
swear it; but you must work, Peter; you must get your degree. You
do nothing; Fate tosses you about from place to place; and that's not
right. It's true what I say, isn't it? And you must do something to your
beard to make it grow better. [*laughing*] I can't help laughing at you.

TROPHIMOF [*picking up the telegram*].   I don't wish to be an
Adonis.

MADAME RANEVSKY.   It's a telegram from Paris. I get them every
day. One came yesterday, another to-day. That savage is ill again; he's
in a bad way. . . . He asks me to forgive him, he begs me to come;
and I really ought to go to Paris and be with him. You look at me
sternly; but what am I to do, Peter? What am I to do? He's ill, he's
lonely, he's unhappy. Who is to look after him? Who is to keep him
from doing stupid things? Who is to give him his medicine when it's
time? After all, why should I be ashamed to say it? I love him, that's
plain. I love him, I love him. . . . My love is like a stone tied round

my neck; it's dragging me down to the bottom; but I love my stone.
I can't live without it. [*squeezing* TROPHIMOF's *hand*] Don't think ill
of me, Peter; don't say anything! Don't say anything!

TROPHIMOF [*crying*].   Forgive my bluntness, for heaven's sake; but
the man has simply robbed you.

MADAME RANEVSKY.   No, no, no! [*stopping her ears*] You mustn't
say that!

TROPHIMOF.   He's a rascal; everybody sees it but yourself; he's a
petty rascal, a ne'er-do-well. . . .

MADAME RANEVSKY [*angry but restrained*].   You're twenty-six or
twenty-seven, and you're still a Lower School boy!

TROPHIMOF.   Who cares?

MADAME RANEVSKY.   You ought to be a man by now; at your
age you ought to understand people who love. You ought to love
someone yourself, you ought to be in love! [*angrily*] Yes, yes! It's not
purity with you; it's simply you're a smug, a figure of fun, a
freak. . . .

TROPHIMOF [*horrified*].   What does she say?

MADAME RANEVSKY.   "I am above love!" You're not above love;
you're simply what Firs calls a "job-lot." At your age you ought to
be ashamed not to have a mistress!

TROPHIMOF [*aghast*].   This is awful! What does she say? [*going
quickly up into the drawing-room, clasping his head with his hands*] This is
something awful! I can't stand it; I'm off . . . [*exit, but returns at once*]
All is over between us! [*exit to landing*]

MADAME RANEVSKY [*calling after him*].   Stop, Peter! Don't be ridiculous; I was only joking! Peter!

[TROPHIMOF *is heard on the landing going quickly down the stairs, and
suddenly falling down them with a crash.* ANYA *and* BARBARA *scream.
A moment later the sound of laughter.*]

MADAME RANEVSKY.   What has happened?

[ANYA *runs in.*]

ANYA [*laughing*].   Peter's tumbled downstairs. [*she runs out again*]
MADAME RANEVSKY.   What a ridiculous fellow he is!

[*The* STATION-MASTER *stands in the middle of the drawing-room behind
the arch and recites Alexey Tolstoi's poem, "The Sinner." Everybody
stops to listen, but after a few lines the sound of a waltz is heard from
the landing and he breaks off. All dance.* TROPHIMOF, ANYA,
BARBARA *and* MADAME RANEVSKY *enter from the landing.*]

MADAME RANEVSKY.   Come, Peter, come, you pure spirit. . . . I beg your pardon. Let's have a dance. [*She dances with* TROPHIMOF. ANYA *and* BARBARA *dance.*]

[*Enter* FIRS, *and stands his walking-stick by the side door. Enter* YASHA *by the drawing-room; he stands looking at the dancers.*]

YASHA.   Well, grandfather?

FIRS.   I'm not feeling well. In the old days it was generals and barons and admirals that danced at our dances, but now we send for the Postmaster and the Station-Master, and even they make a favor of coming. I'm sort of weak all over. The old master, their grandfather, used to give us all sealing wax, when we had anything the matter. I've taken sealing wax every day for twenty years and more. Perhaps that's why I'm still alive.

YASHA.   I'm sick of you, grandfather. [*yawning*] I wish you'd die and have done with it.

FIRS.   Ah! you . . . job-lot! [*he mumbles to himself*]

[TROPHIMOF *and* MADAME RANEVSKY *dance beyond the arch and down into the sitting-room.*]

MADAME RANEVSKY.   Merci. I'll sit down. [*sitting*] I'm tired.

[*Enter* ANYA.]

ANYA [*agitated*].   There was somebody in the kitchen just now saying that the cherry orchard was sold to-day.

MADAME RANEVSKY.   Sold? Who to?

ANYA.   He didn't say who to. He's gone. [*she dances with* TROPHIMOF; *both dance up into the drawing-room*]

YASHA.   It was some old fellow chattering; a stranger.

FIRS.   And still Leonid Andreyitch doesn't come. He's wearing his light overcoat *demi-saison;* he'll catch cold as like as not. Ah, young wood, green wood!

MADAME RANEVSKY.   This is killing me. Yasha, go and find out who it was sold to.

YASHA.   Why, he's gone long ago, the old man. [*laughs*]

MADAME RANEVSKY [*vexed*].   What are you laughing at? What are you glad about?

YASHA.   He's a ridiculous fellow, is Ephikhodof. Nothing in him. Twenty-two misfortunes!

MADAME RANEVSKY.   Firs, if the property is sold, where will you go to?

FIRS.   Wherever you tell me, there I'll go.

MADAME RANEVSKY.   Why do you look like that? Are you ill? You ought to be in bed.

FIRS [*ironically*].   Oh yes, I'll go to bed, and who'll hand the things around, who'll give orders? I've the whole house on my hands.

YASHA.   Lyubof Andreyevna! Let me ask a favor of you; be so kind; if you go to Paris again, take me with you, I beseech you. It's absolutely impossible for me to stay here. [*looking about; sotto voce*] What's the use of talking? You can see for yourself this is a barbarous country; the people have no morals; and the boredom! The food in the kitchen is something shocking, and on the top of it old Firs goes about mumbling irrelevant nonsense. Take me back with you; be so kind!

[*Enter* PISHTCHIK.]

PISHTCHIK.   May I have the pleasure . . . a bit of a waltz, charming lady? [MADAME RANEVSKY *takes his arm*] All the same, enchanting lady, you must let me have eighteen pounds. [*dancing*] Let me have . . . eighteen pounds.

[*Exeunt dancing through the arch.*]

YASHA [*singing to himself*].   "Oh, wilt thou undersand
                                  The turmoil of my soul?"

[*Beyond the arch appears a figure in gray tall hat and check trousers, jumping and waving its arms. Cries of "Bravo, Charlotte Ivanovna."*]

DUNYASHA [*stopping to powder her face*].   Mamselle Anya tells me I'm to dance; there are so many gentlemen and so few ladies. But dancing makes me giddy and makes my heart beat, Firs Nikolayevitch; and just now the gentleman from the post office said something so nice to me, oh, so nice! It quite took my breath away. [*the music stops*]

FIRS.   What did he say to you?

DUNYASHA.   He said, "You are like a flower."

YASHA [*yawning*].   Cad! [*exit*]

DUNYASHA.   Like a flower! I am so ladylike and refined, I dote on compliments.

FIRS.   You'll come to a bad end.

[*Enter* EPHIKHODOF.]

EPHIKHODOF.   You are not pleased to see me. Avdotya Fyodorovna, no more than if I were some sort of insect. [*sighing*] Ah! Life! Life!

DUNYASHA.   What do you want?

EPHIKHODOF.   Undoubtedly perhaps you are right. [*sighing*] But of course, if one regards it, so to speak, from the point of view, if I may allow myself the expression, and with apologies for my frankness, you have finally reduced me to a state of mind. I quite appreciate my destiny; every day some misfortune happens to me, and I have long since grown accustomed to it, and face my fortune with a smile. You have passed your word to me, and although I . . .

DUNYASHA.   Let us talk of this another time, if you please; but now leave me in peace. I am busy meditating. [*playing with her fan*]

EPHIKHODOF.   Every day some misfortune befalls me, and yet, if I may venture to say so, I meet them with smiles and even laughter.

[*Enter* BARBARA *from the drawing-room.*]

BARBARA [*to* EPHIKHODOF].   Haven't you gone yet, Simeon? You seem to pay no attention to what you're told. [*to* DUNYASHA] You get out of here, Dunyasha. [*to* EPHIKHODOF] First you play billiards and break a cue, and then you march about the drawing-room as if you were a guest!

EPHIKHODOF.   Allow me to inform you that it's not your place to call me to account.

BARBARA.   I'm not calling you to account; I'm merely talking to you. All you can do is to walk about from one place to another, without ever doing a stroke of work; and why on earth we keep a clerk at all heaven only knows.

EPHIKHODOF [*offended*].   Whether I work, or whether I walk, or whether I eat, or whether I play billiards is a question to be decided only by my elders and people who understand.

BARBARA [*furious*].   How dare you talk to me like that! How dare you! I don't understand things, don't I? You clear out of here this minute! Do you hear me? This minute!

EPHIKHODOF [*flinching*].   I must beg you to express yourself in genteeler language.

BARBARA [*beside herself*].   You clear out this instant second! Out you go! [*following him as he retreats towards the door*] Twenty-two misfortunes! Make yourself scarce! Get out of my sight!

[*Exit* EPHIKHODOF.]

EPHIKHODOF [*without*].   I shall lodge a complaint against you.

BARBARA.   What! You're coming back, are you? [*seizing the walking-stick left at the door by* FIRS] Come on! Come on! Come on! I'll teach you! Are you coming? Are you coming? Then take that. [*she slashes with the stick.*]

[*Enter* LOPAKHIN.]

LOPAKHIN.   Many thanks; much obliged.

BARBARA [*still angry, but ironical*].   Sorry!

LOPAKHIN.   Don't mention it. I'm very grateful for your warm reception.

BARBARA.   It's not worth thanking me for. [*she walks away, then looks round and asks in a gentle voice*] I didn't hurt you?

LOPAKHIN.   Oh, no, nothing to matter. I shall have a bump like a goose's egg, that's all.

[*Voices from the drawing-room: "Lopakhin has arrived! Yermolai Alexeyitch!"*]

PISHTCHIK.   Let my eyes see him, let my ears hear him! [*he and LOPAKHIN kiss*] You smell of brandy, old man. We're having a high time, too.

[*Enter* MADAME RANEVSKY.]

MADAME RANEVSKY.   Is it you, Yermolai Alexeyitch? Why have you been so long? Where is Leonid?

LOPAKHIN.   Leonid Andreyitch came back with me. He's just coming.

MADAME RANEVSKY [*agitated*].   What happened? Did the sale come off? Tell me, tell me!

LOPAKHIN [*embarrassed, afraid of showing his pleasure*].   The sale was all over by four o'clock. We missed the train and had to wait till half-past eight. [*sighing heavily*] Ouf! I'm rather giddy. . . .

[*Enter* GAYEF. *In one hand he carries parcels; with the other he wipes away his tears.*]

MADAME RANEVSKY.   What happened, Lenya? Come, Lenya! [*impatiently, crying*] Be quick, be quick, for heaven's sake!

GAYEF [*answering her only with an up and down gesture of the hand; to* FIRS, *crying*].   Here, take these. . . . Here are some anchovies and Black Sea herrings. I've had nothing to eat all day, Lord, what I've been through! [*through the open door of the billiard-room comes the click of the billiard balls and* YASHA's *voice: "Seven, eighteen!"* GAYEF's *expression changes; he stops crying*] I'm frightfully tired. Come and help me change, Firs. [*he goes up through the drawing-room,* FIRS *following*]

PISHTCHIK.   What about the sale? Come on, tell us all about it.

MADAME RANEVSKY.   Was the cherry orchard sold?

LOPAKHIN.   Yes.

MADAME RANEVSKY.   Who bought it?

LOPAKHIN.   I did. [*pause;* MADAME RANEVSKY *is overwhelmed at the news; she would fall to the ground but for the chair and table by her;* BARBARA *takes the keys from her belt, throws them on the floor in the middle of the sitting-room, and exits.*] I bought it. Wait a bit; don't hurry me; my head's in a whirl; I can't speak. . . . [*laughing*] When we got to the sale, Deriganof was there already. Leonid Andreyitch had only fifteen hundred pounds, and Deriganof bid three thousand more than the mortgage right away. When I saw how things stood, I went for him and bid four thousand. He said four thousand five hundred. I said five thousand five hundred. He went up by five hundreds, you see, and I went up by thousands. . . . Well, it was soon over. I bid nine thousand more than the mortgage, and got it; and now the cherry orchard is mine! Mine! [*laughing*] Heaven's alive! Just think of it! The cherry orchard is mine! Tell me that I'm drunk; tell me that I'm off my head; tell me that it's all a dream! . . . [*stamping his feet*] Don't laugh at me! If only my father and my grandfather could rise from their graves and see the whole affair, how their Yermolai, their flogged and ignorant Yermolai, who used to run about barefooted in the winter, how this same Yermolai had bought a property that hasn't its equal for beauty anywhere in the whole world! I have bought the property where my father and grandfather were slaves, where they weren't even allowed into the kitchen. I'm asleep, it's only a vision, it isn't real. . . . 'Tis the fruit of imagination, wrapped in the mists of ignorance. [*picking up the keys and smiling affectionately*] She's thrown down her keys; she wants to show that she's no longer mistress here. . . . [*jingling them together*] Well, well, what's the odds? [*the musicians are heard tuning up*] Hey, musicians, play! I want to hear you. Come everyone and see Yermolai Lopakhin lay his axe to the cherry orchard, come and see the trees fall down! We'll fill the place with villas; our grandsons and greatsons shall see a new life here. . . . Strike up, music! [*the band plays;* MADAME RANEVSKY *sinks into a chair and weeps bitterly; reproachfully*] Oh, why, why didn't you listen to me? You can't put the clock back now, poor dear. [*crying*] Oh, that all this were past and over! Oh, that our unhappy topsy-turvy life were changed!

PISHTCHIK [*taking him by the arm, sotto voce*].   She's crying. Let's go into the drawing-room and leave her alone to . . . Come on. [*taking him by the arm, and going up towards the drawing-room*]

LOPAKHIN.   What's up? Play your best, musicians! Let everything be as I want. [*ironically*] Here comes the new squire, the owner of the cherry orchard! [*knocking up by accident against a table and nearly throwing down the candelabra*] Never mind, I can pay for everything!

[*Exit with* PISHTCHIK. *Nobody remains in the drawing-room or sitting-room except* MADAME RANEVSKY, *who sits huddled together, weeping bitterly. The band plays softly. Enter* ANYA *and* TROPHIMOF *quickly.*

ANYA *goes to her mother and kneels before her.* TROPHIMOF *stands in the entry to the drawing-room.*]

ANYA.   Mamma! Are you crying, mamma? My dear, good, sweet mamma! Darling, I love you! I bless you! The cherry orchard is sold; it's gone; it's quite true, it's quite true. But don't cry, mamma, you've still got life before you, you've still got your pure and lovely soul. Come with me, darling; come away from here. We'll plant a new garden, still lovelier than this. You will see it and understand, and happiness, deep, tranquil happiness will sink down on your soul, like the sun at eventide, and you'll smile, mamma. Come, darling, come with me!

CURTAIN.

ACT IV

Same scene as Act I. There are no window-curtains, no pictures. The little furniture left is stacked in a corner, as if for sale. A feeling of emptiness. By the door to the hall and at the back of the scene are piled portmanteaux, bundles, etc. The door is open and the voices of BARBARA *and* ANYA *are audible.*

LOPAKHIN *stands waiting.* YASHA *holds a tray with small tumblers full of champagne.* EPHIKHODOF *is tying up a box in the hall. A distant murmur of voices behind the scene, the* PEASANTS *have come to say good-bye.*

GAYEF [*without*].   Thank you, my lads, thank you.

YASHA.   The common people have come to say good-bye. I'll tell you what I think, Yermolai Alexeyitch; they're good fellows but rather stupid.

[*The murmur of voices dies away. Enter* MADAME RANEVSKY *and* GAYEF *from the hall. She is not crying, but she is pale, her face twitches, she cannot speak.*]

GAYEF.   You gave them your purse, Lyuba. That was wrong, very wrong!

MADAME RANEVSKY.   I couldn't help it, I couldn't help it!

[*Exeunt both.*]

LOPAKHIN [*calling after them through the doorway*].   Please come here! Won't you come here? Just a glass to say good-bye. I forgot to bring any from town, and could only raise one bottle at the station. Come along. [*pause*] What, won't you have any? [*returning from the door*] If I'd known, I wouldn't have bought it. I shan't have any either. [YASHA *sets the tray down carefully on a chair*] Drink it yourself, Yasha.

YASHA.   Here's to our departure! Good luck to them that stay! [*drinking*] This isn't real champagne, you take my word for it.

LOPAKHIN.   Sixteen shillings a bottle. [*pause*] It's devilish cold in here.

316

YASHA.   The fires weren't lighted to-day; we're all going away. [*he laughs*]

LOPAKHIN.   What are you laughing for?

YASHA.   Just pleasure.

LOPAKHIN.   Here we are in October, but it's as calm and sunny as summer. Good building weather. [*looking at his watch and speaking off*] Don't forget that there's only forty-seven minutes before the train goes. You must start for the station in twenty minutes. Make haste.

[*Enter* TROPHIMOF *in an overcoat, from out of doors.*]

TROPHIMOF.   I think it's time we were off. The carriages are round. What the deuce has become of my goloshes? I've lost 'em. [*calling off*] Anya, my goloshes have disappeared. I can't find them anywhere!

LOPAKHIN.   I've got to go to Kharkof. I'll start in the same train with you. I'm going to spend the winter in Kharkof. I've been loafing about all this time with you people, eating my head off for want of work. I can't live without work, I don't know what to do with my hands; they dangle about as if they didn't belong to me.

TROPHIMOF.   Well, we're going now, and you'll be able to get back to your beneficent labors.

LOPAKHIN.   Have a glass.

TROPHIMOF.   Not for me.

LOPAKHIN.   Well, so you're off to Moscow?

TROPHIMOF.   Yes, I'll see them into the town, and go on to Moscow to-morrow.

LOPAKHIN.   Well, well. . . . I suppose the professors haven't started their lectures yet; they're waiting till you arrive.

TROPHIMOF.   It is no affair of yours.

LOPAKHIN.   How many years have you been up at the University?

TROPHIMOF.   Try and think of some new joke; this one's getting a bit flat. [*looking for his goloshes*] Look here, I dare say we shan't meet again, so let me give you a bit of advice as a keepsake: Don't flap your hands about! Get out of the habit of flapping. Building villas, prophesying that villa residents will turn into small freeholders, all that sort of thing is flapping too. Well, when all's said and done, I like you. You have thin, delicate, artist fingers; you have a delicate, artist soul.

LOPAKHIN [*embracing him*].   Good-bye, old chap. Thank you for everything. Take some money off me for the journey if you want it.

TROPHIMOF.   What for? I don't want it.

LOPAKHIN.   But you haven't got any.

TROPHIMOF.   Yes, I have. Many thanks. I got some for a translation. Here it is, in my pocket. [*anxiously*] I can't find my goloshes anywhere!

BARBARA [*from the next room*].   Here, take your garbage away! [*she throws a pair of goloshes on the stage*]

TROPHIMOF.   What are you so cross about, Barbara? Humph! . . . But those aren't *my* goloshes!

LOPAKHIN.   In the spring I sowed three thousand acres of poppy and I have cleared four thousand pounds net profit. When my poppies were in flower, what a picture they made! So you see, I cleared four thousand pounds; and I wanted to lend you a bit because I've got it to spare. What's the good of being stuck up? I'm a peasant. . . . As man to man. . . .

TROPHIMOF.   Your father was a peasant; mine was a chemist; it doesn't prove anything. [LOPAKHIN *takes out his pocket-book with paper money*] Shut up, shut up. . . . If you offered me twenty thousand pounds I would not take it. I am a free man; nothing that you value so highly, all of you, rich and poor, has the smallest power over me; it's like thistledown floating on the wind. I can do without you; I can go past you; I'm strong and proud. Mankind marches forward to the highest truth, to the highest happiness possible on earth, and I march in the foremost ranks.

LOPAKHIN.   Will you get there?

TROPHIMOF.   Yes. [*pause*] I will get there myself or I will show others the way.

[*The sound of axes hewing is heard in the distance.*]

LOPAKHIN.   Well, good-bye, old chap; it is time to start. Here we stand swaggering to each other, and life goes by all the time without heeding us. When I work for hours without getting tired, I get easy in my mind and I seem to know why I exist. But God alone knows what most of the people in Russia were born for. . . . Well, who cares? It doesn't affect the circulation of work. They say Leonid Andreyitch has got a place; he's going to be in a bank and get six hundred pounds a year. . . . He won't sit it out, he's too lazy.

ANYA [*in the doorway*].   Mamma says, will you stop cutting down the orchard till she has gone.

TROPHIMOF.   Really, haven't you got tact enough for that? [*exit by the hall*]

LOPAKHIN.   Of course, I'll stop them at once. What fools they are! [*exit after* TROPHIMOF]

ANYA.   Has Firs been sent to the hospital?

YASHA.   I told 'em this morning. They're sure to have sent him.

ANYA [*to* EPHIKHODOF, *who crosses*].   Simeon Panteleyitch, please find out if Firs has been sent to the hospital.

YASHA [*offended*].   I told George this morning. What's the good of asking a dozen times?

EPHIKHODOF.   Our centenarian friend, in my conclusive opinion, is hardly worth tinkering; it's time he was dispatched to his fore-fathers. I can only say I envy him. [*putting down a portmanteau on a bandbox and crushing it flat*] There you are! I knew how it would be! [*exit*]

YASHA [*jeering*].   Twenty-two misfortunes.

BARBARA [*without*].   Has Firs been sent to the hospital?

ANYA.   Yes.

BARBARA.   Why didn't they take the note to the doctor?

ANYA.   We must send it after them. [*exit*]

BARBARA [*from the next room*].   Where's Yasha? Tell him his mother is here. She wants to say good-bye to him.

YASHA [*with a gesture of impatience*].   It's enough to try the patience of a saint!

[DUNYASHA *has been busying herself with the luggage. Seeing* YASHA *alone, she approaches him.*]

DUNYASHA.   You might just look once at me, Yasha. You are going away, you are leaving me. [*crying and throwing her arms round his neck*]

YASHA.   What's the good of crying? [*drinking champagne*] In six days I shall be back in Paris. To-morrow we take the express, off we go, and that's the last of us! I can hardly believe it's true. Vive la France! This place don't suit me. I can't bear it . . . it can't be helped. I have had enough barbarism; I'm fed up. [*drinking champagne*] What's the good of crying? You be a good girl, and you'll have no call to cry.

DUNYASHA [*powdering her face and looking into a glass*].   Write me a letter from Paris. I've been so fond of you, Yasha, ever so fond! I am a delicate creature, Yasha.

YASHA.   Here's somebody coming. [*he busies himself with the luggage, singing under his breath*]

[*Enter* MADAME RANEVSKY, GAYEF, ANYA *and* CHARLOTTE.]

GAYEF.   We'll have to be off; it's nearly time. [*looking at* YASHA] Who is it smells of red herring?

MADAME RANEVSKY.   We must take our seats in ten minutes. [*looking round the room*] Good-bye, dear old house, good-bye, grand-papa! When winter is past and spring comes again, you will be here no more; they will have pulled you down. Oh, think of all these walls have seen! [*kissing* ANYA *passionately*] My treasure, you look radiant, your eyes flash like two diamonds. Are you happy? very happy?

ANYA.   Very, very happy. We're beginning a new life, mamma.

GAYEF [*gaily*].   She's quite right, everything's all right now. Till the cherry orchard was sold we were all agitated and miserable; but once the thing was settled finally and irrevocably, we all calmed down and got jolly again. I'm a bank clerk now; I'm a financier . . . red in the middle! And you, Lyuba, whatever you may say, you're looking ever so much better, not a doubt about it.

MADAME RANEVSKY.   Yes, my nerves are better; it's quite true. [*she is helped on with her hat and coat*] I sleep well now. Take my things out, Yasha. We must be off. [*to* ANYA] We shall soon meet again, darling. . . . I'm off to Paris; I shall live on the money your grandmother sent from Yaroslav to buy the property. God bless your grandmother! I'm afraid it won't last long.

ANYA.   You'll come back very, very soon, won't you, mamma? I'm going to work and pass the examination at the Gymnase and get a place and help you. We'll read all sorts of books together, won't we, mamma? [*kissing her mother's hands*] We'll read in the long autumn evenings, we'll read heaps of books, and a new, wonderful world will open up before us. [*meditating*] . . . Come back, mamma!

MADAME RANEVSKY.   I'll come back, my angel. [*embracing her*]

[*Enter* LOPAKHIN. CHARLOTTE *sings softly.*]

GAYEF.   Happy Charlotte, she's singing.

CHARLOTTE [*taking a bundle of rugs, like a swaddled baby*].   Hush-a-bye, baby, on the tree top . . . [*the baby answers, "Wah, wah."*] Hush, my little one, hush, my pretty one! [*"Wah, wah."*] You'll break your mother's heart. [*she throws the bundle down on the floor again*] Don't forget to find me a new place, please. I can't do without it.

LOPAKHIN.   We'll find you a place, Charlotte Ivanovna, don't be afraid.

GAYEF.   Everybody's deserting us. Barbara's going. Nobody seems to want us.

CHARLOTTE.   There's nowhere for me to live in the town. I'm obliged to go. [*hums a tune*] What's the odds?

[*Enter* PISHTCHIK.]

LOPAKHIN.   Nature's masterpiece!

PISHTCHIK [*panting*].   Oy, oy, let me get my breath again! . . . I'm done up! . . . My noble friends! . . . Give me some water.

GAYEF.   Wants some money, I suppose. No, thank you; I'll keep out of harm's way. [*exit*]

PISHTCHIK.   It's ages since I have been here, fairest lady. [*to* LOPAKHIN] You here? Glad to see you, you man of gigantic intellect. Take this; it's for you. [*giving* LOPAKHIN *money*] Forty pounds! I still owe you eighty-four.

LOPAKHIN [*amazed, shrugging his shoulders*].   It's like a thing in a dream! Where did you get it from?

PISHTCHIK.   Wait a bit. . . . I'm hot. . . . A most remarkable thing! Some Englishmen came and found some sort of white clay on my land. [*to* MADAME RANEVSKY] And here's forty pounds for you, lovely, wonderful lady. [*giving her money*] The rest another time. [*drinking water*] Only just now a young man in the train was saying that some . . . some great philosopher advises us all to jump off roofs. . . . Jump, he says, and there's an end of it. [*with an astonished air*] Just think of that! More water!

LOPAKHIN.   Who were the Englishmen?

PISHTCHIK.   I leased them the plot with the clay on it for twenty-four years. But I haven't any time now   I must be getting on. I must go to Znoikof's, to Kardamonof's. . . . I owe everybody money. [*drinking*] Good-bye to everyone; I'll look in on Thursday.

MADAME RANEVSKY.   We're just moving into town, and to-morrow I go abroad.

PISHTCHIK.   What! [*alarmed*] What are you going into town for? Why, what's happened to the furniture? . . . Trunks? . . . Oh, it's all right. [*crying*] It's all right. People of powerful intellect . . . those Englishmen. It's all right. Be happy . . . God be with you . . . it's all right. Everything in this world has come to an end. [*kissing* MADAME RANEVSKY*'s hand*] If ever the news reaches you that *I* have come to an end, give a thought to the old . . . horse, and say, "Once there lived a certain Simeonof-Pishtchik, Heaven rest his soul." . . . Remarkable weather we're having. . . . Yes. . . . [*goes out deeply moved; returns at once and says from the doorway*] Dashenka sent her compliments. [*exit*]

MADAME RANEVSKY.   Now we can go. I have only two things on my mind. One is poor old Firs. [*looking at her watch*] We can still stay five minutes.

ANYA.   Firs has been sent to the hospital already, mamma. Yasha sent him off this morning.

MADAME RANEVSKY.   My second anxiety is Barbara. She's used to getting up early and working, and now that she has no work to do she's like a fish out of water. She has grown thin and pale and taken to crying, poor dear. . . . [*pause*] You know very well, Yermolai

Alexeyitch, I always hoped . . . to see her married to you, and as far as I can see, you're looking out for a wife. [_she whispers to_ ANYA, _who nods to_ CHARLOTTE, _and both exeunt_] She loves you; you like her; and I can't make out why you seem to fight shy of each other. I don't understand it.

LOPAKHIN. I don't understand it either, to tell you the truth. It all seems so odd. If there's still time, I'll do it this moment. Let's get it over and have done with it; without you there, I feel as if I should never propose to her.

MADAME RANEVSKY. A capital idea! After all, it doesn't take more than a minute. I'll call her at once.

LOPAKHIN. And here's the champagne all ready. [_looking at the glasses_] Empty; someone's drunk it. [YASHA _coughs_] That's what they call lapping it up and no mistake!

MADAME RANEVSKY [_animated_]. Capital! We'll all go away. . . . _Allez,_ Yasha. I'll call her. [_at the door_] Barbara, leave all that and come here. Come along!

[_Exeunt_ MADAME RANEVSKY _and_ YASHA.]

LOPAKHIN [_looking at his watch_]. Yes.

[_Pause. A stifled laugh behind the door; whispering; at last enter_ BARBARA.]

BARBARA [_examining the luggage_]. Very odd; I can't find it any-where . . .

LOPAKHIN. What are you looking for?

BARBARA. I packed it myself, and can't remember. [_pause_]

LOPAKHIN. Where are you going to-day, Varvara Mikhailovna?

BARBARA. Me? I'm going to the Ragulins'. I'm engaged to go and keep house for them, to be housekeeper or whatever it is.

LOPAKHIN. Oh, at Yashnevo? That's about fifty miles from here. [_pause_] Well, so life in this house is over now.

BARBARA [_looking at the luggage_]. Wherever can it be? Perhaps I put it in the trunk. . . . Yes, life here is over now; there won't be any more . . .

LOPAKHIN. And I'm off to Kharkof at once . . . by the same train. A lot of business to do. I'm leaving Ephikhodof to look after this place. I've taken him on.

BARBARA. Have you?

LOPAKHIN. At this time last year snow was falling already, if you remember; but now it's fine and sunny. Still, it's cold for all that. Three degrees of frost.

BARBARA.   Were there? I didn't look. [*pause*] Besides, the ther-
mometer's broken. [*pause*]

A VOICE [*at the outer door*].   Yermolai Alexeyitch!

LOPAKHIN [*as if he had only been waiting to be called*].   I'm just coming! [*exit* LOPAKHIN *quickly*]

[BARBARA *sits on the floor, puts her head on a bundle and sobs softly.
The door opens and* MADAME RANEVSKY *comes in cautiously.*]

MADAME RANEVSKY.   Well? [*pause*] We must be off.

BARBARA [*no longer crying, wiping her eyes*].   Yes, it's time, mamma.
I shall get to the Ragulins' all right to-day, so long as I don't miss the
train.

MADAME RANEVSKY [*calling off*].   Put on your things, Anya.

[*Enter* ANYA, *then* GAYEF *and* CHARLOTTE. GAYEF *wears a warm
overcoat with a hood. The servants and drivers come in.* EPHIKHODOF
busies himself about the luggage.]

MADAME RANEVSKY.   Now we can start on our journey.

ANYA [*delighted*].   We can start on our journey!

GAYEF.   My friends, my dear, beloved friends! Now that I am
leaving this house for ever, can I keep silence? Can I refrain from
expressing those emotions which fill my whole being at such a
moment?

ANYA [*pleadingly*].   Uncle!

BARBARA.   Uncle, what's the good?

GAYEF [*sadly*].   Double the red in the middle pocket. I'll hold my
tongue.

[*Enter* TROPHIMOF, *then* LOPAKHIN.]

TROPHIMOF.   Come along, it's time to start.

LOPAKHIN.   Ephikhodof, my coat.

MADAME RANEVSKY.   I must sit here another minute. It's just as
if I had never noticed before what the walls and ceilings of the house
were like. I look at them hungrily, with such tender love. . . .

GAYEF.   I remember, when I was six years old, how I sat in this
window on Trinity Sunday, and watched father starting out for
church.

MADAME RANEVSKY.   Has everything been cleared out?

LOPAKHIN.   Apparently everything. [*to* EPHIKHODOF, *putting on his
overcoat*] See that everything's in order, Ephikhodof.

EPHIKHODOF [*in a hoarse voice*].   You trust me, Yermolai
Alexeyitch.

LOPAKHIN. What's up with your voice?

EPHIKHODOF. I was just having a drink of water. I swallowed something.

YASHA [*contemptuously*]. Cad!

MADAME RANEVSKY. We're going, and not a soul will be left here.

LOPAKHIN. Until the spring.

[BARBARA *pulls an umbrella out of a bundle of rugs, as if she were brandishing it to strike.* LOPAKHIN *pretends to be frightened.*]

BARBARA. Don't be so silly! I never thought of such a thing.

TROPHIMOF. Come, we'd better go and get in. It's time to start. The train will be in immediately.

BARBARA. There are your goloshes, Peter, by that portmanteau. [*crying*] What dirty old things they are!

TROPHIMOF [*putting on his goloshes*]. Come along.

GAYEF [*much moved, afraid of crying*]. The train . . . the station . . . double the red in the middle; doublette to pot the white in the corner. . . .

MADAME RANEVSKY. Come on!

LOPAKHIN. Is everyone here? No one left in there? [*locking the door*] There are things stacked in there; I must lock them up. Come on!

ANYA. Good-bye, house! good-bye, old life!

TROPHIMOF. Welcome, new life! [*Exit with* ANYA.]

[BARBARA *looks round the room, and exit slowly. Exeunt* YASHA, *and* CHARLOTTE *with her dog.*]

LOPAKHIN. Till the spring, then. Go on, everybody. So-long! [*exit*]

[MADAME RANEVSKY *and* GAYEF *remain alone. They seem to have been waiting for this, throw their arms round each other's necks and sob restrainedly and gently, afraid of being overheard.*]

GAYEF [*in despair*]. My sister! my sister!

MADAME RANEVSKY. Oh, my dear, sweet lovely orchard! My life, my youth, my happiness, farewell! Farewell!

ANYA [*calling gaily, without*]. Mamma!

TROPHIMOF [*gay and excited*]. Aoo!

MADAME RANEVSKY. One last look at the walls and the windows. . . . Our dear mother used to walk up and down this room.

GAYEF. My sister! my sister!

ANYA [*without*]. Aoo!

MADAME RANEVSKY.   We're coming. [*exeunt*]

[*The stage is empty. One hears all the doors being locked, and the carriages driving away. All is quiet. Amid the silence the thud of the axes on the trees echoes sad and lonely. The sound of footsteps.* FIRS *appears in the doorway* R. *He is dressed, as always, in his long coat and white waistcoat; he wears slippers. He is ill.*]

FIRS [*going to the door* L. *and trying the handle*].   Locked. They've gone. [*sitting on the sofa*] They've forgotten me. Never mind! I'll sit here. Leonid Andreyitch is sure to have put on his cloth coat instead of his fur. [*he sighs anxiously*] He hadn't me to see. Young wood, green wood! [*he mumbles something incomprehensible*] Life has gone by as if I'd never lived. [*lying down*] I'll lie down. There's no strength left in you; there's nothing, nothing. Ah, you . . . job-lot!

[*He lies motionless. A distant sound is heard, as if from the sky, the sound of a string breaking, dying away, melancholy. Silence ensues, broken only by the stroke of the axe on the trees far away in the cherry orchard.*]

CURTAIN.